JERSEY SAILING SHIPS

Nothing is wasted, nothing is in vain,
The seas roll over but the rocks remain.

A. P. Herbert

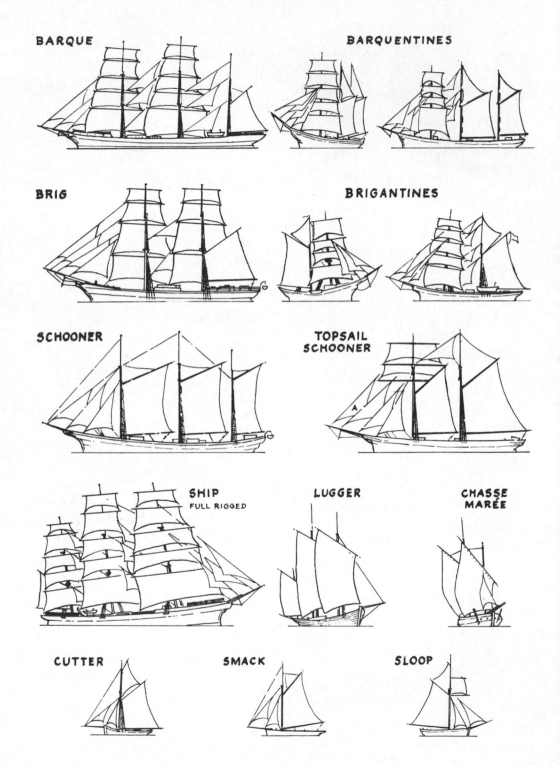

BARQUE

BARQUENTINES

BRIG

BRIGANTINES

SCHOONER

TOPSAIL
SCHOONER

SHIP
FULL RIGGED

LUGGER

CHASSE
MARÉE

CUTTER

SMACK

SLOOP

JERSEY
SAILING SHIPS

John Jean

PHILLIMORE

1982
Published by
PHILLIMORE & CO. LTD.
Shopwyke Hall, Chichester, Sussex

ISBN 0 85033 464 0

Typeset by Fidelity Processes
Printed and bound in Great Britain by
THE CAMELOT PRESS LTD.,
Southampton, Hampshire

CONTENTS

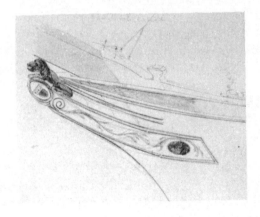

Figurehead of 'Kitten', a schooner of 139 tons.

LIST OF ILLUSTRATIONS

Colour Plates

Monochrome Plates

Line drawings in the text of figureheads from the sketchbook of P. J. Ouless are reproduced by courtesy of La Société Jersiaise.

SOURCES OF ILLUSTRATIONS

Colour Plates
Société Jersiaise, 1, 2, 3, 4, 6; Marjorie Syvret, 5; F. J. Lucas, 7
Monochrome Plates
Author's collection, 1, 2, 3, 4, 5, 6, 8, 13, 16, 19, 22, 23, 24, 26, 27, 28, 29, 31, 32, 33, 37, 45
H. de G. Gaudin, 42, 50
Pauline Hacquoil, 17
Jersey Evening Post, 35
B. Le Marquand, 14
R. Mayne, 9, 10, 11, 12, 15, 20, 21
Dawn Pallot, 39, 43, 44, 46, 47, 48, 49
P. Robeson, 18
Société Jersiaise, 7, 25, 30, 34, 36, 38, 40, 41

FOREWORD

At long last we have a concise record of the era of Jersey's sailing ships, a period when Jersey, incredibly, was sixth in the world shipbuilding league. John Jean's painstaking research not only names hundreds of sailing ships, but gives full details of the shipyards where they were built, their size, tonnage, and date of manufacture, and of their owners, masters and builders. All the allied trades are discussed, and there are also chapters on privateering, ports and harbours, and the cod-fishing industry of Newfoundland, which provided a livelihood for thousands of our seafaring ancestors.

This splendid book is essential reading not only for Islanders, but for all who are drawn by the romance of the sea. The index and tables are of inestimable value; but more, Mr Jean is to be congratulated on being the first author to present such a detailed account, vividly reminding those who walk our coastline, where deckchairs have replaced shipyards, of the smell of pitch and the sound of the caulking hammer. This book is an enormous contribution to the history of our island whose economic life and security depended so greatly on those wooden ships and their stout-hearted crews.

RICHARD MAYNE

MERCHANT'S SIGNALS OR HOUSE FLAGS 1792 - 1900

E. Renouf   Carre   Pellier   Esnouf & Mauger

Le Rossignol   De Ste Croix   Fruing   Earles   De Garis   Le Feuvre

E. Gallichan   Bertram   Carrel   G. Allix   E. Bellingham   W. Bisson

Collas   Huelin   De La Perrelle   F. Allix

Le Boutillier   De Faye   De La Taste   J. Renouf   Barreau   W. Bryant

Deslandes   Daly   De Gruchy Renouf-Clement   Pirouet

P. Le Quesne   J. Orange   Le Vesconte   P. Gavey   C. Le Sueur   E. Gallichan

F. Le Sueur   M. Gallichan   J.F. Picot   Mitchell   Tocque   Laurains

Colour Key   RED   BLUE   YELLOW   GREEN   BLACK

INTRODUCTION

In compiling this volume, no attempt has been made to write a full and complete maritime history; rather is it a book for the descendants of those Jersey families who had a grandfather, a great uncle, father or brother at sea, or one of the ubiquitous paintings of local vessels hiding in some half-forgotten corner of the house. Herein will be found the names of some 1,400 Jersey captains and nearly 1,500 of their ships, which the writer hopes will provide the missing links in numerous family histories. Many were the trades involved in the construction and fitting out of a sailing vessel, and here will be found details of shipwrights, sailmakers, ropemakers and anchorsmiths, etc., and the shipyards where many fine ships began their lives.

What made many a young lad of twelve years leave a comfortable and loving home for a hard and sometimes dangerous life aboard a small vessel which was often at the mercy of the elements? Was it the romantic 'call of the sea', or the more practical reason of too many sons to inherit too few farms? It certainly was a hard and often dangerous life, with cramped living quarters and unwholesome food, plus the ever-present fear of being swept overboard during one of the violent storms encountered at sea. The lure of foreign lands surely appealed to young lads brought up in a small island and the possibility of riches may have enticed the ambitious and thrifty Jerseyman.

Whether fishing the Newfoundland waters or searching the seas for enemy shipping, in the China tea trade or on the Australian wool run, local ships and sailors were to be counted. To the shores of Russia and other Baltic ports went the Jersey ships, returning with cargoes of hemp and timber; from South America came shiploads of fine mahogany, wine from France and Italy, much of it to be re-exported. Island vessels traded with the coast of West Africa, dealing both in goods and in slaves. The transporting of the plenteous codfish to the Catholic countries of Italy, Portugal, Spain and the countries of Latin America occupied local companies for long periods, the ships often returning with cargoes of fruit or salt. The trade that existed between the Island and the nearby French ports, and with towns on the mainland, engaged large numbers of the smaller craft such as cutters, ketches and small schooners; these boats were owned either by small shipping companies or often belonged to the captain. These, and similar craft owned on the mainland, were the forerunners of the 'dirty British coasters' of the later steam age.

As this volume concerns the merchant shipping of Jersey, little or no mention is made of the Royal Navy or of the many Jerseymen who served with honour in the fleet, often reaching high rank. For no other place of equal size can ever have produced so many seamen, not only for crewing the merchant ships, but also so large a number of volunteers for the vessels of the Navy that the notorious press gangs were not allowed to operate in the Island. Certainly no other community gave birth to so many admirals: men such as Admiral Philip Durell, who supported General Wolfe at Quebec; the family of Le Hardy who gave us at least three admirals; Philip de Carteret, of the 'Swallow', who has been described as to rank among the greatest geographical explorers of his time; Rear-Admiral Charles Bertram; Admiral Philip d'Auvergne, and many, many more. Other Jerseymen served aboard naval vessels as pilots, not only in Channel Islands waters but also on the seas of France and North America. In fact, so many Jerseymen were at sea at one time that the ranks of the Island Militia were seriously depleted, which aroused grave concern for the defence of the Island.

The well-known custom of bestowing the father's name upon the eldest son for several generations was likewise used in the naming of their ships, causing some confusion when two or more vessels bearing the same name were registered by the same owners, and the constant repetition of the popular names such as John, Philip and Thomas does not make the identification of captains any easier. Great care has been taken in researching this book, particularly in drawing up the lists of vessels and of persons contained in these pages; however, the writer apologizes in advance for any errors or omissions. Further information will be welcomed.

JOHN JEAN

Le Tilleul,
St Lawrence,
Jersey.

ACKNOWLEDGEMENTS

To Mrs Joan Stevens, M.B.E., F.S.A., for her encouragement, help and for reading of the material. For her kindness in loaning the excellent drawings of the different rigs of vessels drawn by her husband, the late Mr C. G. Stevens. To Richard Mayne, for writing the Foreword, for his faith in my work, and his never-failing help and advice; also for the loan of notes and photographic material. Mr V. H. Palmer and his staff, of the Jersey Shipping Register, for their courtesy and interest. Mr George Drew, for giving me so much of his valuable time, and the staff of the Museum of La Société Jersiaise, for their help with so many things; Mr Michael Dun, for the loan of so much valuable material, Mr Reg Queree, for his trials and tribulations in processing the photographs; also Mr Robin Briault, for his photographic work. To Mr J. Cutler Vincent, for his interest and his valuable lists of ships that saved me hours of research. My thanks also to the many kind persons who have given me family information, and allowed me to examine documents and personal treasures, including Mr John A'Court, Mr John Benest, Mrs Clement-Robson, Mr George Croad, Mr Charles L. Gruchy, B.Sc., M.R.C.V.S., Mrs O. Kerley, Mr C. Langlois, Mrs D. Pallot, Mr G. S. M. Pontius, Mr P. Robson, B.Sc., M.I.Biol., Mrs G. G. Stent, and to the many other kind persons whom I have badgered for information.

I wish to extend my especial thanks to my wife, Betty, without whose encouragement and support this book would not have been written.

MERCHANT'S SIGNALS OR HOUSE FLAGS 1792 - 1900

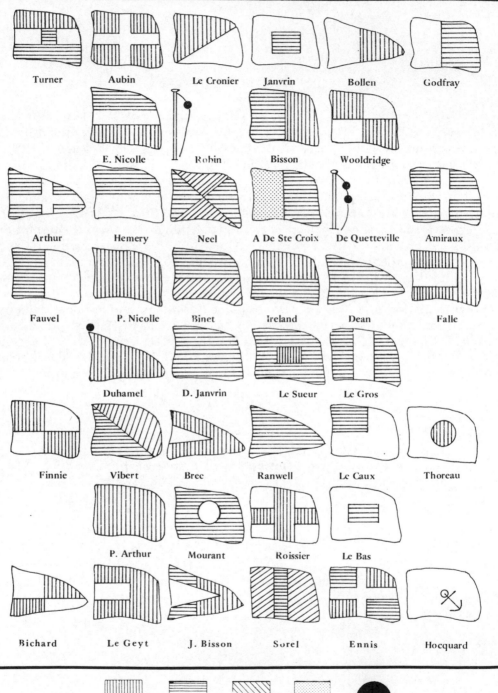

Turner   Aubin   Le Cronier   Janvrin   Bollen   Godfray

E. Nicolle   Robin   Bisson   Wooldridge

Arthur   Hemery   Neel   A De Ste Croix   De Quetteville   Amiraux

Fauvel   P. Nicolle   Binet   Ireland   Dean   Falle

Duhamel   D. Janvrin   Le Sueur   Le Gros

Finnie   Vibert   Brec   Ranwell   Le Caux   Thoreau

P. Arthur   Mourant   Roissier   Le Bas

Bichard   Le Geyt   J. Bisson   Sorel   Ennis   Hocquard

Colour Key   RED   BLUE   YELLOW   GREEN   BLACK

Chapter One

THE SHIPBUILDERS AND THE SHIPBUILDING SITES

The Jersey Shipbuilders

THE EARLIEST RECORD of a vessel being constructed in Jersey is in 1468,[1] when Mont Orgueil Castle lay under siege to Vice-Admiral Sir Richard Harliston; the defenders are described as building two boats within the Castle. In 1480 when the 'Sovereign' was built for the Crown at Southampton, the sails were made from canvas supplied by the Island of Guernsey. Later, in 1617, we have a report of one John Beauchamp, shipwright, and two other men repairing a boat at Elizabeth Castle, but no tonnage of these vessels, which were probably of small design, is given.

The records of Grouville church concerning a giant oak in the churchyard in 1704[2] state that it was sold by auction for 44 crowns and produced 50 tons of wood. The purchaser, one Jean du Boulivot, secured from this timber four beams of 22 feet long, 14 beams for cider presses, 480 spokes for wheels, a large quantity of cask staves and tub bottoms, an 'immense amount of wood for shipbuilding' and six cartloads of bark for tanning. Falle in his *History* (1739) says most wood in the Island is knotty but here and there 'sticks' are found fit for building good ships. A shipbuilder of Southampton, Moody Janverin,[3] built ships at Hamble, Burlesdon, Eape and Buckler's Hard from 1739 to 1755 and was of the Jersey family of Janvrin, which might suggest that the Janvrin family may have built their own ships.

When Captain Le Cronier, commanding 'La Defiance', captured a Swedish prize in 1757, the new owners ran the vessel ashore and added 12 feet to the length, a feat requiring a fair knowledge of shipbuilding expertise, if not of design.

Pierre Mallet in 1773 bought land to the south of Chapelle Des Pas, a field adjoining land belonging to Brelade Valpy dit Janvrin, a wealthy shipowner who 'had shipyards there';[4] a survey of Fowey-registered vessels, 1786 to 1802, shows one ship as Jersey built;[5] again Balleine in his *The Bailiwick of Jersey* (2nd edition, page 31) states that in the '18th century four shipyards occupied the foreshore' at Havre des Pas.

The States in 1796[6] petitioned the British Government to allow further cargoes of coal to be imported into the Island as, due to the diminished amount of wood fuel available, larger supplies of coal were needed. The shortage of timber was caused by the great amounts used for the building of merchant ships and other vessels. Some of these vessels have been recorded in the earlier Lloyds Lists and are:

———	EGMONT	70 tons	Owned by	Janvrin
1763	INDUSTRY	50 tons	Owned by	Janvrin
1773	PITT	70 tons	Owned by	Thoreau
1775	ELIZABETH	60 tons	Owned by	Durell
1776	HOPE	60 tons	Owned by	?
1776	SWIFT	35 tons	Owned by	?
———	MINERVA	70 tons	Owned by	?
1783	PRUDENT	57 tons	Owned by	Le Brun
1789	ELISHA TUPPER	208 tons	Owned by	Janvrin
1791	PRINCESS ROYAL	103 tons	Owned by	Hemery Bros
1792	ENTERPRISE	80 tons	Owned by	Chevalier
1794	DE JERSEY	219 tons	Owned by	Janvrin
1798	ROWCLIFFE	354 tons	Owned by	Durell & De Ste Croix
1800	SPEEDY	72 tons	Owned by	Chevalier & Nicolle

The 'Elisha Tupper' was built for Janvrin at Bel Royal of oak grown in the parish of St Lawrence, and the report in the *Gazette de L'île de Jersey* records that this vessel, a smaller unnamed ship, and a boat were constructed at the same time. Elisha Tupper was a Guernsey merchant, who owned several vessels in partnership with Janvrin for many years until his death in 1809.

During the 19th century over seven hundred ships were built in the Island, some for mainland or Guernsey owners, but mostly for Jersey owners, and locally-built vessels were noted for their craftsmanship and especially for the finish of the fine mahogany woodwork. Many fine pieces of furniture are believed to have been made in the shipyards; some Jersey houses have doors and beautiful stair-cases which were undoubtedly the work of men from the yards. The shipbuilders can be roughly classed in two groups, firstly the owners who, in the latter part of the 18th and at the beginning of the 19th century, built their own vessels, and other independent builders who exercised their trades where and when the need arose.

In the second group are the large and permanent yards such as those of Clarke, Deslandes, Le Vesconte, Esnouf, Picot and others. Ships for different purposes and of various rigs were built: fast sailing schooners for the fruit and meat trades, clipper ships for the Australian wool run, such as the 'Evening Star' (848 tons) owned by J. Le Bas and built at St Aubin by Ed. Allen, and tea clippers such as the 'Fort Regent' (655 tons) owned by Orange and Briard which carried 1,060 tons of tea, and 'Chieftain' (579 tons) owned by W. Fruing & Co. This last ship had been reported as having once beaten the famous 'Cutty Sark' by two days.

In the second half of the 18th century four sources of supply were available to Jersey shipowners: firstly, prize ships taken at war; secondly, vessels built in the American colonies and described as 'British plantation built'; thirdly, boats built on the South Coast at ports such as Plymouth, Southampton, Brixham and Cowes, and lastly, locally-built vessels.

After Waterloo the supply of prize ships ceased and more and more vessels were built in the Island, resulting in more permanent yards being established by such as Ph. Nicolle, Ed. Nicolle, Aaron de Ste Croix, Fr. Grellier, leading to the well known and larger yards of Geo. Deslandes, F. C. Clarke, Dan Le Vesconte, Esnouf and many others. The main sites were at St Aubin, First Tower, Patriotic Place, the Harbour, Havre-des-Pas, Gorey and St Catherine, until the merchant fleet consisted almost entirely of locally-built vessels. Many ships were also constructed for Guernsey and mainland companies, and at one time the field now known as the Triangle Park was stacked high with timber for the yards.

Francis Grellier, the elder, was building vessels in Jersey between 1813 and 1817, and Francis Grellier junior was surveyor of shipping for Jersey from 1814 to 1828, and he too was constructing ships locally in the 1830s and 1840s. George Hamptonne was acting surveyor during the 1820s, and vessels built by him at La Folie are recorded from 1826 to 1849. At times it is difficult to distinguish between the shipwright and the owner, as in the case of Aaron de Ste Croix, who in some newspaper reports is given the credit for building a number of fine vessels, while the shipping register lists John Baxter as being the actual builder. Again we find Denis Blampied and Jean Jope at Bouley Bay described as the makers of several small vessels; this is presumably because one person financed the work and the shipwright was the actual builder.

No doubt in the earlier days ships were built by 'rule of thumb', but later drawings and wooden patterns or models were used, though unfortunately few such articles have survived. We read that in 1876 the brigantine 'Laurel' of 113 tons was designed and built by Daniel Le Vesconte at First Tower, and that in 1881 a Daniel Le Sueur became a naval architect. This Daniel was possibly the son of Daniel Le Sueur who built many boats at La Rocque.

Jerseymen have long been renowned for their adaptability, and this is well illustrated in a list of the diverse activities of George Asplet of Gorey who, as well as being a shipbuilder in 1843,[7] was recorded as a grocer, a shipowner, a broker, a coal merchant, an oyster merchant, and an omnibus owner.

Many vessels were launched on rollers, some were 'fully rigged' when launched, and at least one ship, the 'Highlander' built at St Aubin in 1840, was sent off to a fanfare of guns. Others were launched by well known local personages and were watched by large crowds. Torchlights were used for launchings which had to take place during the hours of darkness because the state of the tide was of the utmost importance. The workmanship and finish of local ships was well thought of; some vessels were decorated with a billethead, others a scrollhead, while the more important vessels bore a more elaborate figurehead, such as the barque 'Ceres' (280 tons), the 'Crusader' (130 tons) and the 'Rowcliffe' (343 tons), which carried a lionhead, the 'Janvrin', 'Brutus' and the 'Warrior' which proudly bore male figures at their heads, and others such as the 'Hebe', 'Minerva', 'Ocean' and 'St Aubin', all of which had ornate womanheads and busts. The barque 'Blue Jacket' (266 tons), built by Le Vesconte and Vautier at Havre-des-Pas and launched on 11 August 1856, was adorned with a figure of a blue jacket, while King George II pointed the way ahead for the 473-ton barque 'George', built with iron masts and constructed in 1865 by F. C. Clarke at West Park.

It is not surprising to find, knowing the close ties between the Channel Islands and 'La Côte' that builders with Island names built vessels for Jersey owners, both in Newfoundland and Canada,[8] such as Thomas Silk at Fortune Bay in 1818, Francis Collas at Fortune Bay in 1827, Nicolas le Masurier at Ship Harbour, Cap Breton in 1828, and Samuel Collas at Gaspé in 1840. A Thomas Silk was building at Patriotic Place from 1826 to 1828 and Nicolas Le Masurier at West Park.

As the rate of shipbuilding in the Island increased, so did many other trades necessary for the completion of the ships, such as anchor smiths, blockmakers, boatbuilders, mast and oar makers, sailmakers, hemp merchants, and ropemakers etc. During the 18th century ropewalks were established by Rowcliffe at Havre-des-Pas, Brine in the High Street at St Aubin, both before 1770, and Aaron de Ste Croix, also at Havre-des-Pas, and in 1773 Pierre Mallet bought additional land in Green Street called 'Le Clos de la Chapelle ou de Boutillier' near the Chapelle-des-Pas and adjacent to the shipyard of Brelade Valpy dit Janvrin. A newspaper report of 1797 advertised 'A vessel to be sold at Mr. Mallet's ropeyard at St Helier'.

In 1804 Pierre Mallet, his son Thomas, and Philippe Janvrin son of Brelade Janvrin, ceded their ropewalks to the British Government for the construction of Fort Regent. Thomas Mallet was also a dealer in hemp, for in 1821 he was import-ing hemp from France, Russia, Italy and the Philippines. A ropemaker by the name of John Armstrong was brought before the Police Court in 1817 and was found guilty of stealing a large quantity of hemp from 'Mr. Janvrin's store in the Parade'. F. Laurens owned a ropewalk in 1790, stated to be in the area of what is now the Green Street Cemetery. Alongside was another walk owned by James Boielle, c. 1811, while George Deslandes at sometime operated a ropeyard at the rear of the Seaforth Hotel at Lower Green Street.

George Deslandes Laurens had established in 1860 the largest ropewalk in Green Street, where the house known as 'La Corderie' was later built. This walk was reputed to be a quarter of a mile long and at one time was roofed. Philip Nicolle had owned a ropewalk in the area which is now called Kensington Place in about 1809 and when in 1817 he built his house in Pier Road, the front garden of which was his shipbuilding yard, he transferred his activities to Patriotic Place and built several vessels there.

The Constable of St Helier, Edward Nicolle, 1818–1827, also ran a ropemaking business, possibly in the same area. One of the last to make rope in Jersey was Jerrom and Son, who had taken over one of the walks in Green Street. Many other merchants were concerned in supplying the shipbuilders, such as Edward Marett of the 'Speedy Packet Office', 5 Church Street, whose advertisement in the *Jersey Times and British Press* of 1865 offers for sale copper sheathing, copper nails and spikes, deck nails, bolts, keel staples and clench rings etc., while the Beaumont Shipyard had for sale pitch pine logs, masts, planks, spars, locust wood, Canadian Spruce, wrought iron, zinc nails, coir rope, ash oars, bar and rod iron, washers and chains. The well-known timber merchants of Commercial Buildings was founded by John Norman about 1840, making fresh water casks for ships and wooden tubs for packing dried codfish.

Information about insurance charges and building costs is rather scarce, but Jersey ships were, or could be, insured as early as 1738,[9] when Abraham Malzard instructed Jean Seale to 'insure his share of the vessel "Pipon Galley" for £100 at 1½ per cent for the journey to Terreneuve'.

No figures have yet been found regarding the building costs of local vessels, but in *South Eastern Sail* by Michael Bouquet costs of mainland-built vessels are quoted — Brig 'Bluebell' (198 tons) cost £2,558 in 1854, and in 1856 the cost of building the schooner 'Osprey' (220 tons) was £3,164. One of the largest yards, that of Clarke's at West Park.[10] employed upwards of 400 men, pay being two shillings and sixpence (12½p) per day for work starting at 6 a.m. until 6 p.m. Clarke told Joseph Hume, M.P. for Montrose, during his visit to Jersey in 1849, 'We can build more cheaply than Liverpool because Jerseymen are sober, frugal and industrious, work six days a week, with no unions to cause strikes and with no idlers to maintain'.

Mainland owners soon found that Jersey-built ships made sound economic sense as, owing to the privilege granted to the Island in the Middle Ages, no dues were paid on goods that had been constructed in the Island when sold to the United Kingdom. This fact, and the superior materials and craftsmanship going into local vessels, made a very attractive proposition to English companies and a number of them had some fine, large vessels from the Jersey stocks.

Melhuish & Company of Liverpool bought the 'Helen Heigers' of 1,100 tons, 'Jane Pratt' (729 tons); 'John Melhuish' (672 tons), 'Matilda Wattenbach' (1,077 tons), 'William Melhuish' (681 tons), and the 'Ann Holtzburg' (705 tons), all built by Clarke during the 1850s. The screw brig 'Joseph Hume' (480 tons). 'Mignonette', a barque of 284 tons, and 'St Vincent' (462 tons), were built by Clarke for Scrutton & Company of London and Asplet built the 'Montrose' (365 tons), launched 23 July 1861, for the same Company. Other mainland firms who bought local ships were Thomas Kaye & Company, Ashton & Company, Redfern & Alexander & Company, all of London and Bristol, Greenock, Plymouth, Dartmouth and Guernsey owners.

The advent and increasing use of steel caused some concern to local builders, and some tentative ventures were made into these realms. F. C. Clarke of West Park in 1851 built the first steamship to be constructed locally, called the 'Rose' (84 tons), using the boiler of the 'Superb' which had been wrecked on the Minquiers the previous year. The boiler of the tug 'Polka' wrecked alongside the 'Superb' was put that same year into a smaller ship of 24 tons named the 'Don'. Both these early steamers were owned by Thomas Rose. Messrs. Esnouf & Mauger of Patriotic Place launched on 20 January 1859 a screw barque of 449 tons. She was built for a mainland buyer and called 'Jeddo', and was noted for her fast sailing.

Both Grandin and Clarke also built screw sailing vessels of small size, but the first iron hulled steam ship in the Island was built by George Ennis, the Iron Founder (and maker of the treadmill for the local prison, which is now in the Jersey Museum). This vessel was of 35 tons, named 'Experiment', and launched on 31 July 1859. Philip Grandin built another screw steamer called 'Surprise' (71 tons) which was launched on 7 March 1872, while Edward Huelin of Kensington Place built 'Eureka' in 1890, which he later sold to Plymouth.

The era of the wooden sailing ship was now ending after a peak reached in 1865, when Daniel Le Vesconte's yard had eight vessels on the stocks at the same time, and ships of 800, 900 and even 1,000 tons had been constructed. Altogether well over six hundred vessels of all classes had come off the stocks in some 90 years, but the once thriving shipbuilding industry died almost overnight, and little remains to be seen today.

However the Public Works Dept. of the States of Jersey has recently erected at Gorey a fountain recording the names of 16 ships that were built in the area. This reminder of the shipbuilding industry shows the formation of a ship's keel. The site of Francis Allix's former yard at Havre-des-Pas has been purchased by the Procureurs of the Vingtain de La Ville of the Parish of St Helier, and a commemorative plaque has been erected to record the position of this once busy shipyard. The last vessel built by Allix was the 'Florida', which was launched on 22 September 1877.

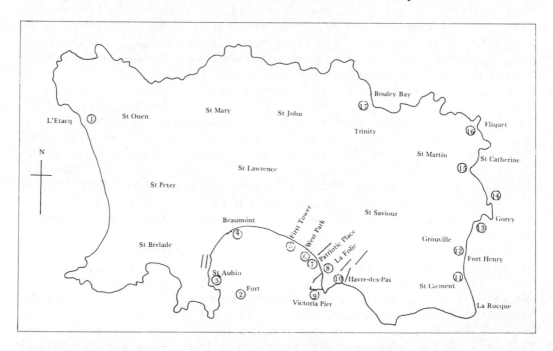

Shipyards and Ropewalks: 1. Hacquoil; 2. Laing; 3. Allen, Du Val, Le Feuvre, Giffard & Laurens, Sauvage; 4. Bartlett, Hayley; 5. Deslandes, Grandin, Le Vesconte; 6. Clarke; 7. Esnouf & Mauger, Gavey, Grellier, Hamon, Le Masurier, Nicolson, Le Rougetel, Silk, Vautier; 8. Le Bouef, Deslandes, Hamptonne; 9. Le Masurier; 10. Allix, Baxter, Clarke, de Ste Croix, Nicolle, Valpy, Vautier, Le Vesconte & Vautier; 11. Filleul & de La Mare, D. Le Sueur; 12. P. J. Le Sueur; 13. Asplet, Aubin, Bellot, Cantel, Fauvel, Messervy, Picot; 14. Vardon; 15. Le Huquet, Vardon & Le Huquet; 16. Richardson; 17. Blampied, Jope. —— Ropewalks.

LIST OF LOCAL SHIPBUILDERS

			vessel(s)	
ALLEN Edward	St Aubin	1837–1854	9	1 built Havre-des-Pas
ALLIX Francis	Havre-des-Pas	1842–1877	18	last built 1877
ARTHUR Charles	St Aubin	1822–1827	3	also built Gaspé 1838
ASPLET George	Gorey	1858–1861	7	
AUBIN Charles W.	Gorey	1866–1877	22	opp. Village
BARTLETT Thomas Leigh	Beaumont	1840–1848	20	
BAXTER John	Havre-des-Pas	1824–1833	5	
BELLOT Philip	Gorey	1858–1878	24	near Tennis Courts
BISSON Thomas	Havre-des-Pas	1856–1875	4	1 built Beaumont
BLAMPIED Denis	Trinity	1824–1829	4	Bouley Bay ?
BOEUF (LE) Mathew	?	1810–1815	7	
CANTEL Mark	Gorey	1862–1863	4	
CLARKE F. C.	Havre-des-Pas	1839–1845	12	2 built La Folie
CLARKE F. C.	West Park	1844–1867	62	
DEAN Philip	St Aubin	1833–1837	2	with John Leigh
DE GRUCHY Thomas	Patriotic Pl.	1848–1849	2	
DESLANDES George	La Folie	1824–1843	27	
DESLANDES George	First Tower	1827–1879	79	
DE STE CROIX Aaron	Fort d'Auvergnc	1815–1828	6	
DU VAL Amice	St Aubin	1833–1848	7	
ENNIS George	Old Harbour	1859–	1	plus 1 steamer
ENO John	Patriotic Pl.	1846–	1	
ESNOUF, Edward	Patriotic Pl.	1834–1842	16	opp. Castle Bridge
ESNOUF & MAUGER	Patriotic Pl.	1847–1867	21	opp. Castle Bridge
FARLEY J.	St Aubin	1866–1888	2	
FAUVEL John	Gorey Pier	1842–1858	4	
FEUVRE (LE) Fr & J.	St Aubin	1843–1860	5	
FILLEUL John	Grouville	1827–1829	7	1 built at St Brelade
FILLEUL & DE LA MARE	La Rocque	1836–1837	3	
GAVEY John	?	1820–1826	11	also built Paspebiac '48
GAVEY Philip	?	1852–1855	3	
GAVEY Thomas	Patriotic Pl.	1856–1866	7	4 built on other sites
GIFFARD & LAURENS	St Aubin	1826–1829	6	
GRANDIN Philip J.	First Tower	1855–1874	11	3 built on other sites
GRAY ?	Havre-des-Pas	1841–1842	3	
GRELLIER Francis (Sen.)	?	1809–1817	7	
GRELLIER Francis (Jun.)	Patriotic Place	1826–1841	9	Surveyor of Shipping, 1814–1824
HACQUOIL Philip	St Ouen (l'Etacq)	1825–1828	3	
HAMON, BARTLETT & BISSON	Beaumont	1840–	1	
HAMON & ESNOUF	Patriotic Pl.	1827–1834	4	
HAMON Philip	Patriotic Pl.	1835–1845	4	also built Quebec ?
HAMPTONNE George	La Folie	1826–1841	20	died 1842
HAYLEY Thomas	Beaumont	1860–1861	2	
HELGREN C. P.	?	1838–1841	6	
HERAULT Philip	?	1813–	1	
HUQUET (LE) Edward	?	1824–1836	5	

List of Local Shipbuilders — continued

			vessel(s)	
HUQUET (LE) J. & T.	St Catherine	1850–1879	31	near the White Tower
JOPE Jean	Bouley Bay	1826	2	with Blampied
KING William	?	1821	1	
LAING Philip	St Aubin	1834–1838	11	St Aubin's Fort
LANE George B.	Gorey	1824–1825	2	
LUCE Francis	St Aubin	1838–1840	2	also built Gaspé 1832
MALLET Francis	Gorey	1862–1865	3	
MASURIER (LE) Nicolas	West Park	1837–1842	4	also built C.B. 1825
MASURIER (LE) Philip	Victoria Pier	1869–1874	5	
MASURIER (LE) Thomas	Trinity	1826	1	
MESSERVY John	Gorey	1854–1865	13	
NEVEU (LE) Philip	?	1807–1819	2	
NICOLLE Edward	Havre-des-Pas	1825–1835	5	
NICOLLE Philip	Patriotic Pl.	1816–1830	7	various sites
NICOLSON George	Patriotic Pl.	1847–1861	3	
NOEL George	Gorey	1858–1865	4	with Bellot
ORANGE Charles	St Aubin	1841	1	
PICOT John F.	Gorey	1858–1883	43	
RICHARDSON Clement	Fliquet Bay	1842–1845	3	
RICHARDSON J. W.	St Martin	1822	3	
ROISSIER ?	Patriotic Pl.	1856	1	
ROUGETEL (LE) Thomas	Patriotic Pl.	1860–1864	5	
SAUVAGE F. P.	St Aubin	1849–1851	4	
SCELLEUR (LE) Thomas	?	1827	1	
SILK Thomas	Patriotic Pl.	1826–1828	6	also built Fortune Bay, 1818
SUEUR (LE) Daniel	La Rocque	1851–1883	32	
SUEUR (LE) Philip	Gorey	1845–1857	10	near Fort Henry
VALPY John	?	1815–1819	4	
VALPY Mathew Ph.	Havre-des-Pas	1840–1868	22	2 built La Folie
VARDON Jean	Gorey	1842–1853	11	rear of Castle
VARDON & LE HUQUET	St Catherine	1837–1864	8	
VAUTIER George	Havre-des-Pas	1861–1875	14	also Fliquet & Beaumont
VESCONTE (LE) Daniel	First Tower	1858–1876	25	Val André
VESCONTE (LE) & VAUTIER	Havre-des-Pas	1854–1858	13	
WALLIS Werter	Commercial St.	1845	1	died 1864

SHIPBUILDERS IN NEWFOUNDLAND OR CANADA OF C.I. ORIGIN OR BUILDING FOR LOCAL OWNERS

ACHE Francis	New Brunswick	1829	
ASCATE Robert	Gaspé	1830	
BECHERVAISE Philip	Gaspé	1821	Jerseyman
BIGLORN Reuben	Nova Scotia	1829	

Shipbuilders in Newfoundland or Canada of C.I. origin — continued

BISSON Edward	Cheticamp C.B.	1832	Jerseyman ?
BOUTILLIER (LE) Josué	Cap Rosier, Gaspé	1832	Jerseyman ?
BOYLE Philip	Gaspé	1842	
BRENTON John	Fortune Bay	1823	Jerseyman ?
BRIARD Peter	Gaspé	1894	Jerseyman
BROURD Peter J.	Cap Breton	1841	Guernseyman
BROWN George	Gaspé	1842	
BRUN (LE) Francis	?	?	Jerseyman ?
COLLAS Francis	Fortune Bay	1827–40	Jerseyman
COLLAS James	Arichat	1831	Jerseyman
COLLAS Samuel	M⁻lbaye Gaspé	1832–40	Jerseyman
CORMIE Ambroise	St Peter's, N.B.	1828	
COUTEUR (LE) Daniel	La Poele Bay	1832	Jerseyman ?
DADRIDGE John	Gaspé	1830	
DAY James	Paspébiac	1825–29	
DUMAS Pierre	Bonaventure ?	?	
ENGLISH Thomas	Gaspé	1831	Jerseyman ?
FALLE Josué	Gaspé	1861–71	Jerseyman ?
GAVEY John	Paspébiac	1848	Jerseyman
GIRARD John	Malbaye, Gaspé	1831	Jerseyman ?
HAMON Philip	Newport, Quebec	?	Jerseyman
HENRY James	Shippigan N.B.	1849–95	Jerseyman
INGOUVILLE Philip	Sydney Harbour, C.B.	1790	Jerseyman
JARRETT (DE)	Arichat	1800	
LANGLOIS Charles	Arichat	1868	Jerseyman ?
LINDRILL & BRIARD	?	1834	
LUCE Francis	St Geo's Cove, Gaspe	1833	Jerseyman
MABE Peter	Gaspé	1825–28	Guernseyman
MARMAUD Fr. & Jas	Arichat	?	Jerseyman ?
MASURIER (LE) J.	Shippigan N.B.	?	Jerseyman ?
MASURIER (LE) Nicolas	Ship Harbor C.B.	1825–28	Jerseyman
MARTEL Isaac	Isle Madame C.B.	?	Guernseyman
MOIGNAN (LE) Pierre	Grand Rivierre	1830	Jerseyman
QUESNE (LE) ?	Quebec	1763	Jerseyman
RICHE (LE) P. J.	Cap Breton	1845	Jerseyman ?
SALTER Joseph & Sons	Monkton N.B.	1800	
SILK Thomas	Fortune Bay	1818	Jerseyman
TOUZEL Thomas John	Gaspé	1844–54	Jerseyman ?
TRACHY John	?	?	Jerseyman ?
VACHE (LE) Francis	Arichat	1828	Jerseyman ?
VAUTIER Philip	Gaspé	1837	Jerseyman ?
VESCONTE (LE) Peter & Isaac	?	1800	Jerseymen ?
VIBERT Philip	St Geo's Cove, Gaspé	1841	Jerseyman
VINCENT J. A. F.	Shippigan N.B. & Paspébiac	1803–39	Jerseyman
ARTHUR Charles	Gaspé	1838	Jerseyman

N.B. The following Builders are found both in Jersey and North America:

GAVEY John	JERSEY 1820–25	Paspébiac, 1848
HAMON Philip	JERSEY 1827–45	Newport, Quebec ?
LUCE Francis	JERSEY 1838–40	Gaspé, 1833
MASURIER Nicolas	JERSEY 1837–42	Cap Breton, 1825–28
SILK Thomas	JERSEY 1826–30	Fortune Bay, 1818
ARTHUR Charles	JERSEY 1822–27	Gaspé, 1838

JERSEY SHIPBUILDERS IN AMERICA

BACON Daniel	Born Jersey 1641	Salem 1664 (Le Porcq ?)
BECKETT (Becquet) ?		Salem ?
LANGLOIS Philip	Born Trinity 1651	Salem 1670
MESSERVY Clement		Boston ?
MESSERVY Nathaniel	Born Jersey	Portsmouth, New Hampshire, c. 1740
STEVENS William	Jersey	Built at Salem for Bailache 1661

NUMBERS AND TONNAGE OF RECORDED VESSELS BUILT LOCALLY

Year	No.	Tons	Year	No.	Tons	Year	No.	Tons
1763	1	50 tons	1823	1	268 tons	1855	10	1,920 tons
1773	1	70 tons	1824	8	760 tons	1856	13	3,150 tons
1776	2	95 tons	1825	11	924 tons	1857	20	4,360 tons
1783	1	57 tons	1826	13	1,346 tons	1858	20	3,245 tons
1789	2	208 tons	1827	8	1,094 tons	1859	14	3,020 tons
1791	1	? tons	1828	11	1,017 tons	1860	15	1,720 tons
1792	2	? tons	1829	8	660 tons	1861	15	2,970 tons
1794	1	219 tons	1830	7	814 tons	1862	18	2,465 tons
1798	1	354 tons	1831	6	1,400 tons	1863	17	3,150 tons
1800	4	185 tons	1832	8	1,166 tons	1864	19	5,265 tons
1801	2	27 tons	1833	6	970 tons	1865	22	4,390 tons
1802	3	295 tons	1834	6	886 tons	1866	12	1,800 tons
1803	2	115 tons	1835	14	1,422 tons	1867	11	3,490 tons
1804	1	65 tons	1836	17	1,679 tons	1868	14	1,260 tons
1805	1	13 tons	1837	18	1,890 tons	1869	8	680 tons
1806	—	— tons	1838	5	793 tons	1870	6	430 tons
1807	1	16 tons	1839	21	2,918 tons	1871	6	450 tons
1808	—	— tons	1840	21	2,972 tons	1872	10	758 tons
1809	1	19 tons	1841	25	3,440 tons	1873	13	1,080 tons
1810	1	12 tons	1842	7	735 tons	1874	7	515 tons
1811	1	130 tons	1843	11	1,939 tons	1875	12	1,000 tons
1812	1	6 tons	1844	4	112 tons	1876	7	460 tons
1813	2	80 tons	1845	9	759 tons	1877	15	595 tons
1814	1	62 tons	1846	7	916 tons	1878	5	388 tons
1815	6	556 tons	1847	14	1,727 tons	1879	3	193 tons
1816	3	56 tons	1848	11	1,665 tons	1880	1	79 tons
1817	2	187 tons	1849	14	2,390 tons	1881	2	60 tons
1818	1	? tons	1850	16	2,935 tons	1882	—	— tons
1819	2	155 tons	1851	11	1,520 tons	1883	3	108 tons
1820	2	300 tons	1852	11	2,510 tons	1884	1	49 tons
1821	5	368 tons	1853	13	3,010 tons			
1822	4	294 tons	1854	15	4,140 tons	Total	733	103,369 tons

SOME JERSEY CLIPPER SHIPS

ALBATROSS	79 tons Schooner	Owned by J. Wright, built by Bellot 1872.
CHIEFTAIN	579 tons Ship	Owned by Wm. Fruing & Co., built by Clarke 1857. Tea Clipper.
EVENING STAR	1,000 tons Ship	Owned by J. Le Bas, built by Allen 1854. Australian wool run.
FORT REGENT	655 tons Ship	Owned by Orange & Briard, built by Le Vesconte 1863. Tea Clipper
JEDDO	449 tons Ship	Not Registered Jersey, built by Esnouf & Mauger 1859, noted for fast sailing.
PERCY DOUGLAS	780 tons Ship	Owned by a Liverpool Company, built by Hayley 1861. Tea Clipper.
RESCUE	1,187 tons Ship	Owned by Ph. Pellier, American built. Australian wool run.
SEABIRD	79 tons Schooner	Owned by G. & F. de Ste Croix, built by Le Vesconte & Vautier 1857.

SHIPBUILDING SITES

BEAUMONT

BARTLETT Th. L.		1840-1848	20
BISSON Th.		1856	4
HAMON, BARTLETT, BISSON		1840	1
HAYLEY Th.		1860-1861	2
			27

BEL ROYAL

BUILDER UNKNOWN		1789	2

BOULEY BAY

BLAMPIED Denis		1826	2
JOPE Jean		1826	2
MASURIER (LE) Th.		1826	1
			5

FIRST TOWER

DESLANDES George		1827-1879	79
GRANDIN Ph. J.	opposite Bay View Hotel	1855-1872	11
VESCONTE (LE) Daniel	Val André	1858-1867	25
			115

GOREY

ASPLET George		1858-1861	7
AUBIN Chas. W.	Gorey Village	1866-1877	21
BELLOT Philip	near Tennis Courts	1858-1878	24
CANTEL Mark		1862-1863	2
FAUVEL John		1830-	4

Continued on following pages

Shipbuilding Sites — Gorey — continued

MALLET Fr.		1858–1865	4
MESSERVY John		1845–1865	13
NOEL George	built with Bellot	1865–	4
PICOT John F.	Gorey Village Slip	1858–1883	40
SUEUR (LE) Ph. J.	Fort Henry	1845–1857	7
VARDON John	rear of Gorey Castle	1943–1855	5
			131

HARBOUR AREA

BOEUF (LE) Matt		1810–1823	7
CLARKE F. C.	La Folie	1845–	2
DESLANDES George	La Folie	1824–1843	27
ENNIS George	Old Harbour	1859–	2
GAVEY John	English Harbour	1820–1826	11
GAVEY Thomas	La Folie	1852–1866	7
HAMPTONNE George	La Folie	1826–1841	20
MASURIER (LE) Phil	Victoria Pier	1869–1874	5
NICOLLE Philip	'New Quay'	1830–	3
SILK Thomas	Quai des Marchands	1826–1830	6
VALPY Matt Ph.	La Folie	1847–	2
WALLIS Werter	Commercial Street	1845–	1
			93

HAVRE-DES-PAS

ALLEN Edward		1840–	1
ALLIX Francis		1842–1877	18
BAXTER John		1824–1833	5
BISSON Thomas		1856–1878	3
CLARKE F. C.		1839–1845	12
DE STE CROIX Aaron	Fort d' Auvergne	1815–1828	4
GAVEY Thomas		1863–	2
GRANDIN Ph. J.		1856–	1
GRAY (?)		1842–1843	3
NICOLLE Edward		1825–1835	6
VALPY Matt. Ph.		1840–1868	22
VESCONTE (LE) & VAUTIER		1854–1858	13
			89

PATRIOTIC PLACE

CLARKE F. C.	opposite Gallows Hill	1844–1867	62
DE GRUCHY Thomas		1848–	2
ENO John	Sand Street	1846–	1
ESNOUF Edward	opposite Castle Bridge	1834–1842	16
ESNOUF & MAUGER	opposite Castle Bridge	1847–1868	21
GAVEY Thomas		1856–1860	3
GRANDIN Phil. J.		1855–1857	2
GRELLIER Fr.		1826–1841	9
HAMON & ESNOUF		1827–1831	4
HAMON Philip		1835–1844	4
MASURIER (LE) Nic.		1837–1839	4

Continued on following page

Shipbuilding Sites — Patriotic Place — continued

NICOLLE Edward		1829–	1
NICOLLE Philip		1822–1824	2
NICOLSON George		1847–1861	3
ROSSIER (?)		1856–	1
ROUGETEL Thomas		1860–1864	4
SILK Thomas		1826–1830	6
VAUTIER George		1861–1871	7
			153

LA ROCQUE

FILLEUL & DE LA MARE		1836–1837	3
SUEUR (LE) Daniel		1858–1883	27
			30

ST AUBIN

ALLEN Edward	end of Bulwarks	1837–1854	8
ARTHUR Charles		1822–1827	3
DEAN Philip		1833–1837	2
DU VAL Amice		1833–1848	7
FEUVRE (LE) Fr. Ph.		1849–1850	4
GIFFARD & LAURENS		1826–1832	6
LAING Philip	St Aubin's Fort	1834–1837	11
LUCE Francis		1838–1840	2
ORANGE Charles		1841–	1
SAUVAGE Fr. Ph.		1849–1851	4
			48

ST CATHERINE

GAVEY Thomas		1861–	1
HUQUET (LE) J. & T.	near White Tower	1850–1879	28
RICHARDSON Clement	Fliquet Bay	1842–1859	3
VARDON & LE HUQUET		1837–1859	8
			40

ST OUEN

HACQUOIL Philip		1825–1829	3
		Total	735

ANCHOR SMITHS

BINET Philip	Pier	1837
ENNIS George	Quai des Marchands	1856
GRANDIN F.	Quai des Marchands	1856–1874
JUENE Philip	Pier	1837
MARQUAND (LE)	North Pier	1856–1874
MASURIER (LE) G.	28 Quai des Marchands	1874
McALLEN C.	Esplanade	1856–1874
McALLEN J.	26 Conway Street	1874

BLOCKMAKERS

DALLAIN C.	Pier	1837–1847
DE LA COUR J.	28 Quai des Marchands	1899
DE STE CROIX J.	17 Aquila Road	1879
MOURANT Josué	22½ Quai des Marchands	1879–1885
SMITH J.	8 Quai des Marchands	1860
STEENE J.	7 Quai des Marchands	1860
TERRY D.	North Pier	1856–1860
TERRY J. D.	16 Quai des Marchands	1879–1885
VESCONTE (LE) N.	3 Quai des Marchands	1856–1885
VESCONTE (LE) Ph.	6 Quai des Marchands	1885–1905

MASTS AND OAR MAKERS

DALLAIN	Quai des Marchands	1856–1860
DE LA COUR J.	28 Quai des Marchands	1899
SMITH C.	Quai des Marchands	1856–1860
STEENE J.	Quai des Marchands	1856–1860
TERRY D.	3 Quai des Marchands	1860
VESCONTE (LE) N.	8 Quai des Marchands	1860

BOATBUILDERS

ALLIX Fr.	Havre-des-Pas	1879
ARROWSMITH C. J.	North Pier	1843
BAKER	Gorey	—
BISSON Th.	Green Street	1879
CLARKE H.	Pier Road	1843–1846
DOWNER J. P.	6 Quai des Marchands	1879
GAVEY J.	28 Seaton Place	1860
GAVEY P.	19 Quai des Marchands	1860–1879
GLENDEWAR O.	28½ Quai des Marchands	1879
GODFRAY F.	27 Quai des Marchands	1874
GRANDIN P.	North Pier	1834–1860
GRELLIER Fr.	North Pier	1843–1846
HUXFORD J.		1879
LEIGH J.	Bulwarks, St Aubin	1834–1845
NICOLSON Geo.	North Pier	1843–1846
NOEL Ph.	Gorey	1841
OATLEY J.	1 Quai des Marchands	1874
PICOT F.	North Pier	1843–1860
SILK J.	Quai des Marchands	1843–1846
VALPY	6 Quai des Marchands	1860

ROPEWALKS AND ROPEMAKERS

BARREAU Barnaby	Bath Street	1827	now Blue Coach Garage
BOIELLE James	Green Street	1811	alongside Cemetery
BRINE William	High Street, St Aubin	1770	from La Haule Manor to opposite first house in High Street
DESLANDERS Geo.	Havre-des-Pas		rear of Seaforth Hotel
DE STE CROIX A.	Havre-des-Pas		rear of Seaforth Hotel
HEMERY C. & T. MALLET	18 Quai des Marchands		
JANVRIN & MALLET	Green Street	1804	
JANVRIN Brelade	Green Street	1773	near Chapelle des Pas
JANVRIN Philippe	Green Street	1804	ceded to Government
JERROM & SON	Havre-des-Pas		rear of Seaforth Hotel
LAURENS F.	Green Street	1790	near Cemetery
LAURENS Geo. D.	Green Street	1860	Last and Largest — ¼-mile long roofed. House 'La Corderie'.
MALLET Pierre	Green Street	1773	near Chappelle des Pas
MALLET Thomas	Green Street	1804	ceded to Government
MARETT	St Aubin	1820–1834	Seafront West of La Haule Manor
NICOLLE Edward	Kensington Place	1820	
NICOLLE Philip	Kensington Place	1809	
ROWCLIFFE George	Havre-des-Pas	1760–1770	

SAILMAKERS

BAUDAINS	Caledonia Place	1843–1846
BERTRAM, Auguste	Liverpool (from Jersey)	1870–
BINGHAM	Pier	1837–
CUMMINS, T. B.	24 Quai des Marchands	1874–1899 also Gorey
DE GARIS & BAUDAINS	24 Quai des Marchands	1837–
DE GARIS & CO.	24 Quai des Marchands	1843–1848
FAUVEL, J.	21 Quai des Marchands	1874
FEUVRE (LE) Philip	21 Quai des Marchands	1870
FRUING	3 Pier Road	1837– Sailcloth maker
GRUCHY, J. E.	Quai des Marchands	1826–1860
HENRY & DE GARIS	Quai des Marchands	1847
HENRY & LE FEUVRE	18 Quai des Marchands	1860–1885
HENRY, J.	13 Quai des Marchands	1843–1899
HUBERT & LE SUEUR	13 Quai des Marchands	1860–
HUTCHINGS	Pier	1837–
JEUNE, J.	10 Le Geyt Street	1879–
LAVAN, Thomas	9 Quai des Marchands	1869–1885
OVENING & LE FEUVRE	9 Quai des Marchands	1843–1846
ROBILLIARD, H.	9 Quai des Marchands	1843–1874
SHERWOOD & OVENING	9 Quai des Marchands	1860–
TOCQUE BROS.	5 Quai des Marchands	1885–
TOCQUE, J. D.	5 Quai des Marchands	1870–
TOCQUE, T.	St Aubin	1843

SHIPWRIGHTS

AMY J.	Gorey	1843–	
BEER		1826	drowned Bouley Bay
CHEVALIER Francis		1819–	with P. J. Le Neveu
CLERC (LE) Thomas		1827–	
COUTANCHE Philip		1836–	with Chas. Hamon
DORWARD John		1821–	
GAVEY Joshua		1827–	
GRELLIER Francis	St Helier	1808–	
GRESLEY John	Canada	1819–	returned to Jersey
LANE Geo. B.	Gorey	1824–	
LUCE Francis	St Aubin	1837–	for M. Alexandre
LAURENS Abraham	Liverpool	1867–	and Shipowner
MAISTRE Edward		1818–	
MONTAIS (LE) Edward		1808–	
RICOU William	Trinity	1836–	
ROUX (LE) Philip		1830	
SCELLEUR (LE) J.	Gorey	1843–	
SCELLEUR (LE) Charles		1870–	

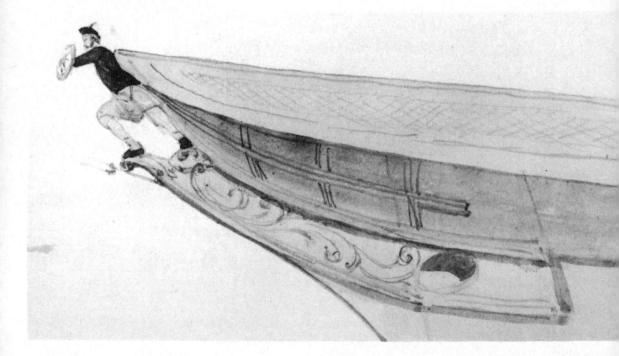

Figurehead of 'Chieftain', a tea clipper of 579 tons, built by Clarke, West Park 1857. Owner W M Fruing & Co. Lost in the Indian Ocean 1 December, 1859 with a cargo of tea and silk from Shanghai.

Chapter Two

PORTS AND HARBOURS

Jersey's Harbours and Piers

THE EARLIEST HARBOURS around the Island coast were natural havens which provided a little shelter from the wild south-westerly gales and a sand bed on which small vessels could lie without damage to their keels. Coves such as Havre-des-Pas, La Rocque, St Brelade and St Aubin gave shelter for many years but, as the vessels grew both larger and more numerous, increased anchorage was needed and more shelter was required.

In the extente of 1274 the 'Portus Gorryk' or Port of Gorey is mentioned and later in 1617 the harbour is described as 'not good'. In 1685 Dumaresq wrote: 'at the foot of the Castle is the most ancient harbour in the island, an old decayed pier, where small boats as use the Normandy coast resort'. St Helier was still harbour-less at this time. 'Under the churchyard', he said, 'is a shelter for boats'.

St Aubin offered the safest anchorage, sheltered as it was by Noirmont from the south-west gales and from southerly winds; protection was given by the islet on which the Fort was built, and on the north and east by hills and the sweep of the shore. Moreover at low tides ships could rest on the ample sands and discharge their cargo into carts.

The Chronicler tells how in 1533 'a Spanish merchant had laden his barque with wheat in the harbour of St Obin'. A time came when the natural shelter given was insufficient and the Newfoundland fishing fleet began to winter at St Malo. So in 1649, when Charles II was in Jersey, he offered 500 pistoles towards a pier to be built at St Aubin. Twenty years later, when restored to his throne, he ordered part of the import duties to be used for this purpose. The States adopted a plan for the pier to be built slightly south of the present pier, and one Nicolas Bailhache[1] contracted to build it. But nothing was done until three years later, when the Governor, Sir Thomas Morgan, took on the work and built it in 1675, projecting from St Aubin's Fort. It has stood the test of some 300 years.

The States implemented an Order in Council to appropriate the Impôt revenue for the construction of a harbour at St Helier, after St Aubin's pier should be completed. The pier was finished in 1700 and the same year the States chose a site at St Helier, known as Le Havre Neuf,[2] a small creek under Le Petit Mont de la Ville, to the south west of La Folie. A screen or pier was started here but money from the duties on goods was poor and the work progressed very slowly.

17

In 1720[3] notes to the amount of 50,000 livres tournois were issued by the States to continue the work, and in 1749[4] a States Lottery was started to raise more revenue, while two years later £300 was given by King George II towards the costs, the grateful States thereupon erecting a statue of him in the Royal Square.

1754 saw the start of the South Pier[5] at St Aubin's, and a new construction at Le Havre Neuf, to join the pier to the New Quay where the house 'La Folie' now stands, was begun in 1765. However, the work at Le Havre Neuf was of poor quality and in spite of repairs it became dangerous to shipping and there was no proper access to the quay, pedestrians reaching the harbour by a small road skirting the Mont de la Ville, whilst carts had to go along the beach at low tide to unload vessels.

In 1788 the Island shipping had so increased that a larger and better harbour was needed, and the celebrated engineer, Smeaton, builder of the Eddystone Lighthouse, came to Jersey to advise the States on the building of new harbours, at both St Helier and St Aubin. However, the States did not adopt Smeaton's plan and on 8 February 1790[6] approved a plan of their own. On 19 April the following year they laid the foundation stone of the New North Pier, starting from in front of the Southampton Hotel. The Havre Neuf now became known as the South Pier. This work dragged on slowly because of lack of money but was finished by 1819 at a cost of £80,000.

Meanwhile the merchants at St Aubin, who owned land facing the harbour, built a quay in 1790[7] for their own use and thereby reclaimed a large area from the sea, as can be seen today by the length of the front gardens; the North Pier was added in 1818. This harbour, though small, attracted shipping merchants to St Aubin where they built their houses, and so a small township sprang up and many of these fine old houses can still be seen today.

The Chamber of Commerce voted 15,000 livres tournois in 1803[8] to build a quay on the south of the Havre des Anglais, and the owners of land on the roadway leading to the Havre Neuf started in 1811 to build a row of houses now known as Commercial Buildings. Later, in 1814, the foundation stone for a quay was laid. This new quay was named Quai des Marchands and the work was undertaken by Abraham de la Mare and Son, supervised by David de Quetteville, and completed on 1 May 1818. The States on 2 January 1817 adopted a report to extend the Quai des Marchands to link up with the Rue du Port and to build a slip in the Havre aux Anglais; this extra work was carried out by Abraham de la Mare, whose tender was accepted on 21 January 1818. The States agreed to repair and rebuild the old South Pier and this started in 1820, together with a low water landing place for passengers in what is now the middle of Victoria Pier. The work was again undertaken by Abraham de la Mare, who in 1819[9] had a sloop of 25 tons built by Philip J. Le Neveu. This vessel was named 'Father and Son' and was lost in 1821 while transporting stone for the South Pier.

The construction of a public Weighbridge at the entrance to the quay, close to the town, was ordered by the States on 7 January 1825[10] and the following year a pier to shelter the oyster boats at Gorey was erected, followed by a pier at

1. Figurehead of the *Evening Star*, a clippership of 847 tons. Built by Allen, St Aubin 1854, owner Jean Le Bas, master Philip R. De Ste Croix.

2. Stern of the *Evening Star*. Her maiden voyage was to Australia with ninety-five Jersey emigrants in 1854.

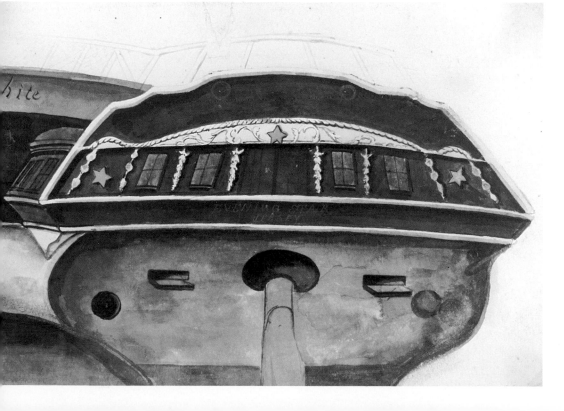

3. Built by F.C. Clarke at West Park, and launched on 26 May 1865, the ship *Georges*, 473 tons was owned by Orange and Briard. Lost off Maryport, Cumberland, 1 March, 1871.

4. The fine barque *Alexandre*, 306 tons, built by Mallet 1865, Signal Letters H.B.Q.M. official no. 51256. Owned by Le Quesne, Pallot and Mallet, this vessel was sold to New South Wales in 1877.

5. *(right)* Captain Philip Le Blancq, master of the topsail schooner *Adelina*, 1855. Also master of the brigantine *Reaper*. Believed drowned at sea.

6. Wearing the Janvrin colours on her foremast this fine ship of 228 tons was named *Janvrin*. Built in 1821 by Matthew Le Boeuf, St Helier and owned by P & F Janvrin for many years, and was commanded by Jean Piton from 1834-44.

7. The schooner *Royal Blue Jacket*, 93 tons, built by J & R White, Cowes, 1854. At the masthead the house flag of the owners 1870-79, de Gruchy, Renouf and Clement, master Frank Le Marquand. Sold to Cork, 1888.

Bouley Bay, work on which started in 1827, being entrusted to another Abraham de la Mare. This breakwater was 120 feet long and 46 feet high, and the cost was £2,500. The States voted £8,000 for building the Esplanade, the report being adopted on 15 May 1829, and work was completed by 1835. The congestion of oyster boats at Gorey caused the States to build a quay at Rozel, 200 feet long and 26 feet high. The advent of a gas supply to Jersey in 1831 led to the harbour at St Helier being lit by this medium. A slaughter house and a cattle market were added in 1834, built at the end of the North Pier.

All these works were inadequate for the rapid increase in local shipping, and a harbour of some substance became an urgent necessity. So a new South Pier was started by the States, the contract being agreed on 10 August 1841 at a cost of £56,000; the builders were Thomas Le Gros and John de Gruchy, Junr. and no time was lost in making a start, as the foundation stone was laid with great ceremony on 29 September 1841[11] (a painting by Reynolds of this scene can be seen in the Museum of the Société Jersiaise). The new South Pier was completed by 10 August 1846 and was named Victoria by the Queen during her visit to Jersey on 3 September 1846. This fine pier was followed the next year by a new North Pier, the contractors being Thomas Le Gros and Francis de la Mare, for a sum of £109,000; the foundation stone was laid on 18th March 1847 and the work completed in July 1853. This new North Pier was re-named Albert Pier in 1859 in honour of the Queen's Consort after their second visit.

Another harbour was started at St Catherine,[12] in 1847, designed as a naval harbour for sheltering vessels of the Royal Navy, to counter the growing threat from the enlarged French Navy. The British Government was responsible for this harbour which consisted of a pier at St Catherine (Verclut) 2,700 feet long, and a proposed second arm at Archirondel. After some eight years work at a cost of £250,000, the harbour was abandoned in 1855 and was transferred to the States on 12 April 1878, the reason being that, with the coming of steam, it was no longer necessary to keep a squadron of ships this side of the Channel. This fine breakwater today provides the keen angler with an excellent position for fishing but otherwise is of little use.

Further improvements were made from time to time. On 24 March 1849 a lighthouse was placed on Gorey Pier, and a wooden landing stage on the Victoria Pier was completed on 25 May 1860. The Harbours Committee of the States decided in 1861 to acquire a lifeboat and a steam tug. Thomas Le Gros was granted £3,200 for building the new Esplanade in 1865. However, the problem of the harbour drying out at low tides had not been overcome and merchants and shipowners were again calling for a deep water harbour. Ever increasing numbers of local vessels using the harbour again caused difficulties and a new harbour plan was adopted by the States in 1871.[13] Of the 42 plans submitted, Sir John Coode's was accepted, which entailed building a great breakwater stretching from Elizabeth Castle in a southerly direction, and another, three quarters of a mile long, from La Collette. The foundation stone was laid by the Bailiff on 29 August 1872. The work on the breakwater at the Castle was in granite and proved satisfactory, but the pier at La Collette was constructed of concrete blocks and suffered badly from storm damage. In December 1874 a south-west gale caused a great breach in the pier which was repaired, but the following winter another large section collapsed. When a third breach occurred in 1876, the States abandoned the work after paying out £16,000

1872 saw other works started: a jetty at La Rocque, and harbours at Bonne Nuit and Grève de Lecq. The Pier at Grève de Lecq also suffered storm damage. Firstly, early in 1879, gales caused the wall to crack along the whole length of the structure, and a week later 40 yards of wall completely collapsed and the stones were littered across the beach, where they remained for the next hundred years.

Another project undertaken in 1872, after much debate and delay, was the building of a lighthouse at La Corbière. Again a plan submitted by Sir John Coode was adopted. This was to be the first lighthouse in the world build in concrete. All the building materials were carried to the chosen site by sea and the construction was supervised by Mr. Imrie Bell, the States Engineer. The light was first lit on 26 April 1874, the total cost being £8,000.

Further dredging was undertaken in 1882 in an endeavour to overcome the bogey of low tides and constant silting of the harbour. Part of the old harbour was filled in at the north end in 1884, and a circular garden was laid out on the reclaimed area, while the Westaway Monument was moved to a new position beside the Normandy Monument near the Victoria Pier. The old North Pier was widened and was now known as the New North Quay, while yet more dredging took place and a 500-ft. extension to the Elizabeth Castle breakwater was undertaken in 1887, again in granite, which protected the small or inner road from south-westerly gales.

Owing to the constant dredging, the head of the old North Pier collapsed on 9 November 1889, and was rebuilt in 1894. With much ceremony a statue of Queen Victoria was placed in the circular garden on reclaimed land in 1890, where it remained for the next 85 years, surveying the comings and goings in the harbour with all-seeing eyes and unsmiling countenance, until it was removed recently to a more peaceful scene at West Park.

The rebuilding of the Albert Pierhead took place in 1902, and a private company built a jetty at Ronez to facilitate the export of granite direct by sea to many countries all over the world. A grand harbour improvement plan costing £250,000 took two years to complete, starting in 1928, and involved the dredging of the harbour approaches, the making of the deep water berths along the Victoria Pier, the rebuilding of the Victoria Pierhead, filling in the slipway at the end of the Albert Pier, thus providing the No. 1 Berth, and further in-filling of the old harbour. A modern plan to build a deep water tanker berth, a yacht marina, and further land reclamation costing many millions was undertaken in the late 1970s — but that is another story.

HAROUR MASTERS

St Aubin

1720	Thomas Denton
1772	Jean le Boutillier
1778	Pierre Cabot
1788	Elie Vibert
1799	Philippe Bichard
1809-1834	Jean Luce
1834-1841	Philippe Hamon; died 1841
1841-1851	Nicolas Clement
1852-1873	Edward le Feuvre
1873-1884	Philippe de Ste Croix
1884-1899	Jean Vautier; died 5 January 1899
1899-1903	Albert Briard
1904-1913	P. C. Langlois; died 1913

Gorey

Before 8 April 1816 dues received by Jean Chevalier or Jean Asplet.

1816-1836	Philippe Bertram; resigned 1836
1839-1853	James Luce; resigned 1853
1855-1885	Jean Amy
1886-1902	Charles Pallot
1902-1903	George Noel

Rozel

1845-1893	George Noel. First established 1845
1893	Thomas Ph. Renouf

St Helier

1763-1783	Jean Lys
1785	Jean Poingdestre
1787	Joshua Mollet
1792-1809	David Mauger
1809-1819	Jean Chevalier; resigned 1819, died 1825
1819-1831	Philippe Dupont; died 1831
1831-1843	Thomas Lerrier; replaced 1843
1843-1861	Jean Chevalier; drowned 1861 (buried Green Street Cemetery)
1861-1873	Peter Briard; resigned 1873
1873-1883	James Hamon
1883-1896	William Bichard
1896-1926	F. J. Renouf
1926	William le Seelleur

DEPUTY HARBOUR MASTERS

1838	Henry Gillman
	Pierre Le Bas
1849-1850	Jean Sohier
1850	Edward Romeril
1873	J. D. Le Couteur
1871	James Hamon

JERSEY PILOTS

Name	Year	Coast
ALLIX, Francis	1879	West
ALLIX, George	1840–1860	West
ALLIX, Philippe	1860–1879	West
ADAMS, William	1879	East
BATTAM, John	1840	West
BATTAM, John (Junr.)	1840–1860	West
BATTAM, William	1840	West
BLAMPIED, Jean	1840–1879	East
BRACHE, John	1840–1860	West
BRACHE, Nicolas	1840–1860	West
BULCAN, Nicolas	1840–1860	West
CHAMBERS, James	1879	East
DE LA MARE, John	1860	West
DE LA MARE, Peter	1860	West
DE LA MARE, Thomas	1840–1860	West
DE LA RUE, Nicolas	1840–1860	West
DOWNER, James	1840–1843	East
DU FRESNE, Philippe	1840	East
DU FRESNE, Phil (Junr.)	1840	East
DU HEAUME, John	1840–1860	West
DU HEAUME, Phil (Junr.)	1860	West
FINNIE, J...	1860	West
GALLICHAN, Elie	1840–1843	East
GOTTREL, Francis	1840	West
GOTTREL, Fr. (Junr.)	1840–1860	West
GIRARD, Daniel	1860	West
JENNE, John	1840	East
LARBALESTIER, Chas.	1860–1879	West
LARBALESTIER, E. C.	1879	West
KEEPING, William	1879	West
MARETT, Joshué	1840–1860	West
MARIE, George	1860	West
MARIE, Philippe	1840	East
MAUGER, Philip	1840–1860	East
MOLLET, Philip (Junr.)	1840–1860	East
PAYN, Philip	1840–1860	East
PERCHARD, John	1879	East
PERCHARD, Philip	1840	East
RENOUF, Edward	1879	West
RENOUF, Francis	1840	East
RENOUF, Philip	1840–1860	West
RENOUF, Philip	1840	East
RENOUF, Philip (Junr.)	1879	West
RENOUF, P. C.	1879	West
RICHARDSON, Abraham	1840	East
ROBERT, P.	1879	West
ROBERT, Thomas	1879	West
SAINTHILL, Thomas	1840–1843	East
SALTEE, Thomas	1840	East
SAMPSON, John	1860	West
STREET, Stephen	1840	West
SYVRET, Jean	1840	West

JERSEY PILOTS

Year	No.	Coast	Year	No.	Coast
1841	18	West	1841	15	East
1842	18	West	1842	15	East
1845	23	West	1845	13	East
1852	28	West	1852	8	East
1863	22	West	1863	6	East
1865	27	West	1865	7	East
1873	26	West	1873	4	East
1879	10	West	1879	4	East
1886	10	West	1886	3	East

Pilot Boat Number One, 30 tons. Built by Thomas Silk, 1830. Master: Philip Renour.
Pilot Boat Number Two, 30 tons. Built by Geo. Deslandes 1830. Master: Francis Gottrell.

The Jersey Impôt (Local Customs)

The origin of the Impôt dates from Elizabethan times; in the year 1585 the States appointed George Messervy, the Attorney-General, to collect the dues. An Act of the States in 1602 appointed Edouard Le Porq 'Superviseur pour les coustimes des Etats au Havre de St. Aubin'. Likewise Pierre d'Auvergne for St Ouen, Jean du Parq for La Rocque and Nicholas Richardson for Rozel, Bouley and St Catherine. The first duty on wine was established in 1618 on a grant from the Crown. Letters patent granting to the Bailiff and Jurats the right to levy duty on wine and cider was given in 1669. These Impôts were appropriated for the building of a harbour at St Aubin's Tower and, after the completion of this pier, the States set apart the Impôts for building a pier at St Helier.

OFFICERS OF IMPÔT
COLLECTEUR OR TRESORIER

1585	George Messervy	1729	Matthew Le Geyt
1602	Nicholas Durell	1746	Thomas Le Breton
1673	David Bandinel	1750	Jean Le Couteur
1687	George Le Brun	1774	Philip Lerrier
1696	Charles Dumaresq	1790	Clement Hemery
1700	Michel Du Pré		

FERMIERS

1789	Francis Janvrin	1809	David de Quetteville
	Philip Janvrin		Jean Winter
	Aaron de Ste Croix		Jean Benest
	Jean Benest		Jacques Remon
1806	Charles Chevalier	1819	Jacques Remon
	Philip Janvrin		Clement Bailhache
	Jean Janvrin		Josué Pipon
	George Ingouville		Thomas Duhamel
	Louis Poignard		

OFFICERS OF IMPÔT

1826	Thomas Durell, Jacques Remon, Clement Bailhache, Joeué Pipon
1829	Thomas Duhamel, Jacques Remon, Clement Bailhache, Josué Pipon
1832	Edward Nicolle, Philip Le Geyt
1840	Clement Sorel, Philip Le Geyt, Philip Dean
1849	Clement Sorel, Edward de la Taste, Josué M. Nicolle, Jean Le B. Chevalier, John Purchase
1851	H. C. Bertram, J. E. Lesbirel, W. E. Burke
1863	Clement Sorel (Principal), H. C. Bertram (Chief Agent), Philip Gallichan (Agent), James Corbell (Agent), E. J. Bertram (Distillery), Josué Mauger Nicolle (Treasurer), John Le Boutillier (Auditor), C. J. Hocquard (Jaugeur, i.e. Surveyor).
1874	Clement Sorel (Principal), H. C. Bertram (Chief Agent), Philip Gallichan (Agent), James Corbell (Agent), Josué Mauger Nicolle (Treasurer), J. Le B. Chevalier (Auditor).

Customs and Smuggling

Smuggling was rife in the Channel Islands for many years, both between the isles and France, and also on the mainland coasts, particularly in the south west. Only a few Jersey sea-captains actually became engaged in the trade, although ships were built locally with false bottoms for concealing contraband, but the Islanders played a large part in this illegal but profitable trade by supplying the English smugglers with their cargoes. The quiet bays of the Island were excellent places for small English vessels to put into at dead of night, grounding their boats on the sandy shores and quickly loading cargoes of spirits and tobacco, standing ready on the beach by arrangement with the local smugglers. Most of the bays used were unlikely places to come under the eyes of the British Customs Officers appointed by the Crown. In early Stuart days the 'Customer' of Jersey was appointed by the Governor of the island or directly by the Crown, and as far as can be ascertained the first mention of the holder of this office was on 16 April 1632, when one Edmund Dean granted a certificate to John Hardy.

A report of 1689 states that an immense smuggling trade existed between France and England, and the 'Customer' was not above taking part in these activities: a report of 1693 shows that a vessel took brandy and wine from Guernsey to Plymouth without paying duty, with the connivance of Wm. Hely, the Customer in Jersey, who had also sent lead to France illegally. William Chamberlain, the Customer for Jersey c. 1700, brought to the notice of the States an Order-in-Council relating to the unlimited practice of small craft from Jersey running French goods upon the coast of England. Another Order-in-Council was issued in 1767 establishing a permanent Officer of Customs in the Island, and also a Registrar's Office. At this period smuggling was still rife in the island. The peak was reached in the first part of the 19th century, especially after the end of the Napoleonic Wars, and Custom records are full of complaints of the 'doings' of the smugglers, such as that for 1823 which states: 'March 17th,[15] A Cawsand boat loaded in St Brelade's bay, 300 ankers of brandy. March 31st A Plymouth cutter in the same bay took on some 600 ankers of brandy and gin. An East Looe cutter, on the 19th of June also loaded in St. Brelade's bay 690 casks of brandy, and a Cawsand boat took on another large cargo of spirits'.

However, local ships were not slow to participate in this lucrative trade as is shown by the statement of a crew member of the Jersey-owned vessel 'Eliza' in 1863. This vessel loaded at Bonne Nuit 2½ tons of tobacco, snuff, spirits and 'segars'. After a long chase of several house by a Customs cutter, this cargo was landed on the coast near Fishguard.

CUSTOMS OFFICERS

1632	Edmund Dean		
1665–79	Sir Thomas Morgan		
1680	Laurence Cole, Registrar		
1685–93	William Hely, Registrar		
1694–	Francis Watts, Registrar		
1696–1700	William Chamberlain & Samuel Dassel, Registrar		
1704–	John Robertson, Registrar		
1744–	Dixey Coddington, last customer appointed by Privy Council		
1767	First Permanent Officer Appointed		
1829	John Durell	James Rider	Henry Warne (also acted as Deputy Surveyor of Shipping)
	James Hardie	Joseph Beaton	
1840	Joseph Rider	G. P. Prittle	James Rider
	Peter Warne	James Hardie	Joseph Beaton
	John Cocke	Joseph Hussey	
1849	George Radford	James Rider	M. J. D. Dumaresq
	James Hardie	John Rawling	David Mackay (Gorey)
	Philip Vontom (Gorey)	John Squib	G. T. Hamilton
	David Squibb		
1863	George Radford	T. W. Clarke	G. P. Charlton
	N. C, Hunter	Ph. Vonton	W. Mackay
	A. W. Flann	H. C. Amy	D. Squibb (Gorey)
	G. S. Brett (Gorey)	T. H. Baker	
1874	George Clayton	G. P. Charlton	Jas. Cooper
	R. K. Troon	F. W. Hawkins	H. C. Amy
	J. D Henry	R. K. Troon (Jr.)	W. Mackay
	J. H. Baker	A. W. Flann	H. C. Amy
	D. Squibb (Gorey)	G. S. Brett (Gorey)	

The Port of St Aubin

The Port of St Aubin at one time was of greater importance than St Helier since, before the building of a permanent harbour, ships could anchor in the lee of the hills which protected St Aubin from the prevailing westerly winds, and could discharge their cargoes at low water on the wide expanses of firm sand in the bay. St Aubin had the right to be called a township, because of the market which had existed there for many years. This market was already well established in Elizabethan times; it is recorded in 1584 that Monday was market day, and in 1602 the States appointed Edward Le Porcq 'Superviseur pour les coustumes des etats du havre de St Aubin'. Foreign vessels as well as local ships were using this anchorage as early as 1533;[16] in that year 'a Spanish merchant had loaded his barque with wheat in the harbour of St Obin'. To give a measure of security to vessels riding at anchor, the States established a tower on the islet and a two-gun bulwark on the shoreline.

As the Newfoundland fishing fleet began to expand, the shelter provided by nature became insufficient and the vessels began to winter at St Malo. So the States decided to build a pier at St Aubin and, when King Charles was in Jersey in 1649, he offered 500 pistoles towards the cost of construction. When, 20 years later, nothing had been done, Charles ordered that part of the import duties should be used, but the work did not begin until 1675 when the Governor, Sir Thomas Morgan, took over the construction and a pier was built projecting from the fort. This work can still be seen today, having withstood the fury of the waves for over three hundred years. The existence of a pier encouraged the merchants to add to the houses already along the foreshore and on the surrounding hills, and a small township sprang up. The oldest house standing today is dated 1611 and was the home of P. Seale, a merchant and shipowner, and was once called Osborne House. This dwelling, during the Civil War, was the Prize Court where captured vessels were brought to be judged and sold, and it is now the Old Court House Hotel.

The majority of the houses along the Boulevards were built at the end of the 17th century, and among the merchants living there then were Thomas Pipon, Constable of St Brelade, Merchant and Shipowner, at Elliston House, 1678; Pierre Le Bailly, Merchant and Shipowner, of La Vielle Maison, c. 1687, and Francois Kastel, Merchant, L'Armistice, c. 1700. Thomas Denton was probably the first Harbour Master to be appointed, c. 1720, to St Aubin, and his son Thomas, born in 1801, married Jeanne Le Bailly and became a wealthy merchant and shipowner, one of the founders of St Aubin's church and left a sum of money to establish a hospital for old people in St Aubin. Francis Bartlett, an English merchant, who settled at St Aubin and married Marie Mauger, daughter of Captain Jean Mauger, died childless in 1734, but his widow carried on the business and when she died she left a large sum of money to start a hospital, which after much delay was built at St Helier and is now part of the General Hospital there. Jean Villeneuve was at La Vielle Maison by 1705, and he with other merchants used to gather on the quay every morning to conduct business.

Some of the vessels based at St Aubin at this period include 'The Golden Lion' (Master Philip Pipon), *c.* 1668; 'Rachel' (Jean Vincent), trading with Virginia, *c.* 1701; 'Marie' (Owned by Jean Villeneuve, Master Wm. Snow); 'L'Accident' (Sam. Perrand), *c.* 1721; 'Adventure' (Peter Fiott); 'Thomas & Jane' (Carteret Dean); 'Jersey' (Jean Pipon); 'William' (Thom. Snow), all in 1737. The building of a new pier commenced in 1754, and this pier to the south provided further shelter, thereby encouraging more and bigger ships to lay up at St Aubin, particularly in the 1770s and 1780s. Among these vessels were 'Aigle' (Master Ph. Dean); 'Alert' (Wm. Snow); 'L'Arme' (owned by Ph. Dean, Master Jean Fiott); 'L'Industrie' (Jean Herault); 'Mercury'; 'Dauphin'; 'Kingfisher'; 'Marie'; 'Beaver'; and 'Betsy'. The merchants who owned land facing the harbour constructed the quay now known as the Bulwarks; building was started *c.* 1790 and a considerable amount of land was reclaimed from the sea as can be seen today by the length of the front gardens belonging to some of the houses. The existence of this quay brought further increases in the number of vessels using the harbour, and by 1798 as many as 30 were to be seen at one time at rest in the harbour.

A further pier, called the north arm, was added to the harbour in 1818, completely enclosing the anchorage. The building of this pier may have been financed by Jean Janvrin, Shipowner and Merchant, of L'Ancienneté, as his name appears on a commemorative stone set in the wall of the quay. Charles Robin of the famous C.R.C. company of the Canadian Fisheries retired to St Aubin, probably to a house called St Magloire, until his death in 1824. Though it is likely that shipbuilding took place at St Aubin for many years before the siting of permanent yards, by the 1820s and 1830s the industry had greatly expanded and many yards were building vessels. Philip Laing sited his yard at St Aubin's Fort in 1834, turning out ships for local owners and also for export, but most yards were sited at the end of the bulwarks, where the terminus of the Jersey Railways Co. was later built. Here were the yards of A. Duval, F. P. Sauvage, Fr. Le Feuvre, Dean & Leigh, while that of E. P. Allen was at the far end of the Bulwarks. Yet another yard, that of Thomas Leigh Bartlett, was placed at Beaumont. Charles Arthur, Francis Luce and John Farley also built vessels at St Aubin. Ropewalks were in existence at St Aubin, one which was leased to William Brine, *c.* 1770 reaching from the top of the High Street down to La Haule Manor, and another on the foreshore to the west of La Haule Manor, which was in used in 1834. Some of the earlier ships that were fashioned at St Aubin may have been built by the Janvrins, or by the Dean family who had used the harbour at St Aubin since 1737, or even earlier. Matthew Alexandre, an owner of a number of ships, lived at St Peter but based his vessels at St Aubin for many years, as did Edward and Francis Le Feuvre.

The Harbours Committee of the States established a fresh water pump at the foot of Mont Les Vaux to enable the crews of the many ships using the harbour to draw drinking water for use on their long journeys at sea. This pump can still be seen today inscribed 'Harbours 1862'.

Two of the last sailing vessels to use St Aubin's harbour were the 'Bolivia' and 'St Brelade' in 1870, although photographs show sailing vessels berthed in the harbour much later than this date. The last vessel to be built at St Aubin was the 'Wyvern', a yacht of seven tons, built by Farley in 1880. The harbour today is given over to pleasure craft and small fishing boats, but still retains its old world charm.

The Port of Gorey

There has been a port of some description at Gorey for hundreds of years; in 1274 the King received 'La Coustume du port de Gorrey, pres du Château', and in 1531 there was mention of a little harbour under the castle walls. A jetty or shelter for small boats had existed there for many years. However, the pier of the present day was not built until 1826 to provide shelter for the hundreds of cutters and small schooners employed in dredging the oyster banks. Further harbours were built as the oyster fishing fleet continued to expand; that at Bouley Bay was commenced in 1827, and two years later a pier was built at Rozel in efforts to relieve the congestion of boats at Gorey.

Jerseymen had known of and fished the oyster banks from the middle ages, and although the Governor in 1606[17] tried to claim the banks as crown property, the Court ruled otherwise and the local boats continued to bring back the oysters in small numbers, until the discovery in 1797 of several new banks to the north-west of the French-owned island of Chausey. The industry started to expand and attracted to Gorey large numbers of boats belonging to English companies, particularly from Kent and Sussex and even as far afield as Colchester, as well as growing numbers of local boats. By 1810, over 300 vessels were employed, manned by nearly 1,000 seamen, in the regular fishing of the banks. But unfortunately some boats started to poach on beds in French water inside the three mile limit and this poaching soon led to trouble. In 1821 the French[18] sent armed vessels to patrol the beds and they seized several smacks and took them into Granville. Again in 1822 the French fired broadsides on the British boats and chased them from the banks as far as the Jersey coast. The States were alarmed by the action of the French and in April 1822 they made a representation to the King in council, with the result that H.M.S. 'Fly', a sloop of 10 guns, was stationed off Jersey to prevent further French aggression and to discourage any retaliation by local fishermen.

Then, in 1824, the States heard of the doubling of the limits to six miles and that the Royal Navy Commander had orders not to protect any boats fishing within these limits. This proved disastrous for the British boats as the best part of the banks came within this limit, so they continued to operate in the same area, especially at night. Their operations culminated in yet another fight with the French in 1828, when an English boat was captured by two French men-of-war. When the news reached Gorey, all the fishing boats sailed over to the French coast, boarded the warships and took the English boat back to Jersey, but several fishermen lost their lives and some were taken prisoners. In spite of a protest by the States, the British Government would not sanction this poaching and the fishery began to decline; exports of 300,000 bushels in 1833 fell to 147,000 bushels in 1835.

In 1834 the States decided to lay down new beds in Grouville bay, and a sum of £3,866 was spent buying oysters and for the work entailed. These beds were not to be fished until 1837,[19] and then only under strict control of the periods of fishing and of the size of fish taken. However, unlawful dredging of these reserved beds led to serious trouble with the local authorities, as the Constables of St Martin and Grouville, unable to control the fishermen or to put a stop to the continued raids, appealed to the States for help, who in turn appealed to the Lieutenant-Governor. On 14 April 1838 a large number of boats was dredging in the reserves without permission, so the Lieutenant-Governor, Major General Campbell, marched to Gorey with the St Helier Battalion of the Royal Jersey Militia, a battery of artillery and a detachment of the 60th Regiment of Foot. After several rounds had been fired the boats returned to the harbour, where 97 masters were arrested and presented before the court and each was fined 300 Livres (about £17). Unfortunately the Lieutenant-Governor caught a chill from which he died on 12 May, and was buried in the Town church.

The fishing industry caused the village of Gorey to expand, houses were built for the newcomers and a considerable shipbuilding industry developed to supply vessels for the fishing fleet. Among the first of the builders in the 1820s were Edward Le Huquet, John Filleul and George Lane. The shipyards continued to multiply and were soon turning out schooners and brigs of up to 250 tons both for local owners and for export to the mainland. Perhaps the largest vessel to be built at Gorey was the barque 'Montrose' of 365 tons, built for Scrutton & Sons of London by George Asplet in 1861. Some yards extended from that of Daniel Le Sueur at La Rocque (from 1858 to 1883) as far as John and Thomas Le Huquet's near the White Tower at St Catherine (1850–79). Other builders at Gorey were Charles W. Aubin (1866–77) opposite the village, Philip Bellot (1854–65) near Gorey Village station, John Fauvel (1842–58), adjacent to the pier, J. Messervy (1854–65), J. F. Picot (1858–83), Philip J. Le Sueur, at Fort Henry (1845–57), Vardon & Le Huquet (1837–64), and Jean Vardon (1842–55), who built at the rear of Mont Orgueil Castle. A few small vessels were also built in the 1830s by Filleul and de La Mare at La Rocque, and by Clem Richardson at Flicquet, while in the 1860s some ships were built by Mark Cantell, and yet another builder was George Noel, who worked in partnership with Bellot. All together well over two hundred vessels were built between 1820 and 1885 in the Gorey yards.

Though the output of the yards at Gorey was mostly cutters and small schooners of under 100 tons for the fishing fleet, some larger vessels were turned out; in particular, Bellot launched several ships of over 100 tons, such as the brig 'Advance' of 229 tons, built in 1858 for George Asplet, and J. & T. Le Huquet built the fine brig 'Britain's Pride' of 182 tons for Pallot & Co. also in that year.

The biggest vessel constructed by J. Messervy was a brig named 'Morning Star' of 178 tons, built in 1859, having built two years earlier a brigantine of 140 tons, the 'John & Eliza'. Picot in the 1860s turned out two stout brigs, the 'Gazelle' (242 tons), and the 193-ton 'Union'. Earlier in 1845 Jean Vardon built for J. Taylor a fine schooner of 180 tons, the 'Elizabeth Taylor'. This vessel after launching was towed around to the harbour at St Helier, and there suffered damage by vandals, who mutilated the figurehead. These are only a few examples of the vessels built at Gorey and adjacent sites.

Alongside the oyster trade, other vessels based at Gorey carried on a normal trade of exports of wool, hides, apples and cider and imports of meat, coal and grain.

SOME JERSEY OYSTER BOATS

ANT	George Noel (26 tons, built by Th. Silk)	GEORGE & ELIZABETH	Th. Fieldgate
AUORE	Philip Noel	LAUREL	William Haddon
BRANDY	Amice Bertram	MARS	Ph. Mourant (Junr.)
CHARLES	Nicolas Pallot	MARY	Helier Bertram
CHARLES	Charles Messervy	MARY	James Cort
DOLPHIN	Edward Noel (cutter)	MARY ANN	James Brookes
'D'	Jackson Downer	MINERVA	Philip Perchard
EBENEZER	John Le Gros (13 tons, built by Le Huquet)	PELICAN	Th. Journeaux
		ROSE	Clem Le Huquet (cutter)
FRIENDS	Th. Ph. Richardson	SEA SEAL	Philip Noel
FRIENDS	Josue Valpy	TWO BROTHERS	William Adams
GEORGE	John Langlois (Junr.)	TRAVELLER	Thomas Renouf
		WILLIAM	Charles Mallet

OYSTER BOATS 1838 AND 1843

	1838	1843		1838	1843
Colchester	41	70	Maldon	—	3
Jersey	24	137	Ipswich	1	—
Portsmouth. . . .	6	11	Sark	—	1
Faversham	6	7	London	1	—
Southampton . . .	4	1	Poole.	—	1
Guernsey	—	5	Rochester	1	3
Milton	2	—	Shoreham	—	2
			Total	101	241

(Among the oyster fishermen at Gorey was Captain Henry A. Butt, the father of Dame Clara Butt, the famous operatic singer. Capt. Butt was born in the parish of St Martin and was master of the cutter 'Osprey' (42 tons) in 1848. He later owned and skippered the 'Cristal', a ketch of 35 tons. A Captain Edward Butt (? brother of Henry) was master of the 34-ton cutter 'Victory' in 1852.)

Chapter Three

THE JERSEY PRIVATEERS

IT HAS BEEN SAID that privateering was started in the Channel Islands, and certainly one of the earliest recorded British privateers was John Briard of Guernsey, merchant and owner of a vessel named 'Dove' (not the most appropriate name for a privateer) who received a Letter of Marque from Queen Elizabeth in 1578 giving him permission to attack the French. Records show that it was often at the request of the King that vessels were sent from the Islands to reinforce the English navy, and it could be that these same ships became auxiliary vessels of the navy while an emergency existed, but kept their independence in the operations. However, privateering soon became a way of life for the Islanders.

During the civil war[1] Sir George Carteret, while holding the Island for King Charles, formed a force of some 13 ships that caused havoc among the parliamentarian shipping. These vessels were manned by masters and crews of several nationalities including Dutch, English, and French, but contained also a fair proportion of local seamen. Partly financing Carteret's stand for the King, these privateers had many successes and became very daring, cutting out enemy vessels lying at anchor under the protection of the guns of the forts in the hands of the parliamentarians. Reports to Cromwell record:

Feb 21st Several merchants taken on the western coast by 'Jersey Pirates'.
Feb 26th Two dutchmen, laden with salt at anchor with half a league of Dartmouth Castle, had their cables cut and the vessels taken by Jersey privateers, the castle opened fire without effect.
Mar 1st Jersey pirates very bold upon the western coast.
Mar 6th Several ships taken by the pirates of Jersey.
Mar 17th Jersey pirates taking several merchantmen.
Apr 17th Two laden barques taken by Jersey pirates in sight of Portland.
Apr 21st More prizes taken by Jersey pirates.
Jul 14th Five English vessels taken by boats from Jersey, carrying five or six great guns apiece.
Jul 18th Two prizes taken by a Jersey Frigate, which had eight guns, 24 oars, and eighty men.
Aug 17th Much damage done by Jersey pirates.
Sep 17th Jersey pirates doing much mischief upon the western coasts.
Nov 30th Jersey pirates take two Dartmouth ships and three other vessels.

Apart from prizes sold in foreign ports 125 prizes were taken. Clement Le Montais, Carteret's brother-in-law, looked after the privateers, victualling the ships, paying the crews, and selling the prizes. His large tombstone is to be seen in the south-east corner of St Peter's church. The prizes were sold at the Admiralty Prize Court (now the Old Court House Hotel) at St Aubin.

Most of Carteret's ships were captured prizes which were quickly re-armed and added to his fleet.[2] Such vessels were the 'Francis' of 16 guns, 'Doggerbank', 'Hunter' of 22 guns, 'Iroise', 'Lady' 4 guns, 'Little George', 'Marie' of 10 guns, 'My lord Jermyn', 'Pastris' of 14 guns, 'Patrick' and 'The Hart'. The commodore of the fleet was Capt. George Bowden, an Englishman; Capt. John Jelf and Capt. Charles Cannon were also English, Cannon being a former naval chaplain turned privateer. Other Carteret captains were Amy a Cornishman, Baudains, Collings, and Phil. Mauger, all Jerseymen, Capt. Baudoin (French), Capts. Chamberlain, Dedans, Corneille, Dessourd, Hilt, Jones, Lendall, Lyme, Smith, Sam Tickel, and the Dutchmen, Capts. Martens, Vandersil and Van Diemen.

When privateering became legalized in 1689, Jersey merchants and sailors were not slow to take advantage of the new regulations, for during the 1692–97 war 30 Guernsey and eight Jersey vessels were soon operating, several captains being particularly successful; among them were Capt. William Snow of Lansdown House, Millbrook, and Thomas, possibly a brother of William; Jean Mauger, of Les Prairies, also at Millbrook, was master of the privateer 'Jersey Sloop'; George Bennet of the 'St Albans'; and Captains Edward Browne, Daniel Janvrin, and James Lemprière. The number of prizes taken in this war amounted to forty-six.

The war of 1703–11 saw increasing activity by local privateers, some 151 prizes falling to 38 Jersey captains. Not all local privateers were heavily armed, and some boats had no guns at all but resorted to small arms and by boarding with cutlass. Crews averaged thirty to sixty seamen, unusually large, but necessary to provide prize crews for captured vessels; most ships also carried an officer called a prizemaster whose duty entailed the bringing home of an enemy vessel for the Prize Court. The local privateers were able to intercept enemy ships sailing from French ports, from St Malo to Dunkirk, and by their knowledge of the coasts and tides were able to sail under cover of night into the very harbours of the French and to cut out the enemy vessels. Often landings on the French coast were made, livestock and chattels were carried away and sometimes prisoners were taken. In the many ways that Britain was involved in French, Spanish, Danish, Dutch and American vessels were captured by Jersey vessels and it was said that 'From Drake to Nelson Jersey privateers made the Channel and the Bay of Biscay dangerous for enemy shipping'.[3] The French Commander at Cherbourg in 1778 complained 'there are in St Helier's roads more than 150 french prizes', while during the war of 1797 a captain of a local privateer made himself so formidable that a price of six hundred pounds was put upon his head by the enemy.

Britain was at war again in 1743, firstly with Spain and then France, thus giving the local vessels further opportunities to indulge their favourite sport.[4] Capt. Thomas Snow, master of the 'William', acted with great daring and many prizes soon fell into his hands, including nine French ships valued at £127,600, taken between January and May 1744, and another nine were taken between July and October 1746, valued at £191,800. Capt. Le Cronier of the 'Defiance' returned to the island on 30 June 1757 accompanied by two large prizes which he had taken on their voyage from Bordeaux to America. 'Defiance' sailed again and surprised a Swedish vessel valued at £8,000. Altogether no fewer than nine prizes valued at £486,440 fell to Le Cronier that year. Capt. Nicolas Fiott was master of the local privateer 'Charming Betty' in 1758 when the Jersey boat recaptured from the French the 'Adventure', a London boat, with a valuable cargo of 148 hogsheads of sugar, 22 tons of spice, 20 tons of logwood, £1,000 worth of mahogany, 12 puncheons of rum, coffee, cotton and other goods. While on his way back to Jersey with his prize, Capt. Fiott took a Dutch ship laden with 200 tons of Bordeaux wine, and later that year the 'Charming Betty' surprised and took a French brigantine loaded with sugar. Another Fiott privateer at this time was the 'Charming Nancy' (master Philip Winter), and a number of ships were owned by Daniel Messervy, including 'L'Actif' (Capt. Balleine), 'Balthide', 'Boscawen' (Capt. Labey), 'Le Burnett', 'La Defiance', 'La Delvarde' (Capt. George Messervy), 'The Earl of Granville', 'Elizabeth' (Capt. Arthur), 'Minerva' (Capt. Le Couteur), 'Molly' (Capt. George Bertram), 'Phoenix' (Capt. Richard Le Quesne), 'Revenge' (Capt. Charles Alexandre), 'Roy De Prusse' and the 'Tartar'. Many of these ships carried a normal cargo as well as their privateering effects, trading in Jersey stockings to the mainland and with the new world. Other privateers operating from Jersey at this period were 'The Duke of Cumberland' (Capt. Philip Seward), 'Fox' (Capt. Labey), 'Jersey Galley' (Capt. Amice Vincent), 'King George' (Capt. John Le Gros), 'Squirrel' (Capt. Nicolas Le Courteur), 'The Willing Mind' (Capt. Daniel Le Preveu), 'Pierre', and 'The Duke of Northumberland'. The actions of the privateers together with ships of the Royal Navy provoked the French into plans for the capture of the Islands. An attempt made in 1779 ending in complete failure, but another attempt in 1781 led to the now famous Battle of Jersey, but this attack, too, after some initial success, failed. Undaunted, the privateers kept up the pressure on the enemy. A squadron of the Royal Navy, 'Rodney', 'Union', 'Crescent', 'Hydra', 'Cabot', 'Wasp', 'Rattlesnake' and 'Cormorant', together with the local privateers from Jersey, 'Beazely', 'Defiance', 'Endeavour', 'Minerva', 'Nancy', and 'York' operated in 1799 against the French.

Some 22 privateers were based in Jersey in 1778, rising to 38 as the war progressed, and many successes were made by the enterprising Jersey captains, like that in July 1780, when the privateer 'Mars' (Capt. Tocque) sighted nine French ships; seven ships were destroyed by 'Mars' and the two that remained were taken as prizes into Jersey. After the attempt on the Island in 1781, the States employed guard boats to cruise around the island and off the French coast to give warning of any further attacks. The first vessel to be appointed was the 'Nonsuch' under Capt. Philip Robin.

The advantages of privateering were offset by many losses suffered by the Islanders, particularly during the war of 1793, when in the first two years 42 local boats were captured by the French, and some 900 Jerseymen were in French prisons. Jersey privateers took every opportunity to harass the enemy vessels, and many were the battles that took place; one famous encounter was that between Capt. Thomas Pickstock,[5] master of J. & C. Hemery's vessel 'Herald', and three French ships, which attacked him off Naples. After a fight of some three hours the Jersey boat beat off the enemy ships, leaving them with shattered hulls and 30 men killed or wounded, while the local vessel of 80 tons, 10 guns and 28 crew suffered no loss. The enemy guns were of superior weight and more numerous than those of the 'Herald' and their crews totalled 180 men. That same night the 'Herald' beat off yet another attack, sinking a Frenchman and her crew of 22 men. At a meeting on 13 March 1799, the Jersey Chamber of Commerce decided to present Capt. Pickstock with a piece of silver valued at £500, in recognition of his bravery both when defending his ship against a superior force of three French ships, and also when attacking the French on the island of Newfoundland, and retaking from them the captured brigantine 'Princess Royal' and her crew.

Captain Peter Duval,[6] master of the 'Vulture', a lugger of 100 tons, four guns, and 27 crew became the terror of the Bay of Biscay, so the Merchants of Bayonne fitted out a brig of 180 tons, armed with 16 guns and a crew of 80 men, and sent her out when the 'Vulture' was about, hoping to trap the Jersey boat. Capt. Duval soon spotted the Frenchman and quickly gave chase. Rapidly coming alongside, he called upon her to surrender. The French opened fire at once with all their guns but were unable to depress the guns to do any real damage to the Jersey boat, who replied with her four guns, doing great damage to the hull of the enemy and killing or wounding many of her crew. Upon this the brig ran for home and was glad to escape from Capt. Duval and his gallant ship. The 'Vulture' continued to be a thorn in the side of the French for many years, firstly with Peter Duval still in command, later under Daniel Hamon, who took a large number of valuable prizes, and later still with Capt. Samuel Gasnier at the helm.

Captain Daniel Hamon had earlier commanded the 'Phoenix', again with much success. Other privateers bringing in numerous prizes at this time were 'Neptune' (Capt. William Du Heaume), 'Success' (Capt. Philip Payn), 'Union' (Capt. Francis Hocquard), 'Hope' (Capt. Elias L'Amy), 'Ceres' (Capt. George Messervy), 'Hazard' (Capt. Francis Marie), 'Lottery' (Capt. Philip Hacquoil, whose sword is preserved in the Museum of La Société Jersiaise), 'Rose' (Capt. Philip Du Pont), 'Mary' (Capt. J. Th. Bréhaut), the 'Marquis of Townsend', 'Comus', 'Jersey', 'Gen. Gordon', 'Lord Nelson', and many others.

On Thursday 14 December 1809,[7] Jurat Aaron De Ste Croix was in his shipyard at Havre-des-Pas when he noticed a vessel in distress some four miles out to sea. Taking four of his men from the yard they set out in an open boat, and discovered that she was an enemy ship named 'Calista', armed with eight guns, and carrying a cargo of sugar and coffee. The 'rescuers' boarded the ship and piloted her into St Helier where the crew were taken prisoner (much to their disgust), and the vessel was declared a prize. Two of the 'Calista's' guns stood outside the entrance to Jurat de Ste Croix's house 'The Limes' in Green Street for some years. Privateering continued until Waterloo in 1815, but the granting of Letters of Marque was not finally abolished until the Peace of Paris in 1856, though not before many Jersey families had founded their fortunes. The Island produced a number of fine captains, fearless and ready to tackle any enemy vessels where and when they appeared. These masters commanded loyal and able crews, ready to board enemy ships with cutlass and small arms, and ready to fight to the last.

The laws for privateering vessels during the Napoleonic Wars were[8] that ships with Letters of Marque paid one-fifth of the total prize money to the king, and of the remaining four-fifths, two thirds went to the owner of the vessel and the remaining third was divided among the captain and crew in varying amounts, according to seniority. The list of officers and crew of the privateer 'Corbet' in 1799 is a typical example:[9]

Captain	Jean Tocque of St Brelade	60 shares
1st Lieut.	Jean Le Feuvre of St Peter	30 shares
2nd Lieut.	George ? of St Brelade	30 shares
Mate	Noé Corbet of St Lawrence	30 shares
Doctor	Amice Du Heaume of St Ouen	15 shares
1st Gunner	Josué Laffoley of St Peter	14 shares
2nd Gunner	Jean Jean of St Ouen	12 shares
Boatswain	? ? of St Helier	15 shares
Seaman	Jean Le Brun of St Ouen	12 shares
Seaman	Jean Du Val of St Peter	10 shares
Seaman	Benjamin Trachy of St Peter	10 shares
Seaman	Philip Perreé of St Ouen	10 shares
Remainder of crew . .	(Boys)	3 shares

THE JERSEY PRIVATEERING CAPTAINS

Captain	Date	Vessel(s)
AHIER, Jean	1758	Mary
AHIER, Philip	1778–1814	Fox
ALEXANDER, Charles	1751–1763	Revenge
AMIRAUX, Pierre	1781–1801	Gen. Gordon, Revenge
AMY, Thomas	1646	(a Royalist Capt.), Little George
ARTHUR, Jean	1756–1758	Duke of Cumberland, Elizabeth
ASPLET, Elias	1803–1815	Young Phoenix
AUBIN, Germaine	1782–1792	Surprise
BALLEINE, Edward	1802	Hazard
BALLEINE, Jacques	1729–1763	L'Actif
BARBIER, Robert	1756	Phoenix
BAUDAINS, ?	1646	(a Royalist Capt.)
BAUDION, ?	1646	(a Royalist Capt.)
BENNET, George	1695	St Albans
BENNET, Philip	1794–1803	Dundas, Rover

Continued on following pages

The Jersey Privateering Captains — continued

Captain	Date	Vessel(s)
BERTRAM, Charles	1812	——
BERTRAM, George	1736	Molly
BERTRAM, Philip	1803	Expedition Packet
BOWDEN, George	1646	(a Royalist Capt.)
BREHAUT, Thomas	1807–1813	Mary, St Vincent
BROCQ (LE), Philip	1801–1808	Gen. Gordon
BROWNE, Edward	1692–1698	Two Brothers
BRUE, ?	1646	(a Royalist Capt.)
BUSHELL, Thomas	1746	Expedition Packet
BUSHELL, William	1703–1745	Three Eagles, Expedition Packet
CABOT, Peter	1747–1758	Prince of Wales
CANNON, Charles	1647	(a Royalist Capt.)
CHAMBERLAIN, ?	1666	(a Royalist Capt.)
CLEMENT, John	1812–1836	Eliza
CLEMENT, Peter	1805–1820	Venus
COLLAS, George	1803–1806	Ceres
COLLINGS, Nehemiah	1649	(a Royalist Capt.)
CORNEILLE, ?	1649	(a Royalist Capt.)
COUTANCHE, Jean	1802	Vulture
COUTANCHE, Charles	1778	Gen. Conway
COUTEUR (LE), Jean	1757	Minerve
COURTEUR (LE), Nicolas	1737–1746	Squirrel
CRAS (LE), James	1741	Charming Betty
CRONIER (LE), George	1756–1757	La Defiance
DEAN, Philip	1778–1788	Aigle
DE STE CROIX, Andre	1703–1711	Capré
DESSOURD, ?	1646	(a Royalist Capt.)
DOBELL, Nicolas	1801–1803	Mayflower
DU HEAUME, William	1802–1805	Neptune
DUMARESQ, Edward	1703–1717	Concorde
DUFONT, Philip	1803–1813	Hope, Phoenix, Rose
DURANT, Abraham	1703–1711	——
DUVAL, Jean	1800–1804	Vulture
DUVAL, Peter	1803–1815	Aeolus, Phoenix, Vulture
FEUVRE (LE) ?	1795	Boston (spy ship for D'Auvergne)
FILLEUL, Thomas	1778	Revenge
FIOTT, Edward	1766–1779	Tartar
FIOTT, Nicolas	1734–1763	Charming Betty, Charming Nancy
FITZHUGH, Robert	1703–1711	——
GALLAIS (LE), Richard	1801–1803	Comus
GALLIE, Jean	1803–1804	Comus
GASNIER, Samuel	1798–1813	Hazard, Lottery, Robert & Jane, Vulture
GEYT (LE), James	1800–1803	Tartar
GERNET, Francis	1646	(a Royalist Capt.)
GIFFARD, Philip	1778–1780	Eole, Aeolus
GROS (LE), Elias	1737	Elizabeth, Hope
GROS (LE), Jean	1747	King George

Continued on following pages

The Jersey Privateering Captains — continued

Captain	Date	Vessel(s)
GROS (LE), ?	1812	Lord Gambier
GRUCHY, ?	1705–1715	Defiance
HACQUOIL, Philip	1810–1814	Lottery, Phoenix
HAMON, Charles	1802–1842	North Star
HAMON, Daniel	1790–1812	Neptune, Phoenix, Vulture
HEMERY, James	1801	Lovely Emily
HILT, ?	1646	(a Royalist Capt.)
HOCQUARD, Francois	1790–1824	Marquis of Townsend, Union
HOCQUARD, George	1803	Comus
HUBERT, Philip	1790–1810	Rose
JANVRIN, Daniel	1692	——
JELF, John	1649	(a Royalist Capt.)
JONES, ?	1646	(a Royalist Capt.)
LABEY, Pierre	1759–1763	Boscawen, Le Burnett, Fox
LABEY, Thomas	1757–1763	Boscawen
LACHEUR (LE), Pierre	1804	Lord Nelson
L'AMY, Elias	1808–1810	Hope, Gen. Don
LAWRENCE, Abraham	1803–1804	Lady Sarah
LEMPRIÈRE, James	1692	Dolphin
LENDALL, ?	1646	(a Royalist Capt.)
MALLET, Nicolas	1778	La Defiance
MALZARD, Isaac	1790–1820	Lottery
MARIE, Francis	1813–1814	Hazard
MARTENS, ?	1646	(a Royalist Capt.)
MASURIER (LE), Jean	1806–1815	Peggy, Papillion
MASURIER (LE), Josué	1803–1809	Gen. Doyle
MAUGER, Jean	1677–1692	(Jersey Sloop)
MAUGER, Peter	1705	——
MAUGER, Philip	1649	——
MESSERVY, Clement	1757	Dragon of Guernsey
MESSERVY, George	1763–1808	Ceres, La Delvarde
MOURANT, Peter	1810	Queen
OGRAUD, John	1710	——
ORANGE, Jean	1705	——
PALLOT, Clement	1779	Fox
PAYN, Philip	1804–1815	Success, Venus
PERCHARD, Philip	1703–1737	Hope
PERRAND, Samuel	1703–1721	Hope
PICKSTOCK, Thomas	1798–1800	Herald, Queen
PICOT, D.	1801	Ajax
PIPON, Josué	1746	Charming Nancy
PIPON, Richard	1707–1708	George, Capre Prince
PIPON, Thomas	1705	——
PREVEU (LE), Daniel	1757	Willing Mind
QUESNE (LE), Eichard	1757	Phoenix
QUILLER, Richard	1790	Lively
ROMERIL, Abraham	1813	Success

Continued on following page

The Jersey Privateering Captains — continued

ROSSIGNOL	(LE), Jean	1804	Jersey
ROSSIGNOL	(LE), Mathew	1813–1815	Hazard
ROSSIGNOL	(LE), Philip	1792–1815	Masquerade, Success
ROUGETEL (LE), Jean		1800	Jersey
ROUX (LE), Jean		1803–1811	Vulture
ROUX (LE), Philip		1806	Providence
SEWARD, Philip		1756–1757	Duke of Cumberland, Duke of Northumberland
SHOOSMITH, Philip		1703–1711	Jolly Sloope
SMITH, ?		1649	(a Royalist Capt.)
SNOW, Thomas		1692	Marie
SNOW, Thomas		1737–1746	William
SNOW, William		1692–1704	Marie
SUEUR (LE), Noé		1776–1809	Mars, Tartar
SYVRET, Jean		1804	——
THOMAS, ?		1810	Queen Charlotte
TICKELL, Samuel		1646	(a Royalist Capt.)
TOCQUE, Jean		1779	Le Corbet
TORRY, James		1789	Aigle
VAUTIER, Thomas		1810	Success
VANDERSIL, ?		1646	(a Royalist Capt.)
VAN DIEMEN, ?		1646	(a Royalist Capt.)
VIBERT, Jean		1803	Marquis of Townsend
VINCENT, Amice		1744	Jersey Galley
WALKER, Thomas		1803	Mary
WINTER, Philip		1747–	Charming Nancy
WOOLDRIDGE, George		1794–1809	Cumberland

BRITISH WARS AND CAMPAIGNS IN WHICH JERSEY PRIVATEERS WERE ENGAGED

English Civil Wars	1642–1649	With France	1755–1763
With the Netherlands	1651–1654	With U.S.A.	1775–1782
With Spain	1655–1658	With France	1778–1783
With the Netherlands	1665–1667	With Spain	1780–1783
With the Netherlands	1672–1674	With the Netherlands	1780–1782
With France	1692–1697	With France	1793–1802
With Spain and France	1702–1712	With Napoleon	1803–1815
With Spain	1718–1727	With U.S.A.	1812–1814
With France	1742–1748		

JERSEY PRIVATEERS

Vessel	Owner	Dates	Rig/tons	Master
ACTIVE	D. Messervy	1756–94	80 tons	Jacques Balleine
AEOLUS		1760–11	250 tons	Peter Duval
AIGLE	P. & F. Janvrin	1789–06	96 tons	Phil Dean
AJAX		1801–		David Picot
ALARM	Phil Dean	1760–80	132 tons	Jean Fiott
ALERT		1778–87	87 tons	Wm Snow
ALLIGATOR		1796–		
ARGUS	Phil Winter	1760–14	68 ton brig	
BALTHIDE	D. Messervy	1763–	Brig'tine	
BEAZLEY	Mat. Gosset & Co.	1778–80	160 tons	Nic. Vautier
BENNET		1790–	68 ton sch.	
BOSCAWNEN	D. Messervy	1757–63	8 guns	Th. Labey
BOSTON	Le Feuvre	1795–	Sch'r	Le Feuvre
BRETAGNE		1759–	16 guns	
BRILLIANT		1760–80		
BURNETT	D. Messervy	1758–63	27 crew	Pierre Labey
CAPRE		1708–		And. De Ste Croix
CERES	Matt Amiraux	1806–08	119 tons	Geo. Collas
CHARMING BETTY	Lemprière & Fiott	1758–59	Sloop	Nic. Fiott
CHARMING NANCY	Lemprière & Fiott	1747–48	225 tons	Phil Winter
CHARMING NANCY	Lemprière & Fiott	1759–62		Nic. Fiott
COMMERCE	J. & C. Hemery	1784–92	127 tons	Geo. Aubin
COMUS	Dolbel & Giffard	1801–		Ric. Le Gallais
COMUS	Dolbel & Giffard	1803–		Jean Gallie
COMUS	Dolbel & Giffard	1803–		Geo. Hocquard
CORBET	Jean Kerby	1776–92	68 tons	Jean Tocque
CUMBERLAND		1809–		Geo. Wooldridge
DEFIANCE		1715–		Gruchy
DEFIANCE	D. Messervy	1757–	67 t sch.	Le Cronier
DEFIANCE		1778–	40 t, 6 guns	Nic. Mallet
DELVARDE (LA)	D. Messervy	1763–	4 guns	Geo. Messervy
DILIGENT		1778–	76 t brig	Jean Le Brun
DUKE OF CUMBERLAND	D. Messervy	1757–58	70 tons	Jean Arthur (killed in action)
DUKE OF NORTH'L'D		1757–		Philip Seward
DUNDAS		1803–	brig'tine	Phil. Bennett
EAGLE (ex-FOX)	Fr. Janvrin	1778–99	90 t sloop, 8 guns	Phil. Dean
EARL OF GRANVILLE	D. Messervy	1757–		
EARL ST VINCENT		1812–13		J. T. Brehaut
ELIZA	Ph. Nicolle	1807–	170 t, brig	Jean Clement
ELIZABETH	D. Messervy	1756–63	115 t, b'tine	Jean Arthur
ENDEAVOUR	Ph. Winter	1778–79	110 tons	Edward Helleur
ENTERPRIZE	Lys & Messervy	1778–97	40 tons	Elie Messervy
EOLE		1778–		Phil. Giffard
EXPEDITION PKT		1746	36 tons	Th. Bushell
EXPEDITION PKT	Geo. Hooper	1803–		Phil Bertram

Continued on following pages

Jersey Privateers — continued

Vessel	Owner	Dates	Rig/tons	Master
FERRET		1780–		
FOX	Guillaume Patriarche	1759–80	9 tons	Pierre Labey
GEN. CONWAY	J. Remon & Co.	1778–81	119 tons	Ch. Coutanche
GEN. GORDON		1799–01		Phil. Le Brocq
GEN. GORDON		1801–		Pierre Amiraux
GOREY		1760–80	25 tons	
GREYHOUND		1760–80		
HAZARD		1798–		Samuel Gasnier
HAZARD		1798		Jean Coutanche
HAZARD	Hammond, Pipon & Remon	1802–		Edward Balleine
HAZARD	Aug. Le Rossignol	1813–14		Francis Marie
HERALD	J. & C. Hemery	1798–	80 tons	Thomas Pickstock
HERO		1780–09	50 tons, 4 guns	Nicolle
HOPE		1703–37	Sloop	Samuel Perrand
HOPE	Ch. Robin & Co.	1768–08	110 tons	Philip Jean
HOPE	Ch. Robin & Co.	1808–		Elie L'amy
HUNTER		1760–80		
JERSEY	Ed. Robinson	1781–85	50 t, sloop, 4 guns	Ahier
JERSEY		1760–80		Jean Le Rougetel
JERSEY		1804–		Jean Le Rossignol
JERSEY GALLEY		1744–48		Amice Vincent
JERSEY SLOOP		1692–	30 tons	Jean Mauger
KING GEORGE		1747–		Jean Le Gros
LADY SARAH	Cabot & Le Vesconte	1803–	23 tons	Abrm. Lawrence
LIVELY	Patriarche & Co.	1790–	120 tons	Richard Quiller
LORD GAMBLER	P. Bishop	1812–	52 tons	Le Gros
LORD NELSON	Chevalier, Wooldridge & Nicolle	1804	71 t sch'r	Pierre La Cheur
LOTTERY	Mallet, Thoreau, Hooper	1797–99	24 tons	Samuel Gasnier
LOTTERY	Janvrin	1803–	Chasse marée 52 t	Isaac Malzard
LOTTERY	Janvrin	1814–	Chasse marée 52 t	Philip Hacquoil
LOVELY EMILY		1801–		James Hemery
MARIE		1692–04		William Snow
MARQUIS OF TOWNSEND		1792–01	71 t lugger	Francis Hocquard
MARQUIS OF TOWNSEND	Remon, Pipon, Hammond	1803–	71 t lugger	Jean Vibert
MARS	Edward Renouf	1760–15	272 tons	Noé Le Sueur
MARY		1741–47	Sloop	Jean Ahier
MARY	Thomas Mallet	1803–	74 t sloop	Thomas Mallet
MARY		1806–07		Thomas Brehaut

Continued on following page

Jersey Privateers — continued

Vessel	Owner	Dates	Rig/tons	Master
MASQUERADE	Geo. Le Cronier	1803–12	Lugger	Philip Le Rossignol
MAYFLOWER		1801–	30 t brig	Nicolas Dolbel
MINERVA	D. Messervy	1757–81	180 tons	Jean Le Couteur
MOLLY	D. Messervy	1756–72	80 tons	George Bertram
NANCY	P. Mallet	1777–86	200 t brig	Philip Tocque
NEPTUNE	Fr. Janvrin	1802–04		William Du Heaume
NEPTUNE	Fr. Janvrin	1790–92	131 tons	Daniel Hamon
NONSUCH	Ph. Robin	1760–81		Philip Robin
NORTH STAR		1812–	Cutter	Charles Hamon
PETIT JULIE (LE)		1780–		Poingdestre
PHOENIX	D. Messervy	1756–	Snow	Robert Barbier
PHOENIX	D. Messervy	1757–		Richard Le Quesne
PHOENIX	D. Messervy	1799–08		Daniel Hamon
PHOENIX	Cosnard & Janvrin	1813–		Philip Hacquoil
PHOENIX	Cosnard & Janvrin	1813–		Philip Dupont
PIERRE		1757–		Daniel Le Preveu
PITT	J. Thoreau	1778–99	Sloop, 6 guns	J. De Ste Croix
PROVIDENCE	J. Roissier	1806–	Sch'r/brig	Philip Le Roux (killed in action)
QUEEN	J. & C. Hemery	1792–	144 tons	Thomas Pickstock
QUEEN		1810–		Peter Mourant
QUEEN CHARLOTTE		1810–	Sloop, 8 guns	Thomas
REGULATOR		1783–94	36 tons	Philip Dolbel
REVENGE	D. Messervy	1751–63	150 t l'ger, 20 guns	Chas. Alexandre
REVENGE		1781–82	150 t l'ger, 20 guns	Pierre Amiraux
REVENGE		1778	150 t l'ger 20 guns	Thomas Filleul
REVENGE	Matt. Gossett	1778–	120 t brig, 10 guns	Noé Vautier
ROBERT & JANE	Mallet & De Gruchy	1798–	38 tons	Samuel Gasnier
ROSE	Cosnard & Janvrin	1810–		Philip Hubert
ROSE	Cosnard & Janvrin	1811–12		Philip Dupont
ROYAL CHARLOTTE		1772–	200 tons	George Hamel
ROY DE PRUSSE	D. Messervy	1757–		Edward Mourant
ST ALBANS		1695–		George Bennett
SPEEDWELL		1813–		
SQUIRREL		1747–		Nicolas Le Couteur
STAG		1779–95	130 tons	Francis Le Feuvre
SUCCESS	Le Mottee, Le Brun, Millais	1803	51 t smack	Philip Le Rossignol
SUCCESS	Le Mottee, Le Brun, Millais	1810	51 t smack	Thomas Vautier

Jersey Privateers — continued

Vessel	Owner	Dates	Rig/tons	Master
SUCCESS	Ph. Payn	1806–09		Philip Payn
SUCCESS	Renouf & Duhamel	1813–		Abraham Romeril
SURPRISE	Fiott & Co.	1778–94	50 t sloop 6 guns	Clement Le Quesne
TARTAR	D. Messervy	1757–80	100 t snow	Richard Le Quesne
TARTAR	Nic. Fiott	1778–	200 t snow 10 guns	Edward Fiott
TARTAR	E. D. Fiott	1779–	600 t, 40 guns, 230 crew	Edward Fiott
TARTAR		1800–		James Le Geyt
UNION		1760–	65 t, sloop 2 guns	Charles Alexandre
UNION	Villeneuve & Mallet	1805–08	84 t lug'r	Francis Hocquard
VENUS	Winter & Nicolle	1814	215 t brig, 8 guns	Peter Clement
VENUS	Durel & De Ste Croix	1814–	65 t b'tine	Philip Payn
VICTORY		1779		
VOLUNTEER		1760–80		
VULTURE		1760–		
VULTURE	Janvrin & Durell	1776–	100 tons	Peter Duval
VULTURE	Janvrin & Durell	1800–	Lugger	Jean Duval
VULTURE	Janvrin & Durell	1813–		Samuel Gasnier
VULTURE	Janvrin & Durell	1809–12		Daniel Hamon
WILLIAM		1737–44		Thomas Snow
WILLING MIND		1748–60		Daniel Le Preveu
WILLING MIND	Nic. Fiott	1766–80	180 tons	Edward Fiott
YORK	Edw. Remon	1760–79	130 t brig	Jean Remon
YOUNG PHOENIX	P. & F. & J. Janvrin	1803–	183 t b'que	Elias Asplet

N.B. Some Guernsey owned vessels are included in this list, as they were either owned in partnership with Jersey or commanded by Jersey captains.

Chapter Four

JERSEY AND THE COD FISHERIES OF
NORTH AMERICA

HISTORIANS have looked for the motives that brought the Jerseymen to the shores of Newfoundland so early, about a hundred years before colonization began. It must be remembered that they had the blood of the Vikings still coursing through their veins, and the tales of these famous sea-rovers, who had discovered North America hundreds of years before Columbus, may have been handed down through the generations. The Channel Islanders were naturally strong in the ways of the sea, and undoubtedly Jersey ships could have extended their fishing trade to Icelandic waters, in an endeavour to catch the quantity of fish needed to fulfil their trading contracts with the Mediterranean ports, which Jersey fishermen had supplied from earliest times.

Legend handed down in Jersey families long settled in Newfoundland state that this Icelandic fishery was an important occupation for islanders from the earliest times, and that they had fished as far north as Greenland. They also had a tradition that north-east gales drove some vessels over the Grand Banks to within sight of the coast of Newfoundland, 'where the seas teemed with fish'. Old and well established names, like Jerseyside and Jersey Harbour, are proof that the men from the Norman Isles were very active on the 'Coast' long before the English awakened to the value of the fishing grounds. The people of the Channel Islands left their mark on the province, firstly in the naming of sites and locations used by them, and in the many stories and legends of Island origin. One of the most interesting, documented stories, is that of the Colours of the Royal Newfoundland Regiment,[1] which fought in upper Canada in 1812–1814, and were found in St Brelade's parish church in Jersey almost a century later where they had been taken by the son of an officer in the regiment at that time. This regiment had been commanded by Major Elias Pipon, and the Colour was laid up in the parish church on 14 September 1882, together with the Colours of the old 5th (Southwest) Regiment of the Royal Jersey Militia.

C. D. Howe in his book *Newfoundland, An Introduction to Canada's New Province* says: 'There is a tale that Channel Island boats in the latter part of the 15th century were blown off course westward until they came to a strange land where the sea was abounding with fish'. When Jacques Cartier[2] sailed from St Malo in 1534 to discover 'the new found land', among his crew were Guillaume de Guerneze, Anthoine, Fleury, Ollivier, Le Breton and Colas, all thought to be

Jerseymen, and some evidence exists that Islanders and French seamen mixed freely at that time. Certainly Jerseymen were eating codfish as early as the reign of King Henry VIII. Island fishermen in 1562 had been noted on the Grand Banks, south of Newfoundland, and it would seem that small but sturdy boats had regularly sailed in North American waters a hundred years or more before the Pilgrims sailed from Plymouth. The islanders were thus among the first settlers in New England, arriving via the Grand Banks and Newfoundland.

Jean Guilleaume is credited with having brought to Jersey in 1596 the first cargo of fish from the Newfoundland grounds, and on arrival at the island was ordered to pay dues on the fish as though locally caught. Guilleaume objected to paying tax, so he proceeded to St Malo to sell his cargo, but there his ship and cargo was arrested by order of the Jersey Governor for 'the public good of the Inhabitants of Jersey'. Guilleaume's complaints were not settled until Sir Walter Ralegh was appointed Governor of Jersey in 1600.

Harbor Grace[3] has claims as being the first permanent settlement in Newfoundland, where Jerseymen were the earliest settlers, and possibly the discoverers of Harbor Grace, where the remains of several small stone houses were still to be seen as late as 1936, which were roofed in red tiles and said to have belonged to the Jersey settlers. They took a very important part in the first colonization of Conception Bay, but it is thought that Harbor Grace may have been their headquarters. History tells us that there were no more enterprising people anywhere between the years 1500 and 1600, and that Jerseymen were willing to travel anywhere, so it is only natural that the first houses were erected near the fishing grounds, where most of the fishermen lived in boats or temporary dwellings.

For the first hundred years after the discovery of the country fishing was carried out by adventurers coming out yearly in the spring in their small vessels averaging less than 50 tons, and returning home in September or October. These vessels wintered at St Malo in the earlier years, as little shelter was available in Jersey, and sailed again when winter had passed and the better spring weather arrived. The first ship to arrive on the coast was saluted by the firing of guns and the master named 'Admiral' for that year. The 'Admiral' held his court at Mosquito Cove, a suburb of Harbor Grace; unfortunately little is known about this court's activities, or whether the title of 'Admiral' was just a courtesy or if any real power could be exercised. Jersey Rock was a large boulder fitted with a huge ring bolt where the Jersey boats tied up. This rock has long disappeared under land reclamation, and all direct trade connections between Jersey and Harbor Grace were lost many years ago. Folklore has it that at one time a Jerseyman could be seen jumping over a puncheon of water, believing that in this way he could spend the weekend with his family back in Jersey. Another tradition, that of the Batten family who came from Jersey and settled at Port De Grave early in the 1500s, states 'that when Grandfather settled here, there was an Indian encampment just where our kitchen garden is now'.

Sir Walter Ralegh, while governor of the island, encouraged the Jersey sailors in 1600 to trade and fish the Newfoundland waters, and the islanders soon dominated the east coast, even as far as the Labrador coast. This trade continued to prove profitable and by 1731 Falle records some 17 vessels engaged in the fishing grounds, and by 1737 ships to the number of 30 left the shelter of St Aubin, mostly for Newfoundland or Virginia. The year 1771 saw 45 boats leaving for 'La Côte', increasing to some 59 by 1785.

A custom had arisen in 1611,[4] called 'Le Communion des Terreneuviers' whereby all the crews of the fishing fleet of St Aubin attended communion at St Brelade's church before the annual spring sailing to Newfoundland. During times when Britain was at war, the fleet often sailed in convoy protected by a British man of war. This manoeuvre was not always infallible, as in May 1794[5] 14 Jersey vessels sailing in convoy with H.M.S. 'Castor' ran into the French Fleet, and 'Castor' and nine of the local ships fell to the enemy. One of these ships, the 'Success' (Capt. Le Capelain) was re-taken from the French by the action of the mate, a seaman and two boys, and the ship was then safely taken into Guernsey. A report of 1775 claims that 1,500 to 2,000 local men were employed in the fisheries, and the cod trade at this time seemed to be of uppermost import-ance to Jersey shipping. Each year the first vessel back from the fishing grounds had the right to tie up at La Boue Du Roi,[6] The King's Buoy, immediately east of the pier at St Aubin, as it remained drier than any other mooring. The cod trade in the 19th century lost some of its importance to the Jersey merchants as the local shipping industry expanded, and other markets became more attrac-tive, but as late as 1896 at least 25 ships were still going out from Jersey, and many were the goods carried by these boats on the outward journey including: boots and shoes,[7] cotton, salt, tin, and tinware, files, pipes and tobacco, gun-powder, candles, earthenware, soap, cordage, paint, seeds, nails, cider, coaltar, glass, gloves, calfskins, lead, brushes, nets and hooks, and many foodstuffs includ-ing sugar, cheese, mustard, tea, etc. Thousands of Jersey-made bricks were also carried as ballast and numerous brick-built houses with a Jersey name stamped on them can still be found on 'La Côte'.

Many trading posts and fisheries were established by Jersey merchants and traders, both small and large, among the earliest being Henry & John Le Cras with Nicolas Bailhache at Bonaventure (c. 1674) and John Mahie & François Messervy (c. 1691), and a vessel called 'L'Orange' (master Jean Le Cras), owned by Edward Touzel and Philip & Jean Orange, was also trading that same year. Other early traders were Carteret Dean, of St Aubin, De Carteret & Co., Thomas Denton, also from St Aubin, Marett, and another merchant from St Aubin, Thomas Seale. All these merchants were trading before 1718. 'Thomas & Jane', a brigantine owned by Carteret Dean, 'La Bonne Industrie' and 'John' (master Jacques Balleine) were some of the first vessels recorded on the North American scene before 1730. The brigantine 'Philip' (70 tons, master Jean Du Parq, 1737–40), was another ship trading in these early years. Robin, Pipon & Co. had a number of boats going out to the coast in the middle of the 18th century, includ-ing the 'Endeavour' (1767), 'Bee' (1777), and the 'Seaflower' of 41 tons, the first of four Robin vessels with that name. Other Robin boats at this time were

'Recovery' (118 tons), 'Hope' (a brig of 100 tons, 1770–1779), and 'Mercury' (54 tons), Nicolas Fiott & Co. were trading at Gaspé c. 1743, Valpy & Le Bas were also at Gaspé in the 1770s, John Le Breton (1766) at Newfoundland, Le Couteur (1770) and De La Perrelle Bros & Co. at Cave Cove, Gaspé (1770–1800), Jean Morel, at Louisbourg, Nova Scotia, in 1740, and Philip Nicolle, at Fortune Bay in 1740s, as was John Giffard.

After 1783 the Robin, Pipon & Co. business was divided, the Pipons retaining the Newfoundland trade, while the Canadian posts were owned and developed by Charles Robin & Co. whose activities expanded and swallowed up many smaller rival firms. The first part of the 19th century saw further companies on 'La Côte': Janvrin Bros. & Co., at Gaspé and Cape Breton, Bertram, Godfray, Grey & Co. at Quebec, John Le Boutillier at Paspébiac (a great rival of Robin), De Carteret and Le Vesconte at Arichat, William Fruing and many more. Some of these merchants took advantage of the plentiful supply of timber available so close to the shore to set up ship-building yards for further vessels to enlarge their fleets. Many of these shipwrights were from Jersey or Guernsey, and later returned to the Islands to take part in the expanding market for Channel Islands-built ships. Charles Robin had many of his boats built at Paspébiac;[8] in fact some 35–40 of the nearly 100 vessels recorded as owned by Robin at one time or another were built in Gaspé.

Philipe Nicolle also had a number of ships built in Newfoundland for his own use and J. & F. Perreé & Co. had ships constructed at Malbaie by the Collas brothers, Francis, James and Samuel. This firm known as J. & E. Collas had a family connection with the Perreés, and the two companies joined forces. The Collas Company came to the rescue of Robin Co. in 1866, when the Robin bank (The Commercial Bank of Jersey) failed. The company then became known as Robin, Collas & Co. and continued to trade under that name until 1914 brought further amalgamations, and the company became Robin, Jones & Whitman. One of the very last companies from Jersey to trade with Newfoundland was De Gruchy, Renouf & Clement, who had a number of fine vessels plying to the coast well into the twentieth century, and they were almost the last of Jersey's once large and successful maritime fleet.

JERSEY MERCHANTS IN NEWFOUNDLAND AND CANADA

ALEXANDRE, James	Malbaie, Gaspé	1830–
ALEXANDRE & LE MARQUAND	Malbaie, Gaspé	? –1914
AMY, Philip	Nova Scotia	1800s
ANLEY & CO.	Newfoundland	1717–
BANDINEL, Thomas	Harbor Grace	1675–
BAS (LE), & VALPY	Gaspé	1770
BERTRAM, GODFRAY, GREY & CO.	Quebec	1830–1860
BEST	Newfoundland	?
BIARD, Charles	Perce, Gaspé	?
BOUCHER BROS.	Labrador & Cape Breton	1850–
BRETON (LE), John	Paspébiac	1837–
BRUN (LE), Abraham	Gaspé	1861–
COLLAS, J. & E.	Point St Pierre	1861–

Jersey Merchants in Newfoundland and Canada — continued

COLLAS, James	Gaspé	1883–
COUTEUR (LE)		1770–
CRAS (LE), Henry and John and Nicolas Bailhache	Bonaventure	1675–
DEAN, Carteret	Newfoundland	1717–
DEAN, Philip	N.-E. Gaspé	1840–
DE CARTERET		1717–
DE CARTERET & LE VESCONTE	Arichat	1830–1860
DE GRUCHY	Bonne Bay, Newfoundland	1800s
DE GRUCHY & NICOLLE & CO.	Little St Lawrence, Newfoundland	
DE GRUCHY, RENOUF & CLEMENT		1870–1903
DE LA PERRELLE, Bros. & Co.	Cave Cove, Gaspé	1770–1800
DENTON, Thomas	Newfoundland	1717–
DE QUETTEVILLE	Harbor Grace	1800s
DE QUETTEVILLE	Blanc Sablon, Labrador	1800s
DE ST CROIX	Bonne Bay, Newfoundland	?
DU VAL, Peter & Co.	Cape Breton	1820s
FALLE, Richard	Point George	1830–
FAUVEL, John	Point St Pierre	
FIOTT, Nicolas & Co.	Perce, Gaspé	1743–
FRUING, William & Co.	New Brunswick	1832–
GEYT (LE), John	Red Bay, Labrador	
GIFFARD, John		1785
GIRARD, William	Gaspé	1836–
GODFRAY, Jean & Co.	Shippegan	1832–1854
GROS (LE), John	Point St Pierre, Gaspé	1850s
GROS (LE), Peter	Eskimo Point, Quebec	?
GRUCHY, David, Peter, Philip	Nova Scotia	1883
HAMMOND, DUMARESQ & CO.	Bonaventure Island	?
HAMON	Gaspé	1830
HUELIN, John	Sandy Pit, Newfoundland	1800
JANVRIN, BROS & CO.	Gaspé	1770–1816
JANVRIN, John	Arichat	c. 1836
JANVRIN, Peter	Cape Breton	c. 1836
JANVRIN, Philip	Cape Breton	c. 1836
JANVRIN, Frederic & Co.		1880
MAHIE, John & MESSERVY, Fr.		1691
MARETT	Newfoundland	c. 1717
MAUGER, Joshua	Nova Scotia	c. 1754
MARQUAND, Ernest & Eloysius	Newport	
MESURIER (LE)	Gaspé	c. 1826
MOREL, Jean	Louisbourg, N.S.	1740–
NICOLLE, Philip	Fortune Bay	1740
PATRIARCHE, William & Co.	Maritimes	1770
PAYN	Newfoundland	
PERREÉ, John & John (Junr.)	Malbaie, Gaspé	1800s
REMON, James & Thomas	Pabos, Gaspé	
ROBIN, PIPON & CO.	Gaspé	1767–
ROBIN, Charles & Co.	Canada	1783–
ROBIN, JONES & WHITMAN	Canada	1914–
SAUVAGE, Thomas	Gaspé	1800s
SEALE,		1717
TOCQUE	Gaspé	1880s
VALPY & LE BAS	Gaspé	1770–
VILLENEUVE	Newfoundland	1800s

VESSELS TRADING TO NEWFOUNDLAND 1780-92

Date	Vessel	Tons	Owners	Master
1790	Angelicque	42	Mathew Gosset	Abraham Gaudin
1792	Angelicque		Mallet & Fiott	Thomas Blampied
1790	Anne	45	Phil. Ahier	George Marett
1792	Anne		Phil. Janvrin	Jean Marett
1790	Bacchus	80	Ch. Robin & Co.	Jean De Caen
1790	Beaver	38	Jacques Remon	Jean Hamon
1790	Betsy	77	Edward Coombes	Jean Le Quesne
1790	La Concorde	126	Geo. Rowcliffe	Jean De Ste Croix
1790	Corbet	68	Poingdestre & Robinson	Francis Le Four
1792	Corbet	68	Poingdestre & Robinson	Germaine Aubin
1790	Cornhill	192	Francis Janvrin	Thomas Bishop
1790	Elisha Tupper	280	Francis Janvrin	Philip Vibert
1790	Expedient	49	Ch. Robin & Co.	Jean Alexandre
1780	Friendship	51	Jean Le Feuvre	Edward Le Feuvre
1790	Gaspé	?	Jean Kirby	?
1790	Good Friends	58	Francis Amy	Philip Le Couteur
1790	Hercules	161	Mathew Gossett	Clement Durell
1790	Hilton	178	Ch. Robin & Co.	Philip Bisson
1790	Industrie	68	Philip Janvrin	Philip Dean
1790	Jenny	54	J. & C. Hemery	Philip Billot
1790	Jupiter	58	Ed. Du Heaume	Clement Messervy
1790	Kenton	113	Ingouville & De Ste Croix	Philip Ingouville
1790	Kingfisher	57	Mathew Gossett	Moise Steele
1790	Liberté	69	Pierre Mallet	Charles Hocquard
1790	Lynx	183	Jean Le Vesconte	Jean Du Heaume
1790	Major Pierson	172	Ch. Robin & Co.	Philip Jean
1790	Magdaleine	38	Pierre Mallet	Francis Noel
1790	Mary	60	Pierre Mallet	Edward Noel
1790	Nancy	64	Pierre Le Brun	Jean Le Quesne
1792	Neptune	131	Francis Janvrin	Jean Hocquard
1792	Paspébiac	133	Ch. Robin & Co.	Thomas Hacquoil
1790	Peace	72	Ch. Robin & Co.	Isaac Malzard
1790	Peirson	90	Francis Janvrin	Philip Benest
1790	Preference	59	Brun Benest	Brun Benest
1790	Providence	72	Jean Roissier	Jean Roissier
1790	Prudent	57	Pierre Le Brun	Clement Le Quesne
1790	Queen	144	J. & C. Hemery	Thomas Pickstock
1790	Resolution	70	Thomas De La Garde	Jean Dolbel
1792	Resolution	70	J. & C. Hemery	Jean Dolbel
1790	St Lawrence	145	Ch. Robin & Co.	Jean Alexandre
1790	St Peter	210	Ch. Robin & Co.	Philip De Caux
1790	Success	110	Poingdestre & De Ste Croix	B. Le Capelain
1790	Union	?	?	Jean Bichard
1790	Vine	129	Poingdestre & De Ste Croix	Thomas Falle
1792	Vine	129	Poingdestre & De Ste Croix	Francis Le Four

ROBIN—OWNED VESSELS

Vessel	Tons	Rig	Built		Master
ADMIRAL SPROUL	70	schooner	1901–03	—	
ANDES	212	brig	1840–	Grellier '39 Jy	John Gavey
ANT	53	schooner	1854--99	Paspébiac '54	
AURORA	73	schooner	1824–34	Canada '28	Phil Briard
BACCHUS	80	?	1790–	—	J. De Caen
BEE	160	?	1777–90	Boston '73	Ph. Fainton
BEE	58	schooner	1863–70	Paspébiac '50	J. De la Perrelle
BRIARD	121	brig't	1846–	Bartlett '45 Jy	Ed. Briard
BROAD AXE	142	brig	1823–30	Paspébiac '21	Hacquoil
BROTHERS	173	brig	1858–63	Gaspé '58	D. Collas
CALM	48	schooner	1826–31	Paspébiac '26	J. Flannegan
CAP BRETON	122	schooner	1812–19	Cheticamp '12	Ph. Brouard
CHAGAMAU	84	?	1829–	Paspébiac	Ed. Du Heaume
CHAGAMAU	83	schooner	1878–	Bellot '78 Jy	
CENTURY	186	brig't	1866–96	Le Vesconte '66 Jy	Am. Le Moignan
C. COLUMBUS	253	barque	1825–	Paspébiac '25	Helier Vibert
COMMANDER	12	schooner	1865–	Vardon Jy '45	Phil. Hamon
CORONATION	70	schooner	1903–	—	
C.R.C.	261	barque	1827–67	Paspébiac '27	
C.R.C.	260	barque	1871–1900	Gaspé '71	J. Balleine
C.R.C.	300	barque't	1902–	St Malo '02	Brehaut
DAWN	168	brig't	1874–1902	Gaspé '74	Geo. Noel
DAY	186	barque	1816–34	Gaspé '06	Pet. Briard
DIT-ON	95	schooner	1831–34	Paspébiac '31	J. Le Feuvre
DITTO	162	brig	1831–34	Paspébiac '30	J. Luce
ELLEN MARY	66	schooner	1899–02	Cheticamp '78	Ed. de la Perrelle
ENDEAVOUR	121	brig	1767–	—	Balleine
FANNY BRESLAUER	295	barque't	1890–08	Plymouth '71	C. Le Sueur
FARRAGO	163	brig	1843–	Paspébiac '43	Jean Piton
FISHERMAN	196	barque	1832–45	Paspébiac '32	Moses Gibaut
FLY	59	schooner	1858–	Paspébiac '58	Baker
GASPÉ	243	barque	1812–26	Paspébiac '12	E. de la Perrelle
GLENVILLE	325	barque	1890–02	Sunderland '74	Ph. Hamon
GROG	150	brig't	1817–34	Paspébiac '10	John Vibert
HABNAB	138	brig	1811–34	Paspébiac '08	Ph. Poingdestre
HARRIET	22	schooner	1840–	Dublin '31	J. W. Deveau
HEMATOPE	81	schooner	1845–79	Paspébiac '45	Ph. Briard
HERO	40	schooner	1840–	Gorey ?	
HIBERNICA	165	brig't	1863–	Shippegan '63	J. Le Gresley
HILTON	178	—	1790–94	—	Pierre Bisson
HIRONDELLE	36	schooner	1845–	Cap Breton '45	James Le Couteur
HOMELY	256	barque	1841–79	Paspébiac '41	J. A. F. Vincent
HOPE	110	brig	1768–85	American Colony	Ph. Jean
IF	196	barque	1803–	Newfoundland 1794	Pet. Briard
JOHN BULL	12	cutter	1901–	—	
LARCH	249	barque	1819–26	Paspébiac '15	Phil. Le Geyt
LUCIE	30	schooner	1863–70	—	
MAGOT	—	—	1792–	—	Fr. Le Feuvre

Continued on following page

Robin-owned Vessels — continued

Vessel	Tons	Rig		Built	Master
MAJOR PIERSON	172	—	1792–	—	Ph. Jean
MARKWELL	290	barque	1853–	Gaspé	
MARY	22	schooner	1852–79	?	
MERCURY	54	—	1788–90	—	Clem. Hubert
MESSENGER	?	schooner	1820–24	Arichat '16	Elias Briard
N.B.	254	barque	1849–51	Paspébiac '48	John Huelin
OLIVER BLANCH'D	250	barque	1822–38	? '22 ?	Ed. Orange
OLIVER BLANCH'D	268	barque	1857–66	Paspébiac '55	Giffard
OLIVER BLANCH'D	257	barque	1868–98	Paspébiac '68	
OLD TOM	120	schooner	1834–	Gaspé '34	James Balleine
PALM	176	brig	1819–26	Gaspé '17	Alexandre
PARVENU	16	schooner	1865–	—	
PASPÉBIAC	57	schooner	1872–1901	Paspébiac '72	
PASPÉBIAC	135	schooner	1785–92	—	Thom. Hacquoil
PATRUUS	206	brig	1839–60	Canada '39	Fr. Gibaut
PEACE	72	brig	1790–94	—	Neel
PEACE	60	schooner	1817–31	Paspébiac '71	Pet. Le G. Bisson
P.R.C.	111	brig	1830–66	Paspébiac '28	John Le Bas
RANGER	138	brig't	1863–79	Paspébiac '63	
REAPER	137	brig't	1864–95	Paspébiac '64	Jean Le Blancq
RECOVERY	118	snow	1768–89	—	Phil. Fainton
REDBREAST	97	schooner	1824–26	Paspébiac '24	Chas Le Boeuf
ROBIN	150	brig't	1879–96	Paspébiac '66	
ST LAWRENCE	145	—	1785–92	—	Ph. Fainton
ST PETER	210	—	1785–92	—	Ph. De Caux
SCATARI	104	brig	1823–26	Cape Breton '21	Th. Simon
SEAFLOWER	41	brig	1768–79	—	
SEAFLOWER	163	brig	1831–34	Gaspé '26, '39	Huelin
SEAFLOWER	126	brig	1865–	Paspébiac '56	Geo. Le Brocq
SEAFLOWER	352	barque	1875–85	Paspébiac '73	
SHIFT	49	—	1792–94	—	Jean Alexandre
SPEEDY	74	schooner	1872–	Gaspé	
SQUAW	57	schooner	1826–41	Bonaventure '14	Abrm. Asplet.
STORM	45	schooner	1826–31	Paspébiac '23	Ph. Vautier
SWALLOW	45	schooner	1831–	—	
SWALLOW	62	—	1888–03	Cap Breton '88	
TELEGRAPH	162	brig	1847–53	Ex-Slaveship '44	Jean Larbalestier
THREE BROTHERS	30	schooner	1865–79	—	
TRUE FRIEND	59	schooner	1804–10	Canada 1797	James Journeaux
UNION	193	brig	1865–01	Picot '65 Jy	Davey
URUGUAY	68	schooner	1903–	—	
VENUS	197	brig	1840–	Gavey '22 Jy	Jean Hamon
VINCENT	63	schooner	1837–40	Gaspé '37	John Hardeley
WAG	71	brig't	1815–20	Paspébiac '15	Elias Slous
WASP	36	schooner	1840–	Paspébiac '40	John Fauvel
WITCH	46	schooner	1831–	—	
YOUNG MESSENGER	84	schooner	1823–26	Cheticamp '23	Briard
YOUNG WITCH	51	schooner	1832–	Cheticamp, C.B. '32	Ed. Briard
"85"	138	brig't	1863–85	Paspébiac '60	John Romeril

Fort Regent, St. Helier's, Jersey.

1. St Helier Harbour c1840, showing the mast on Fort Regent which signalled the arrival of all vessels.

2. Weighbridge and quay, St Helier c1830, showing Philip Nicolle's house and garden, built on the site of his shipyard, now the museum of the Société Jersiaise.

3. Ropewalk in Green Street, c1855.

4.   View of Albert Pier and town of St Helier, c1860.

5.   View of Albert Pier, St Helier, c1860.

6. St Aubin's Harbour c1900, showing guns reputed to have once formed the armament of a Jersey privateer, in use as bollards until quite recently. The Admiralty Prize Court (now the Old Court House Hotel) can be seen on the left. A merchant's house (La Vielle Maison) with a sail loft alongside is on the right.

7. Round the Island Race c1865. Won by the schooner *Why Not?*, 105 tons, master and owner John Pallot.

Shipbuilding yards at St Aubin, c1840.

Ships on the stocks at First Tower, Le Vesconte's yard nearest the camera. Eight large vessels were on these stocks at the same time in 1863.

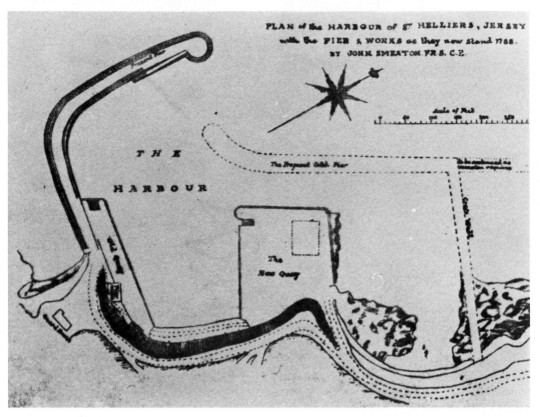

10.   Plan of St Helier harbour, c1788.

11.   Plan of St Helier harbour, c1843.

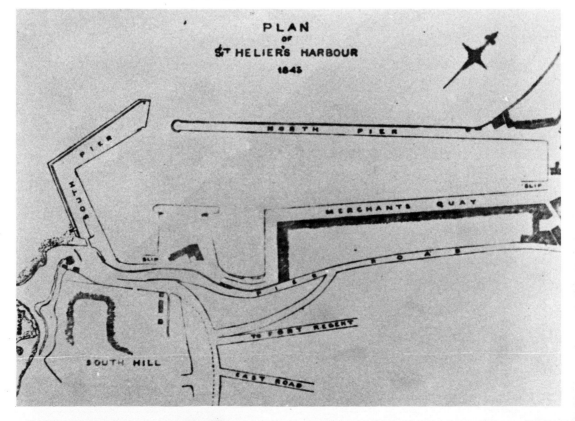

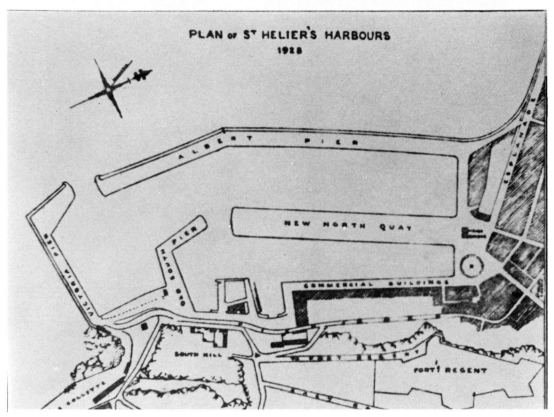

12.   Plan of St Helier harbour, c1928.

13.   Laying the Foundation Stone of the new harbour works, c1872.

LAYING THE FOUNDATION-STONE OF NEW HARBOUR WORKS AT JERSEY.

14. Captain John Le Marchand, master of the brig *Hebe*, c1867.

15. Unknown local master and his father?

16. *(right)* Captain John Read, master of the *Flying Foam*, c1900, his wife (nee Hacquoil) and daughter Annie.

17. *(below left)* A rather delightful study of Captain Peter Hacquoil, master of the brig *Telegraph*, c1853.

18. *(below right)* Figurehead of the brig *Prospero*, 190 tons. Built by Clarke at West Park, 1862, for Captain George Malzard. Signal Letters V.C.P.F.

19. The barque *Gladiateur*, 427 tons, built by F.C. Clarke, Jersey 1866. Official number 55271, Signal Letters H.K.P.T.

20. *(above)* The brig *Argo*, 238 tons, built by Grandin, First Tower, 1862. Signal Letters T.Q.P.D., official number 43848. Owned by Gallichan & Co., later by R. Allix.

21. *(left)* The barquentine *Fanny Breslauer*, 295 tons, built at Stonehouse, Plymouth, 1871. Owned by Robin, Collas & Co., 1890. Towed into Milford Haven after storm damage on 7 January 1908.

22.   Topsail schooner under tow to a steam tug in St Ouen's Bay, passing the lighthouse at La Corbiere which was built by the States of Jersey. The lighthouse was the first to be built in concrete and came into operation in 1874.

23.   Topsail schooner *Red Gauntlet*, 65 tons, built by Aubin, Gorey, 1876, **official number 75263**, owner J.Adams of Guernsey. The vessel is tied up near the premises of W.T. Pugsley & Co., who were the owners from 1877 until the vessel was lost 1906.

3454. **Jersey** — Pier Road G. F.

24. Work in progress on widening of the North Pier, c1887. Right foreground, schooner *Dart*, 64 tons, built by Le Vesconte, owner G.W. Young. Topsail schooner *Charlotte*, built by Bellot at Gorey, owner Cantell & Co. Dandy *Hannah*, 41 tons, owner A.C. Querrée.

25. Shipping in St Helier c1885. Angle of the Quai des Marchands known as 'de Quetteville's Corner.'

26. Crew of unidentified local vessel in St Helier.

27. Crew of another unidentified local vessel in St Helier.

28. Crew of unknown Jersey vessel in a mainland port.

29. *(left) Oliver Blanchard,* in St Helier harbo[ur] This name was used three times for vessels owne[d] by Charles Robin & Co. All were around 250 tons, the first was built in 1822, the second built at Gaspe in 1855, and the third (shown here) also at Gaspe in 1868.

30. *(below) Oliver Blanchard,* a ship of 250 tons built in 1821/22. Owned by Charles Robin & Co., 1822, until her loss in 1838. Masters - 1822 Elias de La Perelle, 1828-31 Edward Orange and 1834-36 Francis Gibaut.

31. and 33. *(right and below right)* Two interesting tombstones ornamented with symbolic ship carvings, Below, that of Captain Jean Le Huquet in St. Martin's Churchyard, and right, the obelisk erected in Almorah cemetary to the memory of Captain Josue Pallot and his twin sons.

32. A pump installed by the Harbours Committee to aid the drawing of drinking water for vessels in St Aubin's harbour, 1862.

34. *(left)* Ropewalk chimney, Green Street, St Helier, c 1929. On the left can be seen La Maison du Mont (The Cedars), which belonged to the Mallet family who were ropemakers. Behind the chimney is The Limes, one time home of Aaron de Ste Croix, ship-owner and shipbuilder.

35. *(below)* H.E. the Lieutenant Governor of Jersey, Sir Peter Whiteley, unveiling a plaque at the site of Allix's shipyard, Havre des Pas on 1 August 1980.

36. Timber used for 'Stocks' and launching slipway at Gorey.

37. Early photograph of vessels in St Helier, before infilling had taken place.

38.   The brig *Stratton*, 181 tons, built by George Deslandes, Jersey 1847. Owners Ennis & Jean, master Philip C. Jean. Lost 14 September 1876.

39.   Cup and saucer with a picture of the schooner *St Catherine*, winner of around the Island Race, master and owner Clement Pallot.

10. The barque *Echo*, 422 tons, built in New Brunwick in 1841. Owned by De Quetteville & Co. for over 25 years. Lost off the Humber, 1868.

11. The brig *Brothers*, 173 tons, built at Gaspe 1858. Owned in 1863 by J&E Collas, this vessel was sold to a French owner in 1888 and re named *Gaston Albert*. Official number 27021, Signal Letters P.N.M.H.

42. Captain James R. Gaudin, born Jersey, 1807, master of the *Lady Lampson*, 1869-77, later a Pilot in B.C. waters and later still in command of lighthouse tenders.

43. Captain Elias Nicolas Pallot, born 1849, son of Elias George. Master of *Wilhelmina*, c1870.

44. Captain Nicolas Pallot, born 1793. Son of Philip. Master of *John*, 1825, *Charles*, 1836, *John & Mary*, 1844, *Queen*, 1847.

45. Captain Philip Le Rossignol, born 1798, lived at 22 St Saviour's Road, master of *Clio*, 1835, and *Commodore*, 1845.

46. Captain Charles Pallot, born 1833 son of Nicolas, lived at Elm Bank, Gorey Pier.

47. Captain F. Downer, born 1846.

48. Captain Clement Pallot, born 1826, son of Nicolas, lived at St Martin, master of *St Catherine*, shipowner.

49. Captain Elias George Pallot, born 1829, son of Nicolas, lived at Welton House, St Martin.

50. The Hudson's Bay Company's barque *Lady Lampson*, 426 tons, built by John Mills at Sunderland 1869, master Captain James R Gaudin. Here seen in the harbour at Victoria, British Columbia.

SOME ROBIN CAPTAINS

Master	Dates	Vessels
Ahier, Fred J.	1873	
Alexandre, Jean	1792	St Lawrence, Expedient
Asplet, Abraham	1826	Squaw
Baker, ?	1859	Fly
Balleine, Jean	1834–39	C.R.C., Seaflower
Bas (Le), Jean	1834–36	P.R.C.
Bas (Le), Richard	1827	Scatari
Bertram, ?	1859	Telegraph
Blancq (Le)	1868	Reaper
Boeuf (Le)	1824	Redbreast
Brehaut, T. J.	1900	C.R.C., Dawn
Briard, Edward	1822	Young Witch
Briard, Elias	1820	Messenger
Briard, Peter	1803	Day, If
Briard, Philip	1813	Cap Breton
Burgreen, Nicolas	1826	Peace
Butel, J. W.	1900	Glenville
Carrel, Francis	1821	Wag
Couilliard (Le), Jean	?	C.R.C.
Couteur (Le), J. D.	1863	C. Columbus
Dain (Le), ?	1896	
De Caen, Jean	1790	Bacchus
De Caux	1790	St Peter
De La Mare, Thom.	1827	Larch
De La Perrelle, El.	1821	Oliver Blanchard
Davey, ?	1900	Dawn, Union
Du Heaume, Edward	1829	Chagamau
Fainton, Philip	1767–77	Recovery
Le Feuvre, ?	1846	Seaflower
Flannegan, John	?	Calm
Gibaut, Francis	1834–39	Fisherman, Oliver Blanchard, Patruus
Giffard, ?	1860	Oliver Blanchard
Gresley (Le), J. F.	1900	Fanny Breslauer
Hacquoil, Peter	1853	Telegraph
Hacquoil, Thom.	1790	Paspébiac
Hamon, Philip	?	Glenville
Hawes, G. C.	?	Glenville
Hocquard, Thom.	1792	Paspébiac
Hubert, Clement	1792	Mercury
Huelin, ?	1831–34	Seaflower
Jean, Philip	1790–92	Major Pierson
Journeaux, Jam.	1804	True Friends
Luce, ?	1831–34	C. Columbus, Ditto
Malzard, Isaac	1790–92	Peace
Malzard, Nicolas	1790	Mercury
Moignard (Le), Amice	1866	Century
Noel, George	?	Dawn
Orange, Edward	1828–31	Day, Oliver Blanchard
Park, S. H.	?	Dawn
Paten, J.	1851	C. Columbus
Poingdestre, Ph.	1811	Habnab
Romeril, Jean	1866	"85"
Slous, Elias	1816	Wag
Sueur (Le), Chas.	1900	Fanny Breslauer, Union
Syvret, Philip	1850	Century
Tibot, Peter	1820	Cap Breton
Tocque, Philip	1826	Cap Breton
Vautier, Philip	1826	Storm
Vibert, Helier	1826	C. Columbus
Vibert, Philip	1830	Gaspé
Weary, Philip	1827	Grog

Chapter Five

MERCHANTS AND SHIPOWNERS AND THEIR
VESSELS BEFORE 1800

Local Exports

FROM EARLIEST TIMES Jersey merchants and seamen have been in the forefront of maritime trade, and with their well known versatility have always maintained a steady flow of exports, mostly to the mainland and France, but also to other countries, particularly to the Mediterranean ports. As early as 1294[1] islanders were trading with the south coast ports of Southampton, Weymouth, Dartmouth and Lyme, cargoes consisting at this time most of conger, which were found in large numbers in local waters. King Edward II in 1320 instructed the Governor of the island to receive the local taxes in whatever coin was being circulated, as many different species of coins were being taken in trade by the island merchants, thus confirming that a considerable foreign trade existed at this period.

The islands became free ports of the realm in 1392,[2] in consideration of the liberal services granted to the King, to carry him overseas whenever the necessity arose, and also to assist at his coronation. The Islanders' large fleet of sea-going vessels was held in high esteem by the Crown at this time and the importance of the islands, situated astride the British trade routes to their lands in the south of France, was widely known on the mainland. Local merchants in 1442 had cause to complain to King Henry IV that they were being obstructed by the Custom Officers of the ports of Plymouth, Poole and Southampton, which was a violation of their privileges. The King rectified the matter at once, declaring that the Channel Islanders were not to be treated as foreigners.

Knitted woollen goods became another export of importance. William Camden's *Britannia*, referring to Jersey in 1586, said 'Their women gained considerably by knitting of stockings, which we therefore call Jersey'. A year later Harrison's *England*[3] spoke of coloured hose of silk Jersey. That same year an account of Mary Queen of Scots' execution stated that she wore stockings 'Silk about the clocks and white Jersey under them'. Jersey knitted goods were much in demand in France at this time; French merchants came from Rouen, Paris, Carteret and Coutance in 1628 to buy bales of stockings knitted in the island. In 1670 ten thousand pairs were sold in the market place each week, mostly to local merchants for export to France and small amounts to Spain, while waistcoats were sent to England.

By 1680[4] two thousand tons of wool were being imported annually to supplement locally produced wool. The population of the island in 1685 was estimated at 15,000, of whom at least half depended upon the knitting of stockings and other woollen goods for their living. David Patriarche, a local merchant, was dealing in woollens in 1650, and Philip Pipon, another Jersey merchant based in London, was selling Island stockings to Portugal in 1693. When trade was bad, he had two thousand pairs dyed and sent them to Lisbon, where they sold at a good profit.

Jean Martel,[5] of brandy fame and a Jerseyman born at St Brelade, exported large amounts of spirits to Jersey, building up a good trade with Channel Island smugglers who carried his brandy to the mainland and to America, and indeed all over the world. The Martel boats returned to France with Jersey stockings for sale at the French markets. Jersey stockings were also well known in America and were imported by Philip Langlois (English) of Salem in 1670, who had at least two of his vessels trading regularly with his native island. Capt. Jean Mauger in 1741 said that 'Jean Le Gros had shipped on the "Jane" of Jersey, of which he was master, 120 trees grown in the island, one hogshead of cider, and five bales containing 145 dozen worsted stockings, 15 knitted waistcoats, 4 pairs of knitted breeches, 11 knitted caps, and two dozen knitted gloves, all for the port of Dartmouth'. 1748 saw 168,364 pairs of stockings exported to Southampton in a 12-month period. A consignment of 44 dozen stockings and 30 dozen balls of wool was shipped on the 'Esther' (Capt. Lys, master)[6] in the year 1759 by one Jean Simon, Carpenter, Undertaker, and export merchant. A report of 1788 states that 312,000 pairs of stockings were exported annually. Many other local merchants became established in London and other ports on the mainland over the years; some became prominent citizens of their adopted cities, some were elected mayors, or held other positions of high office.

In modern times the Jersey cow has become world famous, and a steady and lucrative export trade has been built up, both in cows and bulls. Many fine herds of 'Jerseys' have been established in many countries, originally with stock from island farms. Although early reports of the exports of cattle are few, we do know that in 1657 George Poindexter (Poingdestre) and Peter Effard were sending cows to America in small numbers. In the early 1700s cattle were being shipped to ports on the south coast of England, where they were shod like horses and driven to markets further inland. Custom house books tell of exports of cattle to various English ports in 1724, and again in 1729, of 25 black cattle shipped from Jersey. Again a report of September 1742 says that the sloop 'Jane' of Guernsey left for Southampton with eight Jersey cows. The end of the 18th century saw the trade well established and increasing numbers were shipped, as the following figures show:[7]

1803	408 head	1829	1,491 head	1852	1,752 head	1862	2,144 head
1804	269 head	1830	1,168 head	1853	1,930 head	1863	2,070 head
1805	434 head	1831	1,328 head	1854	1,699 head	1864	3,015 head
1806	409 head	1832	1,700 head				

Apple growing and cider making played a large part in island life from the middle of the 16th century and by 1625 had become a very profitable business. It was rapidly ousting corn growing on Jersey farms and by 1670 led to the export of large quantities of cider to England, while in 1680 so much cider was produced that there were not enough barrels in the island to contain it, and great quantities of apples rotted. Falle, in his 1692 history of Jersey, writes, 'I do not think there is any country in the world that (in the same extent of ground) produces so much cider as Jersey does'. The port of Southampton by 1748 was receiving regular shipments, and by 1801, according to Rev. F. Le Couteur that great expert on cider, average annual production was 30,000 barrels, of which 20,000 were consumed locally, and the rest exported to the mainland.

Plees in *An Account of the Island* (1817) writes: '1800 hogsheads (97,000 gallons) were exported yearly during the years 1809–1813. The fruit was exported and the remainder used for cidermaking. Most of these apples were sent to Devonshire for mixing with Devon grown fruit so as to improve the flavour of their local cider. The amounts of apple and cider sent to the mainland varied from year to year; 142,240 gallons of cider and 99,700 bushels of apples were exported in 1853, while the following year 89,790 gallons of cider and 179,600 bushels of apples were sent away'. After 1855, a steady decline is recorded until 1875, when exports had dwindled to 2,880 gallons only. During this period exports of potatoes were rising from 2,000 to 3,000 tons annually in the 1850s to 54,000 tons in 1890. Over the years many varieties of cider apple trees were developed locally, and some were particularly noted for their flavour and heavy cropping. Small quantities of these trees were sold to mainland growers for the Devonshire orchards.

When in 1797 banks of oysters were discovered off Jersey,[8] a new export trade opened up, and the port of Gorey grew into a small town to cater for the influx of oyster boats from the mainland in addition to the local vessels. By 1830 upwards of 250 ships, mostly cutters or small schooners, were engaged in dredging the banks. Hundreds of women and girls were employed in packing the oysters into tubs ready for shipping to the mainland, and there were nearly 2,000 men employed on the boats. In the peak year of 1834, 305,000 bushels were exported and oysters at this time were so cheap and plentiful that Gorey hotels served them free to their customers. Unfortunately, owing to severe over-fishing, the shellfish started to dwindle and by 1835 exports had dropped to 149,860 bushels. Despite attempts by the States to lay down new beds, poaching became commonplace and the garrison and militia had to be called out to stop the riots. The fishermen then turned to poaching the French beds, which led to trouble with the French, and a British naval station had to be established at Gorey to protect the local boats. However, the fish continued to dwindle and by 1864 this industry had all but ended.

The export of potatoes in the 1830s averaged 17,000 tons annually, but this dropped to about 3,500 tons until the coming of 'New Potatoes', when exports in the 1870s started to rise and soon averaged 20,000 tons yearly; the tonnage increased annually until by 1890 it had reached 54,000 tons, but by then most sailing vessels had left this trade and the steamships had taken over. Other agricultural exports were butter, grapes, pears and a variety of fruits. The export of butter reached a peak of 106,388 lbs in 1865. Grapes topped 10,000 lbs in 1859. The growing of choice fruits such as pears, grapes, dessert apples, plums and peaches for export had been established for many years, being a speciality of vineries or graperies on the island's sunny south coast. One of the more famous was Fennimore's at Bel Royal,[9] of whom Col. Le Couteur said: 'They must come to Fennimore's to see the finest grapes in the world'. This vinery changed hands in about 1862, and was taken over by a Mr. Pond, who continued to grow delicious fruits of many varieties for export, and it was at Mr. Pond's hands that the writer's grandfather, James Jean, learnt the art of fruit growing, and himself continued to grow and export fruit to Covent Garden as late as the 1930s.

Jersey-made bricks were exported in substantial quantities, and a number of brickfields were established, mainly in the Mont à L'Abbé area and also in the parish of St Saviour, at Five Oaks, at Croix Besnard, and at Longueville. These bricks were often used as ballast by vessels sailing light, particularly as a ready market was to be had in Newfoundland and on the Canadian coast. Quantities of china clay from the quarries at Handois in the parish of St Lawrence were exported. Granite from the quarries at La Moye and Corbière was shipped from the port of St Aubin; the transport of this granite to St Aubin was by the local railway to be shipped out by sailing ships. An earlier export trade in granite had been built up in the 18th century, and consisted of cargoes of pebble stones; such stones were loaded in various amounts of up to 50 tons and were certainly part of a vessel's cargo and not its ballast, and were used for paving. Granite was also cut into squares for use as paving stones and shipped mostly to south coast ports, but also as far afield as London.

Southampton had been the major port to which local goods were exported from as early as the 15th century, and certainly Channel Island vessels made up a very large share of that port's maritime trade, as the following figures taken from Southampton port books show:

	1733	1744	1748	1756	1763	1772	
Total	204	211	212	211	324	257	vessels
C.I.	123	170	139	170	249	223	vessels

AGRICULTURAL EXPORTS ETC — 1803–1865

Year	Cattle Head	Potatoes Tons	Butter Lbs	Grapes Lbs	Cider Gallons	Apples Bushels	Bricks Nos.
1803	408				100,626		
1805	434				174,258		
1806	409				185,000		
1829	1,491				—		

Continued on following page

Agricultural Exports etc — 1803-1865 — continued

Year	Cattle Head	Potatoes Tons	Butter Lbs	Grapes Lbs	Cider Gallons	Apples Bushels	Bricks Nos.
1830	1,168	10,852					
1832	1,353	8,679	27,968	1,823	191,477	220,377	187,750
1833	1,771	1,859	16,522	1,777	316,893	228,860	49,700
1837	1,060	10,951	3,203	1,585	360,700	138,770	41,000
1838	1,257	12,032	5,784	1,016	253,772	29,492	46,500
1839	1,504	17,648	10,559	659	208,534	70,645	84,600
1841	1,744	17,670	12,152	587	129,442	285,656	36,700
1843	1,846	18,560	9,560	634	110,534	215,876	21,000
1845	1,540	—	10,978	1,245	106,600	169,470	268,620
1846	1,801	3,822	3,044	1,594	209,393	139,907	221,600
1849	1,521	5,990	3,816	2,320	114,772	259,904	268,600
1850	1,817	4,992	2,543	4,640	216,625	157,710	—
1851	1,402	5,622	6,778	3,728	97,874	216,704	1,308,280
1852	1,752	3,354	1,540	2,549	164,607	36,619	1,764,750
1853	1,930	3,776	10,528	4,938	139,903	138,904	2,168,450
1854	1,699	4,330	60,846	1,465	150,260	137,034	1,899,000
1858	1,567	3,093	52,788	6,689	64,989	237,680	1,712,100
1859	1,602	2,211	64,580	10,302	121,410	138,037	1,200,890
1862	2,144	2,803	63,588	4,526	96,029	130,370	2,798,371
1863	2,070	3,908	84,868	2,204	62,506	62,449	1,827,780
1864	3,015	6,705	87,936	9,762	84,873	83,615	2,235,400
1856	2,510	3,216	106,288	1,373	72,466	81,212	2,195,600

MERCHANTS AND SHIPOWNERS OF LOCAL ORIGIN BEFORE 1800

ANLEY, David, *c.* 1730. Merchant, Constable of St John, grandfather of Thomas Anley.

ANLEY, J. & CO., *c.* 1720-37. Woolmerchants, Southampton.

AUBIN, Germain, *c.* 1730. Merchant, Jersey.

BAILLY (LE), Pierre, 1687. Merchant and Shipowner, La Vielle Maison, St Aubin.

BALLEINE, John, *c.* 1690. Shipowner, Salem, America.

BARTLETT, Marie, 1734–41. Widow of Francis, continued trading in foreign spirits after husband's death. Left money for building of Hospital. Daughter of Capt. Jean Mauger. Born 1677.

BAUDAINS, Edouard, *c.* 1546. Farmer and Merchant, St Martin.

BENEST, Brun, *c.* 1730. Merchant, based St Aubin. Father of Col. George Benest, Commanding Officer of St Lawrence Militia 1781.

BENEYT, John, *c.* 1409. Merchant, Mayor of Southampton 1409.

BERTRAM, Le BRETON & CO. (late 18th century ?). Merchants, Montevideo, South America.

BISSON, Philip, *c.* 1749. Merchant and Shipowner, Marblehead, America. Born Trinity 1729. Owner of 'Peacock' and 'Patty'.

BRETON (LE), David, *c.* 1680. Merchant and Shipowner, Jersey.

BRETON (LE), Edward, *c.* 1730. Merchant, Jersey. Importer of tobacco from Virginia.

BROHIER, Cyrus, *c.* 1730. Merchant, Jersey.

BROHIER, P. M. & CO., *c.* 1720-37. Woolmerchant, Southampton.

Continued on following pages

Merchants and Shipowners of Local Origin before 1800 — continued

BROUGHTON, John. Merchant and Shipowner, Marblehead, America.

CABOT, Francis, 1716–25. Merchant, Southampton. Born Trinity. Sheriff of Southampton, 1716, Mayor 1725.

CABOT, Francis, *c.* 1733. Merchant, Sheriff of Southampton. Fils of Francis.

CABOT, Joseph, *c.* 1730. Cattle importer, Southampton.

CAILLETEAU, P., *c.* 1758. Merchant, Jersey ?

CAUX (LE), John ? Merchant, Boston, America.

CHEVALIER, John, *c.* 1684. Merchant, Born Jersey 1659.

CHEVALIER, Raulin, *c.* 1564. Shipowner, Jersey.

CLEMENT, Nicolas, *c.* 1656. Merchant. Born St Brelade. Sheriff of Southampton, 1656, Mayor 1658.

CORBET, Moise, 1730–46. Merchant and Shipowner, St Aubin.

COUTEUR (LE), J., *c.* 1730. Merchant, Jersey.

CRAS (LE), Noé, *c.* 1763. Merchant, London.

DAMPTON, Thomas, *c.* 1730. Merchant, Jersey.

d'AUVERGNE, J. 1730–57. Merchant, Jersey and London.

d'AUVERGNE, General James 1792–94. Merchant. Fils de Charles d'Auvergne of St Helier. Sheriff of Southampton, 1792, Mayor 1795.

d'AUVERGNE, Philip, *c.* 1671. Merchant Jersey. Importer of tobacco from Virginia.

DEAN, Carteret, 1717–37. Merchant and Shipowner, St Aubin. Trading with Newfoundland 1717. Master of 'Thomas & Jane'.

DEAN, Philip 1778–81. Merchant and Shipowner, St Aubin. Fils Carteret ?? master of 'Aigle' and owner of 'L'Alarme' 1780.

de CARTERET, J. *c.* 1730. Merchant, Jersey.

de GRUCHY, Elias 1677–97. Merchant. Fils de Gilles de Gruchy, Constable of St Lawrence. Sheriff of Southampton, 1677. Mayor 1682 and 1697.

de LA PERRELLE, Philip, *c.* 1730. Merchant, Jersey.

DENTON, Thomas 1701–1770. Merchant and Shipowner, St Aubin. Fils de Thomas, harbourmaster St Aubin. Married Jeanne Le Bailly. Founder of St Aubin's church. Provided money for St Aubin's Hospital. Owner of Newfoundland fishery 1717.

de SOULEMONT, Guillaume, *c.* 1537. Merchant and Shipowner, Master of 'La Marie De Jersey' robbed by Spanish mariners.

de VEULLE, Aaron, 1686–1705. Merchant of St Clement. Sheriff of Southampton 1696. Mayor 1705.

DURELL, Thomas, 1787–1804. Merchant, Fils de Thomas Durell, Vicomte. Sheriff of Southampton 1792. Mayor 1790, 1794, 1804.

DURELL (LE VAVOUR dit), Thomas, *c.* 1813. Merchant. Sheriff of Southampton 1813.

ESTUR, Richard 1587–1602. Merchant, Southampton.

FAVOUR, John, *c.* 1576. Merchant, Fils de Jean Le Feuvre ?. Sheriff of Southampton.

FAVOUR. John, 1509–14. Merchant. Jean Le Feuvre of St Ouen. Sheriff of Southampton 1508, Mayor 1514.

GALLAIS (LE) David, *c.* 1755. Shipowner, Marblehead, America. Born Jersey.

GOSSET, Abraham 1730–46. Merchant and Shipowner, Jersey.

GOSSET, Matthew, 1778–1790. Merchant and Shipowner, Pier Road, Jersey.

GRUCHY, Thomas, *c.* 1730. Merchant, Jersey.

GRUCHY, Thomas, *c.* 1741. Shipping Magnate, Boston, America. Born Jersey 1709.

GUILLELAUME, Thomas, 1755–79. Merchant. Fils de Aaron ?; Sheriff of Southampton, 1755–77.

HAMON or HAMMOND, Jacques Jean, *c.* 1753. Merchant, London.

HAMON, Philip, *c.* 1730. Merchant, Jersey.

Continued on following pages

Merchants and Shipowners of Local Origin before 1800 – continued

HARDY (LE), Thomas, *c.*1738. Merchant, St Aubin.

HILGROVE, Clement, 1769–85. Merchant, of St Helier, Sheriff of Southampton, 1796–82–85. Mayor 1778–89.

HUE, Jacques, *c.* 1779. Merchant, St Helier.

JANVRIN, Brelade, 1773. Shipowner, of St Brelade. Shipyard at Havre-des-Pas.

JANVRIN, Daniel, ?. Shipowner, Salem, America.

JANEVRIN, Peter, 1581. Merchant, of St Brelade, married Marie Markant (Marquand). Sheriff of Southampton, 1581.

JANVRIN, Philip Valpy, dit. *c.* 1720. Shipowner and master of St Brelade. Died on board his ship 'Esther', Buried on Isle au Guerdain, Portelet.

JANVRIN, Philip, 1768. Shipowner, Jersey.

JUSTISE, William, *c.* 1495. Merchant, of Grouville. Sheriff of Southampton, 1495.

KASTEL, Francois, *c.* 1700. Merchant, lived L'Armistice, St Aubin.

LANGLOIS (ENGLISH), Philip, *c.* 1670. Merchant, owner and builder. Born Trinity 1651, owned 27 vessels in Salem. First American millionaire ?

LAURENS, Henry, *c.*1769. Merchant in slave traffic, noted for high prices obtained for slaves. High office in Charleston, South Carolina. Said to have come from Jersey.

LEMPRIÈRE, Jacques, 1730–41. Merchant and shipowner, Jersey and London 1753).

LEMPRIÈRE, Thomas, *c.* 1671. Merchant, Jersey. Importer of tobacco from Virginia.

LESBIREL, J. *c.* 1730. Merchant, Jersey.

LYS, Philip, 1768–96. Shipowner, Jersey.

MALLET, Pierre, 1790–92. Merchant and Shipowner, Jersey.

MAISTRE (LE), J. T. *c.* 1730. Merchant, Jersey.

MARETT, Henry, *c.* 1730. Merchant, Jersey.

MARETT, Philip, *c.* 1792. Merchant and Banker, Boston, America. Born St Helier, 1742.

MARKANT (MARQUAND), Edward, 1530–37 Merchant, Sheriff of Southampton 1530–37.

MARRINEL, William, *c.* 1609. Merchant. William Le Marinel of St John. Sheriff of Southampton, 1609.

MARTEL, Jean, *c.* 1720. Brandy merchant, Cognac, France. Born St Brelade, 1694.

MARTEL, J. *c.* 1775. Merchant, St Aubin. Fils de Jean ?

MAUGER, Elias, *c.* 1720. Woolmerchant, Southampton.

MAUGER, Joshua, 1740–88. Merchant. First Jerseyman elected to House of Commons, M.P. for Poole.

MAUGER, Pierre, *c.* 1763. Merchant, London.

MESSERVY, Daniel, 1757–75. Merchant and Shipowner, Linden Hall, Mont au Pretre. Owner of a number of privateering vessels.

MONTESQUIET, A., *c.* 1730. Merchant Jersey.

MONTESQUIET, P., *c.* 1730. Merchant, Jersey.

NICOLLE, Elie, *c.* 1730. Merchant, Jersey.

NICOLLE, Philip, *c.* 1769. Woolmerchant, Herupe, St John.

OVERY, Thomas, *c.* 1487. Merchant, Sheriff of Southampton 1487, Mayor 1488–90.

PATRIARCHE, David, *c.* 1650. Woolmerchant, Jersey.

PATRIARCHE, Richard, *c.* 1706. Merchant and Shipowner, Jersey.

PELLIER, Daniel, *c.* 1728. Merchant and Shipowner of 'Seven Sisters'.

PERCHARD, John, *c.*. 1512–33. Merchant, of St Saviour. Sheriff of Southampton 1512, Mayor 1524–33.

PERCHARD, William, *c.* 1485. Merchant, Sheriff of Southampton 1485.

PIPON, Jacques, 1733–46. Merchant and Shipowner, Elliston House, St Aubin, and London 1763.

PIPON, Philip, 1693–1726. Woolmerchant, London.

Continued on following page

Merchants and Shipowners of Local Origin before 1800 — continued

PIPON, Thomas, 1678-1735. Merchant, St Aubin. Constable of St Brelade. Died in England.

PIPON, Thomas, c. 1817, Merchant and Shipowner, Sussex. Director of Charles Robin & Co.

POINGDESTRE, George, c. 1656. Shipowner and Slaveholder, Virginia, America. Born St Saviour.

POINGDESTRE, James and John, c. 1814. Merchants, London.

PROUINGS, Henry, c. 1641. Shipowner, Maine, America.

RENAUD, John, c. 1415. Merchant, Mayor of Southampton, 1415.

RICHARDSON, Amis, c. 1730. Merchant, Jersey.

ROBIN, Charles, c. 1766. Principal of famous Robin, Pipon & Co. (Later Ch. Robin & Co.) of Jersey and Gaspé.

ROBIN, George, c. 1730. Merchant, Jersey.

ROBIN, Magdolain, c. 1551. Merchant and Shipowner, Augerez, St Peter. Brought to Jersey the artillery for St Peter and St Lawrence 1551. Cannon at Beaumont only surviving parish gun.

ROBIN, James and Philip, c. 1811. Merchants in Canada.

ROBIN, John, c. 1816. Merchant and Shipowner, Liverpool. Director and Agent of Charles Robin & Co.

ROBIN, Thomas, c. 1816. Merchant, Sussex.

ROWCLIFFE, George, 1757-1790. Merchant, Shipowner and Ropemaker, Havre-des-Pas, Jersey.

ROWCLIFFE, John, 1804-13. Merchant. Sheriff of Southampton 1804, Mayor 1807-13.

SEALE, Peter, 1628-42. Merchant, Fils de Germain of St Brelade. Sheriff of Southampton 1628, Mayor 1642.

SEWARD, William, c. 1767. Merchant. Married Jeanne Queripel of St Helier. Sheriff of Southampton 1767.

SEWARD & PIPON, c. 1790. Merchants, Southampton.

SIMON, Jean, c. 1759. Carpenter, Undertaker and Woolmerchant, Jersey.

TEHY, Vincent, 1474-98, Wool and Cloth merchant. Sheriff of Southampton 1474. Mayor 1484 and 1498. Co-founder of St Mannelier school. St Saviour.

VILLENEUVE, Gideon, c. 1730. Merchant, St Aubin, Jersey.

VILLENEUVE, Jean, c. 1704. Merchant and Shipowner, La Vielle Maison, St Aubin. Master of 'Marie'.

N.B. See under the Newfoundland Fisheries & Shipowners in the 19th century for names of other merchants (pp. 00-00).

JERSEY OWNED VESSELS 1537-1699

Vessel	Date	Master	Rig, Tonnage, etc.
AMITÉ	1603	Peter Seale	40 tons, based St Aubin
ANN	1693	Owned by 6 Jerseymen	25 tons, ex-prize 'Mary'
BENEDITION (LA)	?	Edward de Carteret	—
BONA SPERA	1587	Jean Guillaume	40 tons, trading Swansea
BONAVENTURE	1587-89	Jean Filleul	20 tons, trading Swansea
DRAGON	1595	Matthew Harry	50 tons, trading Swansea
DYAMONT	1587	Thomas Guillaume	20 tons, trading Swansea
EDWARD	1603	Helier de Gall	20 tons, trading Swansea
ELIZABETH	1595	Nicolas Bailhache	20 tons, trading Swansea

Continued on following page

Jersey Owned Vessels 1537-1699 — continued

Vessel	Date	Master	Rig, Tonnage, etc.
FALCON	1603	Jean Oliver	20 tons, trading Swansea
FIDELITE (LA)	1690	Thomas Martel	—
FLEUR (LA)	1619	J. Bailhache	Master and owner
FLOWER DE LUCE	1600	Peter Syvrett	20 tons, trading Swansea
FRANCIS	1600	Nicolas Le Bas	15 tons, trading Swansea
FRANCOIS (LE)	1644	Jeremie Grandin	—
GABRIELL	1587	Richard Jean ?	16 tons, trading Swansea
GEORGE	1588	Jean Balleine	20 tons, trading Swansea
GOLDEN LION	1668	Philip Pipon	Based St Aubin
GOOD HOPE	1587	Richard de Carteret	30 tons, trading Swansea
GRACE OF GOD	1690	Nicolas Bichard	20 tons, trading Swansea
HOPEWELL	1655	?	—
JERSEY SLOOP	1692-93	Jean Mauger	Master and owner, Privateer
JOHN	1580	? Perrott	24 tons, trading Swansea
JOHN	1674	Clement Lempriére	—
JONAT	1595	Peter Le Brocq	70 tons, trading Swansea
LYON	1588-95	Jean Marett	24 tons, trading Swansea
LYTELLA	1587	Andrew Filleul	18 tons, trading Swansea
MAIDA	1600	?	40 tons, trading Swansea
MAIOR	1600	Edward Parke	Trading Swansea
MARGARETT	1580	William Le Marinel	20 tons, trading Swansea
MARIE	1692	William Snow	Privateer, St Aubin
MARIE (LA)	1537	Guillaume de Soulement	Robbed of ship and cargo by Spanish
MARY	1587-00	?	Trading Swansea
MICHEL	1600	Thomas Janvrin	20 tons, trading Swansea
MICHEL RICARD	1591	?	Sold by auction
MINION	1580-95	J. Bailhache	20 tons, trading Swansea
ORANGE (L')	1649-91	J. Le Cras	40 tons, Touzel & Orange owners
PELLICANE	1580	Guillaume Neel	14 tons, trading Swansea
PRIMROSE	1595	Peter Janvrin	58 tons, trading Swansea
RICHARD	1691-96	?	Elias Pipon, owner
ST ALBANS	1695	George Bennet	Privateer
SARAH	1628	?	Taken by pirates
SOLOMON	1600	Solomon Blondel	30 tons, Privateer
STARE	1588	George Le Boutillier	18 tons, trading Swansea
SUSAN	1588-03	Michel Le Phon	19 tons, trading Swansea
THOMAS	1696	Elias Pipon	Taken by the French
TWO BROTHERS	?	Edward Browne	Privateer

JERSEY OWNED VESSELS IN THE 18TH CENTURY

Vessel	Date	Master	Owner	Rig, Tonnage, etc.
ACCIDENT (L')	1721	Samuel Perrand	Samuel Perrand	Based St Aubin
ACTIF (L')	1753–78	James Balleine	Daniel Messervy	80 t, 6 guns, Privateer
ACTIF (L')	1778	C. Messervy	Daniel Messervy	Taken by enemy 1778
ACTIVE	1796	? Shoosmith	Thomas Mallet	Brig, 67 t, French built, 1792
ACTIVE	1785	Philip Le Vesconte	Jean Le Vesconte	Brig, 42 t, American built
ACTIVE	1792	Jean Noel	Hemery Bros.	Brig, 42 t, American built
ADMIRAL BARRINGTON	1786	? Janvrin	Francis Janvrin	Brig, 108 t, built Dartmouth 1785
ADMIRAL BARRINGTON	1790	Francis Hocquard	Francis Janvrin	Brig, 108 t, built Dartmouth 1785
ADMIRAL BARRINGTON	1792	Philip Winter	Philip Winter	Brig, trading N'foundland
ADMIRAL DURELL	1773	? Cabot	—	60 t, French built 1756
ADMIRAL DURELL	1778	Philip Dean	Francis Janvrin	60 t, French built 1756
ADMIRAL DURELL	1780	Jean Cabot	—	60 t, French built 1756
ADVENTURE	1737	Peter Fiott	—	Sloop, 58 t
ADVENTURE	1777	? Poingdestre	—	Sloop, 58 t
ADVENTURE	1790–92	James Torrey	Philip Winter	Sloop, 58 t
ADVENTURE	1786	Jean de Feu	—	120 t, British built 1761
AEOLUS	1780	? Giffard	—	Privateer 1780
AIGLE (EAGLE)	1778	Philip Dean	Francis Janvrin	Lugger, 96 t, Privateer
AIGLE (EAGLE)	1789	? Torrey	Francis Janvrin	Based St Aubin
ALARME (L')	1780	Jean Fiott	Philip Dean	132 t, Privateer
ALDERNEY PACKET	1780–90	? Le Ray	—	30 t, Southampton built, 1777?
ALERT	1779	William Snow	—	87 t, Privateer
ALEXANDER	1773–76	? Luce	—	Taken by enemy and retaken 1776
ALEXANDER	1778	? Vibert	—	All crew bar one drowned 1778
ALLIGATOR	1792	—	—	89 t, taken by enemy 1794
AMBITION	1752	Clem. Messervy	—	—
AMELIA	1776	—	—	Trading with Spain
ANGELICQUE	1790	Amice Gaudin	Matthew Gosset	Trading with N'foundland
ANGELICQUE	1792	Thomas Blampied	Mallet & Fiott	Taken by enemy 1793
ANNE	1737	Philip Payn	—	Sloop, 47 t
ANNE	1790	George Marett	Philip Ahier	45 t, trading with Newfoundland
ANNE & MARY	1790	Jean Hamon	Philip Durell	44 t, sold to Bristol 1809
ANNE & MARY	1792	Clement Durell	Philip Durell	44 t, sold to Bristol 1809
ARGUS	1780–82	—	Philip Winter	Brig, 68 t
AUBIN	1757	Thomas Blampied	Daniel Messervy	—
AURORA	1786	Thomas Filleul	—	—

Continued on following pages

Jersey Owned Vessels in the 18th Century — continued

Vessel	Date	Master	Owner	Rig, Tonnage, etc.
BACCHUS	1790	Jean de Caen	Ch. Robin & Co.	80 t, trading with Newfoundland
BACHELLEUR	1731	Francis Du Heaume	—	—
BALCANNA	1794	—	—	—
BATHIDE	1763	—	Daniel Messervy	Brigantine, Privateer
BEAVER	1778	Francis Messervy	—	Snow, 166 t, Bristol built 1767
BEAVER	1790	Jean Hamon	James Remon	Schooner, 38 t
BEAZLEY	1778	Nicolas Vautier	Matthew Gosset	160 t, 14 guns, Privateer
BEE	1777-78	Philip Fainton	Ch. Robin & Co.	160 t, 7 guns, Boston built 1773
BEE	1778	M. Dolbel	E. Mauger	Brig, 40 t, French built
BENNET	1780	—	—	Schooner, 68 tons
BETSY	1786	J. Roy	—	Sloop, 26 t, French built 1770
BETSY	1790	Francis Godfray	Francis Godfray	Sloop, 26 t, French built 1770
BETSY	1765	Jean Le Sueur	Jean Le Sueur	Brigantine, 120 t, American built
BETSY	1783	—	Jean Le Gallais	Brigantine, 120 t, American built
BETSY	1790	Francis Journeaux	Jean Journeaux	40 t, taken by enemy 1793
BETSY	1778	Nicolas Chevalier	Geo. Rowcliffe	Brig, 74 t, French built
BETSY	1790-92	Jean Le Quesne	Edward Coombes	Brig, 74 t, French built
BETSY & MARY	1794	—	—	50 t, taken by enemy 1794
BETTY	1786	Daniel Le Geyt	—	Brig, 91 t
BLACK PRINCE	1794	—	—	12 t, taken by enemy 1794
BONAVENTURE	1776	? Journeaux	—	Trading with Spain
BONNE ESPERANCE	1715	Jean Mauger	—	Trading with New England
BONNE INDUSTRIE	1727	—	—	Trading with N'foundland
BONNE SOIESE	1714	Abraham Le Moigne	—	—
BOSCAWNEN	1757	Thomas Labey	Daniel Messervy	Privateer
BOSCAWNEN	1763	Pierre Labey	Daniel Messervy	Privateer
BOSTON	1795	? Le Feuvre	? Le Feuvre	Spy ship for d'Auvergne
BRETAGNE	1759	—	—	Privat'r, 16 guns, lost 1759
BRILLIANT	1780	—	—	Privateer
BURNETT (LE)	1763	—	Daniel Messervy	Privateer, 27 crew
CAESAR	1771	? de Carteret	—	Trading Jamaica
CANADIAN	1778	G. Renouf	? de Gruchy	Brig, 120 t, built 1774 Quebec
CAPRE	1708	Andrew de Ste Croix	—	Privateer and guard boat
CAPRE PRINCE	1708	Richard Pipon	—	Privateer
CAPRE PRINCE	1709-15	Edward Le Brun	—	Privateer
CAPRI L'ESPERANCE	1704	Noé Le Cras	—	—

Continued on following pages

Jersey Owned Vessels in the 18th Century — continued

Vessel	Date	Master	Owner	Rig, Tonnage, etc.
CATHERINE	1786	? Dumaresq	—	Sloop, 80 t
CERES	1790	Philip Bisson	Philip Bisson	29 t, trading with G'sey
CERES	1792	Philip Bisson	Elie Collings	29 t, trading with G'sey
CHARLOTTE	1778-90	P. Gallie	—	Sloop, 40 t, trading with Southampton
CHARLOTTE	1792	Jean Kerby	Durell & Kerby	Sloop, 40 t, trading with Southampton
CHARLOTTE	1776	Jean Falle	Noé Cabot	27 t, French built 1757
CHARLOTTE	1790	Thomas Payn	Thomas Payn	Trading Southampton
CHARMING BETTY	1737-40	Thomas Pipon	Thomas Pipon	Sloop, trading S'hampton
CHARMING BETTY	1741	James Le Cras	James Le Cras	Sloop, trading S'hampton
CHARMING BETTY	1758-59	Nicolas Fiott	Lemprière & Fiott	Privateer, 70 crew
CHARMING BETTY	1776	M. Janvrin	—	60 t, built 1746
CHARMING BETTY	1776-78	William Snow	—	170 t, built Newbury, America 1764
CHARMING JENNY	1751-52	Pierre Labey	—	
CHARMING NANCY	1753-59	Jean Luce	Lemprière & Fiott	225 t, 14 guns, barque
CHARMING NANCY	1759	Nicolas Fio	Lemprière & Fiott	225 t, 14 guns, barque
CHARMING NANCY	1778	Philip Winter	Philip Winter	225 t, 14 guns, barque
CITY OF DERBY	1778	P. Mauger	M. Lemprière	Brig, 120 t, built 1775 Rhode Island
CLEOPATRA	1776	Charles Mauger	James Hemery	260 t, taken by enemy 1804
CLINTON	1780	—	—	Brig, 65 tons
COMMERCE	1786	G. Olsen	J. & G. Hemery	Brig, 127 t, French built 1776
COMMERCE	1790	G. Aubin	J. & G. Hemery	Trading with N'foundland
COMMERCE	1792	Edw. Le Couteur	J. &. G. Hemery	Trading with N'foundland
CONCORD	?	—	—	Brig, 60 t, American built 1773
CONCORDE	1717	Edward Dumaresq	—	—
CONCORDE	1786-90	Jean de Ste Croix	Geo. Rowcliffe	Brig, 126 t, Trading Newfoundland
CONTENT GALLEY	1705	Philip Patriarche	—	
CONWAY	1769	—	—	9 t, guard boat, taken by enemy 1794?
CORBET	1776	Jean Kerby	—	Brig, 68 t, Boston built 1774
CORBET	1778	Jean Tocque	—	Privateer
CORBET	1790	Francis Le Four	Poingdestre & Robinson	—
CORBET	1792	Germaine Aubin	Poingdestre & Robinson	—
CORNWALL	1778	Pierre Janvrin	Francis Janvrin	192 t, trad'g N'foundland
CORNWALL	1786	Jean Vibert	Francis Janvrin	160 men taken to N'f'dland

Continued on following pages

Jersey Owned Vessels in the 18th Century — continued

Vessel	Date	Master	Owner	Rig, Tonnage, etc.
COTTÉE	1757	—	—	Privateer, took French prize in Biscay
CRUSIER	1787	? Le Feuvre	—	—
DARTMOUTH GALLEY	1740–41	Richard Le Feuvre	—	—
DAUPHIN	1765	Clement Gallichan	—	37 t, based St Aubin
DAUPHIN	1786–88	Pierre Le Roux	Philip Winter	Trading with Spain, taken by enemy 1793
DAWKINS (Le)	1792	Francis Le Feuvre	Philip Janvrin	118 t, taken and sunk 1794
DEFIANCE	1715	? Gruchy	—	Privateer ?
DEFIANCE	1757	? Le Cronier	Daniel Messervy	Schooner, 67 t, Privateer
DEFIANCE	1778	Nicolas Mallet	—	40 t, Privateer, 6 guns
DE JERSEY	1794	—	—	208 t
DELVARDE (LA)	1763	Geo. Messervy	Daniel Messervy	Privateer, 4 guns
DILIGENT	1779	Jean Le Brun	—	Brig, 76 t, Privateer
DILIGENT	1790–92	Edward Mourant	Geo. Rowcliffe	Brig, 76 t, taken by French 1792
DISPATCH	1780–90	? Babot	—	60 t, trading Southampton, taken by enemy 1793 ?
DOLPHIN	1737	James Lemprière	—	Snow, taken by Spanish 1741
DOLPHIN	1741	Edward Luce	Jas. Lamprière	Snow
DOLPHIN	1778	Jean Cabot	Jean Thoreau	120 t, Privateer, built Quebec 1770
DOLPHIN	1781	—	—	Brig, 60 t
DOLPHIN	1783	—	—	Sloop, 50 t
DON DE DIEU (LE)	1728	—	—	—
DOROTHY & MAY	1773	? Seward	—	—
DRAGON	1757	Clem. Messervey	Guernsey owned	91 tons
DUKE OF CUMBERLAND	1757	Jean Arthur	Daniel Messervy	70 t, Privateer
DUKE OF NORTHUMB'D	1757	Jean Arthur	—	Privateer
DUKE OF RICHMOND	1763–64	Noé Gautier	G'sey owned ?	Trading Southampton
DUMARESQ	1790	Jean Vibert	Francis Janvrin	180 t
DUMARESQ	1792	Philip Vibert	Francis Janvrin	180 t, taken by enemy 1794
DURELL	1776	Philip Dean	—	Brig, 60 t, French built 1756
DURELL	1778	Edward Mourant	Thomas Durell	Brig, 150 t, built 1767
EAGLE (AIGLE)	1778	Philip Dean	Francis Janvrin	Lugger, 96 t, Privateer
EARL OF GRANVILLE	1758	—	Daniel Messervy	Privateer
ECLIPSE	1796	? Gruchy	C. Hemery	Brig, 74 t, b'lt Plym'th 1790
EFFORT	1762–65	Philip Journeaux	—	Trading Southampton
EGMONT	1778	Jean Janvrin	—	Brig, 70 t, old Jersey-built vessel

Continued on following pages

Jersey Owned Vessels in the 18th Century — continued

Vessel	Date	Master	Owner	Rig, Tonnage, etc.
ELIA	1737	George Hooper	—	Sloop
ELIAS & JAMES	1738	Elias Trachy	—	—
ELISHA TUPPER	1789	Daniel Haines	Francis Janvrin	280 t, Jersey built 1789
ELISHA TUPPER	1790	Philip Vibert	Francis Janvrin	Trading Newfoundland
ELISHA TUPPER	1796	E. Valpy	Francis Janvrin	Trading Newfoundland
ELIZABETH	1778	Jean Fiott	? Fiott	Sloop, 70 t, Brit. b'lt 1765
ELIZABETH	1777-78	? Anquetil	Thomas Durell	Schooner, 60 t, Jersey built 1775
ELIZABETH	1773	? Le Brun	—	Schooner, 25 tons
ELIZABETH	1737	Elias Le Gros	—	Sloop
ELIZABETH	1790	David Mauger	Jean Villeneuve	Brigantine, 115 t, 2 guns
ELIZABETH	1790	Jean Brohier	Daniel Messervy	—
ENDEAVOUR	1767	? Balleine	Ch. Robin & Co.	Brig, 130 t, trading with Newfoundland
ENDEAVOUR	1778	E. Helleur	Philip Winter	Brig, 110 t, Am. b'lt 1759
ENTERPRISE	1794	Elie Messervy	Philip Lys & Nic. Messervy	40 t
ENTERPRISE	1796	? Chevalier	A. de Ste Croix	Brig, 80 t, built 1792
EOLE	1778	Philip Giffard	—	Privateer
ESTHER	1720	Philip Janvrin	Philip Janvrin	Brig, 79 t
ESTHER	1778	? Poingdestre	—	Brig, 50 t, built 1768
ESTIENNE (L')	1712	Rich'd Le Feuvre	—	—
EXPEDITION	1778	J. Geffrard	A. Chevalier	Sloop, 56 t, built 1772
EXPEDITION PACKET	1746	Thomas Bushel	—	Privateer
FAIRY	1792	Abraham Gaudin	Dumaresq & Hammond	66 t
FANNY	1773	Philip Journeaux	—	Trading Plymouth and Southampton
FAVOURITE	1792	Jean Voie	Henri Voie	100 t
FELICITY	1796	Jean Le Roux	? Chevalier	Brig, 186 t, built in France 1790
FERRET	1780	—	—	Privateer
FIOTT	1792	—	—	150 t, taken by enemy 1793
FLORA	1786	S. Wilkins	Geo. Rowcliffe	Schooner, 70 t, built America 1779
FLORISSANT	1780	—	—	Ship, 280 tons
FLY	1783	—	—	72 t
FLYING FISH	1793	—	de Lisle & Bett	184 t
FLYING SCUD	1793	—	—	—
FORTUNE	1786	J. Richardson	J. Richardson	Brig, 37 t
FORTUNE	1790	Abraham Bushell	H. Le Sueur	Sloop, 13 t
FOX	1759	Clement Pallot	—	Lugger, 8 t, 2 guns
FOX	1780	Clement Pallot	Wm. Patriarche	Lugger,
FRANCIS	1747	John Lys	—	Trading Southampton
FRANCIS & ANN	1701	Thomas Snow	—	40 t
FRANCIS & ANN	1710	William Bushell	—	40 t
FRIENDS	1758	Joshua Gabourel	—	Trading Southampton

Continued on following pages

Jersey Owned Vessels in the 18th Century — continued

Vessel	Date	Master	Owner	Rig, Tonnage, etc.
FRIENDS	1776	—	—	Trading Spain
FRIENDS DELIGHT	1744	Philip Luce	—	Trading Southampton
FRIENDS ENDEAVOUR	1779	Charles Renouf	—	—
FRIENDSHIP	1790	Philip Messervy	J. & C. Hemery	Brig, 78 t
FRIENDSHIP	1747	Jean Fauvel	—	51 t, trading S'hampton
FRIENDSHIP	1790	Ed. Le Feuvre	J. Le Feuvre	51 t, trading S'hampton
FRIENDS	1792	Philip Gallie	Dolbel & Gallie	39 t, trading N'f'dland
GASPÉ	1790	—	Jean Kerby	Brig, 35 t, trading with Newfoundland
GAUTIER	1771	? Gautier	? Gautier	Sloop
GEN. CONWAY	1778	Ch. Coutanche	Remon & Co.	Snow, 118 t, Brit. b'lt 1776
GEORGE	1790	Elie Cabot	J. & C. Hemery	65 t
GEORGE	1792	Pierre Le Cronier	Pierre Le Cronier	65 t
GEORGE	1778	E. Le Couteur	T. &. J. Pipon	Brig, 110 t, built in Philadelphia 1769
GEORGE & PHILIP	1737	Philip Robin	—	—
GLOBE	1790	—	—	—
GOOD FRIENDS	1790	Philip Le Cronier	Francis Amy	58 t, took 46 persons to Newfoundland 1790
GOOD INTENT	1778	Ed. de La Taste	T. & J. Pipon	Brig, 148 t
GOOD INTENT	1796	P. Bertram	Philip Bisson	Brig, 52 t, built in Newfoundland 1792
GOREY	1760–80	—	—	25 tons, Privateer
GRATITUDE	1755	Francis Cosnard	—	Based St Aubin
GREYHOUND	1780	—	—	Privateer
GUERNSEY PACKET	1786	Peter Mourant	—	39 t, trading S'hampton
GUERNSEY PACKET	1790	William Kerby	Thomas Tacker	39 t, trading S'hampton
HAPPY RETURN	1783	? Le Vesconte	—	—
HARMONY	1790	James Barbier	Elie de Ste Croix	35 t
HARMONY	1792	? d'Auvergne	James Remon	Brig, 130 t, built 1787
HARMONY	1792	Philip Wright	Elie de Ste Croix	—
HARRIETT	1799	—	—	—
HARTWELL	1787	? Fiott	—	Lost 1787, crew saved
HAWKE	1785	Thomas de La Garde	R. de Jersey, of Guernsey	Sloop, 51 t, Brit. b'lt 1773
HAZARD	1798	Samuel Gasnier	—	Privateer
HENRY & MARY	1796	? Le Feuvre	? Gautier	34 t, built Brixton 1790
HERALD	1798	Thomas Pickstock	J. & C. Hemery	80 t, 10 guns, Privateer
HERCULES	1790	Clement Durell	Matthew Gossett	161 t
HERCULES	1792	Thos. Hocquard	Gossett & Mallet	161 t
HERO	1780	? Nicolle	—	50 t, 4 guns, Privateer, trading S'hampton
HERRIOT	1785–86	—	—	Ship, 300 t
HILTON	1794	Pierre Bisson	Ch. Robin & Co.	178 t
HOPE	1703	Samuel Perrand	—	Sloop, Privateer

Continued on following pages

Jersey Owned Vessels in the 18th Century — continued

Vessel	Date	Master	Owner	Rig, Tonnage, etc.
HOPE	1737	Philip Perchard	—	Sloop Privateer
HOPE	1747	Stephen Mourant	Thomas Mallet	Sloop, 41 t
HOPE	1777	Philip Jean	Ch. Robin & Co.	Brig, 110 t, colonial built
HOPE	1785	? Poingdestre	Ch. Robin & Co.	Snow, 70 t, colonial built 1769
HOPE	1786	J. Le Riche	—	Sloop, 60 t, Jersey built 1776
HUNTER	1760–80	—	—	Privateer
HYNDE	1730–33	—	—	Lost 1733
INDEED	1784	—	—	60 t
INDUSTRIE (L')	1744	Nicolas Dupre	—	—
INDUSTRIE (L')	1790	Philip Dean	Philip Janvrin	Brig, 50 t, Jersey built 1763, based St Aubin
INDUSTRY	1785	E. Remon	E. Remon	Brig, 70 t, colonial built 1764
JAMES	1784–49	—	—	—
JAMES & NANCY	1794	Noé Le Sueur	—	109 t, taken by enemy 1794
JANE	1737–41	Jean Le Gros	Thomas Denton	Sloop, trading S'hampton
JANE	1768	—		Schooner, 45 t
JANE	1776–85	J. Le Sueur	Nicolas Fiott	Brig, 100 t, rebuilt 1774
JANE	1794	—	—	70 t
JANE & ELIZABETH	1777	? Messervy	—	—
JANVRIN	1792	Francis Hocquard	Francis Janvrin	192 t
JEANNE	1799	—	—	—
JENNY	1778–85	E. Le Brocq	Matthew Gossett	Barque, 150 t, 10 guns, built Boston 1764
JENNY	1792	James Gasnier	A. de Ste Croix	57 tons
JERSEY	1737	Jean Pipon	—	Snow
JERSEY	1773	? Fiott	—	Snow, 150 t, built 1767
JERSEY	1776–79	E. de Ste Croix	—	200 t, built N'f'land 1771
JERSEY	1785	? Ahier	E. Robinson	Sloop, 50 t, Brit. b'lt 1770
JERSEY	1785	C. Lemprière	Hemery & Co.	Brig, 180 t, Brit. b'lt 1773
JERSEY	1786	P. Dorey	? de Gruchy	Sloop, 100 t, Scottish built 1780
JERSEY FLOWER	1737	Jean Poingdestre	—	Barque
JERSEY FLOWER	1756–63	Abraham Chevalier	—	Trading with S'hampton
JERSEY GALLEY	1744	Amice Vincent		Privateer
JERSEY PACKET	1787–96	Francis Bichard	E. de Ste Croix	66 t, built Cowes 1787
JERSEY PACKET	1785	Jean Hamon	S. Guillet	45 t, British built 1769
JERSEY PACKET	1796	Philip Asplet	? Poingdestre	45 t, British built 1769
JOHANNA	1790	Henry Wilkins	Bishop & Chevalier	40 t
JOHN	1721	Jean Mauger	—	Sloop, 60 tons
JOHN	1737	Thomas Filleul	—	Sloop, trading with Newfoundland
JOHN	1747	Jean Le Gros	—	Trading with S'hampton
JOHN & MARY	1741	Robert Le Feuvre	—	Brig, 40 t

Continued on following pages

Jersey Owned Vessels in the 18th Century — continued

Vessels	Date	Master	Owner	Rig, Tonnage, etc.
JOHN & MARY	1786	J. Giffard	J. Giffard	Brig, 129 t
JOLLY SLOOPE	1704	Philip Shoosmith	—	
JORGE & JAN	1785	A. Stoodie	A. Stoodie	100 t, Dutch built 1773
JULIA	1762	Philip Le Brocq	—	Trading Southampton
JUNO	1785	P. Gorequer	J. Geffrard	Brig, 140 t, 8 guns, built America 1771
JUPITER	1790-92	Clem. Messervy	Ed. Du Heaume	58 t
KENTON	1790	Phil. Ingouville	Ingouville & de Ste Croix	Brig, 113 t
KINGFISHER	1735	Jean Luce	—	—
KINGFISHER	1786	Jean Le Roux	Dumaresq & Hammond	Sloop, 57 t
KING GEORGE	1747	Jean Le Gros	—	Privateer
KITTY	1787	Philip Dumaresq	—	40 t
KITTY	1792	Clem. Le Couteur	James Remon	100 t, taken by enemy 1794
LIBERTÉ	1786	Moise Steel	—	Brig, 69 t
LIBERTÉ	1790-92	Chas. Hocquard	Pierre Mallet	Brig, 69 t
LIBERTY	1796	—	—	240 t
LIBERTY PACKET	1784	—	—	60 t
LION	1778	John Millais	—	Privateer
LIVELY	1778	Jean Kerby	Patriarche & Co.	120 t, 16 guns, French built 1756
LIVELY	1784	—	—	12 t, taken by enemy 1784
LIVELY	1778	—	—	16 guns, taken by enemy 1778
LONDON	1785	P. Mourant	Le Cras & Co.	70 t, built 1748
LONDON EXPEDITION	1774	Philip Laurens	—	Trading with Boston and Newfoundland
LONDON PACKET	1768	Jean Lys	Philip Lys	Sloop, 88 t, built 1748
LONDON PACKET	1786	? Ingouville	? Le Masurier	Sloop, 88 t, built 1748
LORD DORCHESTER	1792	Philip Hubert	Pierre Mallet	171 tons, taken 1794
LORD NELSON	1789	—	—	83 t
LOTTERY	1797-99	Samuel Gasnier	Mallet, Thoreau & Hooper	24 t
LOVELY	1776	? Kerby	—	Trading with Spain
LYNX	1779	Jean Simonet	—	Brig, 182 t
LYNX	1790	Jean Du Heaume	J. Le Vesconte	Trading with N'f'dland and Labrador
MACARONI	1778	Peter Cabot	Francis Janvrin	60 t, 8 guns, Privateer, built 1774
MAGDELAINE	1786	Edward Noel	—	Barque, 120 t
MAGDELAINE	1790	Francis Noel	Pierre Mallet	38 t, trading with Newfoundland
MAGDELAINE	1792	Thomas Le Cras	Pierre Mallet	38 t, trading with Newfoundland
MAGOT (LE)	1792	Francis Le Feuvre	Ch. Robin & Co.	—

Continued on following pages

Jersey Owned Vessels in the 18th century — continued

Vessel	Date	Master	Owner	Rig, Tonnage, etc.
MAJOR PEIRSON	1786–92	Philip Jean	Ch. Robin & Co.	172 t, trading N'f'dland, taken by enemy 1794
MAKIE	1786	Francis Noel	—	—
MARGUERITE	1794	Jean Le Feuvre	—	120 t, taken by enemy 1794
MARIE	1704	Jean Villeneuve	—	Based St Aubin
MARQUIS OF TOWNSEND	1792	Francis Hocquard	—	Privateer
MARS	1776	Noé Le Sueur	Edward Renouf	165 t, Privateer
MARY	1737–47	Thomas Balleine	—	Trading Virginia
MARY	1778	J. Heraut	T. & J. Pipon	Brig, 70 t, built 1763
MARY	1778	P. Le Cronier	Matthew Gossett	Barque, 150 t, built 1735
MARY	1790	Noé Messervy	Noé Messervy	Cutter, 15 tons
MARY ANN	1739	Jean Ahier	Jean Ahier	90 t, lost 1739
MARY ANN	1789–90	Jean Le Riche	Charles Renouf	Brig, 36 t
MARY ANN	1792	Philip Bisson	Chas. Chevalier	Brig, 36 t
MARY & BETSY	1790	J. Le Gresley	J. Le Gresley	32 t
MAYFLOWER	1768–80	—	—	Schooner, 80 t
MAYFLOWER	1768	—	—	Brig, 60 t
MAYFLOWER	1768–01	Nicolas Dolbel	—	Brig, 30 t, Privateer
MERCURE	1788–90	Clement Hubert	Ch. Robin & Co.	54 t, based at St Aubin
MERMAID	1736	? Lawrence	—	—
MINERVA	1757	—	Daniel Messervy	Brig, 180 t, Privateer, French b't, sold Bristol
MINERVA	1779	Jean Le Couteur	—	—
MINERVA	1778–86	Chas. Ingouville	—	Sloop, 40 t, Jersey built
MINERVA	1780	—	—	Brig, 88 t
MOLLY	1756	George Bertram	Daniel Messervy	Schooner, 80 t, colonial b'lt
MOLLY	1786	Edward Le Geyt	D. Le Geyt	Brig, 130 t, b'lt Lyme 1769
MONT ANLEY	1741	Ric. Le Cras		Schr., tkn by Sp'sh 1741
MOLLY	1783	Geo. Le Geyt	—	Schooner, Privateer
MOLLY	1741	Richard Le Cras	—	Schooner, taken by Spanish 1741
NANCY	1763	H. Vibert	Thomas Pipon	Based St Aubin
NANCY	1778–86	Josue Bouton	Pierre Mallet	Brig, 200 t
NANCY	1786–90	James Simonet	Pierre Le Brun	64 t, trading with Spain
NANCY & MARY	1776	? Le Geyt	—	Brig
NAXOS	1790	Philip Mourant	Philip Mourant	11 tons
NEPTUNE	1768–73	? Messervy	—	Brig, 80 tons
NEPTUNE	1784–90	Daniel Hamon	Francis Janvrin	131 t
NEPTUNE	1784–90	Jean Hocquard	Francis Janvrin	Trading Newfoundland
NEPTUNE	1795	Jean Le Vesconte	—	Schooner, 17 t, taken by enemy 1794
NEPTUNE GALLEY	1709	Thomas Lesbirel	—	—
NONPARIEL	1770	Peter Clement	—	Trading Antigua and South Carolina
NONSUCH	1780	—	Elie Robinson	Guard boat 1781
NUMSLEY CASTLE	1710	Thomas Lesbirel	—	—
NYMPH	1786	? Messervy	—	Lost off Boulogne 1768

Continued on following pages

Jersey Owned Vessels in the 18th Century — continued

Vessel	Date	Master	Owner	Rig, Tonnage, etc.
OWNER'S GOODWILL	1790–91	Clement Pallot	Clement Pallot	27 t
OWNER'S GOODWILL	1792	D. Simpson	Jean Kerby	Trading with Plymouth
PASPEBIAC	1785–92	Thos. Hacquoil	Ch. Robin & Co.	133 t, trading N'f'dland, taken by enemy 1794
PEACE	1790–92	Isaac Malzard	Ch. Robin & Co.	Brig, 72 t, trading Oporto and N'f'dland, tkn 1794
PEARL	1737	Jean Chevalier	Jean Pipon	Sloop
PEGGY	1796	—	? Janvrin	Sloop, 35 t, built Cowes 1791
PEGGY	1799	Aaron Godfray	Geo. Le Cronier	Brig, 62 t
PEGGY	1790	Thos. Bandinel	Thomas Mallet	98 t
PEGGY	1742	William Weeks	—	Sloop
PEIRSON	1786–92	Philip Vibert	Francis Janvrin	Brig, 90 t, colonial built
PERSEVERANCE	1790	Brun Benest	Brun Benest	Cutter, 59 t, based St Aubin
PETIT JULIE (LE)	1780	? Poingdestre	—	Privateer
PHILIP	1737–40	Jean Du Parq	—	Brigantine, 70 t, based St Aubin
PHILIP	1737–40	Thomas Robin	—	Brigantine, trading Newfoundland
PHILIP & JOHN	1737	Richard Le Cras	—	—
PHOENIX	1727–47	Philip Marett	—	Snow
PHOENIX	1756	Robert Barbier	Daniel Messervy	Snow
PHOENIX	1789	Daniel Hamon	? Janvrin	Snow
PHYLIS	1740	—	—	Sloop, 20 tons
PIERRE	1757	John Taylor	—	Privateer
PIGEON	1737	Abraham Malzard	—	—
PINGUIN	—	—	—	Brig, 35 t
PIPON GALLEY	1738	Abraham Malzard	Malzard & Pipon	—
PITT	1778	Elie Le Blanc	J. Thoreau	Sloop, 70 t, 6 guns, built Jersey 1773
POSTILLION PACKET	1785–90	? le Ray	Mat. Gossett	Schooner, 40 t
POSTILLION PACKET	1790	Nicolas Cabot	Mat. Gossett	Schooner, 40 t, trading with Southampton
POSTILLION PACKET	1792	Phil. Le Blanc	Dumaresq & Hammond	Schooner, 40 t, trading with Southampton
PRESS ON	1782–83	—	—	Schooner
PRETTY	1751	M. Le Vesconte	—	—
PRINCE D'AUVERGNE	1794	—	—	150 t
PRINCE OF WALES	1747–51	Peter Cabot	—	Trading with S'hampton
PRINCESS	1778	Nicolas Anthoine	Philip Winter	Brig, 100 t, old colonial built vessel
PRINCESSA	1768	—	—	Brig, 70 t
PRINCESS ROYAL	1796	Thos. Pickstock	Hemery Bros	Brig, 103 t, built 1791
PRINCE WILLIAM	1747	William Coombes	—	—

Continued on following pages

Jersey Owned Vessels in the 18th Century — continued

Vessel	Date	Master	Owner	Rig, Tonnage, etc
PROSPECT	—	—	—	Brig, 40 t
PROSPER	1775	Clem. Lemprière	? Janvrin	—
PROVIDENCE	1737	Nic. Le Vesconte	—	—
PROVIDENCE	1790	Jean Roissier	Jean Roissier	Sloop, 72 t, trading with Newfoundland
PROVIDENCE	1790-92	Philip Bouton	Aaron de Ste Croix	Brig, 51 t, built Bristol 1783
PROVIDENCE	1796	P. Gaudin	J. Mauger	Brig, 51 t, trading with Rotterdam
PRUDENT	1790	Clem. Le Quesne	Pierre Le Brun	Sloop, 57 t, b'lt Jersey 1783
QUEBEC	1792	Thos. Le Feuvre	Mallet & Fiott	Brig, 60 t, French built
QUEEN	1789	—	—	38 t, taken by enemy 1793
QUEEN	1790-92	Thos. Pickstock	J. & C. Hemery	144 t, Privateer
RACHEL	1701-37	Jean Vincent	—	Brig'tine, trading Virginia
RECOVERY	1768-89	Philip Fainton	Ch. Robin & Co.	Snow, 118 t, trading with Newfoundland
REGULATOR	1783-90	Philip Dolbel	—	36 t, Privateer
RESOLUTION	1778	P. Mauger	? Lemprière	110 t, Boston built 1768
RESOLUTION	1778-92	Jean Dolbel	J. & C. Hemery	70 t
RESOLUTION	1778-93	Edward Gallie	J. Thoreau	Sloop, 40 t, old vessel
REVENGE	1763	Chas. Alexandre	Daniel Messervy	Lugger, 150 t, Am. built
REVENGE	1778	Thomas Filleul	Gosset & Janvrin	20 guns
REVENGE	1778-86	P. Clement	Philip Winter	Brig, 60 t, built France 1763
REVENGE	1778	Noé Vautier	Matthew Gossett	Brig, 120 t, built France
REWARD	1792	Abraham Le Sueur	Jean Dumaresq	25 t
ROBERT & JANE	1798	Samuel Gasnier	Mallet & De Gruchy	38 t, Privateer
RODNEY	1780	—	—	Sloop
ROSE	1793	Thos. de Gruchy	Thos. de Gruchy	Cutter, 80 t, trading with Southampton
ROYAL CHARLOTTE	1772	George Hamel	—	200 t, sunk of Boulogne 1772
ROYAL SOPHIA	1785	—	—	Sloop
ROYAL VOLUNTEER	1796	P. Benest	Bisson & Co.	Brig, 39 t, French built
ROY DE PRUSSE	1757	Edward Mourant	Daniel Messervy	Privateer
ST ANTONIO	1786	? Du Heaume	—	Lugger, 45 t, French built
ST AUBIN	1780	—	—	Privateer
ST CHARLES	1780	Clem. Messervy	—	Brig, 81 t
ST LAWRENCE	1783	Philip Fainton	Ch. Robin & Co.	145 t
ST LAWRENCE	1790-92	J. Alexandre	Ch. Robin & Co.	145 t
ST PETER	1790-94	Philip de Caux	Ch. Robin & Co.	210 t
SALLY	1776	—	—	Barque, 160 t, trading with Spain
SAMARITAN	1796	Frances Pirouet	A. Carrel	Brig, 83 t
SARAH	1757	Daniel Le Preveu	Daniel Messervy	—
SEAFLOWER	1735	Charles Pinel	Rachel Hardy	100 t

Continued on following pages

Jersey Owned Vessels in the 18th Century — continued

Vessel	Date	Master	Owner	Rig, Tonnage, etc.
SEAFLOWER	1768-79	—	Ch. Robin & Co.	Brig, 41 t
SEAFLOWER	1778	John Filleux	Brelade Janvrin	Brig, 70 t, old vessel
SEVEN SISTERS	1728-37	Peter Quetyvel	Daniel Pellier	Sloop
SHIFT (LE)	1792	Jean Alexandre	Ch. Robin & Co.	49 t, taken by enemy 1794
SINCERITY	1786	—	de Ste Croix	Sloop, 50 t, built I.o.W'ht
SOLIDE (LE)	1790-92	Laurens Remon	Francis Janvrin	130 t, trading West Indies
SOUTHAMPTON PACKET	1780-90	Philip Neel	Philip Neel	Sloop, 36 t
SOUTHAMPTON PACKET	1792	Josue Bouton	Neel & Bouton	Sloop, trading S'hampton
SOUTH ?	1778	Jean Le Sueur	Nicolas Fiott	Brig, 130 t, col'l b'lt 1767
SPECULATION	1794	Philip Jean	—	—
SPEEDWELL	1768-82	—	—	Brig, 80 t
SPEEDY PACKET	1793-14	Henry Wilkins	Amiraux & Co.	Sloop, 80 t
SPIDER & THE FLY	1737	Amice Laffoley	—	—
SPRIGHTLY	1793	—	—	70 t
SPY	1780	—	—	54 t
SQUIRREL	1747	Nic. Le Couteur	—	Privateer
STAG	1779-94	Francis Le Feuvre	—	130 t, Privateer
STAGG	1794	—	—	47 t
STEPHEN GALLEY	1711	Richard De Feu	—	—
SUCCESS	1747	Edward Le Gresley	—	Trading with S'hampton
SUCCESS	1773-76	? Cabot	—	Sloop, 20 t, taken by e'my and retaken 1776
SUCCESS	1783-90	C. Le Couteur	Poingdestre & de Ste Croix	110 t
SUCCESS	1790-92	B. Le Caplain	J. de La Taste	144 t
SUKEY	1778	J. Le Brun	Durell & Co.	Snow, 46 t, b't Spain 1773
SUKEY (LA)	1777-78	C. Nicolle	C. Gautier	Sloop, 46 t, built 1763
SUKEY (LA)	1790	Charles Bertram	Charles Bertram	Sloop, 46 t, built 1763
SUKEY (LA)	1792	Jean Le Feuvre	Nicolle & Simonet	Sloop, 46 t, built 1763
SULTANA	1777	? Janvrin	—	—
SURPRISE	1778	J. Thompson	Fiott & Co.	Sloop, 50 t, 6 guns, taken by enemy 1794
SURPRISE	1780	—	—	65 t, Privateer
SUSAN	1796	? Vautier	P. Robin	Brig, 30 t, built 1720
SWALLOW	1783-92	Abraham Huelin	Pierre Mallet	89 t, taken by enemy 1794
SWAN	1790	Josue Cabot	Josue Cabot	37 t, trading with G'sey
SWIFT	1778	G. De Feu	—	Sloop, 35 t, Jersey built 1776
SWIFT	1792	Ph. Le Rossingnol	de Quetteville	Brig, 126 t
TAPON (LE)	1784-85	Philip Ahier	—	Sloop, 12 t
TARTAR	1757	—	Daniel Messervy	Snow, 100 t, old colonial built vessel
TARTAR	1778	Edward Fiott	Nicolas Fiott	Snow, 200 t, 10 guns, old French-built vessel

Continued on following pages

Jersey Owned Vessels in the 18th Century — continued

Vessel	Date	Master	Owner	Rig, Tonnage, etc.
TARTAR	1779	Edward Fiott	Edward Fiott	600 t, captured French frigate, 40 guns, P'teer
TARTAR	1778	R. Le Quesne	Matthew Gossett	Snow
THOMAS & JANE	1737–40	Carteret Dean	Carteret Dean	Brigantine, 60 t, trading with Maryland
THREE BROTHERS	1727	Nic. Le Couteur	—	—
THREE BROTHERS	1796	John Lys	? Messervy	Brig, 57 t, French built
THREE FRIENDS	1740	Philip Mourant	Philip Mourant	30 t
THREE PARTNERS	1771	? Anquetil	—	Schooner
THREE SISTERS	1793	—	—	—
TRIAL	1747	Jean Brunet	—	Brig, 120 t
TRINIDAD	1780	—	—	Sold to London 1780
TRITON	1778	James Remon	? Le Masurier	Brig, 160 t, 6 guns, British built 1774
TWO BROTHERS	1778	—	Hue & Co.	Brig, 150 t, old vessel
TWO BROTHERS	1778	Edward Touzel	J. de La Taste	Sloop, 47 t, old French-built vessel
TWO BROTHERS	1790	Jean Voie	Henri Voie	Sloop, 47 t, old French-built vessel
TWO BROTHERS	1747	Jean Poingdestre	—	—
TWO BROTHERS	1778	? Brunet	? Brunet	50 t, b'lt N'f'dland 1776
TWO BROTHERS	1778	—	Hue & Co.	Brig, 150 t, an old vessel
TWO COUSINS	1757–59	Jean de Caen	—	
TWO FRIENDS	1790	Thos. Anquetil	Thos. Anquetil	Brig, 17 t, French built
TWO FRIENDS	1796	R. Mauger	? de Ste Croix	50 t, b'lt Newfoundland
TWO FRIENDS	1792	Josué Hocquard	Chevalier & Robinson	35 t
UNION	1796	Nicolas Vautier	? Janvrin	Brig, 71 t
UNION	1785	—	—	132 t
UNION	1787–82	George Le Geyt	Fiott & Gossett	115 t, trading Virginia
UNION	1790–92	Jean Bichard	Jean Villeneuve	2 guns, taken by enemy 1794
UNION	1737	Jean Le Vesconte	—	65 t
UNITY	1737–50	Philip Ahier	—	Snow, trading Virginia
UNITY	1785	—	—	Ship, 280 t
UNITY	1788	D. Simpson	—	Sloop, 80 t, built 1767
UNITY	1778	H. Le Brun	Pierre Mallet	Brig, 80 t, old Spanish-built vessel
VENUS	1774	Ric. de Carteret	Ric. de Carteret	—
VINE	1790–92	Thomas Falle	Poingdestre & Robinson	129 t, trading N'f'dland, lost Scillies 1796
VULTURE	1776–88	Peter Du Val	Janvrin & Durell	Lugger, 100 t, Privateer
WEAZEL	1752	Francis Cosnard	—	—
WEYMOUTH	1796	—	—	Lugger, Privateer
WHEAT	1780	—	—	Sloop
WILLIAM	1737–44	Thomas Snow	—	—
WILLIAM	1778	Jean Luce	Ch. Robin & Co.	Brig, 100 t, colonial built 1773

Continued on following page

Jersey Owned Vessels in the 18th Century — continued

Vessel	Date	Master	Owner	Rig, Tonnage, etc.
WILLIAM	1792	Laurens Ahier	Jean Benest	Brig, 100 t, colonial built 1773
WILLIAM & ELIZABETH	1774–78	William Snow	William Snow	Snow, 110 t, built at Barnstaple 1767
WILLING ENDEAVOUR	1737	Peter Maynard	—	Sloop
WILLING MIND	1748–60	Dan. Le Preveu	—	—
WILLING MIND	1766–80	Edward Fiott	Nicolas Fiott	Snow, 180 t, built 1749
YORK	1782	Jean Remon	Edward Remon	Brig, 130 t, built France 1776
YOUNG MARY	1792	Philip Lair	M. Quesnel	80 tons, trading Bristol
ZEPHYR	1796	—	—	—

Rigs of Jersey Sailing Vessels

The rigs of Jersey sailing vessels are set out in a table below. There were many variations on these basic rigs, such as Clipper ships, fast sailing vessels with finer lines, built and much used for the Chine tea trade and on the Australian wool run. Clipper rigged schooners were also built and these fast ships were used in the Meat and Fruit trades before the advent of refrigerated ships, their speed was essential. A snow was rigged similar to a brig but with the additional small trysail just aft of the mainmast. Luggers were two or three masted, with quadrilateral sails. The rig of a Chasse marée was unique to the Channel Islands and the adjacent French coast and was like a lugger. Sloop and smack rigs were variations of the rig of a cutter, while a dandy was a similar rig to a ketch. Unfortunately the reasons for many of these rigs have been lost to the modern day landlubber more used to filling his car with a gallon of petrol.

RIGS OF JERSEY SAILING VESSELS

SHIP	3-Masted. Square rigged on all three.
BARQUE	3-Masted. Square rigged on fore and mainmast.
BARQUENTINE	3-Masted. Square rigged on rore mast only.
BRIG	2-Masted. Square rigged on both.
BRIGANTINE	2-Masted. Square rigged on fore mast only.
SCHOONER	2-Masted. Fore and aft rigged.
SCHOONER (3-masted)	3-Masted. Fore and aft rigged on all three.
TOPSAIL SCHOONER	2-Masted. Partly square rigged on fore mast.
KETCH	2-Masted. Fore and aft rigged but aft mast shorter than fore.
CUTTER	Single-masted. Fore and aft rigged.

Chapter Six

A LIST OF THE PRINCIPAL VESSELS AND THEIR OWNERS IN THE 19TH CENTURY

ORIGIN OF 19TH CENTURY JERSEY OWNED VESSELS[1]

Built in Jersey	684
Built in Canada and Newfoundland	241
Built in England	201
Captured enemy ships	146
Built in France	34
Built in Guernsey	21
Built in Scotland	13
Built in Wales	12
Built in Ireland	5
Built in U.S.A.	5
Built in Sweden	3
Built in Germany	2
Built in Bermuda	2
Built in Finland	1
Built in Sark	1
Builder unknown	5
	1,374
Unverified	206
Total	1,580

A list of the Principal Vessels and their Owners in the 19th century is given which is divided into two areas.

A. List of some 1,580 Jersey owned vessels from 1800 to the first part of the 20th century.

B. List of the principal shipowners for the same period.

These lists give in the first column the name of each vessel, followed by the registered tonnage at the first Jersey registration. Thirdly the rig of each vessel is given and fourthly the place of building and the name of the builder if known. The fifth column gives the date of building. In the sixth column the name of the owner at the time of the first Jersey registration and lastly the dates of that first ownership. These facts have been verified by examination of the Jersey Shipping Register held at the Office of the Impot, St Helier, Jersey, by permission of Mr V. H. Palmer, the then Chief Agent of the Impot. In some cases alterations in rig were quite considerable over the time that a particular vessel remained on the Register, but other ships retained the original rig throughout their working life.

Changes in tonnage show frequent variations, due not only to alterations in the superstructure of a vessel, but also to the different methods used, at different periods, to calculate a ship's tonnage. The figures given in these lists are the tonnage given on the builder's certificate. Vessels under twenty tons are not listed. Not all Jersey owned vessels were locally registered; many were registered at Guernsey and some at mainland ports such as London, Liverpool or Cardiff. Numbers were also registered at ports in Canada and never crossed the Atlantic to reach the Islands' waters.

JERSEY OWNED VESSELS IN THE 19TH CENTURY

Name of Vessel	Tons Rig	Where built	When	Owners	Years
ABEONA	158 brig	Silk, Jersey	1827	Ph. Pellier	1827–38
ABROTA	300 barq	Sunderland	1851	Orange & Co.	1851–55
ACCRA	138 brigt	Deslandes, Jersey	1857	Geo. Deslandes	1857–74
ACHILLES	289 barq	Grellier, Jersey	1841	Ph. Pellier	1841–50
ACIS	113 schr	Deslandes, Jersey	1850	Geo. Deslandes	1850–53
ACTIVE	100 brig	ex-prize	—	Janvrin & Amiraux	1813–14
ACTIVE	80 smack	Lyme Regis	1810	Abm Millias & others	1813–26
ACTIVE	46 cutt	T. Gavey, Jersey	1849	P. & J. Renouf	1849–50
ACTIVE	29 ketch	J. F. Picot, Jersey	1864	C. Whitley	1870–79
ACTIVE	21 sloop	Southampton	1776	Jacob Voisin	1800–07
ADA	243 brig	Clarke, Jersey	1847	P. Arthur	1847–49
ADA	109 brig	Nova Scotia	1851	Gaudin & Renouf	1858–
ADAM SEDGWICK	459 barq	Aberdeen, Scotland	1861	P. Le Maistre	1879–
ADELAIDE	81 schr	Deslandes, Jersey	1831	J. E. Martel	1831–35
ADELE	121 brig	St Malo, France	1836	Buesnel & Le Quesne	1865–66
ADELINA	105 schr	?	1852	Wm. Fruing & Co.	1852–55
ADMIRAL	215 barq	Dunkirk, France	1841	de Gruchy & Gallichan	1863–
ADMIRAL	60 cutt	Clarke, Jersey	1847	E. J. Gallichan	1849–57
ADMIRAL NELSON	184 brigt	Jersey	1841	Chas. Mauger	1841–50
ADMIRAL SPROUL	70 schr	North America ?	?	Robin, Collas & Co.	1901–
ADOLPHOS YATES	106 brigt	Guernsey	1840	S. Gallie	1845–
ADONIS	144 brig	New Brunswick	1832	F. Bertram	1832–43
ADVANCE	229 brig	Bellot, Jersey	1858	Geo. Asplet	1858–62
ADVANCE	117 schr	Pontorson, France	1865	C. Le Quesne	1865–70
ADVANCE	28 cutt	Jersey	1865	Proper & Le Masurier	1865–70
ADVENTURE	146 brigt	Whitby, Yorkshire	1818	Fr. Hocquard	1819–35
ADVENTURE	113 brig	Gaspé	1823	Jean Perrée	1823–41
ADVENTURE	73 brigt	ex-prize	—	Hemery Bros.	1804–05
AEOLUS	230 barq	ex-prize	—	P. & F. Janvrin	1815–19
AEOLUS	? cutt	Bartlett, Jersey	1844	Capt. Hamon	1844–
AGENORIA	116 schr	Deslandes, Jersey	1840	J. Renouf	1840–41
AGILIS	238 barq	Guernsey	1860	J. Collings	1887–90
AGRICOLA	63 ketch	Bellot, Jersey	1871	Cantwell & Co.	1879–99
AIMWELL	40 schr	?	—	de Gruchy, Renouf & Clement	1870–
ALABAMA	78 schr	Vautier, Jersey	1873	de Faye & Chevalier	1874–1903
ALABAMA	54 schr	?	—	C. Le Sueur	1905–
ALARM	30 schr	Jersey	1844	J. Asplet & Co.	1856–59
ALBATROSS	79 schr	Bellot, Jersey	1872	J. Wricht	1872–85
ALBATROSS	58 cutt	Valpy, Jersey	1857	?	lost 1858
ALBERT	28 cutt	?	—	J. Baxter	1863–
ALBERT & EDWARD	22 cutt	?	—	Thos. Mauger	1856–59
ALBERTINA	158 brigt	Valpy, Jersey	1868	Jos. Le Bailly	1868–70
ALBINA	135 brigt	Esnouf, Jersey	1835	Esnouf & Mauger	1856–63

Continued on following pages

Jersey Owned Vessels in the 19th Century — continued

Name of Vessel	Tons Rig	Where built	When	Owners	Years
ALBION	321 barq	ex-prize	—	Hemery, Chevalier & Le Breton	1809–
ALBION	108 brig	Bideford, Devon	1819	A. Black	1825–39
ALBION	98 brig	?	—	Collings & McBean	1838–
ALERT	59 schr	Esnouf & Mauger, Jersey	1851	Jos. Renouf & Co.	1856–63
ALERT	53 schr	Nova Scotia	1840	Le Boutillier	1844–49
ALERT	28 ketch	Plymouth	1836	W. T. Pugsley	1864–
ALEXANDER	93 schr	Deslandes, Jersey	1833	Carre & Alexandre	1833–
ALEXANDRE	206 barq	Mallet, Jersey	1865	Le Quesne, Pallot & Mallet	1865–77
ALEXANDRINA	21 cutt	Sidmouth, Devon	1864	Thos. Gavey & Co.	1870–
ALFRED	86 schr	Stockholm, Sweden	1852	H. Godfray	1852–56
ALFRED STORER	1,077 ship	Maine, U.S.A.	1854	Young & Wright	1865–
ALICE	293 brig	Southampton	1847	J. de Ste Croix	1849–56
ALICE	68 schr	P. Gavey, Jersey	1855	Gavey & McKeown	1856–63
ALICE	66 schr	Shippegan, N. Br'w'k	1901	Wm. Fruing & Co.	1901–
ALICE JANE	205 barq	Liverpool	1836	Wm. Fruing & Co.	1857–79
ALICE JANE	198 brigt	?	—	W. F. Stokes	1888–
ALLIANCE	339 barq	Clarke, Jersey	1853	Tocque, Luce & Allen	1853–56
ALLIANCE	207 barq	Legue, France	1837	Falle & Mitchell	1865–68
ALLIANCE	99 schr	Shippegan, N. Br'w'k	1877	A. Hacquoil	1877–
ALLIANCE	53 schr	Jersey	1856	D. Blampied & Co.	1859–77
ALLIANCE	52 brig	ex prize	—	Janvrin & Durell	1804–09
ALLIGATOR	71 brig	British-built man of war	?	Nicolas Le Quesne	1812–
ALMA	41 schr	Jersey	1855	E. Falle	1855–63
ALPHA	56 schr	Le Masurier, Jersey	1842	P. Le Gros	1842–56
ALZINA	26 cutt	Jersey	?	Le Huquet & Perchard	1879–85
AMANDA	28 schr	?	—	de Gruchy, Renouf & Clement	1888
AMAZON	363 barq	Clarke, Jersey	1855	Carrel & Co.	1855–64
AMAZON	50 ketch	Le Sueur, Jersey	1866	J. Wright	1870–79
AMBERWITCH	330 barq	Plymouth	?	J. Dean	1865–70
AMELIA	235 barq	Deslandes, Jersey	1832	Wm. Fruing & Co.	1832–53
AMELIA	185 brig	Shippegan, N. Br'w'k	1840	Wm. Fruing & Co.	1840–56
AMELIA	114 brigt	Deslandes, Jersey	1834	Machon & Henry	1834–35
AMELIA	74 schr	Prince Edward Isle	1818	W. R. Airey	1821–
AMELIA	37 cutt	Southampton	1819	Ch. Le Boutillier	1826–
AMELIA & JANE	62 schr	Allix, Jersey	1874	Wallis & Shapland	1879–85
AMICUS	511 barq	Le Vesconte & Vautier, Jersey	1856	Orange & Briard	1856–59
AMICUS	150 brigt	Hamptonne, Jersey	1839	J. Orange	1839–41
AMITY	106 Brig	Fowey, Cornwall	1812	Janvrin & Duval	1817–32
ANDES	212 brig	Grellier, Jersey	1839	Ch. Robin & Co.	1840–42
ANGELIQUE	72 schr	Cap Breton	1811	P. &. F. Janvrin	1815–
ANGELIQUE	47 schr	Cap Breton	1827	J. Le Boutillier	1830–31
ANLEY	90 schr	Silk, Jersey	1826	Jemes Ennis	1826–31

Continued on following pages

Jersey Owned Vessels in the 19th Century — continued

Name of Vessel	Tons Rig	Where built	When	Owners	Years
ANN	179 brig	ex-prize	—	A. de Ste Croix	1815–23
ANN	132 brig	ex-prize	—	Ph. Touzel	1831–41
ANN	70 schr	Deslandes, Jersey	1841	Geo. Deslandes	1841–57
ANN	38 cutt	?	—	Touzel & Co.	1856–;
ANNABELLA	90 schr	Gaspé	1818	P. & F. Janvrin	1824–26
ANN & ELIZA	21 cutt	?	—	Le Seelleir & Davis	1841–
ANNA & ELIZABETH	33 cutt	?	—	R. Sanford	1831–
ANNA MARIA	21 cutt	Southampton	1807	Blampied & Machon	1856–
ANN & MARY	44 smack	France (ex-prize)	1726	Durell & Benest	1803–05
ANN AMY	25 cutt	Paspébiac, Gaspé	1847	Le Boutillier	1848–60
ANNE	56 brigt	ex-prize	—	Durell & Alexandre	1807–08
ANNE KAYE	287 barq	Deslandes, Jersey	1862	Peter Le Maistre	1862–
ANNIE	120 ketch	?	—	Capt. J. G. Lr Gros	1904–
ANNIE	91 schr	Le Vesconte, Jersey	1863	Le Vesconte, Sutton & Ahier	1863–
ANNIE	44 ketch	Barnstaple	1872	G. T. Bryant	1885–88
ANNIE EDWIN	48 schr	?	—	J. Le Couteur	1874–
ANNIE GELBERT	112 brigt	Nova Scotia	1857	R. W. Dobson	1865–67
ANT	53 schr	Paspébiac, Gaspé	1854	Ch. Robin & Co.	1856–99
ANT	27 sloop	Cowes	1796	Peter Le Brun	1804–06
ANT	26 cutt	Silk, Jersey	1828	Ph. Nicolle	1828–35
ANTAGONIST	50 cutt	Vardon, Jersey	1855	Esnouf & Mauger	1855–56
ANTELOPE	138 brig	Deslandes, Jersey	1825	Ph. Du Heaume	1825–35
ANVIL	142 brigt	Sunderland	1807	Ph. Le Couteur & Thos. Dubois	1821–22
APOLLO	85 schr	Bristol	1820	de Quetteville	1822–41
APPARITION	137 schr	Clarke, Jersey	1840	Carré & Alexandre	1840–41
AQUILON	83 dandy	Le Masurier, Jersey	1874	Thos. Lavan	1879–82
ARAB	156 barq	?	—	Thos. Rose	1854–56
ARAB	114 schr	Clarke, Jersey	1849	Fr. Carrel & Co.	1849–54
ARABIAN	92 schr	Esnouf & Mauger, Jersey	1849	Chas. Mauger	1849–50
ARCANA	29 cutt	Le Huquet, Jersey	1851?	Du Fresne & Stevens	1851–59
ARCHIBALD	41 cutt	Cowes	1808	A. Black	1840–43
ARGO	238 brig	Grandin, Jersey	1862	Gallichan & Co.	1862–
ARGUS	198 brig	Sunderland	1826	Ph. Perchard	1826–41
ARGYLE	25 cutt	?	1841	Robert Davy	1841–
ARICHAT	76 brigt	Arichat	1815	Remon & Huelin	1816–19
ARIEL	72 schr	Jersey ?	1839	Ph. Nicolle	1840–59
ARROW	26 cutt	Jersey	1855	F. Wright	1856–70
ASHBURTON	104 brigt	ex-prize	—	J. Benest	1818–35
ASIA	97 schr	Allix, Jersey	1850	G. De Garis	1850–59
ASKELON	35 ketch	Mallet, Jersey	1859	H. Mallet	1859–60
ASKELON	23 ketch	?	—	J. C. Blampied	1863–87
ASP	40 cutt	Lymington	1836	W. Metherell	1856–70
ASTREA	164 schr	Deslandes, Jersey	1839	Le Gros & Le Couteur	1840–41
ATALANTA	243 ?	ex-prize	—	J. Benest	1826–27
ATALANTA	89 schr	Laing, Jersey	1837	Thos. Silk	1839–

Continued on following pages

Jersey Owned Vessels in the 19th Century — continued

Name of Vessel	Tons	Rig	Where built	When	Owners	Years
ATLAS	51	cutt	Jersey	1848	M. Walken	1848–50
ATREVIDA	158	brigt	Esnouf & Mauger, Jersey	1854	Esnouf & Mauger	1854–63
AUGIA	178	brig	Silk, Jersey	1829	Ph. Nicolle	1929–59
AUGUSTA	373	barq	Le Vesconte & Vautier, Jersey	1855	Giffard & Le Quesne	1855–59
AURA	94	brigt	Picot, Jersey	1872	J. Fauvel	1872–
AURORA	109	brig	Deslandes, Jersey	1824	Ed. Renouf	1824–38
AURORA	88	schr	?	—	Cooper & Banks	1838–
AURORA	86	brigt	Bridport	1818	Le Rossignol	1841–42
AURORA	73	schr	Canada	1828	Ch. Robin & Co.	1832–35
AZORES	110	brigt	Dunbar, Scotland	1814	Clem. Hemery	1823–
AZUR	44	ketch	Allix, Jersey	1871	Fr. Allix	1871–79
BAGATELLE	21	cutt	Clarke, Jersey	1850	L. Godfray	1850–56
BARON	24	cutt	Clarke, Jersey	1862	G. Allix	1862–1901
BARTLETT	52	schr	Bartlett. Jersey	1843	T. L. Bartlett	1843–46
BEBEC	256	brig	Sunderland	1857	W. Downing	1859–63
BEE	71	schr	Paspébiac, Gaspé	1851	Ph. Briard	1863 68
BEE	58	schr	Paspébiac, Gaspé	1850	Ch. Robin & Co.	1856–70
BEE	39	cutt	?	—	Thos. Huard	1835–41
BEEHIVE	40	cutt	ex-prize	—	Moisson & Co.	1817–26
BELINDA	180	brig	Prince Edward Isle	1856	M. Gallichan & Co.	1859–63
BELLA	228	barq	Le Vesconte, Jersey	1864	Thos. Aubin	1865
BELLADONNA	277	barq	Grandin, Jersey	1863	Pirouet, Le Blancq & Dean	1863–68
BELLADONNA	60	schr	Aubin, Jersey	1877	Ph. Le Gresley	1877–
BELLE ANNE	100	brigt	Denmark (ex prize)	1798	Fr. Le Sueur	1803–11
BELLONA	110	schr	Vardon & Le Huquet, Jersey	1837	Ph. Vardon	1837–41
BELLON	61	brigt	ex-prize	—	?	1811–14
BELLONA	58	dandy	Le Sueur, Jersey	1864	Bisson & Dawe	1864–1903
BELTED WILL	79	schr	Le Sueur, Jersey	1878	F. Godfray	1878–85
BELUS	88	schr	Newfoundland	1840	de Quetteville	1840–59
BERTIE	470	barq	Whitehaven	1868	Le Maistre & Co.	1870–79
BETSY	176	brigt	ex-prize	—	Renour, Collas & Le Sueur	1808–
BETSY	91	brig	?	—	G. Le Gros	1829–35
BETSY	60	schr	ex-prize	—	J. Le Gallais	1810–15
BETSY	53	brigt	ex-prize	—	Ph. Payn	1803–04
BETSY	38	sloop	ex-prize	—	D. Le Ray	1803–04
BETSY	35	smack	Cowes	1800	Joseph Gruchy	1804–07
BETSY & JANE	103	schr	Prince Edward Isle	1849	J. Simon	1850–52
BETSY & JANE	90	brigt	Canada	1817	James Remon	1819–26
BISMARCK	20	?	?	—	Le Boutillier	1888–
BLACK DIAMOND	129	brigt	Fecamp, France	1837	S. Picot	1863–70
BLACK DIAMOND	37	ketch	Southampton	1880	W. Pitman	?
BLACK GRIFFON	30	schr	Newfoundland	1850	Ph. Nicolle	1853–63

Continued on following pages

Jersey Owned Vessels in the 19th Century

Name of Vessel	Tons	Rig	Where built	When	Owners	Years
BLANCHE	190	brig	?	—	P. Asplet	1852–
BLISS	32	cutt	Vardon, Jersey	1845	Ph. Jenne	1859–70
BLOOMING DALE	40	schr	?	—	de Gruchy, Renouf Clement	1870–79
BLONDE	131	schr	Deslandes, Jersey	1851	Geo. Deslandes	1851–63
BLOYE	58	schr	J. Gavey, Jersey	1826	Jos. Blampied	1826–
BLUE EYED MAID	22	cutt	?	1824	Ph. barette & Jos. Picot	1831–35
BLUE JACKET	266	barq	Le Vesconte & Vautier	1858	Dean, Le Caux & Le Maistre	1858–70
BOADICEA	106	schr	Gaspé	1860	J. & E. Collas	1863–70
BOLINA	92	schr	?	—	Valpy & Le Bas	1888–
BOLINA	64	schr	Filleul & Le Rougetel, Jersey	1837	J. Ahier	1837–41
BOLUS	?	schr	?	—	Chas. Renouf	1847–
BONITA	60	ketch	Le Sueur, Jersey	1881	J. C. & G. S. Renouf	1881–1901
BONITA	32	cutt	Clarke, Jersey	1863	Parker & Fuzzard	1863–
BONITTA or BONETTA	37	ketch	Plymouth	1866	F. & J. Blampied	1890–1901
BONNIE LASSIE	351	barq	Dundee, Scotland	1861	Le Maistre & Dean	1863–70
BONNY MARY	149	schr	Bellot, Jersey	1863	Clem. Pallot	1864–65
BRADORE	85	brigt	Deslandes, Jersey	1850	E. Le Feuvre	1850–59
BRANDY	44	cutt	Filleul, Jersey	1827	Thos. Touzel	1827–31
BRAVE	408	barq	Deslandes, Jersey	1867	Geo. Deslandes	1867–70
BRAVE	29	cutt	Jersey	1868	Thos. Messervy	1870–85
BRIARD	121	brigt	Bartlett, Jersey	1845	Ch. Robin & Co.	1846–59
BRIDE	30	schr	Newfoundland	1840	Fr. Collas	1840–63
BRIDE	28	cutt	?	—	G. M. Gregor	1888–
BRIDESMAID	132	schr	Valpy, Jersey	1851	Jos. Deslandes	1856–63
BRIGHT	21	cutt	Jersey	1857	Le Gros & de Gruchy	1870–
BRILLIANT	84	smack	Cowes	1803	? Mourant	1815–
BRILLIANT	37	ketch	Jersey	1856	J. Le Huquet & Co.	1856–59
BRISK	32	schr	?	—	J. Messervy	1870–
BRISTOL	116	brigt	?	—	Thos. Lee	1856–59
BRITAIN'S PRIDE	178	brig	Le Huquet, Jersey	1858	Clem. Pallot	1858–63
BRITANNIA	108	brig	Prince Edward Isle	1816	de Quetteville	1819–26
BRITANNIA	58	ketch	Le Sueur, Jersey	1860	Jemina Swain	1863–79
BRITANNIA	26	cutt	?	—	Ph. Bertram	1835–
BRITTANY	90	schr	St Malo, France	1873	J. Pallot & J. Buths	1879–83
BROAD AXE	142	brig	Pasbébiac, Gaspé	1821	Chas. Robin & Co.	1823–30
BROTHERS	173	brig	Gaspé	1858	Chas. Robin & Co.	1858–63
BROTHERS	136	brig	Arichat	1830	Peter Janvrin	1832–33
BROTHERS	46	schr	?	—	J. Le Sueur	1822–23
BROTHERS	21	schr	Newfoundland	1815	Ph. Nicolle	1826–39
BRUNSWICK	81	schr	ex-prize	—	Elias Durell (Jr.)	1810–11

Continued on following pages

Jersey Owned Vessels in the 19th century - continued

Name of Vessel	Tons	Rig	Where built	When	Owners	Years
BRUTUS	122	schr	J. Gavey, Jersey	1826	Thos. Sorel & Ed. Nicolle	1826–35
BUD	47	cutt	Picot, Jersey	1862	Fr. Hamon & Co.	1863–
BULLA	128	schr	Deslandes, Jersey	1859	J. R. Pickering	1873–
BULLA	79	schr	Deslandes, Jersey	1873	Geo. Deslandes	1873–78
BULWARK	287	barq	Le Feuvre, Jersey	1843	Le Feuvre & Co.	1843–
BUSTLER	74	smack	Lyme Regis	1811	Millias, Labey & Walker	1813–14
BYZANTIUM	179	brig	?	—	J. Larbalestier	1856–59
CAESAR	106	schr	Deslandes, Jersey	1835	Carré & Alexander	1835–41
CAESAREA	342	barq	Bridgewater	1864	P. Briard	1865–69
CAESAREA	173	brigt	Bartlett & Bisson, Jersey	1840	J. Orange	1840–42
CAESAREAN	159	brig	?	—	Hemery Bros.	1826–
CALISTA	202	barq	de Ste Croix, Jersey	1825	A. de Ste Croix	1825–56
CALISTA	26	cutt	Grellier, Jersey	1815	Durell & de Ste Croix	1815–18
CALM	48	schr	Paspébiac, Gaspé	1826	Chas. Robin & Co.	1826–38
CAMBRAI	1,177	ship	Maine U.S.A.	1853	C. Morrison	1865–
CAMBRAI	82	ketch	Le Sueur, Jersey	1870	Ph. Le Masurier	1870–79
CAMELIA	97	schr	Le Sueur, Jersey	1873	Ph. Le Masurier	1879–99
CAMPBELL	79	schr	Deslandes, Jersey	1837	Thos. Messervy	1837–40
CANADA	156	brig	Gaspé	1856	A. de Gruchy	1859–63
CANADA	141	brig	Gaspé	1832	Ph. Pellier	1835–
CANOPUS	120	brig	Giffard & Laurens, Jersey	1828	Jean Bichard	1828–38
CAP BRETON	122	schr	Cap Breton	1812	Chas. Robin & Co.	1812–19
CAROLINE	186	brig	Arichat, N.S.	1843	de Carteret	1843–
CAROLINE	179	brig	Arichat, N.S.	1856	Monck & Lavans	1865–70
CAROLINE	31	cutt	Deslandes, Jersey	1843	?	?
CAROLINE R. FERRIAR	46	cutt	Le Huquet, Jersey	1851	Geo. Asplet	1851–56
CASTELIA	77	schr	Bellot, Jersey	1879?	D. Le Masurier	1879–88
CASTOR	105	schr	Duval, Jersey	1833	Alexandre & Mauger	1833–35
CATHERINE	132	brig	ex-prize	—	Elie Durell	1813–19
CATHERINE	83	schr	?	—	P. & F. Janvrin	1818–26
CATHERINE	60	brigt	Devonshire	1829	R. Hare	1831–
CATHERINE	37	?	Kingswear, Devon	1817	Blampied & Helleur	1830–31
C. COLUMBUS	204	brigt	Paspébiac, Gaspé	1825	J. S. N. Robin	1826–63
C.E.C.C.	47	cutt	Aubin, Jersey	1869	C. Cotgrove	1869–
CECILIA	120	schr	Jersey?	?	Le Masurier	1900–
CECILIA	56	ketch	Le Sueur, Jersey	1867	Ph. Le Masurier	1870–99
CELEBRITY	44	cutt	Lane, Jersey	1824	Lane & Dickenson	1824–26
CENTURION	175	brig	Esnouf, Jersey	1837	Chas. Mauger	1837–48
CENTURY	186	brigt	Le Vesconte, Jersey	1866	Chas. Robin & Co.	1866–96
CERES	280	barq	Baxter, Jersey	1824	A. de Ste Croix	1824–56

Continued on following pages

Jersey Owned Vessels in the 19th Century — continued

Name of vessel	Tons	Rig	Where built	When	Owners	Years
CERES	150	brigt	British built?	1804	Remon, Pipon & Hammond	1804–06
CERES	130	brig	De Ste Croix, Jersey	1811	A. de Ste Croix	1811–19
CERES	125	barq	ex-prize	—	A. de Ste Croix	1807–11
CERES	119	brigt	ex-prize	—	Chevalier, Amiraux & Le Breton	1806–14
CERES	26	cutt	Newfoundland	1834	Ph. Nicolle	1834–63
CERUS	110	?	Newfoundland	1834	Elie Falle	1834–38
CEYLON	265	barq	Le Rougetel, Jersey	1864	Alexandre & Co.	1864–69
CHAGAMAU	84	?	Paspébiad, Gaspé	1829	Chas. Robin & Co.	1829–
CHAGAMAU	83	schr	Bellot, Jersey	1878	Chas. Robin & Co.	1878–
CHALLENGER	62	ketch	Bellot, Jersey	1878	W. P. Sims	1878–79
CHAMPION	486	barq	Vautier, Jersey	1863	Wm. Fruing & Co.	1863–72
CHAMPION	126	schr	Clarke, Jersey	1839	Wm. Ranwell	1839–50
CHAMPION	73	ketch	Le Sueur, Jersey	1875	J. D. Goode	1879–
CHANCE	134	brig	Gaspé	1845	F. Perrée	1845–49
CHANCE	57	chasse marée	ex-prize	—	Durell, Le Brun & Bertaut	1813–15
CHARLES	206	ship	America (ex-prize)	1804	Hemery Bros.	1810–23
CHARLES	190	brig	?	?	Chas. Mauger	1856–
CHARLES	58	brigt	Gaspé	1838	Piton & Bisson	1838–40
CHARLES	34	cutt	?	?	N. Pallot & Co.	1835–38
CHARLES	28	cutt	?	?	Blampied & Le Brun	1831–
CHARLES BUCHAN	130	sche	Deslandes, Jersey	1835	Geo. Deslandes	1835–41
CHARLOTTE	108	schr	Bellot, Jersey	1874	Cantell & Co.	1874–88
CHARLOTTE	88	schr	Nova Scotia	1804	Ph. Dean	1819–31
CHARLOTTE	37	cutt	?	1858	Cantell & Co.	1858–70
CHARLOTTE	21	sloop	Southampton	1801	Le Rossignol & Noel	1803–05
CHARMING MOLLY	30	smack	Rochester, Kent	1786	Norman & Marett	1841–
CHARMING NANCY	177	?	ex-prize		John Dolbell	1810–15
CHARMING NANCY	140	?	Gaspé	1825	James Remon, Bertram & Hamon	1825–26
CHAZALIE	86	?	Le Sueur, Jersey	1878	D. Le Sueur (Jr.)	1878–82
CHESTNUT FARM	62	schr	Cap Breton	1823	Payn, Filleul & Renouf	1824–31
CHIEFTAIN	579	barq	Clarke, Jersey	1857	Wm. Fruing & Co.	1857–59
CHILDERS	30	cutt	builder unknown	1849	Wm. Pitman & Co.	1856–59
CHIN-CHIN	342	barq	Jersey	1881	wrecked 1881	
CHOICE	177	brigt	Southtown, Suffolk	1846	J. de Caen	1849–53
CHRISTIE & JANE	72	brigt	Cap Breton	1821	D. Pellier (Jr.)	1821–23
CINDERELLA	293	barq	Sunderland	1841	F. Le Sueur	1849–52
CIRCASSIAN	106	schr	Granville, France	1854	Thos. Renouf	1854–65
CLACHNACUDDIN	224	schr	Scotland ?	?	R. Allix	1888–
CLARA	98	Brigt	ex-prize (slaver)	—	Geo. Ingouville	1826–28
CLARA	87	schr	?	?	Hardeley & de La Perrelle	1865–79
CLEMATIS	87	schr	St Vaast, France	1861	J. P. Collas	1872–76

Continued on following pages

Jersey Owned Vessels in the 19th Century — continued

Name of Vessel	Tons Rig	Where built	When	Owners	Years
CLEOPATRA	122 snow	Hull	1796	Falle, Durell & Benest	1803–09
CLIO	217 barq	Hamptonne, Jersey	1835	J. Bichard	1835–63
CLIPPER	85 schr	Dumbarton, Scotland	1838	Edw. Jean	1842–45
CLUTHA	34 cutt	?	?	H. Robilliard	1856–59
CLYDE	34 cutt	Jersey	1859	Pirouet, Le Caudey & Davey	1859–79
CŒUR DE LION	847 ship	Le Vesconte, Jersey	1867	Philip Ahier	1870–73
COLOMBINE	21 cutt	Jersey	1864	Coleman & Cole	1869–70
COMET	73 schr	Nicolson, Jersey	1853	James Cort	1870–
COMET	80 yawl	Le Huquet, Jersey	1853	Geo. Noel	1853–54
COMMERCE	112 brig	?	?	H. Vibert	1831–35
COMMERCE	60 cutt	J. Gavey, Jersey	1825	Geo. Asplet	1825–31
COMMODORE	360 barq	Hamptonne, Jersey	1840	J. Bichard	1840–41
COMMODORE	88 schr	Jersey	1845?	Buesnel, Le Quesne & Young	1859–70
COMMODORE	59 cutt	Le Sueur, Jersey	1845	Chas. Mauger	1845–48
COMUS	153 brigt	Hylton, Co. Durham	1810	Perchard & Hall	1821–23
COMUS	58 schr	?	?	Wm. Fruing & Co.	1840–42
COMUS	? lugger	ex-prize	—	Dolbel & Giffard	1803–04
CONCORD	81 brigt	Gaspé	1815	Remon & Le Gresley	1818–19
CONCORD	42 brigt	ex-prize	—	J. Le Riche	1804–
CONCORDE	27 cutt	St Malo, France	1879	Elias Le Bas	1885–88
CONCORDIA	127 schr	Grandin, Jersey	1856	J. P. Filleul	1856–59
CONCORDIA	26 cutt	Malbaye, Canada	1831	J. Perrée (Sr.) & J. Perrée (Jr.)	1834–38
CONQUEROR	112 schr	Grandin, Jersey	1855	J. Le Couteur & J. Le Feuvre	1855–65
CONQUEROR	59 schr	Picot, Jersey	1876	J. Blampied	1876–85
CONQUEST	144 brigt	Gaspé	1841	J. F. Wilson	1841–43
CONRAD	328 barq	Chepstow	1844	Chas. Mauger	1863–70
CONSTANT	230 brig	Sunderland	1839	Harrowing & Banks	1856–
CONSTANT	93 brigt	ex-prize	—	Jean Villeneuve	1807–
CONSTANT PACKET	52 brigt	ex-prize	—	John Mourant	1804–06
CONTEST	41 schr	?	?	Philips & Ouless	1856–
CONTEST	39 cutt	?	?	A. Spence	1859–
CONWAY	54 chasse marée	ex-prize	—	Cosnard & Janvrin	1813–14
CORA	112 brig	ex-prize	—	Geo. Ingouville	1815–19
CORA	111 brig	Giffard & Laurens, Jersey	1829	Le Grand & Bree	1829–35
CORBIERE	249 brig	Deslandes, Jersey	1848	Geo. Deslandes	1848–59
CORNUCOPIA	155 brig	New Brunswick	1859	Wm. Fruing & Co.	1858–63
CORONATION	70 schr	?	?	Robin, Collas & Co.	1903
COURIER	361 barq	Deslandes, Jersey	1863	G. N. Le Quesne	1863–70
COURIER	288 barq	Esnouf, Jersey	1831	N. Le Quesne	1831–63
COURIER	274 barq	Esnouf & Mauger, Jersey	1849	Chas. Mauger	1849–

Continued on following pages

Jersey Owned Vessels in the 19th Century — continued

Name of Vessel	Tons Rig	Where built	When	Owners	Years
COURIER	268 barq	Le Boeuf, Jersey	1823	N. Le Quesne	1823–29
COURIER	236 barq	America (ex-prize)	1810	N. Le Quesne	1815–18
COURIER	92 schr	?	?	Blampied & du Quesne	1859–
CRAPAUD	134 brigt	New Brunswick	1843	Wm. Fruing & Co.	1843–59
C.R.C.	300 barqt	St Malo, France	1902	Robin, Collas & Co.	1902–05
C.R.C.	261 barq	Paspébiac, Gaspé	1827	Chas. Robin & Co.	1827–67
C.R.C.	260 barq	Gaspé	1871	Chas. Robin & Co.	1871–1900
CRICHTON	283 brig	Sunderland	1849	J. de Caen	1850–59
CRIsPIN	136 schr	Fife, Scotland	1841	Ph. Gallichan	1863–64
CRISTAL	35 ketch	Cantell, Jersey	1874	? Barbier	1874–
CRISTAL	25 cutt	Jersey	1863	Ph. Pallot	1863–70
CRITIC	96 schr	St Malo, France	1878	G. de Ste Croix	1878–
CROWN	298 barq	Deslandes, Jersey	1862	Geo. Deslandes	1862–70
CROWN	42 ketch	Le Huquet, Jersey	1863	John Messervy	1863–
CRUSADER	151 brig	Baxter, Jersey	1828	A. de Ste Croix	1828–56
CRUISER	20 cutt	?	?	Geo. Laffoley	1856–59
C. T. SUTTON	200 brig	Gaspé	1845	Ph. Perchard	1845–49
CUPID	98 schr	Le Sueur, Jersey	1865	Bisson & Dawe	1865–85
CURLEW	22 schr	New Brunswick	1872	Ph. Luce	1872–
CURLEW	21 schr	Newfoundland	1843	Ph. Nicolle	1844–57
CYGNET	68 schr	Le Vesconte & Vautier, Jersey	1858	P. M. de La Taste	1858–63
CYGNUS	214 brig	Deslandes, Jersey	1875	Boler, Francis & Ereaut	1879–
CZARINA	64 schr	Le Huquet, Jersey	1874	J. C. Pascoe	1874–79
D	30 cutt	Fauvel, Jersey	1830	Le Vesconte, Le Scelleur & Le Cras	1830–41
DAMON	141 brig	Malbaye, Canada	1831	J. Perrée	1832–41
DAMON	119 brigt	Malbaye, Canada	1832	J. Le Bas	1842–48
DAPPER	68 schr	Hamptonne, Jersey	1835	J. Bichard	1835–41
DAPPER	45 schr	Newfoundland ?	?	Mallet & Villeneuve	1804–07
DARING	60 cutt	Le Huquet, Jersey	1848	Asplet & Le Quesne	1848–63
DART	157 brigt	ex-prize	—	Jean Villeneuve	1803–
DART	64 schr	Le Vesconte, Jersey	1862	Ahier & Co.	1862–70
DART	47 ketch	builder unknown	1835	Ph. Laing	1835–
DART PACKET	57 cutt	Cap Breton	1828	Chas. Bisson	1828–41
DASHING WAVE	222 brig	Jersey	1860	Le Quesne, Dean & Rive	1863–
DAUNTLESS	440 barq	Baxter, Jersey	1831	de Ste Croix	1831–43
DAUPHIN	232 brig	?	?	Ph. Nicolle	1815–32
D'AUVERGNE	440 barq	Baxter, Jersey	1831	de Ste Croix	1831–54
DAWN	168 brigt	Gaudin, Gaspé	1874	Chas. Robin & Co.	1874–92
DAY	186 barq	Gaspé	1815	Chas. Robin & Co.	1815–34
DEAN	103 brigt	Dean & Leigh, Jersey	1833	Philip Dean	1833–41
DEESSÉ	95 schr	Allix, Jersey	1856	Fr. Allix	1856–63
DE JERSEY	219 barq	Jersey	1794	P. & F. Janvrin	1822–29

Continued on following pages

Jersey Owned Vessels in the 19th Century — continued

Name of Vessel	Tons	Rig	Where built	When	Owners	Years
DELIGHT	29	cutt	Le Sueur?, Jersey	1866	J. H. Le Clecq	1870–
DESDEMONA	664	barq	Deslandes, Jersey	1864	Geo. Deslandes	1864–79
DESDEMONA	143	schr	Deslandes, Jersey	1840	Geo. Deslandes	1840–
DESIGN	66	ketch	Aubin, Jersey	1874	Philip Payn & Co.	1879–
DESLANDES	160	brig	Deslandes, Jersey	1837	Geo. Deslandes	1837–59
DESTINY	30	cutt	?	?	Wm. Swain	1859–63
DEWDROP	?	schr	?	?	J. & E. Collas	1873–79
DEWDROP	50	cutt	Jersey	1862	M. Gee	1863–
DIADEM	160	schr	Deslandes, Jersey	1841	Philip Binet	1841–43
DIAMENT	28	cutt	Jersey	1857	Geo. Allix	1859–70
DIAMOND	36	schr	ex-prize	—	Logan Finnie & J. Fauvel	1814–31
DIANA	216	brig	Le Vesconte, Jersey	1861	Le Boutillier & Co.	1863–66
DIANA	177	brigt	ex-prize	—	C. Bayles ?	1810–
DIANA	174	schr	ex-prize	—	Messervy & Le Cronier	1826–
DIDO	71	schr	Filleul & de La Mare, Jersey	1837	J. C. Queree	1837–40
DISPATCH	132	brigt	Hamptonne, Jersey	1841	Hamptonne & Barreau	1841–42
DISPATCH	132	schr	?	?	P. Huelin & Co.	1838–
DISPATCH	58	schr	Jersey	1851	Blampied & Le Marinel	1856–63
DISPATCH	12	cutt	Le Sueur, Jersey	1851	Chas. de Gruchy	1851–
DISPATCH	23	schr	Gaspé	1829	P. & F. Janvrin	1831–35
DISPATCH	23	schr	?	?	Philip Nicolle	1815–
DIT-ON	95	schr	Paspébiac, Gaspé	1831	Chas. Robin & Co.	1831–88
DITTO	162	brig	Paspébiac, Gaspé	1830	Chas. Robin & Co.	1831–98
DOLPHIN	232	brig	ex-prize	—	Janvrin, Benest, Winter & Nicolle	1818–59
DOLPHIN	159	brigt	ex-prize	—	Janvrin, Winter & Nicolle	1803–05
DOLPHIN	54	schr	Picot, Jersey	1862	Thomas Renouf	1862–63
DOLPHIN	40	schr	Newfoundland	1809	Philip Nicolle	1826–33
DOLPHIN	36	schr	Cap Breton	1861	Chas. Robin & Co.	1888–
DON	120	schr	Duval, Jersey	1836	Vautier & Alexandre	1836–40
DON DE DIEU (LE)	66	schr	built 18th century	—	J. Benest	1819–
DONNA MARIA	82	schr	Picot, Jersey	1875	W. Pickford of Newport	1879–88
DORIS	169	brig	Malbaye, Gaspé	1827	P. & F. Janvrin	1828–38
DOVE	53	schr	Malbaye, Gaspé	1840	P. Vardon	1840–42
DOVE	23	cutt	Weymouth	1817	Halsey & Hansford	1826––
DRAGON	23	schr	Le Couteur, Newfoundland	1832	Philip Nicolle	1834–41
DREADNOUGHT	325	barq	Aberdeen, Scotland	1862	Helier Arthur	1862–63
DUKE OF ARGYLL	43	brigt	Newfoundland	1794	John Mahe	1805–
DUKE OF WELLINGTON	130	brig	Plymouth	1814	de Quetteville	1815–31

Continued on following pages

Jersey Owned Vessels in the 19th Century — continued

Name of Vessel	Tons Rig	Where built	When	Owners	Years
DUKE OF WELLINGTON	45 cutt	Guernsey	1825	Wm. Cook	1831–
DUNDAS	172 brig	Guernsey	1794	Renouf, Collas & Duhamel	1803–13
EAGLE	150 schr	Clarke, Jersey	1857	J. J. Le Touzel	1857–63
EAGLE	80 schr	Montrose, Scotland	1803	Wm. Ranwell	1838–40
EBENEZER	86 brig	Cap Breton	1812	J. Benest	1814–21
EBENEZER	59 schr	Le Sueur, Jersey	1847	J. Le Bas	1849–
EBENEZER	23 cutt	Jersey	1836	Amice Bertram	1841–
ECHO	422 barq	New Brunswick	1841	de Quetteville	1841–63
ECHO	36 cutt	?	?	J. F. Bailhache	1831–
ECHO	22 cutt	Dartmouth, Devon	1823	J. Benest	1825–26
ECLAIR	68 cutt	Jersey	1856	Mary Barbier	1856–59
ECLIPSE	? cutt	Clarke, Jersey	1852	Thos. de Faye	1856–63
ECLIPSE	58 schr	Jersey	1873	Thos. de Faye	1873–88
ECLIPSE	59 schr	Picot, Jersey	1879	?	?
EDWARD	25 cutt	Lane, Jersey	1825	Thos. Macpherson	1825–
EGTON	63 schr	Whitby, Yorkshire	1803	Le Couteur & Godfray	1820–
EIGHTY FIVE	139 brigt	Paspébiac, Gaspé	1860	Chas. Robin & Co.	1863–88
ELECTRA	132 schr	Le Vesconte & Vautier, Jersey	1854	Fr. Le Sueur & Son	1854–85
ELECTRIC FLASH	177 schr	Clarke, Jersey	1854	Fr. Carrel & Co.	1854–63
ELFINE	24 cutt	Jersey	1869	Perchard, Le Huquet & de La Mare	1869–88
ELIADA	246 brig	Prince Edward Isle	1864	? de La Taste	1865–
ELIEZER	55 schr	Valpy ? Jersey	?	M. P. Valpy	1842–
ELISHA TUPPER	272 barq	ex-prize	—	Janvrin	1815–
ELIZA	211 brig	Grandin, Jersey	1865	Le Quesne & Buesnel	1870–79
ELIZA	170 brig	ex-prize	—	Nicolle, Janvrin & Geo. Benest	1814–67
ELIZA	119 brig	?	—	J. de Caen	1932–35
ELIZA	105 brig	ex-prize	—	Le Quesne, Le Boeuf, Le Vesconte	
ELIZA	87 brig	British built (ex-prize)	—	P. & F. Janvrin	1810–13
ELIZA	47 cutt	Milford, Wales	1833	Ph. & Geo. Messervy	1843–
ELIZA	35 cutt	Ramsgate	1821	?	?
ELIZA	28 cutt	ex-prize	—	Le Gallais & Aubert	1814–15
ELIZABETH	21 cutt	Fowey, Cornwall	1811	Goldie, Jenkins, Chapman & Currie	1816–18
ELIZABETH	220 brig	Co. Durham	1846	Wm. Bryant	1846–53
ELIZABETH ANN	120 schr	Guernsey	1841	J. &. E. Syvrett	1859–62
ELIZABETH & ANN	20 sloop	Salcombe, Devon	1814	John & George Collas	1823–
ELIZABETH TAYLOR	180 schr	Vardon, Jersey	1845	J. Taylor	1845–
ELIZABETH YOUNG	219 brig	South Shields	1856	George Allix	1865–81

Continued on following pages

Jersey Owned Vessels in the 19th Century — continued

Name of Vessel	Tons Rig	Where built	When	Owners	Years
ELIZA & MARIA	219 barq	Jersey	1864	de Gruchy & Gallichan	1865–70
ELIZA HANDS	264 barq	Clarke, Jersey	1855	Le Maistre & de Gruchy	1863–76
ELIZA JEAN	83 brig	Arichat, Cap Breton	1825	P. & F. Janvrin	1829–
ELIZA JENKINS	230 barq	Newport, Monmouth	1849	P. Le Caux	1852–56
ELLEN	183 brigt	?	?	Philip Luce	1856–
ELLEN	156 brigt	Prince Edward Isle	1850	P. Amy	1851–59
ELLEN	46 cutt	?	?	D. Machon	1834–
ELLEN MARY	35 schr	?	?	Chas. Robin & Co.	1888–
ELLEN MARY	66 schr	Cap Breton	1878	Robin, Collas & Co.	1888–1903
ELLEN MURRAY	116 brigt	Newcastle	1839	Nancy Roberts	1846–
ELLIN	42 cutt	Bristol	1829	Ph. Le Jeune & Co.	1835–41
EMERALD	52 schr	Vardon, Jersey	1846	J. Renouf	1856–57
EMERALD	39 cutt	Cowes	1822	Geo. Asplet	1846–48
EMILY	39 cutt	Picot, Jersey	1869	J. Swain	1870–85
EMILY	26 cutt	?	?	Moses & Swain	1856–59
EMILY COWLET	105 schr	Vautier, Jersey	1861	Buesnel & Le Quesne	1862–63
EMMA	78 schr	Hull	1857	E. J. Bellingham	1870–79
EMMA EDEN	105 schr	Monkwearmouth, D'hm	1840	Thoreau & Co.	1845–56
EMMA JANE	55 dandy	Aubin, Jersey	1872	J. Le Gros	1879–99
EMMA JANE	39 cutt	?	?	Le Couteir & Woods	1856–65
EMMA LOUISE	83 schr	Emsworth, Hampshire	1877	L. Parsons	1885–88
EMMA SUWAROF	170 brig	ex-American prize	—	E. Nicolle	1815–23
EMPEROR	58 cutt	Vardon, Jersey	1847	George Asplet	1847–58
EMPRESS	99 schr	St Malo, France	1876	Buhts, Gavey & Renouf	1879–88
ENCHANTRESS	66 schr	Le Huquet, Jersey	1875	Du Fresne & Becquet	1879–81
ENCORE	257 barq	Esnouf, Jersey	1840	Fr. Hocquard	1840–??
ENDEAVOUR	65 schr	Prince Edward Isle	1808	John Dolbel	1811–1?
ENDORA	45 cutt	Cowes	1838	M. Gee	1861–03
ENERGY	45 schr	Le Huquet, Jersey	1875	R. H. Hooper	1875–79
ENGINEER	65 schr	Le Feuvre, Jersey	1854	Fr. Le Feuvre	1854–63
ENTERPRISE	118 brig	ex-prize	—	P. J. Le Feuvre	1831–36
ENTERPRISE	86 brigt	Nova Scotia	1814	Chevalier & Falle	1823–26
ENTERPRISE	78 ketch	Shoreham	1872	Seager & Payn	1872–79
ENTERPRISE	61 brigt	ex-prize	—	Fr. Amy	1807–08
ENVOY	144 brigt	?	1857	Wm. Fruing & Co.	1857–58
ERATO	60 schr	Le Masurier, Jersey	1871	J. Blampied (Jr.)	1871
ESCAPE	183 brig	Le Huquet, Jersey	1861	G. N. Le Quesne	1861–63
ESCAPE	43 cutt	Calais, France	1847	E. C. Gallichan	1859–63
ESTHER	151 brigt	Nova Scotia	1848	Thayer & Williams	1859–63
ESTHER	107 brig	Hamworthy, Dorset	1846	Philip Nicolle	1846–
ESTHER	88 brig	ex-prize	—	Janvrin, Le Vesconte & Hacquoil	1803–33

Continued on following pages

Jersey Owned Vessels in the 19th Century — continued

Name of Vessel	Tons Rig	Where built	When	Owners	Years
ESTRELLA	233 barq	Redon, France	?	Abraham Laurens	1871–
ETTON	71 schr	Scarborough	1825	J. Fauvel	1831
EVANGELINE	441 barq	Le Vesconte, Jersey	1866	Giffard & Le Quesne	1870–79
EVENING STAR	847 ship	Allen, Jersey	1854	Jean Le Bas	1854–58
EVENING STAR	28 schr	Shippegan, N.B.	18 ?	Philip Luce	1857–
EXACT	220 brig	Deslandes, Jersey	1852	Geo. Deslandes	1852–70
EXCELSIOR	92 schr	Aubin, Jersey	1875	R. Foster	?
EXCHANGE	126 brig	Plymouth	1815	Edward Nicolle	1821–26
EXHIBITION	25 schr	Jersey	1851	Philip Nicolle	1852–63
EXILE	39 schr	?	?	Henry Laming	1856–57
EXPEDITION PACKET	36 cutt	Brixham, Devon	?	George Hooper	1803–04
EXPERIMENT	47 cutt	Arthur, Jersey	1822	J. Ennis	1822–35
EXPRESS	134 brigt	Poole, Dorset	1847	Philip Nicolle	1849–59
EXPRESS	96 schr	Clarke, Jersey	1863	Blampied & Barreau	1863–70
EXPRESS	56 dandy	Messervy, Jersey	1862	Le Gros & Gallichan	1863–70
EXPRESS	22 cutt	Jersey	1856	J. Le Gros	1856–59
FAIRFAX	270 brig	?	?	J. de Caen	1849–50
FAIRLINA	190 brig	Clarke, Jersey	1862	Le Maistre	1863–70
FAIRWATER	68 ketch	Picot, Jersey	1877	Kent & Baker	1977–88
FAIRY	52 cutt	Bartlett, Jersey	1847	G. Le Seelleur	1847–
FAIRY	32 cutt	Guernsey	1846	E. J. Bellingham	1858–79
FALCON	38 cutt	?	?	Le Gros & de La Mare	1856–
FALCON	35 cutt	?	?	W. Downing	1856–59
FANCY	56 schr	Arthur, Jersey	1827	C. Bisson	1831–
FANCY	46 brigt	ex-prize	—	Picot & Bignal	1803–05
FANNY	74 schr	Le Masurier, N'f'dl'd	1823?	Ph. de Quetteville	1835–38
FANNY	69 cutt	?	?	Geo. Le Cronier	1815–
FANNY	68 brig	Bridgewater	1805	E. Le Gros	1814–15
FANNY	63 schr	Newfoundland	1839	Geo. Deslandes	1841–
FANNY	43 ketch	Bellot & Noel, Jersey	1865	J. C. Cartwright	1875–79
FANNY BRESLAUER	295 barqt	Plymouth	1871	Robin, Collas & Co.	1890–1908
FARMER	133 brig	?	1841	J. Perrée	1841–
FARMER	103 brig	Jersey	1802	P. & F. & J. Janvrin	1803–08
FARRAGO	163 brig	Paspébiac	1843	Chas. Robin & Co.	1843–
FATHER MATTHEW	248 brigt	?	?	J. Le Boutillier	1846–
FATHER & SON	25 sloop	Le Nevue, Jersey	1819	Abm. de La Mare	1819–21
FAVORITE	? brig	ex-prize	—	Cabot & Gruchy	1803–05
FAVOURITE	63 schr	Nicolson, Jersey	1847	G. Nicolson & Son	1856–59
FAWN	24 cutt	Le Huquet, Jersey	1858	Jury & Williams	1859–
FELICITY	49 cutt	ex-prize	—	J. de Caen & J. Prouings	1808–15
FIONA	49 ketch	Le Sueur, Jersey	1884	Le Sueur & Le Gros	1885–88

Continued on following pages

Jersey Owned Vessels in the 19th Century — continued

Name of Vessel	Tons	Rig	Where built	When	Owners	Years
FIRM	187	brig	Deslandes, Jersey	1862	de Quetteville	1863–70
FIRST	111	brigt	Prince Edward Isle	1839	Bayfield & Copp	1840–42
FIRST	31	cutt	Le Huquet, Jersey	1852	A. Blampied	1852–56
FISHERMAN	196	barq	Paspébiac, Gaspé	1832	Chas. Robin & Co.	1832–45
FISH HAWK	48	schr	Newfoundland	1818	Philip Nicolle	1826–39
FLAMER	134	schr	Grellier, Jersey	1836	Philip Binet	1837–
FLAMER	110	schr	Deslandes, Jersey	1840	Philip Binet	1840–41
FLEET WING	33	cutt	Jersey	1869	F. Mollet	1870–
FLEUR DE MAURICE	333	barq	Clarke, Jersey	1864	Fr. Carrel & Co.	1864–70
FLORA	95	brigt	Nicolle, Jersey	1835	Philip Bree	1835–38
FLORA	75	schr	Quebec	1835	Philip Le Brocq	1842–
FLORA	72	schr	Jersey	1835	T. & J. Sullivan	1840–56
FLORA	63	brigt	ex-prize (French built)	1794	Mourant & Le Grand	1806–08
FLORIDA	50	schr	Allix, Jersey	1877	Chas. Whitley	1877–
FLY	62	schr	France (ex-prize ?)	1795	Hemery Bros.	1801–
FLY	59	schr	Le Brun, Paspébiac, Gaspé	1858	Chas. Robin & Co.	1858–76
FLY	51	schr	Cap Breton	1826	? Janvrin	1834–41
FLYING CLOUD	70	schr	Messervy, Jersey	1863	John Buhts	1863–99
FLYING DUTCHMAN	66	yawl	Southampton	1859	Mallet & Gavey	1863–
FLYING FISH	99	schr	Clarke, Jersey	1853	J. J. Le Touzel	1853–54
FLYING FISH	74	schr	Picot, Jersey	1878	Picot & Coles	1878–88
FLYING FISH	60	lugger	ex-prize (French)	—	? Seward	1801–
FLYING FOAM	98	schr	Le Huquet, Jersey	1879	P. Noel	1888–
FLYING FOAM	98	schr	Asplet ?, Jersey ?	1861	Chas. Le Quesne	1861–66
FLYING SCUD	160	brig	Jersey	1861	Le Quesne & Labey	1863–66
FOREMAN	169	brigt	Deslandes, Jersey	1854	Geo. Deslandes	1854–59
FOREST GIRL	49	cutt	Picot, Jersey	1863	James H. Young	1863–70
FOREST LAD	63	ketch	Jersey	1865	?	lost '68
FORTITUDE	99	brig	Sunderland	1804	J. Brayn	1853–55
FORT REGENT	655	ship	Le Vesconte, Jersey	1863	Orange & Briard	1863–70
FORTUNE	51	brigt	ex-prize	—	Amy & de La Lande	1803–
FOX	95	schr	Vautier, Jersey	1864	Wm. Fruing & Co.	1864–68
FOX	60	brigt	ex-prize (Spanish)	—	Janvrin & Duheame	1810–11
FOX	30	cutt	Cowes	1806	Aubin & Gallichan	1856–59
FRANCIS	92	schr	Le Sueur, Jersey	1848	F. Le Sueur	1848–49
FRANCIS	21	schr	Newfoundland	1832	Philip Nicolle	1835–63
FRANCIS & MARY	39	cutt	?	?	G. Desreaux	1863–
FRANCIS & ANN	124	brigt	?	?	F. Perrée	1849–56
FRANCIS ANN	98	schr	Bartlett, Jersey	1849	Ph. de La Perrelle	1849–63
FRANCIS & RICHARD	114	schr	Allix, Jersey	1862	Francis Allix	1862–63
FRANCIS JOHN	235	brig	Grandin, Jersey	1869	J. & D. Pallot	1870–79
FRANCIS PHILIP	102	schr	Sauvage, Jersey	1850	Francis Sauvage	1850–52
FREDERICK	30	cutt	?	?	Touzel & Le Rougetel	1841– lost '41
FREE	192	brigt	Deslandes, Jersey	1864	Geo. Deslandes	1864–70

Continued on following pages

Jersey Owned Vessels in the 19th Century — continued

Name of Vessel	Tons	Rig	Where built	When	Owners	Years
FREEDOM	165	brigt	Grellier, Jersey	1841	Jean Le Bas	1841–42
FREEDOM	77	schr	Jersey	1860	Gallichan & Noel	1863–70
FREEDOM	50	cutt	Vardon & Le Huquet	1847	Le Couteur & Bisson	1848–49
FREEDOM	39	ketch	?	?	Wm. Steel	1877–88
FRIEND OF THE ISLES	47	ketch	Le Huquet, Jersey	1852	T. Cabot	1856–59
FRIENDS	287	barq	Deslandes, Jersey	1832	Philip Arthur	1832–
FRIENDS	196	brig	?	?	A. de Gruchy & C. Le Quesne	1856–
FRIENDS	191	brig	Southtown, Suffolk	1834	J. P. Collas	1834–38
FRIENDS	170	brigt	ex-prize (American)	—	Janvrin, Chevalier & Amiraux	1813–23
FRIENDS	115	schr	Canada	1828	Le Veslet & Jeune	1830–31
FRIENDS	42	smack	Isle of Wight	?	Hemery Bros.	1803–
FRIENDS	28	cutt	Hamptonne, Jersey	1832	Philip Arthur	1832–
FRIENDSHIP	207	barq	ex-prize (Dutch)	—	J. Benest	1819–23
FRIENDSHIP	212	barq	ex-prize (American ?)	—	Renouf, Collas & Le Sueur	1809–14
FRIENDSHIP	27	cutt	St Mawes, Cornwall	1816	John Daniels	1823–
FRIENDSHIP	94	brigt	Bonaventure, Canada	1842	Jean Roissier	1842–45
FRUITERER	59	schr	Le Sueur, Jersey	1846	G. de Garis	1846–49
GALATEA	24	cutt	Jersey	1865	Mollet & Edwards	1865–70
GAMBRIA	31	cutt	Arthur, Jersey	1826	Jean Moisson	1826–
GASPÉ	243	barq	Paspébiac, Gaspé	1812	Chas. Robin & Co.	1818–23
GAUNTLET	50	ketch	Bellot, Jersey	1875	J. C. Renouf	1899–1903
GAZELLE	242	barq	Picot, Jersey	1863	Le Gallais & Le Gros	1863–
GAZELLE	65	ketch	Bellot, Jersey	1873	Moses & Baker	1879–88
G.D.T.	124	brigt	New Brunswick	1852	Le Boutillier	1859–83
GEFFRARD	328	brig	Clarke, Jersey	1852	Orange & Pirouet	1852–63
GEM	113	brigt	Poole, Dorset	1848	A. de Gruchy	1849–
GEMINI	426	barq	Le Vesconte, Jersey	1864	Deslandes & Pallot	1865–
GENERAL BROCK	103	brig	Cap Breton	1821	P. & F. Janvrin	1821–26
GENERAL DON	272	barq	ex-prize (French)	—	? Janvrin	1810–12
GENERAL DON	40	cutt	Vardon, Jersey	1844	J. Fauvel	1844–56
GENERAL DOYLE	83	cutt	Cowes	1803	Poignard & Le Masurier	1809–12
GENERAL MACKINTOSH	177	brig	ex-prize (American)	—	Philip Perchard	1822–26
GEORGE	39	brigt	ex-prize	—	Le Cronier & Laugie	1809–19
GEORGE	32	cutt	?	?	William Young	1856–59
GEORGE & ANN	35	cutt	Le Sueur, Jersey	1861	George Wheeler	1861–62
GEORGE & ELIZABETH	41	cutt	Plymouth	1848	Jos. Young	1849–59
GEORGE & HENRY	31	schr	ex-prize (French)	—	Weekes & Osborne	1820–

Continued on following pages

Jersey Owned Vessels in the 19th Century — continued

Name of Vessel	Tons	Rig	Where built	When	Owners	Years
GEORGE & MARY	100	schr	Le Sueur, Jersey	1875	Shapland & Le Four	1879–
GEORGE & MARY	28	cutt	?	?	Philip Asplet	1841–
GEORGE DEAN	150	schr	Dean & Briard, Jersey	1839	Philip Dean	1840–57
GEORGE MAY	43	ketch	Guernsey	?	George May	1870–
GEORGES	473	ship	Clarke, Jersey	1865	Orange & Briard	1865–71
GEORGES	58	schr	Deslandes, Jersey	1839	Geo. Deslandes	1839–41
GEORGY	64	schr	Valpy, Jersey	1847	M. P. Valpy	1848–50
GIPSY	75	schr	Ipswich	1839	William Earles	1846–56
GIPSY	59	schr	?	?	T. & J. Heddle	1859–
GIPSY	37	cutt	?	?	Philip Durell	1835
GIPSY KING	33	cutt	Jersey	1867	Thos. Bennewith	1867–70
GIPSY QUEEN	30	cutt	Jersey	1855	Thos. Bennewith	1856–70
GLADIATEUR	427	barq	Le Vesconte, Jersey	1866	Fr. Carrel & Co.	1866–74
GLADYS	62	ketch	Plymouth	1894	? Mourant	1901–
GLANCE	887	ship	Sunderland	1869	Ph. Pellier & Co.	1869–
GLANCE	33	cutt	Jersey	1864	Philip Messervy	1864–70
GLEANER	60	schr	Le Vesconte, Jersey	1860	Le Boutillier	1888–
GLENVILLE	325	barq	Sunderland	1874	Robin, Collas & Co.	1890–1908
GLOBE	128	schr	?	?	C. Pirouet	1859–
GLORY	250	barq	Deslandes ? Jersey	1855	Geo. Deslandes	1855–59
GOOD INTENT	122	schr	Fowey, Cornwall	1817	J. Moisson & A. Black	1818–23
GOOD INTENT	69	brig	Plymouth	1801	Durell & Gallie	1808–09
GOOD LUCK	232	barq	Deslandes, Jersey	1834	Geo. Deslandes	1834–41
GORDON	300	brig	Clarke, Jersey	1859	Geo. Malzard	1859–64
GOREY LASS	44	dandy	Aubin, Jersey	1868	J. M. Kent	1870–1901
GOVERNOR	60	schr	Vardon, Jersey	1847	Bertram & Noel	1849–56
GOVERNOR LOCK	54	schr	Isle of Man	1865	J. E. Briard	?
GRACE	907	ship	Nova Scotia	1854	J. de Wolf	1863–66
GRACE	40	cutt	Weymouth	1804	Werter Wallis	1859–63
GRAMPUS	22	schr	Newfoundland	1820	Philip Nicolle	1826–34
GRAPHIC	68	schr	Le Huquet, Jersey	1874	Le Huquet, Le Boutillier & Le Scelleur	1879–88
GRECIAN	140	brig	Esnouf & Mauger, Jersey	1851	R. Falle	1851–70
GREENEND	83	schr	Whitby, Yorkshire	1827	William Ranwell	1831–41
GREYHOUND	35	cutt	?	?	Francis Le Sueur	1856–59
GREYHOUND	40	schr	Ryde, Isle of Wight	1830	Philip Nicolle	1840–70
GRIFFIN	98	brigt	Nicolson, Jersey	1861	William Fruing	1861–63
GROG	150	brigt	Paspébiac, Gaspé	1810	Chas. Robin & Co.	1817–41
GROUVILLE	164	brigt	Hamptonne, Jersey	1841	P. Bertram	1841–42
GUERNSEY LILY	235	brig	Guernsey	1828	Nicolas Le Quesne	1831–41
GUERNSEY LILY	28	cutt	Guernsey	1825	Elias de Gruchy	1831–38
GUESS	145	brig	Collas, Malbaye	1836	J. Perrée & J. Perrée (Jr.)	1836–38

Continued on following pages

Jersey owned Vessels in the 19th Century — continued

Name of Vessel	Tons Rig	Where built	When	Owners	Years
GUESS	175 brig	Deslandes, Jersey	1869	Geo. Deslandes	1869–70
GUIDE	161 brigt	Deslandes, Jersey	1863	Geo. Deslandes	1863–
GUIDE	23 cutt	Jersey	1870	Thomas Blampied	1870–99
GUILLELMO	119 schr	Deslandes, Jersey	1835	H. Machon & Co.	1835–42
GULLIVER	54 schr	Le Couteur, La Poele Bay	1832	Philip Nicolle	1834–41
GULNARE	62 schr	Deslandes, Jersey	1848	C. Laurains	1849–53
GULNARE	43 cutt	?	?	Laurains & Bartlett	1835–36
HABNAB	138 brig	Paspébiac, Gaspé	1808	Janvrin, Poingdestre & Robin	1811–14
HALCYON	65 dandy	Jersey	1861	Jacobs, Hambling & Waldren	1861–63
HAMON	188 brig	Le Vesconte & Vautier, Jersey	1857	Hamon & Blampied	1857–59
HANDY	59 cutt	Vardon, Jersey	1846	Drelaud & Anley	1847–55
HANDY	33 ketch	Fauvel, Portbail, France	1852	H. & G. Arthur	1859–63
HANNAH	41 dandy	?	?	A. C. Queree	1889–1901
HAPPY RETURN	199 brig	St Malo, France	1838	Carter & Picot	1865–70
HARE	34 schr	Newfoundland	1838	Philip Nicolle	1838–69
HARE	30 schr	?	?	Chas. Robin & Co.	1888–
HARLEQUIN	20 cutt	Jersey	1866	Coleman & Cole	1866–70
HARMONY	137 brig	Gavey & Nicolle, Jersey	1824	Philip Nicolle	1824–59
HARMONY	27 cutt	Jersey ?	1856?	Denis Blampied	1856–63
HARMONY	? sloop	Sussex	1788	A. Le Rossignol, J. Benest & others	1803–
HARRIET	109 schr	ex-prize	—	Geo. Ingouville	1826–
HARRIET	79 brig	La Vache, Arichat, C.B.	1828	Clem. Hubert	1828–32
HARRIET	56 brigt	Arichat, C.B.	1842	P. Huelin	1842–
HARRIET	59 ketch	?	?	F. F. Mallet & Co.	1888–99
HARRIET	25 ketch	Le Masurier, Jersey	1869	Chas. Mauger	1869–70
HARRIET	22 schr	Dublin	1831	Chas. Robin & Co.	1838–40
HARRIET 'L'	177 schr	Deslandes, Jersey	1840	G. Falle	1840–56
HARVEST LAD	139 schr	Valpy, Jersey	1864	F. & G. de Ste Croix	1865–67
HARVEST MAID	193 brigt	Vautier, Jersey	1865	Cozenz, Carcaud & Blampied	1865–70
HARVEST MAN	140 brigt	Valpy, Jersey	1865	M. P. Valpy	1865–68
HASTY	171 brig	Deslandes, Jersey	1858	Geo. Deslandes	1858–63
HASTY	46 schr	Gaspé	1859	J. & E. Collas	1863–88
HAWK	27 cutt	Guernsey	1824	George Marett	1831–
HAZARD	158 brigt	Gray, Jersey	1842	Deslandes & Nicolle	1842–46
HAZARD	77 sloop	ex-prize (French built)	—	Hammond, Pipon & Remon	1803–04
HAZARD	63 ketch	Clarke, Jersey	1866	J. Le Sueur	1866–70
HAZARD	61 brigt	ex-prize (French)	—	Jean & George Touzel	1811–12

Continued on following pages

Jersey Owned Vessels in the 19th Century — continued

Name of Vessel	Tons Rig	Where built	When	Owners	Years
HAZARD	39 chasse maree	ex-prize (French)	—	Elias Durell	1813–14
HEARTY	36 dandy	Jersey	1849	Le Sueur & Torrens	1856–59
HEBE	240 brig	Le Vesconte, Jersey	1861	J. Le Boutillier	1861–63
HEBE	132 brig	Hamon & Esnouf, Jersey	1827	N. Le Quesne	1827–47
HEBE	132 brig	?	?	J. Le Boutillier	1835–44
HEMATOPE	81 schr	Paspébiac, Gaspé	1845	Chas. Robin & Co.	1845–88
HELEN	191 brig	Chepstow, Wales	1841	Chas. Alexandre	1845–52
HENRY	45 cutt	Nicolle, Jersey	1826	Chas. Bertram	1826–29
HENRY & MARY	54 ?	Plymouth	1803	Jean Benest	1821–
HERALD	183 brig	Le Vesconte & Vautier, Jersey	1857	Orange & Pirouet	1859–
HERBERT	57 schr	Valpy, Jersey	1841	M. P. Valpy	1841–42
HER MAJESTY	80 ketch	Grimsby	1855	John Geo. Le Gros	1890– 1904
HERNHUT	34 cutt	Bellot, Jersey	1877	Philip Wheeler	1877–
HERO	178 brig	Le Boeuf, Jersey	1817	Matthew Le Boeuf	1817–23
HERO	84 schr	Cowes	1805	Nicolle & Amiraux	1805–14
HERO	81 cutt	?	?	Philip Duheaume	1815–19
HERO	80 ketch	Picot, Jersey	1872	C. Whitley & Co.	1872–79
HERO	40 schr	Jersey	1858	C. Whitley & Co.	1858–70
HEROINE	20 cutt	?	?	Henry Arm	1856–70
HIBERNICA	165 brigt	Henry, New Brunswick	1863	Wm. Fruing & Co.	1863–72
HIGHLANDER	147 brigt	Luce, Jersey	1840	M. Alexandre	1840–41
HIND	88 cutt	J. Gavey, Jersey	1821	Nicolle & Duheaume	1821–23
HIPOLYTE	25 cutt	?	?	William Bayfield	1856–59
HIRONELLE	166 brigt	Sweden	1885	Jules Claireaunt	1885– 1907
HIRONDELLE	36 schr	Le Riche, Cap Breton	1845	Chas. Robin & Co.	1845–50
HOMELY	256 barq	Vincent, Gaspé	1841	Chas. Robin & Co.	1841–79
HOMELY	210 barq	Canada	1802	Hemery, Chevalier & Le Breton	1809–
HOMER	162 schr	?	1858?	Le Couteur & Le Feuvre	1859–63
HONOUR	36 cutt	Messervy, Jersey	1861	Chas Hamon & D. Le Gros	1861–63
HOOPOE	86 schr	Clarke, Jersey	1865	Coverly & Westram	1875–78
HOPE	182 brig	Auguste, France	1837	Hocquard & Gaudin	1863–70
HOPE	140 brig	Aberdeen, Scotland	1815	Philip Perchard	1832–38
HOPE	125 brig	Southtown, Suffolk	1810	Deslandes, Neel & Mourant	1818–26
HOPE	114 brig	ex-prize	—	J. Bisson & Co.	1819–
HOPE	77 schr	ex-prize	—	Champion & Butler	1826–31
HOPE	67 schr	Cap Breton	1818	P. & F. & J. Janvrin	1820–23
HOPE	63 cutt	Fowey, Cornwall	1813	Hemery Bros.	1815–19
HOPE	57 brigt	ex-prize (French)	—	Le Rossignol & Bisson	1807–11
HOPE	? lugger	Fowey, Cornwall	1803	Cosnard & Janvrin	1803–09

Continued on following pages

Jersey Owned Vessels in the 19th Century — continued

Name of Vessel	Tons Rig	Where built	When	Owners	Years
HOPE	40 smack	ex-prize (French)	—	Aubin, Touzel & Moisson	1815–20
HOPE	35 sloop	Bermuda	1809	? Janvrin	1815–20
HOPE	24 schr	ex-prize (Spanish)	—	de Ste Croix & Newman	1804–
HOPE	20 cutt	Tracadie, France	1888	J. Alexandre	?
HOPEWELL	67 schr	New Brunswick	1840	Le Boutillier	1840–41
HORATIO	28 cutt	Cowes	1810	John Falle	1820–23
HOWARD	911 ship	Portsmouth, U.S.A.	1854	J. Taylor	? –66
H.R.S.	59 schr	?	?	Wm. Fruing & Co.	1863–65
HUMILITY	175 brig	?	?	G. W. Le Geyt	1831–
HUNDREDTH	200 brig	Deslandes, Jersey	1870	Geo. Deslandes	1870–80
HYDRA	52 cutt	Le Huquet, Jersey	1852	George Noel	1853–54
IBIS	27 cutt	?	?	Francis Picot	1856– lost '56
I.C.U.	48 ketch	Guernsey ?	1884	J. Renouf & Co.	1901–04
IDAS	105 schr	Allix, Jersey	1859	Francis Allix	1859–60
IDEAL	127 schr	Esnouf & Mauger, Jersey	1857	Esnouf & Mauger	1857–59
IF	196 barq	Newfoundland	1794	Chas. Robin & Co.	1803–08
INCA	20 cutt	?	?	Philip Perchard	1841–
INDEX	237 brig	Eno, Jersey	1846	John Eno	1846–
INDIAN	472 barq	de Gruchy, Jersey	1848	Philip Pellier	1848–50
INDUSTRY	209 barq	ex-prize	—	A. de Ste Croix	1803–08
INDUSTRY	97 brig	ex-prize	—	Le Sueur & Le Gallais	1803–05
INDUSTRY	61 schr	ex-prize	—	Renouf, Arthur & Syvret	1818–19
INTEGRITY	35 ?	Weymouth	1802	Edward Purchase	1826–28
INTENDED	111 schr	Prince Edward Isle	1827	de Carteret & Co.	1831–33
INTREPID	69 schr	Gaspé	1849	? Janvrin	1850–55
IRENE	64 schr	Bartlett, Jersey	1847	J. Le Bas	1847–49
IRIS	286 barq	J. Gavey, Jersey	1820	Philip Nicolle	1820–59
IRIS	143 schr	Cap Breton	?	H. B. de Ste Croix	1879–88
ISABEL	42 cutt	Messervy, Jersey	1858	J. Cantell & Co.	1858–70
ISABELLA	59 schr	Clarke, Jersey	1838	Edward Jean	1838–56
ISABELLA	177 brig	Prince Edward Isle	1848	J. Brayn & Co.	1849–56
ISABELLA & JANE	137 brigt	?	?	W. Downing	1856–59
ISLANDER	60 schr	Le Masurier, Jersey	1872	Blampied & Son	1872–88
ISLAND QUEEN	78 ?	Canada	1877	J. C. Le Quesne	1880–
ISLAND QUEEN	47 cutt	Picot, Jersey	1868	Lerrier Godfray	1868–70
JACOB HORTON	1,150 ship	Bridport, U.S.A.	1862	Philip Pellier	1863–
JAMES	101 schr	Bavaria	?	George Asplet	1855–59
JAMES	40 cutt	Isle of Wight	1814	W. Pugsley	1849–52
JAMES & ELLEN	49 brigt	Co. Cork	1807	G. Le Gros & Ph. Le Nevue	1821–41
JAMES & FRANCIS	20 cutt	?	?	James Frost	1859–63
JAMES & MARY	59 dandy	Messervy, Jersey	1865	Gavey & Mckeown	1865–78
JAMES HARMER	58 schr	?	1841	?	1874–

Continued on following pages

Jersey Owned Vessels in the 19th Century — continued

Name of Vessel	Tons	Rig	Where built	When	Owners	Years
JANE	361	barq	Deslandes, Jersey	1846	Josué Deslandes	1846–63
JANE	215	brig	New Brunswick	1857	Wm. Fruing & Co.	1859–63
JANE	169	brig	?	?	Le Vesconte & de Carteret	1831–41
JANE	103	brigt	ex-prize (French)	—	Thomas Mallet & Thomas Mallet	1812–15
JANE	56	cutt	Granville, France	1855	E. & J. Gaudin	1863–64
JANE	42	cutt	Guernsey	1838	Johnson & Miller	1851–52
JANE	29	cutt	?	?	J. Duheaume	1838–41
JANE & LOUISA	40	schr	Saunders, Cap Breton	1837?	de Quetteville	1838–41
JANUS	100	schr	Deslandes, Jersey	1839	Duheaume & Le Brun	1840–41
JANVRIN	228	barq	Le Boeuf, Jersey	1821	P. & F. Janvrin	1821–56
JASON	21	cutt	Jersey	1845	P. J. Le Huquet	1867–70
JEFFERY	70	schr	Asplet, Jersey	1860	Thomas Lavan	1863–70
JEDDO	449	barq	Esnouf & Mauger, Jersey	1859	Esnouf & Mauger	1859–
JENNY LIND	68	schr	Prince Edward Isle	1847	Hougez & Blampied	1849–
JERSEY	56	schr	Sauvage, Jersey	1851	Philip Sauvage	1851–53
JERSEY	44	dandy	Le Sueur, Jersey	1869	Luce & Le Maistre	1870–79
JERSEY	26	schr	Newfoundland	1815	Philip Nicolle	1826–38
JERSEY LASS	132	brigt	Luce, Jersey	1838	Matt Alexandre	1838–48
JERSEY LILY	29	cutt	?	?	Hamon & Pinel	1841–
JERSEY MAID	30	cutt	Filleul, Jersey	1836	John Ahier (Jr.)	1836–38
JERSEY PACKET	60	schr	?	?	Bryant & Wall	1879–88
JERSEY PACKET	40	cutt	Deslandes, Jersey	1837	Chas. Laurains	1837–38
JERSEY TAR	135	schr	Duval, Jersey	1837	Matt Alexandre	1837–40
JESSICA	194	brig	Clarke, Jersey	1849	J. de Ste Croix	1849–52
JESSIE	138	brigt	Le Vesconte & Vautier	1857	Le Boutillier & Co.	1859–
JESSIE	36	schr	Cap Breton ?	?	de Gruchy, Renouf & Clement	1870–
JEUNE LOUISE	178	brigt	Legue, France	1844	Le Huquet & Kingsnorth	1863–
J.F.	?	schr	?	?	John Fauvel	1859–
JIM	97	schr	Valpy, Jersey	1848	M. P. & G. J. Valpy	1848–51
JO	51	schr	Cap Breton	1821	P. & F. Janvrin	1822–23
JOHN	69	schr	Jope, Jersey	1826	J. & L. de La Lande	1826–35
JOHN & ELIZA	141	brigt	Messervy, Jersey	1857	J. Messervy	1857–58
JOHN & MARY	46	cutt	Plymouth	1803	Geo. Nicolson	1821–
JOHN & MARY	50	cutt	Jersey	1841	N. Pallot & Co.	1841–56
JOHN BULL	167	brig	ex-prize	—	Jean & Nicolle	1804–05
JOHN CLARK	86	brig	Bideford, Devon	1863	E. de La Perrelle	1872–80
JOHN MILTON	618	ship	Clarke, Jersey	1865	Josué Le Bailly	1865–70
JOHNNY	58	schr	Newfoundland	1840	de Quetteville	1841–43
JOHN THOMAS	50	brigt	Brenton, Newfoundland	1823	J. Benest (Jr.)	1825–26
JOLLY	25	cutt	Jersey	1853	John Pascoe	1856–70
JOLLY TAR	86	schr	Grellier, Jersey	1826	?	1826–
JOLLY TAR	166	brig	Deslandes, Jersey	1828	M. Le Rossignol	1828–41
JOSEPH	105	brigt	Guernsey	1836	G. de Garis	1843–

Continued on following pages

Jersey Owned Vessels in the 19th Century — continued

Name of vessel	Tons	Rig	Where built	When	Owners	Years
JOSEPH	38	cutt	?	?	Stevenson & Bellingham	1859–60
JOSEPH & JANE	29	smack	Cowes	1810	Dolbel & Others	1818–
JOSEPH H. GRACE	37	sloop	Plymouth	1802	Elias Durell	1809–12
JOSEPH JOHN	35	sloop	Cowes	?	de La Haye, Le Cronier & Gruchy	1803–04
JOSEPHINE	308	barq	Liverpool	1838	A. Laurens	1870–
JUBILEE	112	brigt	Vibert, Newfoundland	1841	J. Le Bas	1841–42
JUBILEE	62	cutt	Mevagissey, Cornwall	1809	Durell & Le Brun	1813–15
JUBILEE	50	schr	Southdown	1886	Jules Claireaunt	? – 1914
JUDGE THOMPSON	67	schr	Canada	1837	I. H. Gosset	1840–41
JUDITH	105	schr	Deslandes, Jersey	1837	Geo. Deslandes	1837–41
JUDITH & ESTHER	83	brigt	Deslandes, Jersey	1827	Geo. Deslandes	1827–31
JUDY	22	cutt	Sark	1829	J. Cort	?
JULIA	307	barq	Deslandes, Jersey	1840	Geo. Deslandes	1840–56
JULIA	59	cutt	Le Sueur, Jersey	1852	J. Chambers	1852–63
JULIA	48	brig	ex-prize (French)	—	Philip Bisson	1811–15
JULIA	45	cutt	Hamptonne, Jersey	1837	Capt. Small	1837–
JUNO	125	brig	Newfoundland	1820	Philip Nicolle	1823–34
JUNO	67	schr	Nova Scotia	1819	Philip Le Caux & others	1820–23
JUNO	20	cutt	Ricou, Jersey	1837	Josue de La Haye	1837–52
JUPITER	302	barq	Finland	1848	J. Brayn & Co.	1853–56
JUPITER	30	cutt	Jersey	1846	George Marie	1846–50
JUPITER	24	cutt	?	?	Fr. Le Feuvre	1856–59
JUST	122	brigt	Deslandes, Jersey	1859	Geo. Deslandes	1859–
JUVENTA	186	brigt	Deslandes, Jersey	1865	Deslandes & Hamon	1865–
KALAMAZOO	35	cutt	?	?	George Falle	1856–
KANAGONA	199	brig	Esnouf & Mauger, Jersey	1860	Philip Romeril	1863–
KASSA	324	barq	Esnouf & Mauger, Jersey	1868	Esnouf & Mauger	1868–
KING	67	schr	Le Sueur, Jersey	1858	? Le Seelleur	1859–70
KINGFISHER	40	schr	Jersey	1839	Philip Nicolle	1839–63
KINGFISHER	34	cutt	Jersey	1822	George Asplet	1825–31
KITE	245	brig	Deslandes, Jersey	1859	Geo. Deslandes	1859–70
KITE	177	brig	?	?	Nicolle & Dreland	1888–
KITTEN	139	schr	Esnouf & Mauger, Jersey	1864	Esnouf & Mauger	1864–65
KITTY	44	sloop	ex-prize	—	Edward Bedford	1817–18
KITTY	?	brigt	ex-prize (French)	—	Ph. Nicolle & Le Rossignol	1809– lost '09
KROO BOY	138	brigt	Le Vesconte, Jersey	1862	Le Vesconte	1862–65
LADY DOUGLAS	188	brig	Jersey	1862	Mallet, Leacroft & Romeril	1863–68
LADY FALKLAND	169	brig	Arichat, Cap Breton	1840	de Carteret & Le Vesconte	1840–56
LADY HARVEY	112	brigt	New Brunswick	1838	Wm Fruing & Co.	1838–41
LADY OF THE ISLES	44	dandy	Aubin, Jersey	1868	P. D. Payn	1868–
LADY SARAH	23	lugger	Jersey	1800	Cabot & Le Vesconte	1803–08

Continued on following pages

Jersey Owned Vessels in the 19th Century — continued

Name of Vessel	Tons Rig	Where built	When	Owners	Years
LALLA ROOKH	32 cutt	Isle of Wight	1828	Pettman & Russel	1859–
LARCH	249 barq	Paspébiac, Gaspé	1815	Chas. Robin & Co.	1819–26
LARCH	63 schr	Paspébiac, Gaspé	1841	Perchard & Vibert	1841–42
LARK	40 cutt	Le Huquet, Jersey	1847	Thomas Aubin	1847–54
LAURA	28 cutt	Jersey	1864	Chas. Whitley	1864–76
LAUREL	284 brig	ex-prize (Spanish)	—	Amiraux, Le Breton & Chevalier	1814–18
LAUREL	114 schr	Nova Scotia	1817	Wm. Le Brocq & N. Le Rossignol	1823–31
LAURITE	59 schr	Bellot, Jersey	1866	W. Downing	1870–77
LAVINIA	255 brig	Sunderland	?	Le Boutillier	1849–59
LAWRENCE	60 brig	ex-prize (French)	—	Bisson, Benest & Finnie	1803–04
LEADER	29 cutt	Jersey	1846	Philip & Thomas Jenne	1856–73
LEICESTER	186 barq	Chatham	1799	Cosnard & Janvrin	1815–19
LEOPARD	300 barq	Cowes	1848	Jean Bichard	1849–60
LEVERET	21 cutt	Plymouth	1838	Matthew Russel	1859–
LIBERTY	40 cutt	?	?	Francis Brown	1856–59
LIBERTY	24 cutt	?	?	George Martin	1835–38
LILIAN	58 schr	Deslandes, Jersey	1873	Elias P. Le Feuvre	1873–
LILY	45 dandy	Jersey	1863	Chas. Pirouet	1863–66
LILY	23 cutt	Picot, Jersey	1871	Delepine & Laffoley	1879–85
LILY OF THE VALLEY	54 dandy	Messervy, Jersey	1864	Cantell & Co.	1864–70
LIVELY	76 brigt	Cap Breton	1811	P. F. & J. Janvrin	1816–
LIVELY	73 schr	Gaspé	1821	Jean & Philip Perrée	1821–26
LIVELY	31 cutt	Jersey	1860	J. Clarey	1860–88
LIVELY	26 cutt	Esnouf & Mauger, Jersey	1863	Philip Renouf	1863–
LIVER	44 schr	Liverpool	1854	R. Alston	1859–60
LIVONIA	199 brig	Grangemouth, Scotland	1833	Le Feuvre & Henry	1859–63
LIVONIA	78 ketch	Le Sueur, Jersey	1872	D. Le Sueur	1872–79
LLOYD	? sloop	?	?	Philip & James Durell	1820–
LONDON	192 barq	America (ex-prize)	1806	A. de Ste Croix	1811–15
LONDON	68 cutt	Messervy, Jersey	1854	Renouf & Co.	1854–56
LONDON	59 dandy	Aubin & Bisson, Jersey	1866	de La Haye & Le Boutillier	1870–
LORD ANSON	133 schr	Deslandes, Jersey	1836	Chas. Mauger & Co.	1838–41
LORD CHARLES SPENCER	205 barq	Falmouth	1801	A. de Ste Croix	1809–15
LORD GAMBIER	35 ketch	Cowes	1807	Peter Bishop	1809–29
LORD JOHN RUSSEL	334 barq	New Brunswick	1835	Thomas Hayley	1849–52
LORD NELSON	85 brigt	ex-prize (Greenock)	1798	D. de Quetteville & others	1812–14
LORD NELSON	74 schr	Le Feuvre, Jersey	?	P. Le Feuvre	1824–26

Continued on following pages

Jersey Owned Vessels in the 19th Century — continued

Name of Vessel	Tons Rig	Where built	When	Owners	Years
LORD NELSON	71 schr	Broadstairs	1799	Chevalier, Nicolle & Wooldridge	1804–05
LORD NELSON	45 sloop	Brixham	1802	? Tonkin	1841–
LORD SAUMAREZ	207 brig	Vincent, New Brunswick	1835	John Godfray	1835–38
LORD SIDMOUTH	192 barq	Le Boeuf, Jersey	1815	Charles Pipon	1815–
LOTTERY	55 lugger	ex-prize	—	F. & P. & J. Janvrin	1803–10
LOTTERY	52 chasse marée	ex-prize (French)	—	Cosnard, Janvrin & Le Feuvre	1813–
LOTUS	41 cutt	?	?	W. Holt	1856–58
LOUISA	279 barq	Llanelly, Wales	1869	Buesnel & Le Quesne	1870–
LOUISA	199 brigt	Deslandes, Jersey	1847	Ennis & Nicolle	1847–
LOUISA	138 brigt	Henry, New Brunswick	1868	Wm. Fruing & Co.	1868–
LOUISA	60 cutt	Le Huquet, Jersey	1850	? Asplet	1850–
LOUISA	52 brigt	Arichat, Cap Breton	1820	Elias Neel & Geo. Macdonald	1821–33
LOUISA	21 cutt	Jersey	1858	Thomas Gore	1859–
LOUISA JANE	49 dandy	Picot, Jersey	1861	Le Couteur	1863–70
LOUISE ERNEST	58 ketch	St Malo, France	1877	? Tope	1920–32
LOUIS JENETT	472 barq	New Brunswick	1854	J. Hardy	1865–70
LOVE	34 cutt	Fauvel, Jersey	1853	Whitley & Co.	1856–63
LOVELY HARRIET	72 brig	ex-prize (French)	—	Renouf & Duhamel	1810–11
LOYAL	222 barq	Deslandes, Jersey	1853	Geo. Deslandes	1853–63
LOYAL WILLIAM	75 schr	Deslandes, Jersey	1831	G. J. Machon	1831–
LUCIE	75 brigt	Deslandes, Jersey	1831	G. J. Machon	1831–
LUCIE	30 schr	?	?	Chas. Robin & Co.	1863–70
LUCINDA	59 schr	Bellot, Jersey	1869	Downing & Morrisey	1869–76
LUCKNOW	641 barq	Sunderland	1858	Pellier & de La Taste	1859–63
LUCY	59 ketch	Salcombe, Devon	1879	S. Wertherall	1899–1906
LUTCHMI	432 barq	Esnouf & Mauger, Jersey	1850	Charles Mauger	1850–53
LYDIA	67 schr	Deslandes, Jersey	1836	Horman & Valpy	1836–40
LYDIA	39 cutt	Aubin, Jersey	1870	W. Wright	1870–88
MABEL	76 schr	Allix, Jersey	1875	H. Shapland	1879–
MAGDALEN	86 brigt	Arichat, Cap Breton	1815	P. & F. & J. Janvrin	1817–18
MAGDALENE	148 brig	ex-prize (Spanish)	—	? Janvrin	1804–07
MAGGIE	335 barq	Ilfracombe	1852	Orange & Co.	1853–63
MAGIC	181 brigt	?	?	Bellingham & Co.	1888–
MAID OF ALICANTE	93 schr	Jersey	1839	Rachel Machon	1846–
MAIN	33 cutt	Picot, Jersey	1860	Wm. Wright	1860–63
MARCO	58 schr	Valpy, Jersey	1854	M. P. Valpy	1854–56
MARGARET	28 cutt	?	?	George Le Seeleur	1835–
MARGARET	44 cutt	?	?	Starck & Messervy	1831–
MARGARET & JANE	36 schr	Gaspé	1833	? Janvrin	1841–
MARGARITTA & ESTHER	26 cutt	Padstow, Cornwall	1827	George Asplet	1838
MARGUERITE	92 brigt	Prince Edward Isle	1818	Peter Duval	1819–20
MARIA	177 schr	Le Masurier, Cap Breton	1830	J. Janvrin	1830–31

Continued on following pages

Jersey Owned Vessels in the 19th Century — continued

Name of Vessel	Tons Rig	Where built	When	Owners	Years
MARIA	51 smack	Cowes	1791	Chevalier & Nicolle	1803–05
MARIA ANGE	274 brig	Llanelly, Wales	1870	Buesnel & Le Quesne	1870–79
MARIA GEORGIANA	101 schr	Canada	1858	Le Boutillier & Co.	1863–79
MARIE	104 brigt	Arichat, Cap Breton	1833	J. Le Bas	1833–41
MARIE	25 schr	?	?	Le Boutillier & Co.	1840–
MARIE EMMA	35 schr	?	?	de Gruchy, Renouf & Clement	1888–
MARIE LOUISE	55 schr	Quebec	1837	Philip Le Brocq	1843–
MARIE VICTOIRE	57 schr	Canada	1823	Chas. Vibert	1829–38
MARINER	200 brig	Sunderland	1828	Philip Perchard	1829–31
MARKWELL	290 barq	Gaspé	1853	Chas. Robin & Co.	1853–63
MARQUIS OF TOWNSEND	71 lugger	ex-prize	—	Remon, Pipon & Hammond	1803–06
MARS	288 barq	Vardon & Le Huquet, Jersey	1839	Philip Pellier	1839–41
MARS	272 barq	ex-prize (American)	—	Renouf, Le Sueur & Collas	1812–15
MARS	104 brigt	Fowey, Cornwall	1799	Hemery Bros.	1807–08
MARS	50 cutt	T. Gavey, Jersey	1861	Bisson & Dawes	1863–70
MARTHA BRUDER	92 schr	Grimsby	1856	Mallet & Le Quesne	1865–76
MARY	120 schr	Deslandes, Jersey	1845	Grandin & Preston	1845–
MARY	84 brigt	Gaspé	1821	J. Bisson	1826–31
MARY	74 sloop	ex-prize	—	Thomas Mallet	1803–19
MARY	68 ketch	Sandwich, Kent	1858	W. Carby	1859–63
MARY	58 schr	Deslandes, Jersey	1843	Le Blancq & Le Riche	1844–56
MARY	37 cutt	?	?	J. Philipps	1856–
MARY	30 cutt	?	?	Philip Bertram	1831–35
MARY	25 schr	Cap Breton?	1843?	P. de Carteret	1845–
MARY	21 cutt	Valpy, Jersey	1816	Dolbel & Le Sueur	1816–21
MARY ANN	298 barq	New Brunswick	1855	Wm. Fruing & Co.	1856–63
MARY ANN	228 brig	Grandin, Jersey	1861	Le Sueur & Le Quesne	1863–70
MARY ANN	137 brig	Nova Scotia	1837	De Carteret	1840–44
MARY ANN	41 schr	Sauvage, Jersey	1850	Francis Sauvage	1850–
MARY ANN	22 cutt	Fauvel, Jersey	1853	J. Wallis	1853–63
MARY & ANNE	21 sloop	Cowes	1790	Anson, Gluyas & Thomas	1820–22
MARY ANN BRUFORD	190 barq	Barnstaple	1854	J. & F. Le Sueur	1859–63
MARY & ELIZABETH	35 cutt	Filleul, Jersey	1829	Payn & Touzel	1831–35
MARY & ELIZABETH	29 cutt	?	?	Sarah Williams	1838–41
MARY ELLEN	25 cutt	Milford, Wales	1835	R. Jenkins	1863–
MARY JANE	77 ketch	Le Sueur, Jersey	1866	Alston, Rumsey & Upton	1870–
MARY WATERS	89 schr	Padstow, Cornwall	1875	J. G. Renouf	1918–25
MASONIC	155 brigt	Grandin, Jersey	1857	Le Couteur	1857–63

Continued on following pages

Jersey Owned Vessels in the 19th Century — continued

Name of Vessel	Tons	Rig	Where built	When	Owners	Years
MASONIC	46	ketch	Le Sueur, Jersey	1862	J. D. Goode	1863–70
MASQUERADE	70	lugger	ex-prize (French)	—	George Le Cronier	1806–08
MASTERY	137	schr	Deslandes, Jersey	1836	Carré & Alexandre	1836–46
MATCHLESS	28	cutt	Jersey	1866	F. Buesnel	1866–70
MAUD	120	schr	Appledore, Devon	1896	J. P. Tocque	1896–1916
MAURICE	68	schr	Cap Breton	1815	Philip Godfray	1820–21
MAYFLOWER	170	schr	Deslandes, Jersey	1832	Geo. Deslandes	1832–35
MAYFLOWER	60	schr	?	?	Misson & Perchard	1835–
MEDEA	44	cutt	Looe, Cornwall	1803	Winter & Nicolle	1803–04
MEDORA	43	cutt	Belfast	1827	J. Blampied	1837–45
MEDUSA	121	brig	J. Valpy, Jersey	1818	N. Le Quesne	1818–35
MELVINA	137	brig	New Brunswick	1842	Wm Fruing & Co.	1842–48
MENAM	469	barq	Sunderland	1869	G. N. Le Quesne	1871–78
MENTOR	226	brig	ex-prize (French)	—	Ph. & Ed. Nicolle	1814–19
MENTOR	123	schr	Deslandes, Jersey	1850	Geo. Deslandes	1850–70
MERCURY	146	schr	Bermuda	1807	? Janvrin	1815–
MERIDA	182	brigt	Valpy, Jersey	1854	de Quetteville	1854–63
MERMAID	52	ketch	Aubin, Jersey	1868	J. Pascoe	1870–79
MERVENIA	97	schr	Aberdovery, Wales	1878	Wm. Fruing & Co.	1878–
MESSENGER	247	barq	Giffard & Laurens, Jersey	1830	P. & F. Janvrin	1830–38
MESSENGER	169	schr	ex-prize	—	Janvrin & others	1814–22
MESSENGER	155	brigt	Hamptonne, Jersey	1841	Balleine & Co.	1841–42
MESSENGER	119	brigt	T. Gavey, Jersey	1856	J. Brayn & Co.	1856–
MESSENGER	?	schr	Arichat, Cap Breton	1816	Robin & Hemery	1820–24
MESSENGER	29	cutt	Jersey	1864	Swain & Moses	1864–70
MIDDLETON	160	brig	Sweden ?	?	W. Bryant	1854–56
MILTON	149	schr	Bellot & Noel, Jersey	1863	Gallichan & Noel	1863–70
MINERVA	307	brig	Virginia, U.S.A. (ex-prize)	1809	Winter & Nicolle	1814–15
MINERVA	136	brig	Hamptonne, Jersey	1826	Jean Perchard	1826–35
MINERVA	62	schr	Cap Breton	1830	H. Vibert	1831–32
MINNIE F	25	schr	?	?	de Gruchy, Renouf & Clement	1888–
MINSTREL	307	barq	?	?	Philip Nicolle	1875–
MINSTREL	182	brig	Clarke, Jersey	1857	Orange & Pirouet	1859–63
MINSTREL	104	schr	?	?	N. Le Quesne	1815–
MIRIAM SMITH	47	schr	?	?	de Gruchy, Renouf & Clement	1888–
MISTLETOE	68	schr	Le Huquet, Jersey	1876	John Le Gros	1876–1901
MIZPAH	57	ketch	Le Sueur, Jersey	1883	Renouf & Sebire	1883–85
MODISTE	89	schr	Deslandes, Jersey	1849	Philip Ahier	1849–52
MONARCH	167	brig	St Malo, France	1822	F. Le Feuvre	1854–78
MORNING STAR	178	brig	Messervy, Jersey	1859	Messervy & Pallot	1859–63
MORNING STAR	51	dandy	Messervy, Jersey	1859	Cantell & Co.	1860–99
MOUNTAINEER	95	ketch	Rostock, France	1886	J. G. Renouf	1917–
MOUNTAINEER	60	schr	Newfoundland	1845	Philip Nicolle	1845–63

Continued on following pages

Jersey Owned Vessels in the 19th Century — continued

Name of Vessel	Tons Rig	Where built	When	Owners	Years
MYSTERY	22 cutt	?	?	William Swain	1856–58
NAGASAKI	1,114 ship	Quebec	1867	J. de Caen	1868–69
NAMELESS	148 brig	Deslandes, Jersey	1825	J. Anthoine	1825–31
NANCY	154 brig	ex-prize (Spanish)	—	Cosnard & Janvrin	1813–15
NANCY	143 ?	Gaspé	1825	Remon & Bertram	1825–26
NANCY	53 schr	Newfoundland	1799	Chas. Bisson	1806–07
NANCY	37 sloop	ex-prize (French)	—	John Sweetland	1808–11
NANCY	21 schr	ex-prize (French)	—	Chas. Dufeu	1815–18
NAPOLEON	233 brig	Esnouf & Mauger, Jersey	1834	C. Ramier	1834–38
NAUTILUS	38 cutt	Silk, Newfoundland	1819	Philip Nicolle	1826–38
NAUTILUS	20 smack	Gosport	1815	Goldie, Ranwell & Jenkins	1816–17
NAVIGATOR	207 barq	Cardiff	1865	J. &. F. Le Feuvre	1865–69
NAVIGATOR	145 brigt	Jersey	1839	Philip Le Caux	1840–41
N.B.	254 barq	Paspébiac, Gaspé	1848	Chas. Robin & Co.	1849–51
NELSON	195 snow	ex-prize (Spanish)	—	Hemery Bros.	1803–19
NELSON	150 brig	Esnouf, Jersey	1835	Edward Renouf	1835–41
NEPTUNE	287 barq	Le Feuvre, Jersey	1843	Le Feuvre & Co.	1856–63
NEPTUNE	259 brig	ex-prize (American)	—	Thomas Boxer Ray	1818–
NEPTUNE	146 brigt	Sunderland	1798	de Carteret & Others	1802–08
NEPTUNE	140 brigt	ex-prize	—	? Janvrin	1802–05
NEPTUNE	102 schr	Brixham	1815	John Chevalier	1819–35
NEPTUNE	88 schr	?	?	Nancy Roberts	1841–
NEPTUNE	68 ketch	ex-prize (French)	—	Renouf & Duhamel	1814–19
NEPTUNE	52 brig	ex-prize	—	Thomas Vibert	1807–08
NERIO	147 brigt	Deslandes, Jersey	1868	Geo. Deslandes	1868–70
NERIO	29 cutt	T. Gavey, Jersey	1861	J. Bisson	1861–88
NESTOR	20 cutt	Filleul, Jersey	1829	J. & N. Le Manquias	1829–
NETLEY	39 cutt	Brixham	1801	Moisson & Durell	1813–15
NEUHA	29 cutt	Isle of Wight	1829	Chas. Picot & Co.	1841–45
NEW EAGLE	23 smack	?	?	J. Chiverton	1831–
NEWHAM	148 brig	Wales	1855	Malzard, Le Maistre & Newham	1855–
NEW LEADER	58 schr	Bisson, Jersey	1873	Thomas Jenne	1873–99
NEWPORT	106 brigt	Le Masurier, Jersey	1847	J. Roissier	1838–44
NIGHTINGALE	21 cutt	?	?	G. Noel & Co.	1829–35
NIMBLE	45 cutt	Dartmouth	1843	de Gruchy, Renouf & Clement	1865–
NIMBLE	33 smack	?	?	J. & G. Bryant	1868–69
NIMBLE	22 cutt	Isle of Wight	1788	Alexandre & Hammond	1815–19
NIMROD	40 cutt	Newfoundland	1834	Philip Nicolle	1826–38
NIMROD	40 cutt	Gavey, Jersey	1864	R. Horner	1870–
NINUS	59 schr	Deslandes, Jersey	1840	de Quetteville	1840–41
NO JOKE	36 cutt	?	?	Wm. Fruing & Co.	1856–
NONPAREIL	23 cutt	?	?	Gore & Cabot	1856–63

Continued on following pages

Jersey Owned Vessels in the 19th Century — continued

Name of Vessel	Tons Rig	Where built	When	Owners	Years
NO ONE	30 pilot cutt	Silk, Jersey	1830	States of Jersey	1830–36
NORA	56 schr	Portsmouth	1845	?	?
NORMANDY	30 cutt	Jersey	1871	J. & A. J. Blampied	1879–
NORMAN GRAY	48 dandy	Rye, Sussex	1860	John Gray	1870–
NORTH STAR	? cutt	ex-prize (Danish)	—	?	1812–
NORTH STAR	169 schr	Deslandes, Jersey	1840	Picot & Tessier	1840–41
NOTTE	? schr	?	1840	John Fauvel	?
NO TWO	30 pilot cutt	Deslandes, Jersey	1830	States of Jersey	1830–
NOX	152	Deslandes, Jersey	1853	F. & N. Le Bas	1853–
NYMPH	449 barq	Laing, Sunderland	1852	Philip Pellier	1852–56
NYMPH	56 ketch	Wivenhoe, Essex	1844	Morgan Davies	1901–
OBEY	271 barq	Deslandes, Jersey	1858	Geo. Deslandes	1858–70
OCEAN	182 brig	Esnouf, Jersey	1828	N. Le Quesne	1828–
OCEAN	93 brigt	ex-prize (French)	—	Benest, Noel & Renouf	1803–
OCEAN BRIDE	334 barq	Clarke, Jersey	1854	Wm. Fruing & Co.	1854–70
OCEAN BRIDE	169 brig	Clarke, Jersey	1850	Le Boutillier & Co.	1850–
OCEAN BRIDE	47 cutt	Picot, Jersey	1858	Philip Wheeler	1859–63
OCEAN PET	83 schr	Picot, Jersey	1876	W. Pickford	1876–89
OCEAN QUEEN	159 brigt	Le Vesconte, Jersey	1865	Payn, Randall & Cantell	1865–
OCEAN QUEEN	122 brigt	Gaspé	1844	Le Boutillier & Co.	1846–
OFFOR	220 brig	Deslandes, Jersey	1861	Geo. Deslandes	1861–65
OLD TOM	120 schr	Gaspé	1834	Chas. Robin & Co.	1834–41
OLIVE BRANCH	196 brig	Esnouf, Jersey	1842	Charles Hamon	1842–
OLIVE BRANCH	125 brig	Gaspé	1821	W. Le Brocq	1822–23
OLIVE BRANCH	61 cutt	Plymouth	1812	John Dorward	1821–38
OLIVE BRANCH	52 cutt	Picot, Jersey	1858	George Wheeler	1859–
OLIVER BLANCHARD	268 barq	Paspébiac, Gaspé	1855	Chas. Robin & Co.	1855–66
OLIVER BLANCHARD	257 barq	Paspébiac, Gaspé	1868	Chas. Robin & Co.	1868–99
OLIVER BLANCHARD	250 barq	Paspébiac, Gaspé	1822	Chas. Robin & Co.	1822–38
ONESIME	62 schr	Gavey, Jersey	1853	Philip Gavey	1853–59
ONWARD	157 schr	Asplet, Jersey	1859	Philip Le Quesne	1859–63
ONWARD	146 brig	?	?	R. & H. Hoskin	1859–
ONWARD	30 cutt	Jersey	1865	Swain & Bishop	1865–70
ORACLE	129 schr	Jersey	1865	Francis Allix	1865–67
ORANGE BLOSSOM	47 cutt	Messervy, Jersey	1861	Cantell & Co.	1863–88
ORIENT	25 cutt	Le Huquet, Jersey	1853	Barbier & Dugué	1853–56
ORIENT STAR	102 schr	Bellot, Jersey	1872	P. Cabot	1872–79
ORIGIN	65 schr	Vautier, Jersey	1864	F. G. de Ste Croix	1864–65
ORLANDO	126 schr	Valpy, Jersey	1860	Francis Allix	1863–
OSPREY	42 cutt	Hamble, Southampton	1848	Bertram & Filleul	1848–59

Continued on following pages

Jersey Owned Vessels in the 19th Century — continued

Name of Vessel	Tons Rig	Where built	When	Owners	Years
OSTRICH	99 schr	Le Vesconte & Vautier, Jersey	1855	Nicolas Allain	1859
OSTRICH	36 cutt	?	?	Wm. Fruing & Co.	1856
OTHELLO	223 barq	Hamptonne, Jersey	1830	Neel & Deslandes	1830–32
OWNY BELLE	127 schr	Cardigan, Wales	1875	J. Vautier	1888–97
PABOS	42 schr	New Brunswick	1859?	Le Boutillier & Co.	1859–79
PAGE	109 schr	Valpy, Jersey	1856	M. P. Valpy	1856–
PALLAS	149 brig	Gavey & Grellier, Jersey	1815	Philip Nicolle	1815–59
PALLAS	62 ketch	Picot, Jersey	1871	Cantell & Co.	1871–1901
PALLAS	33 cutt	Isle of Wight	1837	Cantell & Young	1856–59
PALM	176 brig	Gaspé	1817	Chas. Robin & Co.	1819–26
PANDORA	106 schr	Bartlett, Jersey	1843	Chas. Mauger	1843–
PANDORA	99 schr	Esnouf & Mauger, Jersey	1856	Le Boutillier & Co.	1859–70
PANNY	63 schr	?	?	Geo. Deslandes	1841–42
PANOPE	164 schr	Grellier, Jersey	1840	S. J. Davidson	1840–41
PAPILLION	42 sloop	ex-prize (French)	—	Thos. Le Boutillier	1806–
PARANA	59 ketch	?	?	? le Bas	1853–
PASPÉBIAC	57 schr	Paspébiac, Gaspé	1872	Chas. Robin & Co.	1872–88
PATRIOT	95 schr	Canada	1838	Philip Tocque	1840–41
PATRUUS	206 brig	Vincent, Canada	1839	Chas. Robin & Co.	1839–88
PAVILION	50 schr	New Brunswick	1841	Le Boutillier & Co.	1841–44
P. DEAN	187 schr	Jersey	1841	P. H. Dean	1841–42
PEACE	60 schr	Paspébiac, Gaspé	1817	Chas. Robin & Co.	1826–88
PEARL	44 ketch	Jersey	1858	Le Masurier & de Gruchy	1858–
PEGGY	136 brigt	ex-prize (French)	—	Falle, Durell & Benest	1804–15
PEGGY	33 smack	Cowes	1791	Jean Bichard	1805–09
PEGGY	22 cutt	?	1841?	N. P. Le Vesconte & Son	1841–
PIERSON	49 ketch	?	?	E. Young	1888–
PEIRSON	41 cutt	Clarke, Jersey	1844	Thos. de Faye	1846–49
PELICAN	161 brig	J. Valpy, Jersey	1815	Chevalier, Amiraux & Le Breton	1815–22
PENELOPE	134 brigt	Vardon & Le Huquet, Jersey	1840	Huelin & Le Feuvre	1840–41
PERI	35 cutt	Southampton	1842	Francis Payn	1859–
PERI	34 cutt	?	?	Wm. Metherell	1856–70
PERSEVERANCE	195 brigt	Deslandes, Jersey	1847	Geo. Deslandes	1847–49
PETER & JANE	80 schr	Cap Breton	1823	de Carteret & Le Vesconte	1823–26
PETIT DESGRAT	55 schr	Cap Breton	1819	Godfray, Benest, Le Gresley & Duval	1821–22
PETREL	127 brigt	Prince Edward Isle	1846	E. P. Gaudin	1859–63
PHANTOM	508 barq	Sunderland	1857	Philip Pellier	1859– lost '59
P. H. DEAN	100 brig	Hamptonne, Jersey	1837	P. H. Dean	1837–56

Continued on following pages

Jersey Owned Vessels in the 19th Century — continued

Name of Vessel	Tons Rig	Where built	When	Owners	Years
PHILIPPE	72 schr	Deslandes, Jersey	1841	Geo. Deslandes	1841–
PHOENIX	110 schr	Guernsey	1819	Perchard & Bishop	1823–
PHOENIX	98 brig	?	?	William Holt	1859–
PHOENIX	96 lugger	ex-prize (French)	—	Janvrin & Hamon	1806–08
PILGRIM	43 ketch	Collas, Newfoundland	1830	Philip Nicolle	1830–63
PINK	29 cutt	ex-prize (French)	—	Le Rossignol & Hamon	1811–15
PLENTY TIME	28 cutt	?	?	John de Gruchy	1856–
PLOUGH BOY	111 schr	Valpy, Jersey	1849	M. P. Valpy	1849–55
PLOVER	30 schr	New Brunswick	1872	Philip Luce	1872–
POLPERRO	70 schr	Plymouth	1807	Moisson & Le Rossignol	1820–23
POMONA	190 brig	Hamon & Coutanche, Jersey	1835	Hamon & de Gruchy	1835–38
POMONA	130 brig	J. Gavey, Jersey	1819	Le Quesne & Hamon	1820–32
PORT	62 brigt	Leith, Scotland	1811	P. Le Feuvre	1830–35
POST BOY	96 schr	Topsham, Devon	1831	G. Mallet	1845–53
PRAIRIE FLOWER	138 brigt	Le Vesconte, Jersey	1864	F. Le Sueur	1864–70
PRAIRIE FLOWER	51 dandy	Aubin, Jersey	1868	Newmand & Drummond	1868–70
P.R.C.	111 brig	Paspébiac, Gaspé	1828	Chas. Robin & Co.	1830–66
PRESIDENT	50 cutt	?	?	? Gallichan	1853– lost '53
PRIDE	226 brig	Deslandes, Jersey	1856	Geo. Deslandes	1856–70
PRIDE	24 cutt	?	?	P. D. Payn	1863–
PRIMA	108 brig	Sunderland	1829	William Ranwell	1832–38
PRINCE	73 schr	Deslandes, Jersey	1840	Jean Bichard	1840–41
PRINCE	44 dandy	Aubin, Jersey	1867	Aubin, Richmond & Le Seeleur	1870–
PRINCE	30 cutt	Jersey	1859	Pallot & Co.	1859–
PRINCE OF BOUILLON	62 schr	Grellier, Jersey	1814	Gavey & Grellier	1814–
PRINCE OF THE SEAS	380 barq	Sunderland	1855	J. de Caen	1856–63
PRINCE OF WALES	41 cutt	Jersey	1842	C. Bisson	1842–46
PRINCE REGENT	79 schr	Plymouth	1811	J. Roissier	1829–35
PRINCESS ALEXANDRINA	45 cutt	Jersey	1840	G. Le Seeleur	1840–63
PRINCESS ROYAL	39 brigt	North Shields	1841	Deslandes, Godfray & Ennis	1845–47
PRISCILLA	97 schr	Esnouf & Mauger, Jersey	1848	William Pearce	1849–
PROGRESS	77 schr	Le Huquet, Jersey	1877	Fred Mollet	1877–79
PROPERTY	39 cutt	Brixham, Devon	1795	Aubin, Carrel & Durell	1807–08
PROSERPINE	70 schr	Ipswich	1847	E. Hogge	1870–
PROSPECT	48 cutt	T. Cavey, Jersey	1860	?	?
PROSPERO	192 brig	Clarke, Jersey	1862	Geo. Malzard	1862–70
PROVIDENCE	167 brig	Sandgate, Kent	1783	P. & F. & J. Janvrin	1810–12

Continued on following pages

Jersey Owned Vessels in the 19th Century — continued

Name of Vessel	Tons Rig	Where built	When	Owners	Years
PROVIDENCE	42 cutt	Brixham, Devon	1814	F. Le Caplain	1831–35
PROVIDENCE	? schr	ex-prize (French)	—	Jean Roissier	1808–09
PSYCHE	20 ?	Gaspé	1830	P. & J. Perchard	1836–
QUEEN	253 barq	Esnouf & Mauger, Jersey	1847	C. & W. & G. Le Quesne	1849–56
QUEEN	78 schr	Jersey	1846	Pallot & Le Seelleur	1856–63
QUEEN	60 cutt	Picot, Jersey	1879	P. E. Guille	1879–
QUEEN	31 cutt	Le Sueur, Jersey	1869	J. Vincent	1870–
QUEEN CHARLOTTE	75 cutt	Dover	1801	Alexandre & Co.	1822–26
QUEEN CHARLOTTE	27 smack	Cowes	1797	John Babot	1806–
QUEEN OF THE ISLES	80 ketch	Picot, Jersey	1873	Philip Pallot	1879–87
QUEEN OF THE SEAS	185 brig	Deslandes, Jersey	1865	Blampied, Vautier & Filleul	1865–70
QUICK	228 brig	Deslandes, Jersey	1864	Geo. Deslandes	1864–67
QUIXOTE	120 brig	New Brunswick	1828	P. Duval	1830– lost '30
QUIZ	93 schr	Clarke, Jersey	1841	Philip Binet	1841–42
RACER	147 schr	Grellier, Jersey	1839	Le Bailly & Le Bas	1839–63
RACER	54 ketch	Bellot, Jersey	1869	Chas. Whitley	1869–98
RACER	34 cutt	?	?	Cabot & Godfray	1870–
RACHEL	186 schr	Deslandes, Jersey	1841	Geo. Deslandes	1842–52
RAMBLER	254 barq	Esnouf, Jersey	1841	Edward Nicolle	1841–
RAMBLER	83 schr	Bellot, Jersey	1875	Chas. Whitley	1875 98
RAMBLER	61 schr	Vautier, Jersey	1865	Wm. Fruing & Co.	1865– lost '65
RAMBLER	30 smack	?	?	Richard Butt	1831–
RANAVALA	152 brig	Esnouf & Mauger, Jersey	1855	Esnouf & Mauger	1855–56
RANGER	270 barq	Hamptonne, Jersey	1831	Ph. Duheaume	1831–33
RANGER	185 brig	Stockton	1834	F. Drake	1853–54
RANGER	138 brigt	Paspébiac, Gaspé	1863	Robin, Collas & Co.	1863–79
RAPID	84 schr	Laing, Jersey	1837	Peter Le Bas	1840–41
RAPID	44 ketch	?	?	C. Laraman	1888–99
RAPID	31 cutt	Aubin, Jersey	1866	P. D. Payne	1870–
REAPER	137 brigt	Paspébiac, Gaspé	1864	Chas. Robin & Co.	1864–95
REAPER	68 schr	Valpy, Jersey	1846	M. P. Valpy	1846–48
RECOVERY	46 brigt	ex-prize (French)	—	Philip Bisson	1808–09
RECRUIT	60 schr	Bideford, Devon	1870	P. Luce	1870–71
RED BREAST	97 schr	Paspébiac, Gaspé	1824	Chas. Robin & Co.	1824–26
RED GAUNTLET	65 schr	Aubin, Jersey	1876	J. Adams	1876–77
REDWOOD	207 brigt	?	?	F. Le Sueur	1888–
REFLECT	390 barq	Deslandes, Jersey	1860	Geo. Deslandes	1863–67
REFORMATION	57 brigt	Cowes	1847	W. Downing	1851–62
REGALIA	66 ketch	Picot, Jersey	1872	Picot, Pallot & Erith	1872–79
REGINA	59 schr	Picot, Jersey	1866	H. P. Erith	1866–85
REINDEER	20 cutt	?	?	J. & J. Le Huquet	1856–59
RELIANCE	79 schr	Vautier, Jersey	1871	Wm. Fruing & Co.	1871–
RENARD	142 schr	Jersey	1839	Matt. Alexandre	1840–41
RENOWN	215 brigt	Thom, Guernsey	1867	J. Sebire	1888–

Continued on following pages

Jersey Owned Vessels in the 19th Century — continued

Name of Vessel	Tons	Rig	Where built	When	Owners	Years
RESCUE	1,187	ship	Newberry Port, U.S.A.	1860	Philip Pellier	1860–76
RESCUE	46	ketch	Cantel, Jersey	1866	Chas. Whitley	1866–98
RESOLUTE	76	schr	Le Huquet, Jersey	1877	Geo. Noel	1879–1905
RESOLUTION	41	cutt	ex-prize	—	J. Dorward	1825–38
RESOLUTION	?	sloop	ex-prize	—	Ph. Amy & Elias Gaudin	1815–17
RESOLUTION	37	cutt	ex-prize	—	Le Quesne, Le Rossignol & Noel	1803–07
RESOLUTION	37	cutt	ex-prize	—	Chevalier & Amiraux	1814–
RESULT	280	brig	Clarke, Jersey	1863	Anley & Co.	1863–
REVENUE	797	ship	Sunderland	1859	Philip Pellier	1859–63
REVERIE	53	cutt	Jersey	1866	?	?
REWARD	154	brig	Canada	1834	Fr. Bertram	1835–39
REWARD	76	cutt	?	?	M. Berry	1863–70
REWARD	39	cutt	Picot, Jersey	1870	W. Swain	1870–
RHINE	99	schr	Bavaria	1855	Le Quesne & Asplet	1855–56
RICHARD	95	brigt	Clarke, Jersey	1845	Godfray & Falle	1845–63
RICHARD COBDEN	53	schr	Allix, Jersey	1848	Allix & Amy	1848–49
RICHMOND	576	barqt	New Brunswick	1864	Stewart & Malcolm	1865–67
RIENZA	40	schr	St Vaast, France	1842	W. Bryant	1859–63
RIFLE	41	cutt	Le Huquet, Jersey	1860	J. J. Graut	1860–70
RINGMACHON CASTLE	106	schr	Cork, Ireland	1825	William Ranwell	1842–58
RIPPLE	54	ketch	?	?	—	1905
RISK	20	cutt	?	?	Bellingham & Co.	1888–
RIVAL	153	schr	Clarke, Jersey	1841	? Alexandre	1841–
RIVAL	38	schr	Le Vesconte, Jersey	1860	George Le Four	1860–70
RIVAL	32	cutt	Fauvel, Jersey	1857	John Asplet	1859–
ROBERT & HANNAH	45	ketch	Jersey	1861	Alston & Romney	1861–79
ROBERT WATT	221	brig	Quebec	1830	T. & P. Duhamel	1831–41
ROBIN	150	brigt	Paspébiac, Gaspé	1866	Robin, Collas & Co.	1870–96
ROBINSON	?	brig	?	?	Allix	1888–
ROCOU	154	brigt	ex-prize	—	John Dolbel	1803–06
ROEBUCK	132	brig	ex-prize	—	A. de Ste Croix	1812–13
ROLLA	164	brig	Vardon & Le Huquet, Jersey	1839	Giraudot & Miller	1840–41
ROLLING WAVE	87	schr	Gaurier, St Malo, France	1873	J. Nicolle & ? Ahier	1879–
ROLLO	75	schr	Deslandes, Jersey	1837	de Quetteville	1837–41
ROSAMUND	29	cutt	Brixham, Devon	1807	Chas. Pirouet	1859–63
ROSE	84	brigt	Cowes	1811	Jean Bichard	1826–
ROSE	81	cutt	London	1822	Philip Duheaume	1823–
ROSE	44	smack	Cowes	1802	Gavey & Amy	1808–09
ROSE	44	cutt	Southampton	1802	Hemery Bros.	1803–12
ROSE	80	schr	Cowes ?	?	de Gruchy, Le Vesconte & Le Sueur	1811–

Continued on following pages

Jersey Owned Vessels in the 19th Century — continued

Name of Vessel	Tons Rig	Where built	When	Owners	Years
ROSE	65 cutt	Jersey	1804	de Gruchy & Nicolle	1804–
ROVER	113 cutt	Looe, Cornwall	1808	Janvrin, Amiraux & Chevalier	1813–14
ROVER	66 schr	Esnouf & Mauger, Jersey	1854?	Le Quesne & Mauger	1854–
ROVER	48 lugger	ex-prize	—	Durell, Le Gros & Le Brun	1803–05
ROWCLIFFE	354 barq	Jersey	1798	A. de Ste Croix	1800–26
ROWENA	84 schr	Hamptonne, Jersey	1834	Philip Binet	1835–40
ROYAL	35 cutt	?	?	Pascoe & Le Huquet	1879–
ROYAL ARCH	46 ketch	Picot, Jersey	1866	J. F. Picot	1866–70
ROYAL BLUE JACKET	93 schr	White, Cowes	1854	de Gruchy, Renouf & Clement	1870–79
ROYAL CHARLOTTE	90 sloop	Dover	1795	Godfray, Le Boutillier & Le Couteur	1821–23
ROYAL GEORGE	55 schr	Deslandes, Jersey	1828	Hamon & Co.	1828–35
ROYAL SOVEREIGN	573 barq	Deslandes, Jersey	1848	Geo. Deslandes	1848–59
RUBINA	20 cutt	?	?	Cantel & Triggs	1856–60
ST ANNE	139 brigt	St Anne, Gaspé	1841	Le Boutillier & Co.	1842–61
ST ANNE	53 brig	?	?	P. Dumaresq	1834–
ST AUBIN	104 brigt	Giffard & Laurens, Jersey	1828	Le Caux & Carrel	1828–35
ST BRELADE	120 brigt	Henry, New Brunswick	1849	Wm. Fruing & Co.	1750–63
ST CATHERINE	107 schr	Jersey	1856	Clement Pallot	1856–63
ST CROIX	480 barq	Baxter, Jersey	1827	A. de Ste Croix	1827–63
ST CROIX	34 cutt	?	?	Fruing, Luce & Cort	1856–59
ST DEVENISH	246 schr	Ireland	1864	R. Allix	1887–98
ST GEORGE	127 brig	Luce, Gaspé	1832	Francis Ahier	1832–35
ST GEORGE	123 brig	Bisson, Jersey	1857	William Bisson	1857–59
ST HELIER	148 schr	Deslandes, Jersey	1843	Geo. Deslandes	1843–63
ST JOSEPH	64 ketch	Plymouth	1879	J. Amy	?
ST MARTIN	58 schr	Clarke, Jersey	1849	J. & G. Mallet	1843–49
ST PETER	117 schr	Jersey	1832?	F. Renouf & T. Le Feuvre	1856–63
ST PETER	114 brigt	Giffard & Laurens, Jersey	1832	Chas. Mauger & Dufeu	1832–35
ST SAVIOUR	46 cutt	Jersey	1854	Alexandre & Le Jeune	1854–59
ST VINCENT	478 ship	Clarke, Jersey	1867	Thos. Scrutton	1867–68
SAGE	38 cutt	?1	?	John Asplet	1856–59
SALLY	47 brigt	ex-prize	—	Bailhache & Lawrence	1804–05
SALVADOR PACKET	297 barq	Clarke, Jersey	1854	Josué Deslandes	1863–
SAMUEL	63 schr	England (for Royal Navy)	1809	William Ramwell	1824–28

Continued on following pages

Jersey Owned Vessels in the 19th Century — continued

Name of Vessel	Tons Rig	Where built	When	Owners	Years
SAMUEL	27 schr	Malbaye, Canada	1838	J. Perrée	1838–56
SAMUEL & JULIA	40 cutt	Plymouth	1815	James Sheer	1820–22
SAMUEL & MARY	24 cutt	Jersey	1844	S. Le Four	1848–
SAM WELLER	177 schr	Upham, Brixham, Devon	1864	W. G. Bellingham	1888–1907
SAPPHO	52 ketch	Le Sueur, Jersey	1879	J. Gaudin	1879–99
SARAH	46 schr	?	?	Barreau & de Fresne	1856–
SARAH	35 cutt	?	?	George Picot	1841–
SARAH	131 schr	Prince Edward Isle	1855	P. & E. Le Brocq	1856–
SARAH ANN	146 ?	Fecamp, France	1841	S. A. C. Picot	1865–69
SARAH HORNE	199 barq	Nova Scotia	1846	Renouf, Clement & Mauger	1864–
SARAH JANE	59 ketch	Cantell & Filleul, Jersey	1862	John Wright	1863–99
SARAH JANE	44 ketch	Jersey	1861	W. Pitman	1864–
SATELLITE	245 schr	?	?	R. Allix	1888–
SAUCY LASS	38 cutt	Aubin, Jersey	1870	Harvey & Stacy	1870–
SAUMEREY	37 cutt	ex-prize	—	Samuel Connors	1811–13
SCATARI	104 brig	Cap Breton	1821	Richard Le Bas	1822–23
SCOUT	48 cutt	Rye, Sussex	1859	Paskins & Snell	1860–63
SCUD	58 cutt	Gavey, Jersey	1862	Gavey & McKoewn	1863–70
SEABIRD	71 schr	Le Vesconte & Vautier, Jersey	1857	G. & F. de Ste Croix	1857–63
SEABIRD	70 schr	Aubin, Jersey	1873	Renouf, Oldridge & Le Quesne	1873–82
SEAFLOWER	352 barq	Renouf, Paspébiac, Gaspé	1873	Chas. Robin & Co.	1873–88
SEAFLOWER	163 brig	James Day, Gaspé	1826	Chas. Robin & Co.	1826–41
SEAFLOWER	126 brig	Paspébiac, Gaspé	1856	Chas. Robin & Co.	1856–65
SEAFLOWER	47 schr	Nova Scotia	1817	J. Le Sueur & George Binet	1820–22
SEAFLOWER	36 cutt	Jersey	1868	de La Haye & Le Masurier	1870–74
SEAFLOWER	25 schr	?	?	Chas. Robin & Co.	1888–
SEA LARK	41 cutt	Brixham, Devon	1816	Ireland & Co.	1822–
SEA NYMPH	56 schr	Aubin, Jersey	1877	Arms & Aubin	1877–78
SEA SEAL	42 cutt	Jersey	1865	Cotgrove & Milway	1870–
SECRET	212 barq	Deslandes, Jersey	1833	J. Anthoine	1832–35
SEEKER	58 schr	?	?	Waters & Gill	1901–
SENECA	103 brig	Sunderland	1820	Philip Perchard	1831–35
SEVEN BROTHERS	20 cutt	Deslandes, Jersey	1841	?	?
SHAMROCK	125 brigt	New Brunswick	1852	Wm. Fruing & Co.	1870–
SIBYL	84 schr	Bartlett & Bisson, Jersey	1840	Hamon & Esnouf	1840–41
SILK	110 schr	Thomas Silk, Jersey	1826	J. Ennis & Co.	1826–27
SILVER CLOUD	82 schr	Picot, Jersey	1873	Cantell & Co.	1873–85
SILVER EAGLE	57 schr	Ogier, Guernsey	1875	J. Lafolley	1890–
SILVER FIR	80 ketch	Matthews, Galampton, Devon	1885	P. Langlois	1890–

Continued on following pages

Jersey Owned Vessels in the 19th Century — continued

Name of Vessel	Tons Rig	Where built	When	Owners	Years
SIREN	192 brig	Vincent, New Brunswick	1830	Philip Perchard	1832–40
SIREN	113 brig	Esnouf, Jersey	1836	Edward Esnouf	1836–41
SIR ISAAC NEWTON	406 barq	Clarke, Jersey	1857	J. Le Bailey	1859–63
SIR JOHN FALSTAFF	229 brig	Redon, France	1868	A. Laurens	1870–71
SIR ROBERT PEEL	30 cutt	Le Sueur, Jersey	1868	Wm. Bowyer	1888–
SIR SYDNEY SMITH	112 smack	Isle of Wight	1807	Hemery Bros.	1812–16
SISTERS	73 schr	Prince Edward Isle	1823	J. Le Gros	1826–
SNIPE	37 ?	?	?	Frederic Janvrin	1838–
SNOWDROP	149 brigt	Le Huquet, Jersey	1873	D. Bisson & Co.	1879–88
SNOWDROP	72 schr	Jersey Harbour, Newfoundland	1817	Philip Nicolle	1818–26
SOPHIA	115 schr	J. Gavey, Jersey	1825	J. Moisson & Co.	1825–
SOPHIA	49 schr	Guernsey	1849	Dorey & Leigh	1849–
SOUTHERN CROSS	54 ketch	Barnstaple, Devon	1872	J. Millar	1876–88
SOUVENIR	153 schr	Allix, Jersey	1851	G. de Garis	1851–63
SOVEREIGN	43 dandy	Le Sueur, Jersey	1851	P. de La Cour	1851–56
SPARTAN	52 schr	Canada	1827	Logan Finnie	1835–37
SPECULATION	73 schr	ex-prize	—	Le Cordinier & Aubin	1814–
SPECULATOR	261 barq	ex-prize (French)	—	Janvrin & Others	1810–13
SPECULATOR	129 brig	?	?	J. Brehaut	1831–
SPECULATOR	38 cutt	Moore, Plymouth	1818	Philip Du Pont	1818–20
SPEEDWELL	27 cutt	Guernsey	1828?	Jean Machon	1835–
SPEEDY	74 schr	Gaspé	1872	Chas. Robin & Co.	1872–
SPEEDY	71 cutt	Jersey	1800	Chevalier & Nicolle	1805–07
SPEEDY	27 cutt	Clarke, Jersey	1859	J. Blampied	1873–
SPEEDY PACKET	99 schr	Valpy, Jersey	1842	Marett & Robin	1842–
SPEEDY PACKET	81 cutt	Cowes	1808	Philip Duheaume	1808–23
SPEEDY PACKET	80 cutt	Jersey	1800	Amiraux & Co.	1814–
SPEEDY PACKET	70 cutt	?	?	?	1793–1809
SPEY	167 brig	Garmouth, Scotland	1857	Renouf & Gaudin	1863–
SPITFIRE	75 ketch	Dartmouth	1881	?	?
SPRIGHTLY	25 cutt	Southampton	1805	John Harnett	1825–41
SPY	229 brig	Deslandes, Jersey	1841	Geo. Deslandes	1841–63
SQUAW	57 schr	Newfoundland	1814	Chas. Robin & Co.	1826–41
STAG	92 brigt	ex-prize	—	Geo. Collas & Henri Voy	1807–09
STANDARD	93 brigt	James Henry, New Brunswick	1861	Wm. Fruing & Co.	1861–63
STANDARD	67 ketch	Picot, Jersey	1877	S. P. Wright	1877–88
STAR	233 barq	Bordeaux, France	1853	A. Laurens	1865–66
STAR	24 cutt	?	?	T. D. Milway	1863–66
STELLA	22 dandy	builder unknown	1889	J. Pinel	1894–
STEST	101 brigt	Gainsborough, Lincoln	1753	Geo. Messervy	1803–05
STORM	45 schr	Paspébiac, Gaspé	1823	Chas. Robin & Co.	1826–56
STORMBIRD	113 schr	Picot, Jersey	1862	J. Le Boeuf	1862–63
STRANGER	227 brig	Bayonne, France	1854	Wm. Fruing & Co.	1856–59

Continued on following pages

110

Jersey Owned Vessels in the 19th Century — continued

Name of Vessel	Tons Rig	Where built	When	Owners	Years
STRATTON	181 brigt	Deslandes, Jersey	1847	Ennis & Jean	1847-
SUCCESS	51 smack	ex-prize	—	Le Mottee, Le Brun & Millais	1804-
SUCCESS	40 chasse marée	ex-prize (French)	—	Elias Durell	1812-
SULTAN	65 ketch	Picot, Jersey	1867	Pallot & Gavey	1867-88
SULTANA	153 brigt	Clarke, Jersey	1840	Le Gros & Romeril	1840-41
SUNDA	381 barq	Dumbarton, Scotland	1846	Philip Pellier	1851-56
SUNDERLAND	764 barq	Sunderland, Nova Scotia	1854	J. Wignal	1865-69
SUPERB	86 brig't	Valpy, Jersey	1818	Mauger & Dufeu	1831-
SUPPLY	105 schr	Le Vesconte, Jersey	1865	Thomas Messervy	1865-
SURINAM	169 barq	ex-prize	—	Chas. Hamon & Elias Durell	1811-12
SURPRISE	84 brigt	?	?	G. Le Gros	1826-35
SURPRISE	50 chasse marée	ex-prize (French built)	1805	Cosnard & Janvrin	1813-14
SURPRISE	40 ketch	Le Huquet, Jersey	1858	Henry Newman	1863-88
SUSAN	62 ketch	Picot, Jersey	1876	W. Swain	1879-
SUSAN	37 schr	?	?	W. Alexandre	1835-
SUSAN	87 brigt	?	?	Le Gros & Fruing	1831-41
SUSAN	129 schr	Le Sueur, Jersey	1849	Mallet & Poingdestre	1849-
SWALLOW	70 schr	?	?	Chas. Le Quesne	1856-
SWALLOW	62 schr	Cap Breton	1888	Ph. Le Montais	1888-96
SWALLOW	45 schr	?	?	Chas. Robin & Co.	1829-42
SWALLOW	34 schr	Cap Breton	1851	Chas. Robin & Co.	1856-63
SWALLOW	22 cutt	?	?	G. F. Balleine	1863-
SWAN	54 schr	Vardon & Le Huquet, Jersey	1841	Baudains & de Garis	1841-42
SWAN	46 schr	Picot, Jersey	1875	G. F. Balleine	1888-1901
SWIFT	177 barq	Deslandes, Jersey	1826	de Quetteville	1826-59
SWIFT	154 barq	Cap Breton	1862?	de Quetteville	1863-70
SWIFT	146 schr	Sunderland	1840	? Copp	1849-55
SWIFT	101 brigt	ex-prize	—	de Quetteville	1806-25
SYBIL	99 schr	Jersey	1840	N. J. Le Vesconte	1870-
SYDNEY	61 brigt	ex-prize	—	Chas. Matthews	1805-07
SYLPH	53 schr	Newfoundland	1840?	J. & C. Machon	1840-41
TAKE CARE	21 cutt	?	?	J. J. C. Laffoley	1856-
T.C.B.	27 cutt	Jersey	1863	T. C. Bennewith	1863-
TEASER	131 brig	Canada	1838	Le Boutillier & Co.	1840-63
TEASER	42 cutt	Jersey	1852	J. M. Cantell	1856-70
TELEGRAPH	162 brig	ex-slaver (1844)	—	Chas. Robin & Co.	1846-56
TELEGRAPH	155 brig	?	?	Chas. Robin & Co.	1859-63
TELEGRAPH	99 schr	?	?	Watts & Le Sueur	1870-99
TELEGRAPH	59 schr	Clarke, Jersey	1858	Watts & Le Sueur	1858-63
TELEMACHUS	54 schr	?	?	Dyer Ellyett	1838-
TEMPERANCE	133 schr	Deslandes, Jersey	1834	Jean Anthoine	1834-41
T.G.V.	198 brig	T. Gavey, Jersey	1859	Buesnel & Le Quesne	1859-63

Continued on following pages

Jersey Owned Vessels in the 19th century — continued

Name of Vessel	Tons	Rig	Where built	When	Owners	Years
THE JUST	47	brigt	ex-prize (French)	—	Philip Bisson (Jr.)	1808–09
THEMIS	178	brig	Nicolle, Jersey	1829	D. Janvrin & Le Bas	1829–41
THETIS	179	brig	Grellier, Jersey	1841	J. Sorel	1841–42
THETIS	175	?	Shaldon, Exeter	1812	Philip Perchard	1826– lost '26
THETIS	22	cutt	?	?	Lee & Perham	1835–
THOMAS & KATE	38	dandy	Le Sueur, Jersey	1868	T. J. Luen	1870
THREE BROTHERS	31	sloop	ex-prize	—	Ph. Gallichan	1804– lost '04
THREE BROTHERS	30	schr	?	?	Chas. Robin & Co.	1865–79
THREE FRIENDS	25	cutt	?	?	Ed. Le Rougetel	1835–
THREE SISTERS	220	brig	Guernsey	1820	Philip Arthur	1835–41
THREE SISTERS	76	schr	Nova Scotia	1801	Dean, de Caen & Trachy	1817–19
THRIFTY	22	cutt	?	?	Henry Baker	1863–
TICKLER	96	schr	Le Vesconte & Vautier, Jersey	1858	Le Boutillier & Co.	1858–63
TIDEFORD	40	cutt	Saltash, Plymouth	1832	Mark Walken	1847–58
TIGER (EX TIGRE)	224	barq	builder unknown	—	C. Le Quesne	1865–66
TIPHYS	111	brig	Deslandes, Jersey	1829	de Quetteville	1829–59
TIPHYS	94	schr	Jersey	1827	de Quetteville	1827–
TOKEN	127	schr	Deslandes, Jersey	1850	Geo. Deslandes	1850–63
TOM & MARY	114	brig	Sunderland	1809	Ph. Godfray & Ot's	1818–23
TOM & MARY	60	schr	Jersey	1846	Deslandes & Drelaud	1859–63
TOM & MARY	61	cutt	Jersey	?	Le Huquet & Filleul	1841–56
TOR ABBEY	140	snow	Plinymore, Devon	1799	Nicolle, Winter & Others	1803–12
TRAVELLER	180	brig	Gavey & Nicolle, Jersey	1825	Edward Nicolle	1825–35
TRIAL	40	cutt	Deslandes, Jersey	1843	N. H. Willet	1843–50
TRIO	155	brig	Esnouf & Mauger, Jersey	1857	Aubin, de Quetteville & Deslandes	1857–63
TRIO	81	schr	Le Sueur, Jersey	1877	de La Mare & Le Seeleur	1877–
TRIUMPH	52	ketch	Picot, Jersey	1874	P. J. Le Huquet	1879–
TROJAN	74	ketch	Totnes, Devon	1876	R. Denize	? (8 years)
TRUE BLUE	97	schr	Jersey	1855	N. J. Le Vesconte	1855–67
TRUE FRIEND	59	schr	Canada	1797	Robin, Janvrin & Poingdestre	1804–10
TRUST	79	schr	Deslandes, Jersey	1880	Geo. Deslandes	1880–
TRUST	58	schr	Jersey	1839	Francis Le Sueur	1840–41
TRUST	?	brigt	ex-prize	—	Janvrin, Nicolle & Winter	1810–11
TRUTH	205	barq	Canada	1796	Robin, Hemery & Luce	1803–08
TRY	60	schr	Port des Sables, France	1841	?	1862– lost '62
TURK	59	schr	Gosport, Hampshire	1842	George Asplet	1842–56

Continued on following pages

Jersey Owned Vessels in the 19th Century — continued

Name of Vessel	Tons Rig	Where built	When	Owners	Years
TWENTYNINTH OF MAY	249 barq	Hamon & Esnouf, Jersey	1833	Hamon & de Gruchy	1833–34
TWIG	107 brig	Woodbridge, Suffolk	1812	Philip Dean	1821–35
TWO BROTHERS	173 brig	?	?	J. & E. Collas	1849–59
TWO BROTHERS	160 brigt	ex-prize (Danish)	—	A. De Ste Croix	1808– lost '08
TWO BROTHERS	30 schr	Paspébiac, Gaspé	1880	Chas. Robin & Co.	1888– 1903
TWO BROTHERS	23 cutt	Guernsey	1824?	J. Le Vesconte	1835–
TWO FRIENDS	75 brigt	?	?	Le Vesconte & de Carteret	1831–35
TWO FRIENDS	52 smack	ex-prize	—	Chas. Perchard	1805–07
TWO FRIENDS	102 schr	St Malo, France	1876	E. Le Bas	1879–
TWO FRIENDS	207 brig	Jersey	1836	Francis Hocquard	1838–41
TWO SISTERS	27 cutt	Cantell, Jersey	1863	Cotgrove & Turnidge	1863–82
UBERTY	53 schr	Allix, Jersey	1873	Francis Allix	1873–
ULYSSES	167 barq	?	?	Blampied & Machon	1863–70
ULYSSES	135 brigt	Clarke, Jersey	1845	Pirouet	1845–
UMPIRE	32 cutt	Jersey	1856	W. Sims	1856–85
UNDINE	80 schr	Le Sueur, Jersey	1867	Philip Wheeler	1878–80
UNICORN	136 schr	Brouard, Cap Breton	1840	Edward Nicolle	1841–
UNION	198 brig	Sunderland	1825	Philip Perchard	1826–
UNION	193 brig	Picot, Jersey	1865	Chas. Robin & Co.	1865– 1900
UNION	84 brigt	ex-prize (Spanish)	—	Villeneuve & Mallet	1804–05
UNION	47 chasse marée	ex-prize (French)	—	Cosnard & Janvrin	1811–
UNITED	208 brig	Clarke, Jersey	1841	Jersey Shipping Co.	1841–42
UNITED	58 ketch	Le Sueur, Jersey	1857	Chas. Whitley & Co.	1857–88
UNITY	50 brigt	Gaspé	1839	J. Roissier	1839–42
UNITY	66 schr	Fowey, Cornwall	1811	Geo. Wooldridge	1822–26
UNITY	33 cutt	Le Huquet, Jersey	1870	Amy & Le Seelleur	1870–70
VELOCITY	24 cutt	Wallis, Jersey	1845	J. Barbier	1856–
VENUS	215 brig	ex-prize (French)	—	Winter, Nicolle, Janvrin & Benest	1813–17
VENUS	197 brig	J. Gavey, Jersey	1822	Philip Nicolle	1822–63
VENUS	183 brig	?	?	W. Keane	1863–
VENUS	65 brigt	Grellier, Jersey	1813	Elias Durell & A. de Ste Croix	1813–15
VENUS	50 smack	Cowes	1791	J. Dolbel & P. Le Brun	1803–06
VENUS	33 ketch	Jersey	?	H. P. Erith & S. J. Le Gros Park	1856–63
VESTRAL	54 schr	Newfoundland	1827	Philip Nicolle	1830–33
VIBILIA	94 brigt	Guernsey	1844	Jane Wimble	1844–
VICTORIA	207 brig	Le Vesconte, Jersey	1862	Journeaux & F. Le Sueur	1862–70
VICTORIA	120 schr	Deslandes, Jersey	1843	Geo. Deslandes	1843–59

Continued on following pages

Jersey Owned Vessels in the 19th Century — continued

Name of Vessel	Tons Rig	Where built	When	Owners	Years
VICTORIA	130 schr	Deslandes, Jersey	1838	Geo Deslandes	1838–42
VICTORIA	35 cutt	?	?	J. Blampied	1856–
VICTORIA SUTTON	20 schr	?	?	Le Boutillier & Co.	1863–70
VICTORY	40 cutt	ex-prize	—	Philip Bisson	1814–26
VICTORY	40 cutt	ex-prize (French)	—	Coutanche & Amy	1812–15
VICTORY	36 schr	ex-prize (Spanish)	—	Mourant & Renouf	1806–
VICTORY	34 cutt	Fauvel, Jersey	1852	Chas. Whitley	1852–70
VICTORY	21 cutt	?	?	Dickerson & Luce	1835–
VICTORY	23 cutt	Jope, Jersey	1826	Denis Blampied	1826–
VIGILANT	71 cutt	Cowes	1811	F. Le Sueur & J. Bichard	1826–41
VIGILANT	25 cutt	Jersey	1858	J. Wright & S. Davy	1863–70
VINCENT	68 schr	Vincent, Gaspé	1837	Chas. Robin & Co.	1837–41
VIRGILIA	512 barq	Deslandes, Jersey	1867	Geo. Deslandes	1867–70
VIRGIN BELLE	58 schr	?	?	de Gruchy, Renouf, & Clement	1888– 1901
VIRGINIA	153 brig	Canada	1833	C. F. Ramié	1835–40
VIRGINIA	30 cutt	?	?	Thomas Blampied	1831–
VIRGINIA	29 sloop	ex-prize (French)	—	Thos. Luce & Amice Le Grand	1808–09
VITULA	77 brigt	Cap Breton	1853	Philip Renouf	1859– lost '59
VIVID	197 brig	Asplet, Jersey	1859	George Asplet	1859–62
VIVID	102 schr	?	?	George Asplet	1865–66
VOLANT	226 brig	New Brunswick	1860	F. C. Gallichan	1863–66
VOLANT	52 dandy	Picot, Jersey	1867	A. Anderson	1870–
VOLUNTEER	60 schr	Allix, Jersey	1847	N. J. Le Vesconte	1849–63
VOLUNTEER	20 cutt	?	?	William Bowyer	1863–
VOYAGEUR	295 barq	Esnouf & Mauger, Jersey	1850	J. Le Bailly	1851–59
VULTURE	104 lugger	Jersey	1803	Janvrin & Durell	1807–16
WAG	71 brigt	Paspébiac, Gaspé	1815	Chas. Robin & Co.	1816–
WAR HAWK	66 schr	Martel, Cap Breton	1829	Le Vesconte & de Carteret	1813–
WARRIOR	163 schr	Newport, Mons.	1847	Renouf, Clement & Mauger	1863–70
WARRIOR	146 brig	Hamptonne, Jersey	1828	Philip Arthur	1828–31
WARRIOR	92 schr	Gaspé	1855	J. & E. Collas	1859–79
WASP	36 schr	Vincent, Gaspé	1840	Chas. Robin & Co.	1841–
WATERSPRITE	26 cutt	Jersey ?	1838?	Philip Messervy	1838–45
WATERWITCH	124 brig	Shoreham, Sussex	1831	de Quetteville	1834–41
WATERWITCH	58 schr	Gaspé	1842	Ellyett & Wallis	1842–
WAVE	24 cutt	Jersey	1859	Vincent & Viney	1859–63
WAVE QUEEN	84 schr	Le Vesconte & Vautier, Jersey	1854	Fr. Touzel & Co.	1854–59
WAVERLEY	80 schr	Le Huquet, Jersey	1873	F. J. Mollet	1873–74
WEASEL	76 schr	Tonkin, Cardiff	1871	P. Luce	1871–74
WELCOME	114 brig	Vardon & Le Huquet, Jersey	1840	J. Godfray	1840–41

Continued on following pages

Jersey Owned Vessels in the 19th Century — continued

Name of Vessel	Tons Rig	Where built	When	Owners	Years
WELCOME	130 schr	?	?	M. Morrissey	1888–
WELCOME	38 ketch	Jersey	1866	A. Swanger	1870–99
WELSH GIRL	65 schr	Jersey	1868	Larraman & Paskins	1870–
WESLEY	70 schr	Jersey	1858	Thomas Lavan	1861–63
WESLEY	41 ketch	Le Sueur, Jersey	1865	E. Mourant	1879–
WEST INDIAN	324 barq	Sunderland	1854	J. de Caen	1856–63
WHIFF	22 smack	Jersey	1866?	J. Morel	1866–
WHISPER	27 cutt	?	?	W. F. Helleur	1856–59
WHYDAH	140 brigt	Deslandes, Jersey	1863	Geo. Deslandes	1863–73
WHY NOT?	105 schr	Le Huquet, Jersey	1862	J. Pallot	1862–63
WILD WAVE	? brig	St Malo, France	1875	G. Ahier	1875–
WILLIAM	210 brig	Bisson, Jersey	1856	William Bisson	1856–85
WILLIAM	46 cutt	Grimsby	1853	Bellingham & Co.	1862–65
WILLIAM & FRANK	21 cutt	?	?	Charles Butt	1856–62
WILLIAM & MARIA	22 cutt	?	?	W. S. S. Banks	1856–63
WILLIAM DUMARESQ & CHARLES	37 sloop	ex-prize (Spanish)	—	Philip Bisson	1809–15
WILLIAM FRUING	792 ship	Vautier, Jersey	1867	Wm. Fruing & Co.	1867–70
WILLIAM PITT	198 brig	Collas, Gaspé	1840	J. Perrée	1840–45
WILLIAM'S ADVENTURE	50 schr	Lowestoft	1798	W. Fowler	1853–54
WILLIAM WOOLEY	199 brig	Poole, Dorset	1839	J. Anley	1851–56
WILLING	243 barq	Deslandes, Jersey	1849	Geo. Deslandes	1849–59
WILLING	99 schr	Bellot, Jersey	1868	G. J. Cantell	1868–70
WINDSOR	58 ketch	Gavey, Jersey	1865	? Gavey	1865–
WINDSOR	45 cutt	?	?	C. Pirouet	1863–
WINIFRED	44 ketch	Picot, Jersey	1883	Ph. Bailhache &. Co.	1883–88
WISDOM	23 cutt	Jersey	1860	Mark Cantell	1860–75
WITCH	46 schr	?	?	Chas. Robin & Co.	1829–33
WITCH	42 cutt	Wivenhoe, Essex	1836	W. Swanezy	1848–57
WONDER	20 cutt	?	?	J. Le Masurier	1856–63
WYVERN	83 cutt	?	?	J. Ennis	1834–40
WYVERN	21 cutt	Farley, Jersey	1888	Venables Vernon	1888–
XANTHE	30 schr	?	?	C. de Gruchy	1856–
XARIFA	208 brigt	Bartlett, Jersey	1841	J. Bichard	1847–
YOUNG CHARLES	90 schr	ex-prize	—	A. Le Rossignol & Ph. Hacquoil	1804–09
YOUNG ELIZA	60 sloop	ex-prize	—	Durell & de Gruchy	1808–09
YOUNG LOUISA	178 brig	Legue, France	1844	Kingsworthy, Le Huquet & Barreau	1863–65
YOUNG MESSENGER	84 schr	Cap Breton	1823	Chas. Robin & Co.	1823–32
YOUNG PEGGY	64 brigt	ex-prize	—	G. Le Cronier & J. Laugie	1804–35
YOUNG PHOENIX	183 barq	Jersey	1802	P. & F. & J. Janvrin	1803–18
YOUNG WITCH	51 schr	Bisson, Cap Breton	1832	Chas. Robin & Co.	1832–79
YOUTH	156 brigt	Deslandes, Jersey	1855	Geo. Deslandes	1855–60
ZARAH	347 barq	Sunderland	1846	Philip Pellier	1851–56
ZEAL	144 brigt	Deslandes, Jersey	1858	Geo. Deslandes	1858–70

Continued on following page

Jersey Owned Vessels in the 19th Century — continued

Name of Vessel	Tons Rig	Where built	When	Owners	Years
ZEBRA	58 dandy	Aubin, Jersey	1852	Chas. Aubin	1858–69
ZEBRA	44 cutt	Clarke, Jersey	1852	Philip Gallie	1852–
ZEBRA	29 cutt	?	?	Laurains & Aubin	1841–47
ZEGRI	110 brigt	Liverpool	1859	D. Perchard	1865–
ZEPHYR	161 schr	Laing, Jersey	1837	Thomas Silk	1837–
ZEPHYR	148 schr	Bellot & Noel, Jersey	1865	J. G. Falle	1865–79
ZEPHYR	44 cutt	Allix, Jersey	1850	P. J. Gallie	1850–53
ZEPHYR	28 ketch	Le Sueur, Jersey	1869	L. Gauvrey	1885–
ZIBIAH	105 brigt	Bartlett, Jersey	1848	Tonkin & Robin	1848–63
ZIGZAG	53 schr	?	?	Le Boutillier & Co.	1849–51
ZINGARA	174 brigt	Le Vesconte, Jersey	1865	F. Le Sueur	1865–88
ZIPPORAH	72 schr	Paimpol, France	1892	C. Allen	1892–95

EARLY JERSEY OWNED STEAMSHIPS

Name of Vessel	Tons	When owned	Owners	Further details
ARIADNE	133	1824–31	Ph. Nicolle and Others	built by W. Evans, Surrey, 1824
COMETE			Jersey Steam Packet Co.	re-named 'Granville'
DUMFRIES			Jersey Steam Packet Co.	sold Southampton 1863
DON	24	1851	Clarke & Rose	built by Clarke — first steamer built Jersey
EDINBURGH CASTLE	54	1849	Jersey Steam Navigation Co.	
EUREKA		1890	Edward Huelin	built by Huelin, Kensington Place, sold Plymouth '99
EXPERIMENT		1859	George Ennis	built by Ennis, iron hull
GEORGE CANNING	81	1832	William Ranwell	
LORD BERESFORD	81	1824–31	Matt. Amiraux & Co.	built by W. Scott & Sons, Bristol
POLKA		1850		tug, wrecked on Minquiers
PRINCESS ROYAL	39	1845	Jos. Deslandes	
ROSE	84	1851	Thomas Rose	built by Clarke
SOUTHWESTERN	105	1863	Esnouf & Mauger	
SUPERB		1850		wrecked on Minquiers '50
SURPRISE	71	1872	P. J. Grandin	build by Grandin, first tower 7 March, 1872
TOBY	64	1863	Deslandes, Falle & Le Sueur	built Greenwich 24 November, 1855
VENUS			Jersey Steam Packet Co.	
HEATHER BELL	95	1867	Jersey & Continental Steam Packet Co.	transferred to London '69

PRINCIPAL SHIPOWNERS IN THE 19TH CENTURY

Name	Years	Place of business
Ahier, Philip	1849–79	
Alexandre, Matt. & Co.	1831–49	St Peter
Allix, Francis	1848–79	Havre-des-Pas
Allix, George	1865–85	
Amiraux, & Co.	1793–1831	King Street
Anthoine, Jean	1825–49	41 Quai des Marchands
Arthur, Philip	1826–49	Longueville
Asplet, George	1826–65	Gorey
Le Bas, Jean	1831–54	Linden Hall
Le Bailey, Josua	1839–70	
Bellingham, E. J.	1863–79	St Helier
Benest, Jean (fils Jean)	1814–31	
Benest, Jean (fils Frs.)	1798–1830	
Bertram, Charles	1826–30	
Bertram, Francis	1830–50	Esplanade
Bichard, Jean	1819–50	
Binet, Philip	1840–45	
Bishop, Pierre	1792–1834	
Bisson, Charles	1805–40	
Bisson, James & Co.	1807–26	
Bisson, Philip	1790–1826	
Bisson, William	1857–85	St Aubin
Bisson, Dawe & Co.	1863–1903	
Black, Archibald	1813–42	New Street
Le Boeuf, Matthew	1808–21	St Helier
Le Boutillier, J.	1832–79	
Brayn, J.	1849–56	
Bree, Philip	1830–45	Hill St.
Bryant, G. T.	1875–85	
Bryant, William	1846–63	Bath Street
Buesnel & Le Quesne	1859–79	
Buths, John & Co.	1863–85	Gorey ?
Cantell, & Co.	1863–99	Gorey
Carre, Alexandre & Co.	1833–40	
Carrel, Francis & Co.	1830–70	High Street, St Aubin
Le Caux, P. & Co.	1820–52	High Street, St Aubin
Chevalier Charles	1792–1820	
Collas, George	1808–15	
Collas, J. & E. & Co.	1863–86	St Mary
Collas, J. P.	1812–35	
Cosnard, Jean	1803–20	St Aubin and 2 Quai des Marchands
Le Couteur, Philip	1820	
Le Cronier, George	1804–26	
Dean, Philip	1778–1858	St Aubin
De Caen, Jean	1832–1868	High Street, St Aubin
De Carteret, E.	1830–45	
De Carteret, Philip	1812–15	
De Faye, Thomas	1846–85	

Continued on following pages

Principal Shipowners in the 19th Century — continued

Name	Years	Place of business
De Garis, George	1842–51	
De Gruchy, A.	1849–79	
De Gruchy, Thomas	1793–1811	
De Gruchy, Renouf & Clement	1865–85	
De La Perrelle, E.	1865–80	
De La Taste, P. M.	1858–69	40 Esplanade
Deslandes, George	1827–70	51 vessels owner built
De Ste Croix, Aaron	1790–1828	builder, owner, ropemaker. Green Street
De Ste Croix, P. & J. & F. . .	1828–70	sons of Aaron
Du Hamel, T. & P. & Co. . .	1826–39	cons. of St Helier
Du Heaume, Philip	1807–85	father and son
Dumaresq & Hammond . . .	1786–1800	
Durell, Elie	1792–1819	7 Pier Road
Durell, Philip	1793–1814	
Duval, Peter	1820–30	
Ennis, George	1819–59	1 Quai des Marchands
Ennis, James	1826–31	La Prairie, rue de Haut, St Lawrence
Esnouf & Mauger	1827–70	Esplanade
Falle & Co.	1826–70	
Fauvel, John	1831–72	Gorey
Le Feuvre, F. & J.	1840–70	St Aubin
Filleul, Thomas & Co. . . .	1826–54	
Fruing, William & Co. . . .	1831–1900	30 vessels, 8 Caladonia Pl.
Le Gallais, John	1809–26	
Gallichan, M. & Co.	1849–62	
Gallichan, E. C. & Co. . . .	1863–	
Gaudin, E.	1859–79	
Gavey, P.	1863–70	
Gavey, Thomas & Co. . . .	1865–99	
Giffard & Le Quesne	1855–70	
Godfray, Philip	1819–35	Queen Street
Gosset, I. S.	1831–42	3–4 Quai des Marchands
Le Gros, George	1826–40	
Le Gros, J.	1869–1901	
Hamon, Charles	1826–44	
Hemergy, J. & C. & Co. . . .	1790–1819	Hill Street
Hocquard, Fr.	1819–40	Bulwarks, St Aubin
La Huquet, P. J. & Co. . . .	1863–85	
Janvrin, Daniel	1811–26	Royal Square
Janvrin, Fr.	1790–1830	
Janvrin, Jean	1803–30	High Street, St Aubin
Janvrin, Philip	1790–1830	11 Quai des Marchands
Jean, Edward	1835–49	Quai des Marchands
Lavan, Thomas	1863–79	
Luce, Philip	1852–70	
Machon, J.	1831–87	
Le Maistre, P.	1863–79	also Liverpool ?
Mallet, F.	1842–99	

Continued on following pages

Principal Shipowners in the 19th Century — continued

Name	Years	Place of business
Mallet, Thomas	1792–1819	
Le Masurier, Josua	1804–12	Gorey
Le Masurier, P.	1870–1903	
Mauger, Charles	1832–63	
Messervy, Thomas	1859–99	
Mollet, F.	1870–85	
Mourant, Jean	1804–06	
Moisson, Jean	1813–26	
Neel, Elias & Co.	1814–34	Castle Street
Nicolle, Edward	1792–1830	26 Quai des Marchands
Nicolle, Philip Winter	1803–1850	9 Pier Road, 3, 4, 13, 16, 28, 30 and 31 Quai des Marchands
Noel, George	1849–63	Gorey
Orange, Jean & Co.	1840–63	Bond Street
Orange & Briard & Co.	1863	Esplanade
Pallot, Clement	1858–85	Gorey
Pallot, Philip	1870–85	
Pellier, Philip	1826–63	Wharf Street and London
Perchard, Philip	1821–45	
Perree, Jean	1826–45	St Mary
Picot, J. F.	1870–1902	Gorey
Picot, S. A. C.	1863–79	
Pirouet, C. & Co.	1840–70	
Pugsley, W. T.	1870–1902	Caledonia Pl.
Le Quesne, C.	1863–79	
Le Quesne, Nicolas	1808–50	5 Quai des Marchands
Le Quesne, G. N.	1863–91	
De Quetteville, Philip	1826–70	Quai des Marchands
De Quetteville, David	1792–1830	2, 9, 10 Quai des Marchands
Ramier, C. F.	1832–35	Halket House, King Street
Ranwell, W.	1826–42	ex-naval Officer
Remon, James	1788–1826	St Aubin
Renouf, Edward	1803–26	Bond Street
Renouf, Josua	1840–63	Grove Street
Renouf, J. C. & G. J.	1885–1903	
Robin, Ch. & Co.	c.1760–1910	97 vessels St Aubin and Canada
Roissier, J.	1808–44	Sand Street
Romeril, Philip	1862–1903	
Le Rossignol, Augustin	1803–1819	
Le Rossignol, Matthew	1828–42	
Sauvage, Francis	1850–51	St Aubin
Le Seelleur, George	1846–1900	
Silk, Thomas	1837–	St Helier
Simon, J.	1834–50	St Peter
Le Sueur, Francis	1826–85	
Le Sueur, J.	1822–46	St Lawrence
Swain, W.	1870–85	Gorey
Tocque, J. P.	1853–1914	St James Street

Continued on following page

Principal Shipowners in the 19th Century — continued

Name	Years	Place of business
Turner, J.	1863–79	
Valpy, M. P.	1842–65	
Vautier, J.	1865–85	
Le Vesconte, Philip	1831–63	
Villeneuve, Jean	1792–1809	St Aubin
Whitley, Charles	1857–98	St Martin
Wright, J.	1865–1900	
Wheeler, Philip G.	1863–78	Gorey
Wooldridge, George	1805–26	
Young, G. W.	1862–1900	

SHIPBROKERS, AGENTS, MERCHANTS, ISLANDERS OR WITH ISLAND CONNECTIONS[2]

Name	Location	Occupation	Years (c.)
ALEXANDRE, Joshua	Shippegan, N.B.	Merchant	1847
AMY, John	Bond Street, Jersey	Agent	1866
BARBIER, Philip	15 Mulcaster Street, Jersey	Broker	1863
BELLINGHAM, E. G.	Weighbridge, Jersey	Broker/Owner	1847
BERTRAM, A.	19 Fenwick Street, Liverpool	Broker	
CARREL, F. P.	Bute Street, Cardiff	Broker	
DEAL, J. W.	Southampton	Broker	1865
DEAN & MILLS	41 Chapel Walks, Liverpool	Broker	
DEAN, P. & H.	15 Fenwick Street, Liverpool	Broker	1865
FRANCIS, R. J.	Brunswick Street, Liverpool	Broker	1879
GAMBELL & LE BOUTILLIER	Liverpool	Brokers	
GODFRAY, H. C.	19 Commercial Street	Agent	1837
HACQUOIL, J. P. & F. P.	Cardiff	Coal Merchants	1880
HUE, Charles	Rio de Janeiro	Broker	1878–1880
MAISTRE (LE) & CO.	3 Fenwick Street, Liverpool	Brokers	1879–85
MARETT, Edward	5 Church Street, Jersey	Agent	1865
MOISSON, J.	Weighbridge, Jersey	Broker	1865
MOREL, J.	Cardiff	Brokers/Owners	1866
NOEL, Philip	Bond Street, Jersey	Agent	1866
ORANGE & BRIARD	Bond Street, Jersey	Agent	1866
PUGSLEY, W. G.	Weighbridge	Broker	1881
RAY (LE), J. W.	Bristol	Broker	1858
WIMBLE, John	Bond Street, Jersey	Agent	1860–68

Banks of Local Origin[3]

Some shipowners, needing loans to finance the building of new vessels for their expanding fleets, joined with other merchants to form local banks. The first such bank was known as the Commercial Bank. This company opened its doors in June 1809 and was owned by Hugh Godfray, a wine merchant who had been in that trade since 1797. By 1814 three banks were in business in the Island, and later nearly one hundred banks, parishes, firms, associations and individuals were issuing notes at one period. Sixty of these concerns were in the Town and some thirty-five in the Country. The States brought in measures to control and curtail the indiscriminate issue of paper money and soon only the true banking companies remained until the financial crash of 1873, which came after the failure of the States Harbour Scheme at La Collette and the losses in the sailing ship era as steam took the place of sail.

Channel Islands Bank. Library Place. Owned by Horman, Anthoine, Ahier, Le Gros & Co., bought by the Midland Bank.

Commercial Bank of Jersey. Owned by Hugh Godfray 1809; Janvrin & Durell 1820s; Robin Bros. 1870; bought by the Westminster Bank, 1908.

English & Jersey Union Bank. 5 Brook Street. Owned by Le Nevue, Sorel & Co. 1862; into Liquidation 1873.

Jersey Banking Company. Owned by Nicolle, de Ste Croix, Bertram & Co., known as 'States Bank'.

Jersey Joint Stock Bank. Broad Street. Owned by Elias Neel; bought by Lloyds 1873.

Jersey Mercantile Union Bank. Owned by Josué Le Bailly; into Liquidation 1873.

Jersey Old Bank. Hill Street; owned by Charles Godfray; bought by **Channel Islands Bank** 1879; bought later by the Midland Bank.

Figurehead of 'Reflect', a barque of 390 tons, built & owned by George Deslandes, 1860. Totally wrecked off Buenos Aires 5 February 1867.

Chapter Seven

JERSEY'S SEA CAPTAINS

IN DRAWING UP THIS LIST of Jersey's Sea Captains information has been obtained from many sources, including the records of the Jersey Merchant Seamen's Benefit Society, the Jersey Shipping Register, Bulletins of the Société Jersiaise, movements of shipping published in the local newspapers, and a wealth of data from our Island cemeteries. Much private material has very kindly been loaned to me for examination by descendants of the captains from among their family papers.

Many interesting stories have come to light; for example, the happy event of the birth of twin sons to Anne Deslandes[1] on board her father's vessel 'Jane' in the year 1848 which was commanded by her husband, Captain Josué Pallot. The twins were duly baptised, one being named Josué after his father, and the other taking his mother's maiden name of Deslandes. Both sons later became master mariners, Deslandes Pallot dying at sea in 1878 at the early age of 30, and Josué living until 1913. A fine marble memorial to all three captains can still be seen in Almorah Cemetery.

There is an epic tale of Captain George Malzard[2] and his brig 'Prospero'. After sailing from Jersey, where the vessel had been built in 1862 by F. C. Clarke at West Park, the ship sailed in December 1863 on her maiden voyage from London to the port of Para in Peru laden with supplies for the Government of Peru. On reaching Para, Captain Malzard's brig was taken in tow by a naval paddle steamer for a journey of 2,000 miles up the river Amazon, the first time that a British vessel had penetrated so far into the South American continent, this feat would be unknown today but for Malzard's habit of entering in his log his day to day observations and impressions throughout the four week journey up the river. His logbook makes fascinating reading today, and emphasises the fact that truth is indeed stranger than fiction.

Some stories point to how cruel the sea can be, like the tragedy that overtook the 243 ton barque 'Gaspé' on 6 December 1830.[3] This vessel, owned by T. & P. Du Hamel of Jersey and commanded by Captain Philip Vibert, was hit by a heavy sea which demasted the ship and washed overboard eight of the crew. Among the men that were lost were the captain's son Philip Vibert (Jr.); John Pipon, mate; Philip Després, 2nd mate; John de Ste Croix; Philip Le Sueur; Edward de La Cour and Clement Godfray. Captain Philip Vibert survived, as did Daniel

Deslandes, James de Ste Croix, Francis Dolbel, Philip Binet, Philip Alexandre, John Stratford and John Jandrou.

Another tragic and rather gruesome story tells of the wreck, also in 1830,[4] of the brig 'Quixote', 120 tons and owned by P. Duval, master Francis Bailhache. This vessel, having left Spain on 23 October, experienced very bad weather, which caused the ship to labour heavily. The storm continued till 5 December, when the gale increased almost to hurricane force and the brig was struck amidships by a tremendous sea which threw the ship upon her beam ends and shifted the cargo at the same time. The watch of two men on deck cut the lanyards of the rigging and the masts went over the side, the ship then righted herself but was full of water. Four men were in the fore cuddy when the sea struck, but only one man was able to reach the deck; the other three were drowned. The master and mate were in the cabin and struggled to the deck; the brig was now a complete wreck with the forepart entirely under water, and the sea was now mountainous and continually broke over her. The remainder of the crew, expecting every moment to be their last, held on with great difficulty. The weather was intensely cold, all were drenched to the skin and nearly exhausted by their exertions and after about two hours the master died. Another man worn out with cold and fatigue died the following morning. The misery and deplorable state of the four seamen who still lived when morning dawned cannot be described; the ship was a water-logged wreck, and the men, without food and water and their strength wasted, anxiously gazed at the horizon in hope of seeing a sail; but on 9 December another man died. Those who remained were starving, not having eaten anything since the ship was first struck, and lashed the man's body to the ship to prevent it being washed away in order that they might feed upon it. On the following day, driven to despair, they gnawed part of the arm of their dead shipmate, and on the 11th they were again driven by hunger to eating from the body. On the morning of the 13th the three survivors were lying on the deck completely exhausted and waiting to die when Philip Arthur, with what little strength he had left, looked over the side and saw a sail. The three men were picked up by a French brig and landed at Harfleur, but on the 15th one of them died and only Clement Noel, the mate, and Philip Arthur returned to Jersey.

Captain Elias Nicolas Pallot was sailing off the mouth of the St Lawrence in the 1870s when his ship was cut in two by a steamship. Having lost his own vessel, Captain Pallot transferred to the German owned ship 'Wilhelmina', bound for Antwerp, and acted as a relief captain. The wife of Captain Pallot was also aboard his vessel and, when the ship was off the Scillies, she gave birth to her first child. Wishing to have the baby christened at St Martin, Captain Pallot diverted his ship to Jersey and the child was named Lizette Wilhelmina, and after the ceremony he continued his journey to Antwerp.

Reports of the damage and injury suffered by Jersey vessels in the many storms met with at sea are fairly numerous, and some make rather tedious reading. The following statement or 'Protest' however, is considered by the writer to be of sufficient interest that it is here given in full in the original spelling.

Protest of the brig '85' of Jersey entered in Arichat May 6th 1866
by the Master John Romeril.

Report that on April 15th 1866. First part of this day strong breeze from the south-ward with a heavy sea, running under double reefed sails, vessel shipping much water and labouring heavyly. At 4 p.m. close reefed all sails, fore topmast stay sail having given way unbent it & bent on a new one, at 10 p.m. sea being too dangerous to run the vessel any longer, laid her to under close reefed main stay sail & Fore Topsail, shipped several dangerous seas from 10 p.m. to 5 a.m., at which time wore ship, wind hauling round to Westward with a very dangerous sea running from the Southward. At 7.30 a.m. in Lat 50, Long. 24.40 West, shipped a terrific sea in the Starboard Waist that swept the Deck carrying away Long Boat & Jolly Boat from the deck, then hooking Royal Backstay & thereby breaking Royal Mast on the way overboard also carried away Fore Booby Hatch & Hatchways Lee Gallant sail, Binnicle, eight buckets, two deck tubs, all the untensils for cooking, four studding sails, Fore Topmast stay sail, Main stay sail, six Studding sail halliard & all other moveables about deck, smashing the galley to pieces & broke Seven stanchions we immediately hauled canvas over Fore hatch & other necessary places to prevent water from going down & for safety of crew & vessel. The vessel at this time making about 8 inches of water per hour Pumps attended to with care others damages may be found as soon as weather permits to have a thorough inspection, the Cook laid up having been badly crushed in his galley, but so far as can be seen no limbs are broken. Report for the Brig '85' from Bristol towards Arichat 1866.

The ketch 'Queen of the Isles', owner Philip Pallot, bound for Antwerp with a cargo of figs and almonds, was wrecked on the Westkapelle Dike in Holland on 26 November 1887, and the local people made good use of the cargo, eating figs for weeks on end, and even baking fig bread with no doubt dire results!

After loading some hundred tons of fish off Paspébiac, the brigantine 'G.D.T.', of 124 tons, owned by Le Boutillier and with Captain J. J. Carcaud[5] in command, sailed for Oporto at the end of November 1883, but after several days at sea a series of misfortunes befell this gallant vessel. Firstly, on 3 December a storm arose causing the ship to heel over from side to side. One moment on the crest of a wave, the next wallowing in a trough, the ship took a particularly heavy sea which swept overboard the 2nd mate, Le Quesne, and the wheelhouse, and neither was ever seen again. The captain was thrown between the pumps and was so badly lacerated about the head that he spent the next three or four days in his cabin like a raving madman with the agony of his wounds. Three of the ship's four 120-gallon casks of fresh water went over the side, leaving the seven crew with only 120 gallons of water for the rest of the trip. The boy member of the crew went over the side with one wave and back on deck with the next. On 6 December the brigantine sighted the Belgian steam 'Plantyn' in distress. The steamer's lifeboats were picked up together with 53 passengers and crew, and the steamer sank soon after. For the next 19 days, till the 'G.D.T.' reached Oporto on Christmas Day 1883, the crew and rescued sailors had to exist on a wineglass-ful of water and less than a quarter of a ship's biscuit once every 24 hours. After a rest in an Oporto hotel while the ship was unloaded and repaired, the brigantine sailed for Jersey and home. She arrived off the Island on 26 January and cast anchor in St Aubin's Bay awaiting the tugboat to tow her in. A gale from the south-west arose and despite the two anchors put down by the ship, the brigantine dragged her chain and was stranded on the beach near Beaumont. The crew had to take to the rigging to prevent themselves being washed away. Next morning the crew were lodged at Tom Queree's Sailors Home, the site of which is now the *Swan* hotel in Wharf Street. In recognition of Captain Carcaud's bravery and the devotion to duty of the crew, the Belgian Government made the following awards: The 1st Class Civil Cross to Captain John J. Carcaud, 2nd Class Cross to Charles Hamon, mate, and 1st class medals to Daniel Boudreau, James Farrel, John Gunny, John George Becauet, seamen; and Charles Conner, steward. The 'G.D.T.' was refloated from Beaumont, and sailed the next spring under Captain Cantell until she was finally wrecked in 1887.

The captains, officers, and senior members of the crews were almost entirely Jerseymen during the wars with France, but a search of the record books of the Jersey Merchant Seamen's Benefit Society reveals that by the 1830s/40s crews were recruited from Jersey, Guernsey, France and the mainland including Ireland, and from Canada and Newfoundland, the West Indies, Malta, Gibraltar and the African Territories. Many vessels had at least one African, who was usually the cook. The Africans rejoined in some rather delightful names such as Black Tom, Jack Coffee, Jim Brown, or more often simply 'Kroo Boy'. As the merchant fleet continued to expand, seamen from other countries were also recruited, though in small numbers, from Spain and Portugal, Italy, Norway, Sweden, Denmark and Germany, for the increasing number of local ships.

Due to the lack of communications, before the advent of the telegraph and radio, shipowners had to rely on their captains to act as agents, to obtain the best prices for cargoes, and to arrange further deals for new loads and goods. As a result the masters often held large shares in the vessel under their command. The intermarriage of shipping families in Jersey often strengthened the ties between master and owner, merchant and builder. However, some of the larger owners, such as Janvrin and Robin, had established their own agents in many ports and these agents were often members of the same family or connected by marriage. Local masters' salaries seemed to be on a par with their mainland counterparts, the Jersey captain in the 1830s averaging £100 to £120 per annum, to which was added the commission on the sale of cargoes.

With the introduction of the Merchant Shipping Act of 1854, captains who wished to apply for their 'Master's Ticket' had to sit for an examination at such ports as London, Liverpool, or Plymouth. The successful candidates were entered in the General Registered and Record Office of Seamen at the Board of Trade in London, and were then issued with the Certificate of Competency, the all important 'Master's Ticket'. However, many masters continued to command without a certificate for many years. Another captain's responsibility was, in the event of loss or damage to his vessel whilst at sea, to appear before a person of authority, such as a Justice of the Peace, to swear a full and accurate account of the incidents which occurred during the voyage. Such a declaration (or Protest), concerning the Brig '85' of Jersey, master John Romeril, was made at Arichat in 1866 (see page 123).

JERSEY'S SEA CAPTAINS

To avoid tedious repetition the sea captains are not listed individually in the index but appear alphabetically below. The following abbreviations are used:

b. born; mar. married;	d. died; bur. buried;	cem. cemetery; fils, son of
St B., St Brelade	St J., St John	St O., St Ouen
St C., St Clement	St L., St Lawrence	St P., St Peter
G., Grouville	St Mtn., St Martin	St S., St Saviour
St H., St Helier	St My., St Mary	Ty., Trinity

A'COURT, John	b. 1846, d. 1926, bur. St O., officer on 'Cutty Sark'.
ADAMS, William	b. 1807, Gillingham ?, 'Amelia' 1826, 'Two Brothers' 1836, 'Nymph' 1856.
ADDISON, Abraham	b. 1834, d. 18.11.1909, bur. Mont a L'Abbe, St H, Shipowner 1870-1899
AHIER, Charles	Master's Cert. No. 35210, 'Evelyn' 1864.
AHIER, Charles Philip	Master's Cert. No. 17351, 'Albertina' 1869, 'John Clark' 1872, 'Tiphys' 1877.
AHIER, Francis	'St George' 1834, 'Jubilee' 1842.
AHIER, Frederick John	b. 20.6.1841, d. 14.4.1873, lost en voyage Rio de Janeiro to Paspébiac. Memorial St C's cem. A Robin captain.
AHIER, Jean	d. 1873, Master's Cert. No. 16331, 'Robin' 1867.
AHIER, John	Master's Cert. No. 14545, 'C.R.C.' 1871, 'Aura' 1872.
AHIER, John T.	'Flying Fish' 1900.
AHIER, Jean	A privateer captain, 'Mary Ann' 1739, 'Mary' 1741–. 'Friendship' 1744–48, also 'Charming Betty'.
AHIER, Laurens	'William' 1792.
AHIER, Philip	A privateer captain, 'Unity' 1780, 'Le Tapon' 1784–85.
AHIER, Philip	b. 1778, d. 1855, bur. Green Street cem., 'Ann' 1816.
AHIER, Philip	b. 1845, d. 1885, drowned Southern India.
AHIER, Philip	b. 1820, 'Speedwell' 1840, 'Handy' 1852.
AHIER, Thomas	b. 1794, son of Jean, St Mtn., 'Ant' 1836.
ALEXANDER, A.	From Jersey to Newfoundland, Alexanders came from London to Channel Islands; some bur. Green Street cem.
ALEXANDRE, Charles	A privateer captain, 'Revenge' 1751-63, 'Union' 1750-57, a vessel owned by Charles arrived from Southampton with a cargo of barley in 1757.
ALEXANDRE, Charles	b. 1806, Ty., lived Roseville Street, St H. 1840, 'Caesar' 1836, 'Apparition' 1847.

ALEXANDRE, Charles	son of John, lived St H., ss 'Waishing' 1925.
ALEXANDRE, Francis	b. 1806 Jersey. Robin captain in New Brunswick.
ALEXANDRE, Francois	b. 1807, d. 13.3.1886, bur. Mont a L'Abbe cem., mar. Marie Anne Duret, lived Roseville Street, St H, 1866. 'Dit-On' & 'Ditto' 1826, 'Lady Harvey' 1839, 'Crapaud' 1847.
ALEXANDRE, Frederic	b. 1805, St B., lived Bulwarks 1866, brother of Francois. Many commands, 'Messenger' 1830, 'Adventure' 1836, 'Virginia' 1838, 'Marie' 1841, 'Lady Harvey' 1843, 'Melvina' 1834–44, 'St.Brelade' 1850, 'Amelia' 1851, 'Crapaud' 1857, 'Jane' 1858.
ALEXANDER, George	lived Mont a L'Abbe 1866, 'Othello' 1836–48, retired 1848.
ALEXANDRE, George	Master of brig 'Mary Ann' c. 1833, d. of yellow fever in West Indies. Lived many years in Shippegan.
ALEXANDRE, Jean	'Shift' 1790, 'Paspébiac' 1790, 'St Lawrence' 1792.
ALEXANDRE, Jean	b. 1798, St B., lived St B. 1866, 'Susan' 1836, 'Lady Harvey' 1840, 'Amelia' 1841–49, retired c. 1849.
ALEXANDRE, Joshua	b. 1803, St B. Constable of St B., 'Grog' 1836–38.
ALEXANDRE, Philip	b. 1797, d. 1864, bur. Green Street cem., mar. Elizabeth de Gruchy. 'Tom & Mary' 1821, 'Palm' 1828, 'Rose' 1831.
ALEXANDRE, Walter	Master of 'Sidney Sleece', emigrated to New Zealand c. 1870.
ALEXANDRE, William	'Amity' 1822, 'Lively' 1826, 'Canada' 1833.
ALEXANDRE, Will Milne	b. 1830, son of Captain Philip, d. 1902, bur. Green Street cem., m. Jane Mallet, Master's Cert. No. 21118, 'Conrad' 1868.
ALLEN, John	'Eclipse' 1858.
ALLIX, Francis	b. 1851, d. 1894, bur. Mont a L'Abbe cem.
ALLIX, Frank G.	ss 'Honfleur' 1874, ps 'Alliance'.
ALLIX, George	b. 1813, d. 1884, bur. Mont a L'Abbe cem., mar. Ann Sullivan. Master's Cert. No. 74448, 'Elizabeth Young' 1865.
ALLIX, George	son of George, a London Southwestern Railway master for many years, 'Diament' 1870, ss 'Diana' 1886, ss 'Lydia' and ss 'Fredericia' 1890–1906.
ALLIX, John	'Recovery' and 'Good Intent' 1809.
ALLIX, Philip	Master of steam tug 'Toby' 1864.
AMIRAUX, Pierre	a privateer captain, 'Revenge' 1781.
AMY, Charles	b. 1796, St H., 'Apollo' 1822, 'Charlotte' 1828, 'Three Sisters' 1836, 'Aurore' 1851, 'Ipswich' 1856.
AMY, Daniel Philip	b. 1815, St S.?, drowned St Brieuc, France 1853. 'St Anne' 1839, 'Fanny' 1844, 'Jubilee' 1851–53.
AMY, Francis	'Fortune' 1803, 'Young Peggy' 1805, 'Enterprise' 1808, 'George' 1814–16; prisoner of war 1814, lived St H. 1840.
AMY, John	Master's Cert. -No. 24049, 'Zephyr' 1864, 'Circassian' 1869–73, lived Gorey 1866.
AMY, Philip	'Cousins' 1757–59.
AMY, Philip	b. 1795, son of Philip, Master 1836–48, lived St J.
AMY, Philip	'Julia' 1811, 'Victory' 1813, Resolution & Property' 1815.
AMY, Thomas	b. Cornwall, brought Sir George Carteret to Jersey during Civil War, 'Little George' 1646, one of Carteret's privateers.
AMY, Thomas	'Joseph' and 'Aurore' 1846, 'Jubilee' 1848.
ANDERSON, Lawrence	'Mary' 1744, 'Adventure' 1745–47, 'Two Brothers' 1747–48.
ANLEY, Philip	'William Wooley' 1851, lived St C. 1866.
ANLEY, Richard ?	transported the dolmen from St H. to London for General Conway 1788.
ANLEY, William	'Pavilion' 1842.

ANQUETEL, Thomas	'Ceres' 1784, 'Nancy' 1786, 'Two Friends' 1790.
ANTHOINE, Nicolas	'Princess' 1778.
ANTHOINE, Richard	'Pilgrim' 1830.
ANTHOINE, Thomas	'Catherine' 1819-21.
ARM, James	'Favourite' 1859-77, 'Sea Nymph', based at Gorey.
ARTHUR, Charles	'Heraux' 1813, 'Experimenter' 1822.
ARTHUR, Helier	'Duke of Wellington' 1826, 'Fruiterer' 1846, 'Princess Alexandrina' 1871.
ARTHUR, Jean	a privateer captain, 'Elizabeth' and 'Duke of Cumberland' 1756.
ARTHUR, John George	'Ada' 1847.
ARTHUR, John George le Cain	b. 1858, d. 1925, St B. cem., mar. Mary Esther Le Cappelain.
ARTHUR, Nicolas	'Elizabeth' c. 1744.
ASPLET, Aaron	b. 1793 ?, 'Messenger' 1814.
ASPLET, Abraham	b. 1802, son of Elias, killed at sea 1860. 'Virginia' 1835, 'Pomona' 1837, 'Sultana' 1845, 'Siren' 1846-51, 'Dark Pkt.' 1853, 'Charles' 1856, 'Nelson' 1858, 'Louisa' 1860. Lived St P. ?
ASPLET, Elias	'Esther' 1809, 'Active' and 'Providence' 1810, 'Duke of Wellington' 1815, lived St P.
ASPLET, John	'Medusa' 1818, 'Hope' 1820, 'Atlas' 1848.
ASPLET, Philip	'Providence' 1792, 'Jersey Pkt' 1796.
ASPLET, Philip	Master 1848, drowned on the Goodwins 1860.
AUBIN, Charles	b. 1812, d. 1896, Green Street cem.
AUBIN, Charles	b. 1837, d. 1893, St S.s cem.
AUBIN, Francis	Master 1849-52, lived Clare Vale, St Mtn.
AUBIN, Germain	A privateer captain, 'Hope' 1872, 'Revenge' 1799.
AUBIN, John Richard	killed by U boat, 1917.
AUBIN, Thomas	'Lawrence' 1803.
BABOT, George	Master of ps 'Dispatch', lived 1 Plaisance Terrace, St H., 1866.
BABOT, John B.	Master 'Augusta' 1861.
BAILHACHE, Clement	b. 1808, St O.?, d. 1887, mar. Mary Ann Blampied. 'Exchange' 1836, 'Othello' 1854.
BAILHACHE, Francis	'Quixote' 1830
BAILHACHE, Frederic	'Merida' 1854.
BAILHACHE, Jean	'Fleur' 1579, 'Minion' 1580.
BAILHACHE, Jean	'Venus' 1803
BAILHACHE, Nicholas	'Elizabeth' 1595.
BAILHACHE, Philip	Master 1786.
BAILHACHE, Philip	b. 1801, St O.?, 'Petit Degrat' 1821, 'Twig' 1826, 'Samuel & Julia' 1836, 'Jersey Pkt' 1837, 'Dido' 1838.
BAILLY, Jean	b. 1814, d. 1886, bur. G. cem.
BAILLY (LE), Thomas	'Anne' 1819, 'Harriet' 1826.
BAKER, John	b. 1799, Jersey, Gorey ?, d. 1884 Perce. 'Fly' 1859.
BALCOMBE, John	b. 1697, Jersey, d. U.S.A.
BALLEINE, Archibald	HMT 'Glamorgan', c. 1917.
BALLEINE, Edward	a privateer captain, 'Hazard' 1802.
BALLEINE, Frederic G.	Master and owner of 'Swan' 1874-1902.
BALLEINE, George	'Betsy' 1786.
BALLEINE, Jacques	a privateer captain, 'Active' 1756.
BALLEINE, James	b. 1796, St P.?, 'Old Tom' 1834-35, 'Seaflower' 1839-41, 'Fisherman' 1843, 'C.R.C.' 1849-57.
BALLEINE, John Thomas	mar. Marie Judith Jean, 1833, Arichat.

BALLEINE, Jean	'Lyon and George' 1588.
BALLEINE, Jean	b. 1787, St P., 'Magdalen' 1816, 'Neptune' 1822, 'Janvrin' 1825, 'Messenger' 1836, 'Seaflower' 1839; retired 1842.
BALLEINE, Thomas	'Mary and Anne' 1737, 'Dispatch' 1744.
BANDINEL, F.	'Mary Ann' 1764.
BANDINEL, Thomas	'Peggy' 1790.
BARBIER, Jacques	'Harmony' 1790.
BARBIER, Robert	a privateer captain, 'Phoenix' 1756.
BARRETTE, John C.	Lived Bell Vue, St C., d. 1898.
BARRETT, Joseph Hedley	Master of 'Electric Flash' 1859, built Malta House, St J., lost at sea off Malta.
BARTLETT, Francis	Master 1717.
BAS (LE), Francis	b. 1783, St H., d. 1860. 'Charming Nancy' 1810, 'Mars', 'Olive Branch' 1822–26, 'Themis' 1830.
BAS (LE), Francis	b. 1786, St. P., Master 1836.
BAS (LE), Francis	b. 1809, lived Oxford Place, Pier Road, St H., 1850, d. 1868, bur. Green Street cem., 'Mastery' 1837, 'Themis' 1839, 'Olive Branch' 1846, retired 1848.
BAS (LE), Francois	Master, lived St H., 1840.
BAS (LE), Gedeon	Master of 'Augia' 1823–29; Constable of St. B., 1838–41. Constable of St P., 1852–55, mar.: 1st, Elizabeth Mace; 2nd, Esther Pavn.
BAS (LE) Jean	Lived St B., bur. St P., mar. Marie Anne Pipon. Master of 'Louisa' 1821–23, 'Augia' 1833, 'Marie' 1836.
BAS (LE), Jean	b. 1789, St P., d. 24.7.1840 Cap Breton. 'P.R.C.' 1834–36, 'Aurore' 1838, 'Grog' 1839.
BAS (LE), J.	lived St H., 'Evening Star' 1854, 'Admiral Nelson' 1870.
BAS (LE), Nicholas	'Francis' 1600.
BAS (LE), Peter	Lived St H. 1840, 'Three Sisters' 1824.
BAS (LE), Richard	Lived St H. 1840, 'Scatari', 1822, 'Friends' 1832.
BAS (LE), Thomas Alfred	b. Jersey, lived St J's Road, c. 1880, Master 1860–68.
BAS (LE), Thomas Amice	'Jane' 1868.
BAS (LE), William P.	lived Beaumont 1885, mar. Elvina Sophia Le Quesne, 'Alfred' 1852, 'Glance' 1882.
BASTARD (LE), Jean	Master of 'Ebeneezer' 1826.
BATAILLE, Adophus	'Eclipse' 1878.
BAUDAINS, George	'Henry' 1826.
BAUDAINS, Thomas	ss 'Ibex' 1900.
BAUDAINS, ?	one of Carteret's privateer captains, 1645.
BAYLES, Christopher	'Diana' 1810, 'Betsy' 1816.
BAYLES, Gascoen Noah Edwin	'Betsy' and 'Nautilus' 1817.
BAZIN, Harry	b. Guernsey, 'Speedy Pkt' 1814, ss 'Ariadne' 1824.
BAZIN, Jean	Master c. 1830s, mar. Jane Mauger, bur. Green Street cem.
BEAUGIE, John	Master's Cert. No. 14546, 'Zegri' 1865.
BÉCHERVAISE, John	son of Philip, master, b. 1789 St Aubin.
BÉCHERVAISE, Philip	d. of fever 1811, 'Amazon' 1789, 'Peace' 1786.
BECQUET, J. C.	'Robin' and 'Century' 1898.
BEDBOROUGH ?	'Sir Sydney Smith' 1816, 'Kitty' 1817, 'Nelson' 1819, 'Speedy Pkt', 1824–32.
BEDFORD, Edward	'Albion' 1809, 'Charles' 1810, 'Janvrin' 1821, 'Azores' 1823.
BELLOT, Francis	b. 1797 St H. ?, 'Experiment' 1831, 'Young Peggy' 1836.
BENEST, Brun	lived Bulwarks, St Aubin 1789, Master of 'Perseverance' 1790.

BENEST, Francis Edward	Master's Cert. No. 82023, 'Milton' 1873.
BENEST, Jean	lived near Corn Market 1771, 'Jean' 1731–47, 'Charming Betty'?, 'Phoenix' 1756–65.
BENEST, Jean	'Joseph & Jane' 1819, 'Concord' 1822, 'Echo' 1825, 'Providence' 1828–32.
BENEST, John Thomas	'Atalanta' 1826.
BENEST, J.	'Empress' 1876.
BENEST, Philip	'Alligator', 1780, 'Peirson' 1790–92, 'Royal Volunteer' 1796.
BENEST, Philip Le Geyt	b. 1832 St H., d. 1865, bur. at Shanghai, Master of 'Highflyer' (not a Jersey boat).
BENEST, Thomas	also used name of Bennett?, d. St H.?
BENNETT, George	a privateer captain, 'St Albans' 1695.
BENNETT, George	Master of 'Frolic' 1836, d. 1836.
BENNETT, Henry	b. Jersey 1828, settled Nova Scotia.
BENNETT, Philip	a privateer captain, 'Rover Pkt' 1794, 'Dundas' 1803.
BERRY, Samuel	'Friend's Delight' 1744–47.
BERTEAU, John	'Two Friends' 1786, 'Hope' 1818, 'Hind' 1821.
BERTRAM, Abraham	b. 1801 G., Master 1836–40.
BERTRAM, Charles	Master of 'Sukey' 1790.
BERTRAM, Elias	Master of 'Young Dolphin' 1832.
BERTRAM, George	a privateer captain, 'Molly', c. 1756.
BERTRAM, George	b. 1827, d. 7.4.1907, stone Macpéla cem., Sion.
BERTRAM, Philip	a privateer captain, 'Good Intent' 1796, 'Expedition Pkt' 1803.
BERTRAM, Philip	b. 1794, d. 1869, Mont a L'Abbe cem. 'Grog' 1825.
BERTRAM, Richard	Master of 'Industry', 1803.
BERTRAM, Richard Phil.	b. 1803, St H.?, d. 30.3.1887, mar. Mary Balcam?, Master's Cert. No. 16332, 'Iris' 1840, 'William' 1851, 'Offor' & 'Salvador Pkt' 1860, 'Harmony' 1865.
BERTRAM, Thomas	Master of 'Esther' 1846.
BICHARD, Elias	Master of 'Young Messenger' 1824.
BICHARD, Francis	Master of 'Jersey Pkt' 1780–96.
BICHARD, Jean	Master and owner of barque at St B. (St Aubin?), 1583.
BICHARD, Jean	Master of 'Union' 1790–92, 'Peggy' 1809, 'Prince de Bouillon' 1822.
BICHARD, John	b. 1782, d. 16.4.1850, bur. St B. cem.
BICHARD, John Martell	bur. St B. cem.
BICHARD, Nicolas	Master of 'Lyon' 1595.
BICHARD, Peter	b. 1814, St P.?, lived Savill Street, St H. 1866. 'Canopus' 1835, 'Clio' 1836.
BICHARD, Thomas	Master, c. 1635.
BIGAREAU, George	b. 1790, St B., d. 1840, 'Surprise' 1821, 'Abeona' and 'Seneca' 1836.
BIGREL, George	'Lord Nelson' 1812, 'Laurel' and 'La Dame' 1814.
BILLOT, Edward	Master of 'General Doyle' 1809.
BILLOT, Elias	b. 1787 St Mtn., 'Concorde' 1808, 'Olive Branch' 1826, 'No Two' 1836, ' Virginia' 1836, 'Marie Victoire' 1837, 'Loyal William' 1838, 'Messenger' 1836, 'Marie' 1839, 'Fanny' 1840, 'Diana' 1846.
BILLOT, Philip	Master of 'Jenny' 1790.
BINET, Charles	son of Philip?, d. before 1844, lived St L.?, mar. Elizabeth Rive: mate of 'Rowena'.
BINET, James	lived 13 Duhamel Pl, St H. 1866, Master of 'Ariel' 1859–62.

BINET, Jean	Master of 'Martha' 1763.
BINET, Philip	b. 1811, Ty.?, son of Philip, brother of Charles? living St H. 1840, 'Rowena' 1834–37, 'Flamer' 1837–41, 'Quiz' 1841–46
BINON, P.	b. Guernsey? Master of 'Brave' 1876–77.
BISHOP, Jean	Master or merchant before 1644.
BISHOP, John	Master of 'Faro Pkt' 1764.
BISHOP, John	lived St H. 1840, 'Union' 1794, 'Betsy' 1815, 'Leicester' 1816, 'Othello' 1830.
BISHOP, John	Master of 'Onward' 1865.
BISHOP, Peter	'Betsy' 1804–08, 'Virginia' 1808–09, 'Lord Gambier' 1809–19, 'Phoenix' 1923, 'Othello' 1831, also 'Active' 1809, brother of John?
BISHOP, Pierre	b. 1798, d. 1829, Green Street cem.
BISHOP, Thomas	Master of 'Cornwall' 1790.
BISSON, Charles	lived St H., Master of 'Dart' 1827.
BISSON, Edward	'Charming Betty' 1747, 'George' 1749.
BISSON, J.	b. 1822, d. c. 1912, partner Bisson, Dawe & Co., living Penryn, Cornwall 1880.
BISSON, J. Le Couteur	b. 1808 St H., 'DartPkt' 1835–41, 'Greyhound' 1842–44, 'Freedom' 1848, 'Greyhound' 1852.
BISSON, Peter Le Gros	b. 1796 St P.?, 'Echo' 1835, 'Peace' 1849, also 'Fanny' 1840.
BISSON, Philip	'Ceres' 1790–95, 'Mary & Anne' 1792, 'Good Intent' 1799, 'Hope' 1819.
BISSON, Pierre	Master of 'Hilton' 1790–92.
BLACK, Archibald	'Lord Nelson' 1814, 'Good Intent' 1818.
BLAMPIED, Charles John	b. c. 1828, Master 1866, in Arichat 1854.
BLAMPIED, Denize	Master 1880, lived La Retraite, Ty.
BLAMPIED, Denize	Master of 'Victory' 1824–26.
BLAMPIED, Frederic	Lived Cheapside, St H., 'Aslelon' 1887, ss 'Rossgull' 1900, d. in shipwreck off Corbiere, Jersey, 1900.
BLAMPIED, George	Master's Cert. No. 84313, bur. Almorah cem., 'Erato' 1871. ss 'Progress'?
BLAMPIED, George	b. 1823, d. New Zealand, stone Mont a L'Abbe cem.
BLAMPIED, John	b. 1797 St. P, d. 1843, Master of 'John' 1835–41.
BLAMPIED, Jean	b. 1804 Ty., son of Denize, Master 1836–56.
BLAMPIED, Jean	b. 1814 St P., son of Philip, 'Dart' 1836, 'Masterly' 1838.
BLAMPIED, John	b. 1844 St H., d. 1914, lived Annst, St H. 1895, Master's Cert. No. 88461, 'Conqueror' 1876.
BLAMPIED, Josué	Master of 'Eliza' 1808, A captain J. Blampied was employed as a pilot on Royal Navy vessels around the Jersey coast c. 1778.
BLAMPIED, Josué	Master of 'Bloye' 1826, d. 1860 St. P.
BLAMPIED, Josué	Master's Cert. No. 8072, 'Sir John Falstaff' 1870.
BLAMPIED, Jourdain	b. 1804, St L., d. 1866? lived St H. 1840, 'Diana' 1826, 'Ceres' 1838, 'Calista' 1839, 'St Croix' 1844–56, retired 1856.
BLAMPIED, Philip	b. 1840, d. 21.11.1892. Mont a L'Abbe cem., mar. Elizabeth Hamon, lived Don Road, St H., Master's Cert. No. 8157, 'Alabama' 1873
BLAMPIED, Philip W.	b. 1866, d. Shanghai 21.12.1904.
BLAMPIED, P.	Master of 'Mary' 1825.
BLAMPIED, Thomas	'Aubin' 1757, 'Admiral Durrell' 1761.
BLAMPIED, Thomas	'Angelique' 1831, 'Richard' 1821.

BLAMPIED, Thomas	b. 1839, d. 20.11.1906. Mont a L'Abbe cemetery, mar. Jane Mary Matson, master of 'Askelon' 1864.
BLANCQ (LE), Clement	Master of 'Eliza' 1818–20, 'Polperro' 1826.
BLANCQ (LE), Edward	lived Le Coin, St. B. 1866, Master of 'John Thomas' 1825.
BLANCQ (LE), Elie	Master of 'Pitt' 1799, d. 1850, bur. St. O. cem.
BLANCQ (LE), Jean	Master of 'Telegraph' 1853, 'Reaper' 1866.
BLANCQ (LE), Philip	'Friendship' 1764, 'Postillion Pkt' 1792, 'Fly' 1801.
BLANCQ (LE), Philip	'Adelina' 1855.
BLIAULT, Adolphos	no details.
BLIAULT, Charles	ss 'Atherstone' 1914; also ss 'Gulistan'.
BLONDEL, John	'Pellicane' 1580.
BLONDEL, Solomon	'Solomon' 1600.
BOEUF (LE), Charles	b. 1788 St H., d. 1845 Jersey, 'Red Breast' 1824, 'Quixote' 1829, 'Lord Saumaresq' 1835, 'Lord Anson' 1837, 'Britannia' 1842, 'Larch' 1842, 'Comus' 1845.
BOEUF (LE), F.	Master of 'Syren' 1831, 'Hindustan' 1859.
BOUEF (LE), Frederic	'Queen of the Seas' 1880.
BOEUF (LE), James	lived Payton Terrace, East India Road, London 'Hindustan' 1586, 'Stormbird' 1863.
BOEUF (LE), John Henry	'Stormbird' 1862–63, 'Rambler' 1864.
BOHIER, John	Master of 'Elizabeth' 1737.
BOND, John	'Spitfire' 1901.
BONNEL, ?	'Diament' 1859.
BOSDET, Jean	Master, c. 1812.
BOSDET, Thomas	lived Windsor Cottage, Millbrook, 1800, 'Curlew' 1855, also ? 1850
BOSQUET (LE), Edward	'Three Friends' 1745–47.
BOSQUET (LE), James	'Mary' 1744.
BOSQUET (LE), Philippe	'John' 1747.
BOSQUET (LE), Thomas	'Hope' 1739.
BOUCHERE, Peter	'Minion' 1588.
BOUDIER, Frank	'Priscilla' 1866.
BOULANGER, J. A.	Master 1880.
BOUTILLIER (LE), Amy	b. 1795 St. J., son of Josué, lived Regent Road, St. H., 1866, 'Teaser' 1839, 'Iris' 1840, 'C. T. Sutton' 1845, retired 1847.
BOUTILLIER (LE), Charles	son of Charles lived St Mtn, 'John' 1836, 'Nameless' 1840, 'Ipswich' 1849, 'Voyageur' 1851.
BOUTILLIER (LE), Charles	b. 1838 St. L., d. 1905. St. L cem. Master's Cert. No. 25282, 'Harvest Man' 1864.
BOUTILLIER (LE), David	b. 1824, St My, d. 1897. St My. cem. 'Bridesmaid' 1859. 'Jeddo' 1859, 'Hebe' 1861.
BOUTILLIER (LE), Edward	Master of 'Philip' 1744–45, 'Three Friends' 1747.
BOUTILLIER (LE), Edward	b. 1802 St J., d. 1852 Paspébiac, 'Hebe' 1835–47
BOUTILLIER (LE), Francis	b. 1847, d. 11.4.1902. Mont a L'Abbe cem., mar. Bella Jane Asplet.
BOUTILLIER (LE), George	'Stare' 1588.
BOUTILLIER (LE)', John	'Ocean Queen' 1846, 'Angelique' 1830.
BOUTILLIER (LE), Jean	'Charlotte' 1803, 'Marie' 1808.
BOUTILLIER (LE), Joshua	'Vestal' 1827.
BOUTILLIER (LE), Philip	b. 1814 St H., d. 1864, bur. Green Street cem., 'Dolphin 1840.
BOUTILLIER (LE), Philip	lived Queen's Road, St H., 1866, 'Hero' 1826, 'Sibyl' 1847.
BOUTILLIER (LE), Philip	b. 13.3.1834 St O., passed Master's examination at Plymouth 4.2.1863, No. 82685, lived St O. 1866.

BOUTON, Josué	'Nancy' 1778, 'Southampton Pkt' 1792.
BOUTON, Philip	'Providence' 1790.
BOWDEN, George	One of Carteret's privateer captains 1645.
BRACHE, Henry	Master of 'Commerce' 1874.
BRADLEY, Henry Arthur	b. 1806, G.?, 'Calista' 1836, 'Iris' 1841, 'Ocean' 1842, 'Eliza' 1843, 'St Croix' 1850-64.
BRADLEY, Richard	b. 1798, lived Don Road, St H.. 1866, 'Rowcliffe' 1824, 'St Croix' 1827-60.
BRAND, W. J.	Master of 'Isabella & Jane' 1859.
BREE, Philip	b. 1815 son of Philip, lived St H., 'Flora' 1836, 'Canopus' 1839.
BREHAUT, Thomas John	a privateer captain, 'Mary' 1807--9, 'St Vincent' 1812-13.
BREHAUT, Thomas John	'Dawn' 1900, 'C.R.C.' 1902.
BRETON, Francis André	b. 1798, lived St Mtn., 'Minerva' 1826-36, 'Speedy Pkt' 1838, 'Peggy' 1842, 'Caroline' 1868.
BRIARD, Edward	'Young Witch' 1833, 'Briard' 1846.
BRIARD, Elias	lived Duhamel Pl, St H., 'Messenger' 1820.
BRIARD, Peter	'Peace' 1794, 'If' 1803, 'Cap Breton' 1813, 'Day' 1816, 'Gaspé' 1823-27.
BRIARD, Peter	b. 1797, lived St B., 'C.R.C.' 1831-36, retired 1841.
BRIARD, Peter	'Abrotha' 1851, 'Lady Maxwell' 1855-57.
BRIARD, Philip	'Young Charles' 1804.
BRIARD, Philip	b. 1805, son of Elias, St B., lived Vauxhall 1866. 'Aurore' 1835, 'P.R.C.' 1838, 'Grog' 1841, 'Hemotope' 1849, 'Briard' 1850, 'Fisherman' 1854, 'Quiz' 1855.
BROCQ (LE), Charles	Master of 'Sally' 1804.
BROCQ (LE), Edward	'Seaflower' 1760, 'Jenny' 1785.
BROCQ (LE), Francis	b. 1808, St O., 'Nelson' 1835-37.
BROCQ (LE), George	lived St O., Master's Cert. No. 18435, 'Seaflower' 1862, 'Union' 1865, 'Oliver Blanchard' 1878-80.
BROCQ (LE), Jean	'Friend's Delight' c. 1744.
BROCQ (LE), John	b. 1841, St My., d. 1894 of lockjaw, bur. St My. cem., Master's Cert. No. 17400, 'Royal Blue Jacket' and 'Zibiah' 1860.
BROCQ (LE), John	b. 1837, St J.?, d. 1897, bur, St J.s cem., 'Dewdrop' 1847-79.
BROCQ (LE), John George	b. 1859, d. 1935, bur. Mont a L'Abbe cem., ss 'Upada' 1914.
BROCQ (LE), Peter	Master of 'Jonat' 1595.
BROCQ (LE), Philip	a privateer captain, 'Julia' 1762, 'Phoenix' 1801-04, 'Gen. Gordon' 1799-1801.
BROCQ (LE), Philip	b. 1802 St L., 'Medusa' 1835, 'Guernsey Lily' 1841, 'Courier' 1846, retired 1846.
BROWNE, Eward	a privateer captain, 'Two Brothers' 1692.
BRUN (LE), Abraham	'Egton' 1820.
BRUN (LE), Edward	'Capre Prince' 1708-15, 'Bonne Esperance' 1715.
BRUN (LE), Edward	b. 1801 St P., 'Gambria' 1826, 'Arichat' 1835, 'Charles' 1839, 'Superb' 1841, 'St Peter' 1846-51, also 'Eliza Jean' 1830.
BRUN (LE), F. J.	living St Mark's Road, St H. 1880.
BRUN (LE), H.	'Unity' 1778-79.
BRUN (LE), Jean	'Elizabeth' 1774, 'Sukey' 1778, 'Diligence' 1779.
BRUN (LE), John	'Egton' 1821, 'Parana' 1851-59.
BRUN (LE), Philip	'Hebe' 1874.
BRUNET, Jean	'Trial' 1747, 'Charming Jenny' 1752, 'Phoenix' 1756-65.

BUESNEL, Abraham b. 1806 St B., lived St H. 1840?, 'Tiphys' 1831, 'Abeona' 1836, 'Neptune' 1837, 'Fanny' 1840, 'Emma Eden' 1846, 'St George' 1849.

BUESNEL, John b. 1796 G., 'Nancy' 1818, 'Courier' 1836–43, retired 1843.

BUHTS, J. lived Gorey 1885, shipowner.

BURGREEN, Nicolas 'Peace' 1826.

BURNAL, George 'Fancy' 1803–04, 'Neptune' 1805, 'Flora' 1806, 'Victory' 1809, 'Pink' 1812, 'Flora' 1815.

BUSHELL, Abraham a privateer captain, 'Jersey' 1780, 'Fortune' 1790.

BUSHELL, Thomas a privateer captain, 'Expedition Pkt' 1712–46.

BUSHELL, William a privateer captain, 'Three Eagles' 1709–45, 'Expedition Pkt' 1745, mar. Marie Le Brun.

BUTEL, John W. b. 1842, Ty., d. 1902, bur. at sea, memorial Tr. cem. 'Glenville' 1900–02.

BUTLER, Charles Master of 'Hope' 1826.

BUTLER, John b. 1803 Ireland, d. 1852? 'Albion' 1836, 'Prima' 1841, 'Dart Pkt' 1845, 'Agrenoria' 1848, 'Jersey Lass' 1849, 'Diadem' 1849, 'Corbiere' 1852.

BUTT, Edward 'Victory' 1852.

BUTT, Henry A. b. St Mtn., 'Osprey' 1848, 'Cristal' 1874.

CABOT, Edward 'Enterprise' 1782.

CABOT, Elie 'George' 1790.

CABOT, Jean 'Neptune' 1772, 'Dolphin' 1778, 'Admiral Durell' 1780, 'Jersey Pkt' 1786.

CABOT, Josué Master of 'Swan' 1790.

CABOT, Nicolas b. 1759, d. 1831, bur. Green Street cem., 'Postillion Pkt' 1790, 'Enterprise' 1792.

CABOT, Noé 'Charlotte' 1763–65.

CABOT, Peter a privateer captain, 'Prince of Wales' 1747–48, 'Macaroni' 1778.

CABOT, Philip 'Active' 1813.

CABOT, Thomas 'Duke of Wellington' 1821–25

CAMERON, Archibald 'The Just' 1808–09.

CANNON, ? 'My Lord Jermyn' 1647, one of Carteret's privateers.

CANTELL, Albert Geo. Master's Cert. No. 22344, 'Ocean Queen' 1864, 'Charlotte' 1874.

CANTELL, George Gillis 'Silver Cloud' 1873–92 (owner).

CANTELL, George John Master's Cert. No. 25035, 'Willing' 1868, 'Owny Belles' ?, 'Telegraph' 1899.

CANTELL, Mark 'Ebenezer' 1864.

CAPELAIN (LE), Benjamin 'Success' 1790–92, also Master 1786.

CARCAUD, A. 'Sharston' 1880.

CARCAUD, John J. 'G.D.T.' 1883, 'Sultana' 1844, Captain Carcaud on 21.7.1884 was awarded the first class civil cross by the Belgian Government for his rescue of 53 passengers and crew of the Belgian steamer 'Plantyn' on the night of 6.12.1883.

CARREL, Francis Peter b. St B., 'Anne' 1814, 'Betsy' 1817, 'Ashburton' 1818, 'Wag' 1821, 'Twig' 1824, 'Highlander' 1840.

CARREL, Jean b. 1799 St L., d. 1886, bur. St. L., mar. ? Esnouf, 'Fanny' 1835, 'Waterwitch' 1836, 'Nameless' 1837, 'Harriet' 1839, lived Richmond Pl., Millbrook 1866.

CARREL, Philip 'Spey' 1871.

CARREL, Samuel 'Property' 1808, 'Sylph' 1810.

CARTER, G. F.	'Swan' 1890.
CARTER, Jean	'Master' 1697.
CARTER, Philip	'Elizabeth' 1735.
CARTWRIGHT, J.	son of Joseph Cole Cartwright, 'Fanny' 1870s.
CAVEY, Theodore John	b. 1862, d. 10.12.1901 Rio Grande, Brazil, stone in Macpéla cem., mar. Mary Jane Picot.
CERF (LE), Aaron	Captain or merchant before 1644.
CHAMBERS, James	b. 1805, lived Gorey 1866, 'Julia' 1859-63, 'Atrevida' 1868.
CHEVALIER, Abraham	'Charming Betty' c. 1740, 'Philip' 1744, 'Industry' 1747, 'Jersey Flower' 1756, 'Expedition Pkt' 1763, 'Sukey' 1764-65.
CHEVALIER, Charles	'Catherine' 1745, 'Union' 1764.
CHEVALIER, Charles	'Enterprise' 1823.
CHEVALIER, Francis	'Eclipse' c. 1860.
CHEVALIER, F.	'Success' 1792.
CHEVALIER, Henry	b. 1835, d. 1884, bur. Green Street, Harbourmaster at St H.
CHEVALIER, James Fixott	Master's Cert. No. 3322, 'Josephine' 1869.
CHEVALIER, Jean	'Pearl' 1737.
CHEVALIER, Jean	'Neptune' 1819-22, 'Peirson' 1833-46, 'Eclipse' 1859-60, lived St H. 1840s.
CHEVALIER, Louis John Francis	Master's Cert. No. 83927, 'Eliza' 1869.
CHEVALIER, Nicolas	'Betsy' 1778.
CHEVALIER, Peter John	'William Fruing', 1867.
CHEVALIER, P.	'Neptune' 1826.
CHEVALIER, Thomas	Master of sloop based at Bonne Nuit 1641.
CLARKE, Frederick	b. 1852, d. 1896, bur. St Mtn's cem. Master of 'Lalla Rookh' 1860.
CLARK, John	'Atalanta' 1837.
CLEMENT, John	b. 1715 Jersey, died c. 1805, to America.
CLEMENT, John	a privateer captain, lived Millbrook, St L., 'Stag' 1812, 'Pallas' 1815, 'Eliza' 1836.
CLEMENT, Nicolas	'Fly' 1795, 'Eliza' 1810, 'Friends' 1813-15.
CLEMENT, Peter	a privateer captain, 'Revenge' 1778, 'Charming Nancy' 1786.
CLEMENT, Peter	'Tor Abbey' 1803, 'Speedy' 1805, 'Hero' 1807, 'Venus' 1813-14, 'Pallas' 1817, 'Iris' 1820, 'Nameless' 1825.
CLERCQ (LE), Germain	'Delight' 1866-70.
COCQ (LE), Peter	b. 1808 Guernsey, 'Maria' 1837-39, 'Surprise' 1840.
COFFIN, F.	'Gaspé' 1829.
COLLAS, D.	'Two Brothers' 1853-60.
COLLAS, George	a privateer captain, 'Ceres' 1803-06.
COLLAS, John	'Jersey Lass' 1849.
COLLINGS, Nehemiah	'The Hart' 1649, one of Carteret's privateers.
COLLINGS, Robert Edw.	'Amelia' 1821.
COOMBES, William	'Prince William' 1748-49, 'Endeavour' 1774.
COOPER, D.	'Venus' 1859.
COOPER, Thomas	'Gulliver' 1834.
COPP, Thomas	'Swift' 1844.
CORBEL, Nathaniel	'Elizabeth' 1763.
CORNEILLE, ?	'Patris' 1649, one of Carteret's privateers.
CORNU (LE), Charles John	b. 1839, d. 26.5.1907.
CORNU (LE), Francis	b. 1840, d. 1903, bur. Mont a L'Abbe old cem., lived Prospect Terrace, St Aubin's Road, 'Vivid' 1860, 'Brilliant' 1879.

CORNU (LE), John   b. 1827, St O.?, d. 27.3.1894, bur. St O., medal awarded for services in French merchant navy 1861.
CORNU (LE), Jean   'Fancy' 1808–09, 'Anley' 1826.
CORNU (LE), Thomas   'Betsy' 1803–04.
CORT, James   b. 1803 Portsmouth, 'Favourite' 1847, 'St Croix' and 'Cornucopia' 1859, 'Stranger' c. 1861.
COSNARD, Francis   'Weazel' 1752, 'Gratitude' 1755.
COULLIARD (LE), Jean A.   b. St My., but lived Ty., Master's Cert. No. 25588, obtained 1867, 'C.R.C.' 1867, 'Weasel' 1871–74, 'St Brelade' 1871–80s.
COUTANCHE, Charles   'Magdalen' 1774, 'General Conway' 1778.
COUTANCHE, John   a privateer captain, 'Hazard' 1798, also 'Vulture' ?
COUTANCHE, John Edward   b. 1797 St L., son of Peter, d. Labrador 1840. 'John' 1835, 'Superb' 1838–40.
COUTANCHE, Josué   'William' 1742–43.
COUTANCHE, Philip   b. 1797 St Mtn., 'Speedwell' 1836, ? 1859.
COUTEUR (LE), Clement   'Success' 1790, 'Kitty' 1792.
COUTEUR (LE), Edward   'George' 1778–79, 'Commerce' 1792, 'London' 1811.
COUTEUR (LE), G. E.   'Maud' 1896.
COUTEUR (LE), George Jn   'Emma Eden' 1854, 'Hibernica' 1863.
COUTEUR (LE), James   lived St James Street, St H., 1860s, 'Hirondelle' 1845.
COURTEUR (LE), John B.   'Iris' 1858, 'Channel Queen' 1859.
COUTEUR (LE), John Dubois   lived Tyneville, St Aubin's Road, mar. Jane Curry, 'Emmeline' 1888.
COUTEUR (LE), John D.   b. 1828, d. 1881, 'C. Columbus' 1863.
COUTEUR (LE), Jean   'Mineric' 1779, 'Expedition' 1786.
COUREUR (LE), J. J.   d. 1913.
COUTEUR (LE), Nicolas   'Three Brothers' 1737, 'Squirrel' 1747.
COUTEUR (LE), Nicolas   'Nymph' 1852.
COUTEUR (LE), Philip Edw.   b. 1805 St H., lived Union Street, St H. 1860s, 'Royal George' 1836, 'Astrea' 1841, 'Highlander' 1848, 'George Dean' 1855, 'Nymph' 1856, 'True Blue' 1859, 'Eagle' 1860, 'Jersey Pkt' 1860.
COUTEUR (LE), Thomas   'Déese' 1859–60.
COUTEUR (LE), William   Master's Cert. No. 9235, 'Bertie' 1868.
COUVET (LE), Philip   'General Doyle' 1826.
CRAS (LE), George   b. 1806 St H., 'Three Sisters' 1836.
CRAS (LE), James   a privateer captain, 'Charming Betty' 1737–41, 'Friend's Delight' c. 1744.
CRAS (LE), J.   'Orange' 1649.
CRAS (LE), Philip   Master c. 1744.
CRAS (LE), Richard   'Philip & John' 1737, 'Montanley' 1741, 'Triton' 1746.
CRAS (LE), Thomas   'Magdaliene' 1792.
CROIX (LA), Josue   received an award for bravery, 'Obey' 1853–60, 'Crown' 1865.
CROIX (LA), Charles   'Elizabeth' 1737, 'Squirrel' 1744.
CROIX (LA), Jean   b. 1816, d. 1897, Mont a L'Abbe cem.
CROIX (LA), J.   'Young Peggy' 1813.
CRONIER (LE), George   a successful privateer captain, 'Defiance' 1756–57, 'Betsy & Mary' 1756–57 and others.
CRONIER (LE), Peter   lived Rue á La Greve, St H., 'Anne' 1807, 'Young Charles' 1808, 'Young Peggy' 1811–18.
CRONIER (LE), Philip   'Mary' 1778, 'Good Friends' 1790, 'George' 1792.
CROOME, James   'George & Henry' 1820.

CURTON, Robert	'Centurion' 1744.
DAIN (LE), John	b. 1818, d. 1903, mar. Ann Renouf, lived Rouge Bouillon, St H., bur. Mont á L'Abbe. 'Fanny Breslauer' 1897.
DAIN (LE), N.	'Ranger' and 'Oliver Blanchard' 18 ?
DAIN (LE), Thomas	Master's Cert. No. 8077, 'Oliver Blanchard' 1869, 'Seaflower' 1873.
DANIELS, J.	'Friendship' 1823.
D'AUVERGNE, Philip	b. St O., Master 1682.
D'AUVERGNE, Pierre	Master 1625, captured by Turks.
D'AUVERGNE, ?	Master of 'Harmony' 1792.
DAVEY, Robert	b. 1802, Brightlingsea, 'Mary & Ellen' 1836, 'Virginia' 1842–48.
DAVEY, Walter	awarded Jersey Humane Society medal for his rescue of the crew of an Italian brigantine wrecked off Jersey 1878, 'Albatross' 1878.
DAVEY, William	'Elizabeth' 1814
DAVEY, William	'Silver Cloud' and 'George & Mary' 1892, 'Glenville' 1905.
DEAN, Carteret	'Thomas & Jane' 1737–40, 'Elizabeth' 1729, trading with Newfoundland 1717.
DEAN, John	lived High Street, St Aubin, 'Jersey Lass' 1839, 'P. H. Dean' 1838.
DEAN, Philip	'Durell' 1776, 'Eagle' 1778, 'Industry' 1790.
DE CAEN, Jean	'Cousins' 1757–59.
DE CAEN, Jean	lived High Street, St Aubin, 'Bacchus' 1790, 'Nancy' 1808, 'Stag' 1809, 'Nancy' 1813, 'Felicity' 1815, 'Three Sisters' 1817, 'Jersey Tar' 1837.
DE CAEN, Jean	b. 1816 son of Jean, St B., Master 1836, 'Choice 1846.
DE CARTERET, Edward	'La Benedition' 1634–35.
DE CARTERET, Joseph	'Industry' 1816.
DE CARTERET, J. P.	'Fisherman' 1869, 'Normandy' 1874.
DE CARTERET, Philip	'Swan' 1750.
DE CARTERET, Richard	'Good Hope' 1587.
DE CARTERET, Richard	'Hirondelle' 1767, 'Venus' 1774.
DE CAUX, Philip	'St Peter' 1786–92.
DE FAYE, Francis	Master's Cert. No. 38685.
DE FEU, Alfred	Master's Cert. No. 85720, 'Anne Kay' 1877.
DE FEU, Charles	'Heraux' 1814, 'Nancy' 1815.
DE FEU, G.	'Swift' 1778.
DE FEU, Jean	'Adventure' 1786.
DE FEU, John	'Uberty' 1873.
DE FEU, Laurens	'Endeavour' 1778.
DE FEU, P. W.	bur. Mont á L'Abbe cem., ss 'Victoria' (L. & S.W.R.).
DE GAUL, Helier	'Edward' 1603.
DE GRUCHY, Abraham	drowned off Arichat with vessel 'G. Peabody' 1877; 'P.R.C.' 1869, 'C. Columbus' 1870.
DE GRUCHY, Charles	'Eliza Hands' 1864, 'Caesarea' 1877.
DE GRUCHY, Elias	'Hope' 1808, 'Hazard' 1822, 'Horatio' 1824, lived St H. 1840s.
DE GRUCHY, Elias	b. 1802, son of Philip, St S., mar. Jane Le Geyt. 'Marie' 1836, 'Two Friends' 1839, 'Encore' 1841–44, retired 1844.
DE GRUCHY, Francis	b. 1829, d. 10.1.1900, owner of 'Crown' 1876.
DE GRUCHY, Frederic	son of Jean and Caroline de Quetteville, emigrated to South Africa.
DE GRUCHY, George	no details.

DE GRUCHY, Jean	'Adventure' 1760-64.
DE GRUCHY, Jean	Master and owner of 'Royal George' 1840-56.
DE GRUCHY, Matthew	'Dispatch' 1840-42.
DE GRUCHY, Peter	'Jessie' 1857.
DE GRUCHY, Philip	b. 1801, St H., 'Geo. Canning' 1835, 'Prima' 1836, 'Adonis' 1838, 'Princess Royal' 1845, 'Stark', 'Commodore' and 'Fairy' 1847, 'Gulnare' 1849-51.
DE GRUCHY, Philip	b. 1767, mar. Elizabeth Binet, 'Maria' 1803, 'Comus' 1804, 'Masquerade' 1809-10.
DE GRUCHY, Philip	Master's Cert. No. 15003, 'Thetis' 1869.
DE GRUCHY, Philip	b. 1885, d. 1969, lived Le Catel, Rozel, St Mtn., a Care Line Master.
DE GRUCHY, Thomas	b. 1750 Ty., 'Rose' 1793-1811.
DE GRUCHY, William	son of Jean and Esther de Quetteville, mar. ? Le Gros
DE GRUCHY, W.	'Encore' 1844.
DE LA HAYE, C.	'Messenger' ?
DE LA HAYE, Francis	b. 1821, d. 1868, bur. Green Street cem.
DE LA HAYE, John	b. 1791, son of John, 'Liberty' 1832.
DE LA HAYE, Josué	'Juno' 1837-52, 'Seaflower' 1872.
DE LA MARE, Thomas	'Larch' 1827.
DE LA PERRELLE, Clement	lived Millbrook, St L., 'Francis & Ann' 1859.
DE LA PERRELLE, Elias	'Gaspé' 1814, 'Oliver Blanchard' 1821, also 'Time & Chance', 'Cod Hook', d. 1857, buried St P's cem.
DE LA PERRELLE, Francis	b. 1797, St O., 'Seaflower' 1835-36, 'C. Columbus' 1841, retired 1846.
DE LA PERRELLE, George	b. 1803, St O., son of Francis, 'Egton' 1836, 'Isabella' 1838, retired 1847.
DE LA PERRELLE, John	Bee 1852.
DE LA PERRELLE, Philip	'Francis & Ann' 1849.
DE LA RUE, Nicolas	'Nautilus' 1821, 'Louisa' 1859.
DE LA TASTE, E.	'Good Intent' 1778-79.
DE LA TASTE, Philip Matt	'Cynthie' 1864.
DE QUETTEVILLE, Philip Francis	'Belus' 1840, 'Echo' 1842.
DESLANDES, E. J.	b. 1827, lived St S. Road 1880s, Master c. 1880s.
DESLANDES, G.	d. 1885 ?
DESLANDES, Jean	b. 1810 St H., son of George, d. at Odessa 1840, stone Green Street cem., Master 1838, 'Good Luck' 1840.
DESLANDES, Philip	b. 1825, d. 1854, bur. Green Street cem.
DE SOULEMENT, Guillaume	Master of 'La Marie' 1537. Set upon by Spanish at La Rochelle, ship seized and crew stripped of all but their shirts.
DE STE CROIX, André	'Capré' 1708.
DE STE CROIX, Elie	'Jersey Pkt', 1779-90.
DE STE CROIX, Francis	'Ann' 1821, 'Ceres' 1824.
DE STE CROIX, James	'Success' and 'Mary' c. 1744.
DE STE CROIX, Jean	'Pitt' 1778, 'Concorde' 1790.
DE STE CROIX, Philip Robert ?	lived High Street, St Aubin, 'Elizabeth' 1846, 'Evening Star' 1854, Harbourmaster St Aubin 1873-84.
DE STE CROIX, Thomas	'Concord' 1786, brother of Jean ?
DE STE CROIX, John Thomas Deveau	'Harriet' 1840.
DE VEULLE, John George	Master's Cert. No. 17737, 'Blonde' 1867.

DICKENSON, John   drowned 1850, 'Victory' 1836, 'Virginia' 1839, 'Blue Eyed
(or Dickerson)   Maid' 1841, 'Jane' 1847, 'Admiral' 1850.
DICKENSON, Robert A.   'Celebrity' 1824, 'Henry' 1826.
DOLBEL, George   'Defiance' 1785.
DOLBEL, James   b. 1800, St H., son of Jean, 'Hero' and 'Pallas' 1836, 'Broad-
                          axe' and 'Andes' 1840–41, retired 1845.
DOLBEL, James Graham   'Maggie' 1862.
DOLBEL, Jean   'Resolution' 1790–92.
DOLBEL, Jean   'Isabella' 1838.
DOLBEL, M.   'Bee' 1778.
DOLBEL, Nicolas   A privateer captain, 'Mayflower' 1801–03.
DOLBEL, Philip   'Regulator' 1794, 'Young Peggy' 1804, 'Netley' 1815.
DOREY, George Jourdain   'Navigator' 1851.
DOREY, Henry   b. Jersey, son of George, lived Arichat.
DOREY, John   b. Jersey, 1860, son of George.
DOREY, John Le Couteur   Master's Cert. No. 22867, 'Pandora' 1867.
DOREY, P.   'Jersey' 1786.
DORWARD, John   b. 1783 Devonport, 'Resolution' 1835.
DORWARD, Nicolas Gribble b. 1817 Devonport, lost at sea 1850, 'Olive Branch' 1836.
DOWLE, Richard   'Bon Aventure' 1587.
DOWNER, George   b. 1801 G., son of Charles, lived La Folie ?, 'Grog' 1836,
                          'Peggy' 1840, 'C.R.C.' 1844, 'Jersey Maid' 1845, 'Panope'
                          1846, 'Sarah' 1847, 'Lark' 1848, 'Ellin' 1850, 'Childers'
                          1855, 'Napier' 1859.

DRELAUD, Peter   Master's Cert. Nos. 38321 and 76208, 'Stranger' 1854, 'Tom
                          & Mary' 1859–64, 'Bridemaid' 1867, 'Ocean Bride' 1875.
DU BOIS, Edward   'Hope' 1807, 'Brunswick' 1810, 'Endeavour' 1811.
DU BOIS, Jean   'Anne' 1811.
DU BOIS, Samuel   'Swift' 1790–92.
DU BOIS, Thomas   'Mentor' 1814, 'Anvil' 1821.
DU FRESNE, Francis   b. 1816 St Mtn., son of Philip, d. 1861, Master 1836, 'Courier'
                          1859.
DU HEAUME, Edward   m. Nancy Hubert, 'Chagamau' 1829.
DU HEAUME, Francis   'Bathelleur' 1731, 'Pretty' 1751.
DU HEAUME, George   b. 1810 St O., wife née Janvrin, d. 1857, bur. Almorah cem.
                          'Pelican' 1835, 'Fanny' 1836, 'Adventure' 1939–49, 'Unity'
                          1849, 'Canopus' 1850–56.
DU HEAUME, Jean   'Lynx' 1786–90.
DU HEAUME, Philip   'Antelope' 1825, 'Swift' 1826, 'Ranger' 1831, son of Philip.
DU HEAUME, Philip   son of Jean of St O., 'Active' 1806, 'Apollo' 1823, 'Swift'
                          1835, retired 1841.
DU HEAUME, William   'Neptune' 1803–05.
DU JARDIN, Thomas Ancot   'Brothers' 1826.
DUMARESQ, Clement   lived St My. 1860s, 'Rover' 1854.
DUMARESQ, Edward   'Concorde' 1717.
DUMARESQ, Jean   Master c. 1790.
DUMARESQ, John Felix   Master's Cert. No. 22605, 'Trust' 1881.
DUMARESQ, Nicolas   Captain or merchant before 1644.
DUMARESQ, Philip   'Kitty' 1787.
DUMARESQ, Philip   b. Jersey 1695, son of Elias and Frances de Carteret, d. before
                          1744; to Boston, America c. 1716. Privateer captain from
                          Boston.
DUMARESQ, Philip   Master of 'Express' 1851.

DU PARCQ, Jean — Master of 'Philip' 1737, Captain Jean Du Parc left Jersey 1765 for Norway to buy timber for building the General Hospital, St H. with a draught of £150.

DU PONT, Philip — A privateer captain, 'Hope' 1803–04, 'Rose' 1810–12, 'Phoenix' 1813, 'Surprise' 1813, 'Hero' 1817, 'Speculator' 1818.

DUPRÉ, Edward — Lived St P. *c.* 1880, master of 'Circassian' 1864.

DUPRÉ, Francis — b. 1797 St L., son of George, 'Harmony' 1836, 'Dolphin' 1840.

DUPRÉ, Jean — b. 1808 St L., son of George, 'Pallas' 1836, 'Augia' 1838–, 'Syren' 1840.

DUPRÉ, Nicolas — 'Industry' 1744, 'Jersey Galley' 1748.

DUPRÉ, Philip — Master of 'Adventure' 1856.

DUPRÉ, Philip — 'Elizabeth' *c.* 1744, 'John' *c.* 1744, 'Joseph & Ann' 1746.

DURANT, Abraham — Privateer captain 1703–11.

DURELL, Clement — 'Hercules' 1790, 'Anne & Mary' 1792.

DURELL, Francis — Lived Snow Hill, St H., *c.* 1840, 'Property' 1807, 'Netley' 1813–14, 'Christy & Jane' 1822.

DURELL, James — Master of 'Jubilee' 1813–14.

DURELL, Nathaniel — Master *c.* 1629.

DURELL, Philip — 'Marie' 1786, 'Industry' 1803.

DUVAL, Francis Nicolas — lived Jersey, drowned off brig 'Siren' 1820.

DUVAL, J. — 'Vulture' 1800–04.

DUVAL, Nicolas — 'Amity' 1817–19.

DUVAL, Philip — b. *c.* 1771, 'Esther' 1810, 'De Jersey' 1815, 'Amity' 1825.

DUVAL, Peter John — b. 1794 St B., son of Peter, a very successful privateer captain, 'Farmer' 1803, 'Young Phoenix' 1804–12, 'Vulture' 1815, also 'Messenger', 'Aeolus'. He later became a merchant, ship-owner and owned a fishery company, d. 1835 Bonaventure Island.

EARLES, William — b. 1804, Penzance, 'Green End' 1831–35, 'Champion' 1840, 'Gipsy' 1846–47, retired 1850.

EFFARD, Nicolas — Captain of Frigate (Royal Navy ?) 1684.

ERITH, Elijah — Master of 'Kingfisher' 1834.

ERITH, Henry Philip — b. 1832, d. 1904, bur. Les Croix cem., lived Gorey 1855, mar. Mary Baker of Cornwall, 'Regina' 1866, 'Regalia' 1872.

ESNOUF, Elias — 'Three Brothers' 1804.

ESNOUF, George — b. 1804, St L., 'Charlotte' 1836, 'Rapide' 1838, 'Sibyl' 1840–41, 'Turk' 1845, 'Aurora' 1847, retired 1847.

ESNOUF, Philip — 'Ceres' 1835.

ESTHUR, Richard — 'London Pkt' 1754–65.

EVENDEN, ? — 'Childers' 1840.

FAINTON, Philip — 'Recovery' 1767–77, 'Bee' 1774 and 1778, 'St Lawrence' 1783, 'Aurora' 1786, also 'Orange' 1764.

FALLE, Clement — 'Favorite' 1803.

FALLE, Edward — 'Stag' 1807, 'Friends' 1814.

FALLE, Elias John — 'Lady Falkland' 1840, 'Renard' 1849.

FALLE, George — 'Rover' 1804, 'Fancy' 1805, 'Speedy Pkt' 1807–08, 'Hero' 1815–24.

FALLE, John — 'Phoenix' 1756–65, 'Charlotte' 1776.

FALLE, John — 'Horatio' 1820.

FALLE, Josue — lived St B's Bay, *c.* 1866, 'Anley' 1831, 'Farmer' 1848, 'Atlas' 1853.

FALLE, Philip	Master's Cert. No. 16499, lived Chevalier Road, St H., 'Star' 1866.
FALLE, Philip Clement	b. 1822, d. 1888, Master for the Weymouth and Channel Islands Steam Packet Co.
FALLE, Thomas	Master of 'Vine' 1790.
FALLE, Thomas	b. 1800 St S.? 'Reward' 1836, 'Penelope' 1841.
FAUVEL, Henry	b. 1785 St C., son of Philip, 'Beehive' 1820–46, 'Lark' 1848, 'Witch' 1849.
FAUVEL, John	'Friendship' 1747.
FAUVEL, John	'Diamond' 1817–20.
FAUVEL, John	b. 1794 St S., d. 24.4.1880, mar. Eliza Reynolds. 'Loyal William' 1836, Unicorn' 1850–54, 'Notte' 1840, 'Wasp' 1841, retired 1854.
FAUVEL, Jean	b. 1806, lived St H., c. 1840, 'Etton' 1831, 'Ellin' 1836, 'Mary & Elizabeth' 1836, 'General Don' 1846–54.
FEREY, George	Survivor of wreck of 'Islander' British Columbia.
FEREY, Philip	b. 1813 St Mtn., 'Iris' 1847, 'Willing' 1861, 'Start' 1868.
FEUVRE (LE), Clement	Master of 'Jupiter' 1792.
FEUVRE (LE), Edward	'Friendship' 1790.
FEUVRE (LE), Edward	b. 1799, lived High Street, St Aubin, c. 1866, 'Egton' 1826, 'Duke of Wellington' 1830–31, 'Christy & Jane' 1836, 'Laurel' 1836–41, retired 1841.
FEUVRE (LE), Edward John	b. 1801, St H., son of Jean, 'St Peter' 1832–36.
FEUVRE (LE), Edward	b. 1832 St O., lived St Aubin, Master's Cert. No. 19905 obtained Plymouth 2.2.1859, 'Bolina' 1850–60.
FEUVRE (LE), Elias Phillipe	Master's Cert. No. 84721, 'Warrior' 1868, C. Columbus 1870, 'Lilian' 1873.
FEUVRE (LE), Francis	lived St P.?, drowned 1836, 'Laurel' 1836, 'Port' 1826.
FEUVRE (LE), Francis	'Magot' 1792, 'Dawkins' 1792, 'Stag' 1794, 'Esther' 1805, 'Juno' 1823, also 'Revenge' 1786.
FEUVRE (LE), Francis	b. 1787 St H., lived Sand Street, St H. c. 1866, 'Temperance' 1836, 'Resolution' 1836.
FEUVRE (LE), Francis John	'Spy' 1870, Master's Cert. No. 16090.
FEUVRE (LE), George	'Ceres' 1803, 'Union' 1811.
FEUVRE (LE), Jean	'Friendship' 1786, 'Marguerite' 1794, 'Sukey' 1792, 'Papillion' 1807, 'John' 1813.
FEUVRE (LE), Jean	b. 1793, d. 1870, bur. St B's cem.
FEUVRE (LE), Jean	b. 1802 St B., lived Belmont Road, St H., Master's Cert. No. 43372. 'Dit-On' 1835, 'Navigator' 1841, 'Neptune' 1851 and 1859.
FEUVRE (LE), John	'Great Western Railway' Master, ss 'Ibex' c. 1897, ss 'Roebuck' c. 1911.
FEUVRE (LE), John Fr.	b. 1805 St L., 'Nameless' 1836.
FEUVRE (LE), Peter	'Dean' 1836, 'Bellona' 1838, 'Aurora' 1842, 'Trial' 1846, 'Good Luck' 1848, 'Lord Nelson' 1849, 'Perseverance' 1851, 'Lord Nelson' 1852.
FEUVRE (LE), Philip	'London Pkt' 1754–65, 'Nancy' 1759–63, 'Phoenix' 1756–, 'Esther' 1764.
FEUVRE (LE), Philip	'Lord Nelson' 1804, 'John Bull' 1805, 'Anne' 1813, 'Minerva' 1814–15, 'Venus' 1815, 'Jo' 1824, 'Sophia' 1825, 'Mary' 1816, 'Esther' 1817, 'Sir Sydney Smith' 1819.
FEUVRE (LE), Philip	lived St P., son of Jean, 'Christy & Jane' 1835, 'Laurel' 1837.

FEUVRE (LE), Philip J.	b. 1777 St P., son of Philip, 'Enterprise' 1831, 'Nelson' 1824, retired 1836.
FEUVRE (LE), Richard	'Stephen' 1711, 'L'Estienne' 1712, 'Dartmouth Galley' 1740–41.
FEUVRE (LE), Richard	'Virginia' 1809.
FEUVRE (LE), Robert	'John & Mary' 1741.
FEUVRE (LE), S.	'Jane' 1780–96.
FEUVRE (LE), Thomas	'Dumaresq' and 'Press On' c. 1780–96, lived Quebec?
FILLEUL, Andrew	'Lytella' 1587.
FILLEUL, John	'Bonaventure' 1588.
FILLEUL, John	lived Bulwarks, St Aubin 1789, 'John' 1737–44, 'Vulture' and 'Seaflower' 1778.
FILLEUL, Philip Jn	'Queen of the Seas' 1864, Master's Cert. No. 5376.
FILLEUL, Thomas	'John' 1737–39, brother of John?
FILLEUL, Thomas	'Revenge' 1778, 'Phoenix' 1800, 'Cleopatra' 1803–09.
FILLEUL, Thomas	b. 1796, St C., drowned off Dundee 1848, 'Tiphys' 1836, 'Apollo' 1837, 'Swift' 1839, 'Johnny' 1841, 'Dido' 1842, 'Canopus' 1842, 'Friends' 1842, 'Mary' 1843, 'Beehive' 1844, 'General Don' 1846, 'Tom & Mary' 1847, 'Commodore' 1848.
FINNIE, Logan	b. 1795 St H., son of Logan, 'Diamond' 1814–15, 'Kitty' 1818, 'Charlotte' 1831, 'Spartan' 1835.
FIOTT, Edward	b. 1749, son of Nicolas, Master of his father's vessel 'Willing Mind' 1766–74, 'Tartar' 1774–1778. 'Tartar' (600 tons) 1779–1780.
FIOTT, John	'Adventure' 1737.
FIOTT, John	'Elizabeth' 1778, 'Alarm' 1780, 'Adventure' 1803, also 'Tartar' 1764
FIOTT, Nicolas	'Alligator' 1812.
FIOTT, Nicolas	b. 1704, died 1786 unmar., 'Charming Nancy' 1734, 'Charming Betty' 1759–63.
FLEMING, John	Master's Cert. No. 35988, lived Pomona Road, St H. 1860s, 'Bee' 1868.
FLEURY, René	Master of 'Phoenix' 1751–52.
FONDAN, Philip	lived Bulwarks, St Aubin, 'Le Don De Dieu' 1728, 'Two Partners' 1745.
FORGE (LA), John Fr.	Master's Cert. No. 24693, 'Chance' 1866, 'Ellen' 1872.
FOUR (LE), Francis	'Corbet' 1790, 'Vine' 1792.
FOUR (LE), George	b. 1846, lived Gorey 1885, mar. Mary Louisa Tardif, Master of 'George & Mary' 1875.
FOUR (LE), Samuel	mar. Mary ?, Master of 'Samuel & Mary' 1848.
FRUING, William	Master of 'Success' 1744.
GABOUREL, John	Master of 'John' 1715.
GABOUREL, Josué	'Anne' 1723–29, 'Friend' 1758.
GABOUREL, Thomas	Master c. 1696.
GALLAIS (LE), Aaron	Master c. 1733.
GALLAIS (LE), Jean	'Speedwell' 1745–46, 'Jersey Pkt' 1792.
GALLAIS (LE), Jean	'Joseph & Jane' 1818, 'Samuel' 1824.
GALLAIS (LE), James	'Eliza' 1814.
GALLAIS (LE), Peter	Master of 'Jo' 1825.
GALLAIS (LE), Richard	a privateer captain, 'Comus' 1801, 'Belle Richard' 1803.
GALLICHAN, Abraham	'Alpha' 1842
GALLICHAN, Clement	Master c. 1642.
GALLICHAN, Clement	'Seaflower' 1826.

GALLICHAN, Daniel	'Providence' 1745–46.
GALLICHAN, Edward Jn.	b. St H., 'Waterwitch' 1836, 'Ariel' 1845, 'United' 1847–49.
GALLICHAN, Frederic	Master's Cert. No. 17230, 'Ceylon' 1867.
GALLICHAN, George	Master c. 1851.
GALLICHAN, John	'Dove' 1840.
GALLICHAN, Philip	'Rocou' 1803, 'Friend' 1806.
GALLICHAN, Thomas	ss 'Yarra' c. 1914.
GALLIE, Edward	'Resolution' 1778.
GALLIE, James	'Adventure' 1804.
GALLIE, Jean	a privateer captain, mar. Marie Le Masurier, 'Comus' 1803–05.
GALLIE, J. J.	'Adolphus Yates' 1845.
GALLIE, Philip	'Charlotte' 1785–90, 'Friendship' 1792, 'Chance' 1814, 'Belle Ann' 1815.
GALLIENE, Charles	'Hope' 1764.
GALLIENE, James	d. in wreck off New Zealand, no date.
GASNIER, James	'Jenny' 1792.
GASNIER, Samuel	b. Jersey, very successful privateer captain, 'Lottery' 1798, 'Hazard' 1798–1803, 'Vulture' 1813' also 'Robert & Jane'.
GAUDIN, Abraham	'Angelique' 1790, 'Fairy' 1792.
GAUDIN, David	b. late 1700s, d. 1860, mar.: 1st Elizabeth de Gruchy; 2nd Elizabeth de Quetteville, removed to Canada in his own schooner 1830.
GAUDIN, David	Master c. 1873, mar. Elizabeth Sohier.
GAUDIN, Edward	Master of ss 'Dumfries', mar. D. May, daughter of Captain May of St Malo, d. 1872, stone St P's cem.
GAUDIN, Elias	b. 1811, mar. Elizabeth Hamon, lived Lynwood, G.
GAUDIN, Elias	b. 1843, son of Elias and Elizabeth Hamon, Master of cutter 'Dauntless' c. 1910, d. 1910, stone G. cem., mar. Esther Jane Touzel.
GAUDIN, Elias Ph.	'Hopewell' 1840, 'Trust' 1848.
GAUDIN, Francis	Master of 'Betsy & Jane' 1850, lived Eden Ho., Beaumont.
GAUDIN, Henry	Master of 'Abigail' 1628 and 1635.
GAUDIN, James	b. Jersey 1838, son of James R., d. Victoria, B.C. 1913. Lived at White Horse, B.C. known as the Yukon Navigator.
GAUDIN, James R.	b. Jersey 1807, mar. Agnes Anderson, Master of Hudson Bay Cos. barque 'Lady Lampson' 1869–77. Long career in British Columbia.
GAUDIN, Jean	d. 1873, bur. Mont á L'Abbe.
GAUDIN, John	b. 1847, d. 1927, mar. Elisha Bertram, Master of 'Sappho' 1879–99.
GAUDIN, Philip	b. 1755, mar. Esther de Quetteville, 'Providence' 1796.
GAUDIN, Philip	b. 1808 Jersey, son of David and Elizabeth de Gruchy, lived Herupe, St John, removed to Canada.
GAUDIN, William Chas.	b. 1825 son of William and Ann Bertram, Master of 'Eclipse' 1871, mar. Suzanne Tarr, emigrated to New Zealand.
GAUTIER, Francis	Mary 1757.
GAUTIER, Noé	'Duke of Richmond' 1763–64, 'Sukey' 1772, 'Revenge' 1778.
GAUTIER, Philip	'Diligent' 1780.
GAUTIER, William	ss 'Achibster' c. 1914.
GAUTIER, ?	Master of sloop 1766–69.
GAVEY, Jean	b. 1802 St S., 'Broadaxe' 1836, 'Andes' 1841, 'Collier' 1852.
GAVEY, Josue	Captain or merchant before 1644.
GAVEY, Josua	b. 1764, d. 1833, bur. Green Street cem.

GAVEY, Josua — b. 1769, d. 1861, bur. St S's cem., Master of 'Rose' 1808.

GAVEY, Josua — b. 1796, d. 1865, bur. St S.

GEFFRARD, Charles — Master of 'Hope' 1747–52.

GEFFRARD, J. — 'Three Friends' 1745–47.

GEFFRARD, J. (Jean) — 'Expedition' 1778, 'Aeolus' 1780, 'Rose' 1798.

GEILPH, ? — Master of one of Carteret's privateers, c. 1645.

GEYT (LE), C. M. — Master of 'Fort Regent' 1863.

GEYT (LE), Daniel — Master of Molly & Betsy' 1786, brother of Edward ?

GEYT (LE), Edward — 'Molly' 1783.

GEYT (LE), George — b. 1756, d. 1794, a privateer captain, 'Molly' 1782–83, 'Union' 1787–90.

GEYT (LE), James — Privateer captain, 'Tartar' 1800–03.

GEYT (LE), Jean — 'Dispatch' 1780–96.

GEYT (LE), Peter — 'Hope' c. 1745.

GEYT (LE), Philip — b. 1785, St H., son of Philip, 'Dundas' 1821, 'Phoenix' 1824, 'Larch' 1833–36, 'Rambler' 1844, retired 1844.

GEYT (LE), Thomas — 'Fancy' 1790, 'Liberty' 1798.

GIBAUT, Francis — b. 1804, d. 1849 Naples, mar. Francoise Asplet, 'Oliver Blanchard' 1834–36, 'Patruus' 1839, 'C.R.C.' 1847. Lived G.?

GIBAUT, Jean — 'Elizabeth' 1744.

GIBAUT, Moses Am. — b. 1797 G., 'Larch' 1825, 'Fisherman' 1836, 'Homely' 1842–46.

GIBAUT, Nicolas — 'Expedition Pkt', 1763, 'Industry' 1786.

GIFFARD, Jean — 'John & Mary' 1786.

GIFFARD, John Philip — b. 1826, d. 1892, Master of 'Telegraph' 1851, John Philip was also a stonemason and a Gardien of the prison.

GIFFARD, Philip — Master of 'Eole' 1778.

GIFFARD, Philip — Master's Cert. No. 40282, 'Industry' 1867.

GILLAM, Charles B. — lived St H., d. with ship 9.3.1891, 'Laurite' 1873, 'Aquilon' 1891.

GILMAN, Henry — Master of 'Kroo Boy' 1866, 'Prima' 1836, 'Nameless' 1836, drowned off Lagos, Nigeria 1866.

GODEL, George — 'Trust' 1810.

GODFRAY, Aaron — 'Peggy' 1799, 'Resolution' 1803, 'Constant Pkt' 1806.

GODFRAY, Francis — 'Betsy' 1790, 'Lively' 1803.

GODFRAY, Francis — b. 1834, d. 1899, bur. G. cem., mar. Betsy (Elise) Pepin, Master's Cert. No. 94396, 'Belted Will' 1879.

GODFRAY, Francis — Master's Cert. No. 18429, 'Supply' 1864, 'Zingara' 1864.

GODFRAY, Hugh — b. 1794, St Mtn., son of Hugh, 'Peggy' 1826–45, retired 1840.

GODFRAY, James — lived St H., 'Elizabeth Ann' 1823.

GODFRAY, John — b. 1784, 'Egton' 1821, 'Royal Charlotte' 1821, 'St Anne' 1836, 'Three Friends' 1837, 'Diana' 1837–48, lived St C.?

GODFRAY, John Charles — b. 1813, St Mtn., son of Philip, 'Cerus' 1835–36.

GODFRAY, John Philip — b. 1800, St H., d. at sea 10.10.1856, 'Guillelmo' 1837, 'George' 1842, 'Waterwitch' 1844, 'Richard' 1848–56.

GODFRAY, Lerrier — 'Island Queen' 1867.

GOODRIDGE, James — b. 1782, d. 1855, bur. St S's cem., 'Henry Pkt' 1832, ss 'Courier' 1855.

GOSSET, William — in New Westminster, B.C. c. 1860.

GRAND (LE), Elias — 'Resolution' 1814, 'Cora' 1820–21, 'Britannia' 1831.

GRAND (LE), Frederic — b. 1811 St P., son of Elias, 'Dean' 1833, 'Flora' 1835–37, 'Mary & Joseph' 1838, 'Reward' 1840.

GRAND (LE), John   lived Andover Lodge, St P. 1860s, Master of 'Cora' 1831.
GRANDIN, Collas   Master of vessel going to the Minquiers 1615.
GRANDIN, Jeremie   Master of 'Le Francois' c. 1644.
GRANT, G. W.   'Red Gauntlet' 1881.
GRAUT, Joseph Joshua   'Azur' 1871, 'Rolling Wave' 1873, 'Empress' 1876, 'Wild Wave' 1879, 'Empress' 1890, 'Mermaid' 1903.

GRESLEY (LE), Amice, Ph.   b. St O., 'Twig' 1836, 'Charlotte' 1837, 'Britannia' 1838.
GRESLEY (LE), Edward   'Rambler' 1874.
GRESLEY (LE), Elias   'Success' 1745–48.
GRESLEY (LE), Helier   Master's Cert. No. 51037, 'Guess' 1869.
GRESLEY (LE), Henry   'Donna Maria' 1875, also 'Ocean Pet'.
GRESLEY (LE), John Fr.   lived St P.?, 'Hematope' 1896, also 'Fanny Breslauer', 'Patruus' and 'Robin', d. c. 1905.
GRESLEY (LE), Jean   drowned 5.2.1811 when 'Fox' was lost near Waterford, 'Mary & Betsy' 1790, 'Ocean' 1803, 'Enterprise' 1807, 'Fox' 1811.
GRESLEY (LE), Jean   b. 1780 St O., 'Swift' 1835, 'Pelican' 1836, 'Belus' 1840, 'Nameless' 1844, 'Jersey Maid' 1846.
GRESLEY (LE), Philip   'James Harmer' 1874.
GRESLEY (LE), Philip   'Two Friends' 1809, 'Concord' 1819.
GRESLEY (LE), William   'Rover' 1804.
GROS (LE), Daniel   b. 1802, St Mtn., 'Laurel' 1836, 'Mary Jane' 1847–55.
GROS (LE), Edward   'Fanny' 1810, 'Neptune' 1814–16, 'Sir Sydney Smith' 1820.
GROS (LE), Edward   Master's Cert. No. 6288, 'Nagasaki' 1867.
GROS (LE), Elias   'Elizabeth' 1737–39, 'Hope' 1739–47.
GROS (LE), George   'Dartmouth Galley' 1734–44, 'Matthew' 1744.
GROS (LE), George   b. 1790 Tr.?, son of George, 'Pallas' 1822–26, 'Concord' 1836, 'Newport' 1838–39, lived St H. c. 1840.
GROS (LE), Jean   b. 1799 St Mtn., son of Jean, Master 1836, 'Jim' 1848, drowned 1850.
GROS (LE), John   b. 1797 St L., son of John, 'Ebenezer' 1836, 'Two Friends' 1836, 'Mary Ann' 1840, 'Diadem' 1844, 'Sarah' 1846, 'Sophia' 1854, 'Express' 1859–60.
GROS (LE), John   'Jane' 1737–38, 'Industry' 1744–46, 'Joseph & Ann' 1745–46, 'John' 1747, 'King George' 1747, 'Charming' 1747, 'Sally' 1757, 'John' 1760.
GROS (LE), John   lived St Mtn., c. 1861, obtained Master's Cert. 1861, No. 74106, 'Zephyr' 1874.
GROS (LE), J. G.   Master of 'Mistletoe' 1876, Master and owner of ketch 'Her Majesty' 1890–1904.
GROS (LE), Josiah   'Three Friends' 1745–47.
GROS (LE), Josiah   'Kitten' 1864, lived G. 1880?
GROS (LE), Philip   lived Glenroy, Rue de Haut, St L., 'Freedom' 1842.
GROS (LE), Thomas Nic.   Master's Cert. No. 18480, 'Alice Jane'.
GRUCHY, Elias   'General Hope' 1803–07.
GRUCHY, James   'Expedition Pkt' 1763–64.
GRUCHY, John   b. Trinity, lived Khartoum Villa, Beach Road, ss 'Naparima' 1895–96, ss 'Crown of Grenada' 1902, 'Capt. Gruchy' was awarded a piece of silver by the Russian Government for a rescue he carried out 13.4.1895.
GRUCHY, John   b. 1851, d. 5.12.1913, mar. Mary Ann Valpy, bur. Les Croix cem., G.
GRUCHY, John   b. 1793, lived at Ty., 'Joseph H. Grace' 1809, 'Property' 1811, 'Sisters' 1817, 'Hebe' 1827, 'Thebe' 1835, 'Pomona' 1835–37.

GRUCHY, Philip	'Joseph John' 1803.
GRUCHY, Thomas	'Black Prince' 1780.
GUILLAUME, Francis	'Hope' 1739, 'Joseph & Ann' 1746.
GUILLAUME, Jacques	Captain or merchant before 1644.
GUILLAUME, John	'Bona Spera' 1587.
GUILLAUME, Thomas	'Dyamont' 1587.
GUILLET, George	b. 1804 St. H.?, 'Guernsey Lily' 1836–40.
GUILLET, John	'Dolphin' 1826.
GUILLET, Samuel	'Phoenix' 1756–65.
GUITON, Jean	'Lovely Jane' c. 1737.
HACQUOIL, Edward	b. 1849, lived Homestill, Mont á L'Abbe, mar. Elizabeth Sarre, d. 20.10.1910, Master of 'Tickler' 1870–83.
HACQUOIL, Francis	b. 1801 St B.?, son of Jean, 'Habnab' 1836–48, retired 1848.
HACQUOIL, Francis	b. 1831 L'Etacq, St O., mar. Mary Vibert, d. 1872, bur. St O's Methodist cem.
HACQUOIL, Francis Pet.	coal merchants in Cardiff c. 1880, partnership with Captain J. P. Hacquoil.
HACQUOIL, H.	drowned in storm en voyage from Jersey to Gaspé 1880s.
HACQUOIL, Jean	Master of 'Telegraph' 1847–51.
HACQUOIL, J. P.	coal merchants in Cardiff in partnership with Captain F. P. Hacquoil 1880s, may be connected with Cardiff House, St P.
HACQUOIL, Peter	son of Philip, obtained Master's Cert. 1850, Master of 'Telegraph' 1853, mar. Jane Le Maistre, drowned at sea. 'Amity' 1836, 'Guess' 1839, 'Syrcn' 1840, 'Neptune' 1846, 'United' 1848, 'Navigator' 1853.
HACQUOIL, Philip	lived St O., a successful privateer captain, his sword is now in Société Jersiaise Museum. 'Just' 1810, 'Union' 1811, 'Phoenix' 1812–13, 'Lottery' 1813–14.
HACQUOIL, Philip	b. 1807 St O., son of Philip, 'Concord' 1839, 'Flora' 1843.
HACQUOIL, Philip Wm.	b. 1853, d. at sea off Santos, Brazil 11.2.1896, stone St L. cem., mar. Mary Ann Hamon. 'Oliver Blanchard'.
HACQUOIL, Thomas	Master of 'Paspébiac' 1786–90.
HAMMOND, Henry	'Hero' 1831.
HAMMOND, John	Master of 'Nimble' 1815.
HAMON, Charles	'Young Eliza' 1808, 'Surinam' 1811, 'North Star' 1812, 'Catherine' 1813–15–17, 'Pomona' 1822–26.
HAMON, Daniel	a successful privateer captain, 'Neptune' 1786–90, 'Phoenix' 1798–1803, 'Vulture' 1809' 1809–12.
HAMON, Edward	'General Brock' 1822, 'Lively' 1816, 'Catherine' 1818.
HAMON, Elias	b. 1796 St H., son of Peter, 'Guernsey Lily' 1835, 'Echo' 1837.
HAMON, Francis	'Constant' 1807.
HAMON, Jacques	b. 1834, son of Thomas, a Fruing captain.
HAMON, James	b. 1806 St B., son of Francis, d. 24.11.1884, 'St George' 1836, 'Rollo' 1837, 'Judith' 1838, 'Rachel' 1843, 'Echo' 1852.
HAMON, Jean	'Jersey Pkt' 1785, 'Anne & Mary' 1790, 'Beaver' 1790.
HAMON, Jean	b. 1802 St H., son of Jean, lived Colomberie 1866, 'Venus' 1834–44, 'Iris' 1844, 'Harriet' 1855, 'Iris' 1856.
HAMON, Jean	b. 1808 St B., son of Philip, drowned at sea 1839? 'Prince Regent' 1835, 'Susan' 1837.
HAMON, John Edmund	Master's Cert. No. 4008, Juventa'.
HAMON, J. Fr.	b. 1804 St L., 'Royal George' 1830–35.

HAMON, John Peter	mar. Anne Weary, Master of 'Percy Douglas' 1863, stained glass window to his memory in St Aubin's church.
HAMON, N.	'Nancy' 1764.
HAMON, Philip	lived Bulwarks, St Aubin 1789, 'Hope' 1770–79, 'Kitty' 1794, 'Speculator' 1810, also 'Seaflower'.
HAMON, Philip	Master of 'Charming Nancy' 1825.
HAMON, Philip	b. 1811, lived Gorey 1885, 'Swift' 1856, 'Hearty' 1851, 'Commander' 1847, 'Fearless' 1848, 'Glenville' 1885, son of Philip.
HAMON, Thomas	Master of 'George Dean' 1840.
HARDELEY, John	Master of 'Vincent' 1837, mar. into Collas family.
HARRIS, George Rees	ss 'Wetherpack', c. 1914.
HARRY, Matthew	'Dragon' 1595.
HAWES, G. C.	'Glenville'.
HELLEUR, ?	'Phoenix' 1774.
HELLEUR, Francis	'Sylph' 1809, 'Prince of Bouillon' 1814, 'Richard' 1824.
HELLEUR, Frederic	b. 1798 st B., 'Annabella' 1824–28, 'Catherine' 1830, 'Waterwitch' 1831, 'Amity' 1836.
HEMERY, Charles	b. 1803 St H., Master of 'Antelope' 1831–39, d. at sea 1839?
HENRY, J.	Master c. 1840.
HERAULT, Jean	lived Bulwarks, St Aubin 1775, 'Industry' 1786, 'Lively' 1778.
HOCQUARD, Charles	a privateer captain, 'Liberty' 1790–92, 'Anne' 1810, 'Lovely Harriet' 1810, 'Ceres' 1814–15.
HOCQUARD, Charls Jn.	b. 1840, d. 6.1.1906, bur. St L., mar. Jane Rachel Helleur.
HOCQUARD, Charles Ph.	b. Jersey, lived Les Fiefs, Rozel, Master of 'Newport' 1854.
HOCQUARD, Francis	a successful privateer captain, 'Admiral Barrington' 1790, 'Marquis of Townsend' 1801–03, 'Dart' 1803–04, 'Union' 1804–09, 'Adventure' 1819–24, lived St Aubin?
HOCQUARD, George	a privateer captain, Master of 'Comus' 1803.
HOCQUARD, Jean	'Neptune' 1792–94, 'Betsy' 1810, 'Eliza' 1814, 'Eliza' 1817, 'Harmony' 1824, d. 1829, bur. Green Street cem.
HOCQUARD, John	Master's Cert. No. 31590, Master of 'Hope' 1867.
HOCQUARD, Josua	'Friends' 1792, 'Medea' 1803.
HOCQUARD, Philip J.	b. 1818, drowned in the English Channel 15.12.1874.
HOCQUARD, Philip	Master's Cert. No. 12052, 'Augia' 1869.
HOCQUARD, Thomas	'Paspébiac' 1792, 'Hercules' 1792.
HOOPER, George	Master of 'Elia' 1737, 'Dorchester' 1780.
HORMAN, Jacobus	'Susan' 1603.
HORMAN, John	b. 1807 St S., 'Minerva' 1835, 'Amelia' 1839, 'Lydia' 1839–46.
HORMAN, Peter	Master's Cert. No. 3566, 'Canada' 1859–67, 'Milton' 1869.
HOUSELL, John Edward	b. 1847, d. 1897, bur. G. cem., Master of 'Tickler.
HOUGEZ, Peter	'Jenny Lind' 1848.
HUARD, Thomas	b. 1790, St P., son of Thomas, 'Horatio' 1823, 'Richard' 1824.
HUBERT, Charles	'Fairy' 1780.
HUBERT, Clement	'Mercury' 1792.
HUBERT, John	'Pandora' 1863.
HUBERT, Philip	a privateer captain, sword in Museum of the Société Jersiaise, lived near Corn market, St H., 1771. 'Nancy' 1790, 'Lord Dorchester' 1792, 'Rose' 1800–10.
HUBERT, Victor A. G. F.	Master of 'Commerce' 1835, d. 18.9.1887.
HUE, Jean	'Hope' 1745, 'Betty' 1749–52, 'Sally' 1753–54.
HUELIN, Abraham	'Swallow' 1792.

HUELIN, Amice | b. 1800 St O., son of Philip, 'Betsy' 1836, 'Fanny' 1836, 'Dispatch' 1839, 'Jubilee' 1845, retired 1845.

HUELIN, Francis James | b. 1818 Jersey, 'New Brunswick' 1850, 'Hematope' 1852.

HUELIN, Francis John | 'Dit-On' 1850.

HUELIN, Jean | b. 1800 St B., son of Jean, mar. Marie Piton ?, 'Grog' 1825, 'C. Columbus' 1836, 'C.R.C.' 1843, 'N.B.' 1848, 'Fisherman' 1851, 'Maggie' 1853–58.

HUELIN, John | Master's Cert. No. 2000, 'Homely' 1849, 'N.B.' 1850, 'Telegraph' 1854, 'Jeffery' 1866.

HUELIN, John | 'True Friend' 1805, mar. Marie Duval.

HUELIN, Peter | b. 1800 St O., 'Adelaide' 1836, 'Nelson' 1837, 'Dispatch' 1840, 'Penelope' 1841.

HUELIN, Philip | b. 1790 St. O., son of Philip, 'Day' 1836, 'Caesarea' 1841, retired 1841.

HUELIN, Philip | b. 1802 St P., son of Jean, 'Superb' 1836–43, retired 1843.

HUELIN, Philip | 'Sydney' 1805.

HUQUET (LE), Abraham Jn. | Master's Cert. No. 30166, 'Cornucopia' 1869, 'Orient Star' 1872.

HUQUET (LE), Edward | lived St Mtn, Master c. 1881.

HUQUET (LE), Jean | b. 1764 St Mtn., d. 11.12.1831, 'very nice tombstone embellished with a ship' 'Laurel' 1825.

HUQUET (LE), Philip | lived Les Champ, St Brelade, Master 1820s.

HUQUET (LE), Philip | b. 1795 St Mtn., d. 5.12.1843 Algiers, lived St H., c. 1840, 'Ceres' 1826, 'D'Auvergne' 1832–36, 'Spy' 1843.

HUQUET (LE), Thomas | 'Ceres' 1831, 'Waterwitch' 1840–51, also 'Rollo'.

INGOUVILLE, Charles | 'Minerva' 1786.

INGOUVILLE, Philip | 'London Pkt' 1786, 'Kenton' 1790.

IRELAND, John | Master, c. 1767, mar. Anne Fiott, daughter of Nicolas Fiott and Anne Dumaresq, d. 26.11.1824 ?

IRELAND, John | b. 1815 St H., son of John, Master c. 1836.

JANDRON, J. | lived St B.?, 'Ostrich' 1859.

JANVRIN, D. | a privateer captain, c. 1692, Master of Daniel & Elizabeth' 1680–82. Great Grandfather of Brelade Janvrin, shipowner.

JANVRIN, Daniel | 'Good Intent' 1808.

JANVRIN, John | vessel 'King George' to Boston from Surinam 1715.

JANVRIN, Jean | 'Egmont' 1778.

JANVRIN, M. | 'Charming Betty' 1776.

JANVRIN, Philippe | 'Mynion' 1588.

JANVRIN, Philippe | b. 1677 St B., mar. Elizabeth Orange, Master of 'Esther' 1720, when Philippe d. while vessel in quarantine, bur. Portelet.

JANVRIN, Pierre | 'Primrose' 1595.

JANVRIN, Pierre | 'Unity' 1786, also 'Cornwall'.

JANVRIN, Thomas | 'Michel' 1600.

JEAN, Francis George | b. 1818, d. 1897, bur. St O., mar. Elizabeth Vautier, 'Intrepid' 1850.

JEAN, Frederic | b. 1828, mar. Rachel Sauvage, d. 1917, bur. Almorah cem. lived Greenwood Villas, Roseville Street, St H., obtained ordinary captain's Cert. at London 5.7.1851.

JEAN, James | Master of 'James' 1859.

JEAN, Jean | 'Speedwell' 1745–46, 'Esther' 1756. 'Mary' 1761.

JEAN, Philip | 'Hope' 1777, 'Major Peirson' 1790–02, 'Speculation' 1794.

JEAN, Philip Cooke	b. 1821, St P., son of Edward and Isabell Cooke, daughter of J. Cooke. Obtained Master's Cert. at Liverpool 5.7.1851, d. 22.1.1889, bur. St C's cem. 'Clipper' 1842, 'Newport' 1851, 'Julia' 1855, 'C. T. Sutton' 1856, 'Calista' 1863.
JEAN, Richard	'Gabriell' 1587.
JEHAN, Leonard	'Jersey Pkt' 1755–65.
JELF, ?	Master 1649, one of Carteret's privateers.
JENNE, Philip	b. 1802 St Mtn., 'No. One' 1838, 'Bliss' 1846–69.
JENNE, Thomas	b. 1835, mar. Susan Fauvel, lived New Street, St. H., d. 18.3.1900, bur. Mont á L'Abbe cem., 'Leader' 1864, 'New Leader' 1873.
JEUNE, F.	lived St H., 'Nerio' 1900, 'Gladys' 1901.
JEUNE, Francis	'George and Elizabeth' 1823–26.
JEUNE, Herbert P.	son of G. M. Jeune, lived La Croix, St Mtn., Chief Officer of ss 'Colombo Maru', c. 1904.
JEUNE, John	Master of 'Emma Louise' 1881.
JEUNE, J.	'Lively' 1780–96, 'Friends' 1830?
JEUNE. Philip	lived St H.?, 'Sir Sydney Smith' 1814, 'Hope' 1815, 'Iris' 1826–33.
JEUNE (LE), Philip	b. 1788 St C., 'Ellin' 1836–49.
JOLIN, Peter	'Jersey Flower' 1756–63.
JONES, Matthew	'James & Ellen' 1821, 'Friends' 1826, 'Warrior' 1827.
JONES, Walter Maugier	ss 'Melrose Abbey' c. 1914–18.
JOURNEAUX, Edward	'Dauphin' 1780.
JOURNEAUX, Francis	'Betsy' 1790–92.
JOURNEAUX, James	'True Friend' 1804.
JOURNEAUX, Jean	'Dauphin' 1780 and 1796.
JOURNEAUX, Philip	'Nancy' 1759 and '63, 'Effort' 1762 and '65, 'Fanny' 1765.
JOUET, Clement	'Belle Ann' 1810.
JOYCE, James	b. 1800 Newcastle, lived St H., c. 1840, 'Napoleon' 1834–36, 'Jersey Tar' 1843, 'Siren' 1818.
KEAGEN, J. N.	'Weasel' 1877, also 'Maud' Captain Keagen invented and patented a type of automatic rig for sailing vessels.
KENT, Edward Thomas	b. 1829, mar. Charlotte Rachel Cantwell, lived Gorey c. 1885, d. 29.10.1894.
KENT, G. F.	'Agricola' 1907, drowned off Brest, France 1907.
KENT, James	'Chazalie' 1878–96 lost with ship 1896.
KERBY, Jean	lived Rue Du Pied de la Montagne, St H., Captain Kerby was wounded by enemy action 1.5.1779. 'London Pkt' 1754–65, 'Lively' 1766–78, 'Corbet' 1776, 'Charlotte' 1792.
KERBY, William	'Guernsey Pkt', 1790, 'Ann' 1809.
LABEY, Philip	'Eclipse' 1859.
LABEY, Pierre	a privateer captain, 'Charming Jenny' 1751–52, 'Fox' 1759.
LABEY, Thomas	a privateer captain, 'Boscawen' 1757–63.
LABEY, Thomas	b. 1827 G., d. 1877.
LABEY, Thomas Filleul	b. 1896, d. 1965, bur. St C's cem.
LACHER (LE), Pierre	'Lord Nelson' 1804.
LAFFOLEY, Amice	'The Spider & the Fly' 1737, 'Mary' 1744–61.
LAFFOLEY, John Joseph Clement	'Take Care' 1859, 'Voyageur' 1866.
LAFFOLEY, Josua	'Eagle' 1867, Master's Cert. No. 50955.
LAIR, Philip	'Young Mary' 1790, 'Two Brothers' 1792.

LAMING, Henry — b. 1808, d. 1895, bur. Mont á L'Abbe old cem., Master's Cert. No. 43508, 'Frisk' 1840, 'Exile' 1852, 'Falcon' 1859, 'Charlotte' 1871–80.

L'AMY, Elias — a privateer captain, 'Hope' 1808–1809, 'General Don' 1810.

LANGDON, Charles Hamon — b; 1874, d. at sea 1927 whilst in command of the G.W.R. steamer 'St Julien', ss 'Ibex' c. 1914.

LANGLEY, H. — 'Bolina' 1836–38.

LANGLOIS, Francis — Master's Cert. No. 71742, 'Admiral Nelson' 1843–50, 'Day' 1850, 'Amberwitch' 1865.

LANGLOIS, Helier — 'Nelson' 1803–16, 'Ebenezer' 1818.

LANGLOIS, Helier — b. 1809, St L., son of Francis, 'Siren' 1833, 'Arichat' 1836, 'Bolina' 1837, 'Superb' 1838.

LANGLOIS, John George — Master's Cert No. 43369, 'Weasel' 1871.

LANGLOIS, P. C. — Harbourmaster at St Aubin 1904, d. 1913.

LANGLOIS, Philip — Master in Jersey c. 1674, 'Speedwell' 1676, mar. Mary Hollingworth of Salem, 1675 and settled there and became known as Philip English, owner of 27 vessels, he is reputed to have been America's first millionaire.

LANGLOIS, Philip — 'Peggy' 1804–12, 'Charles' 1817, 'Hope' 1815.

LANGLOIS, Philip P. — Master's Cert. No. 8266, lived Burrard Street, St Helier, 'Oracle' 1865–94, 'Ocean Queen' 1901.

LARBALESTIER, Charles — lived Lempriere Street, c. 1866, 'Charlotte' 1805.

LARBALESTIER, George — Master's Cert. No. 17231, 'Marie Georgiana' 1866–1868.

LARBALESTIER, Jean — b. 1809, St B., 'Dit-On' 1835, 'Minerva' 1837, 'De Jersey' 1839, 'Ceres' 1839, 'D'Auvergne' 1843, 'Crusader' 1844, 'Telegraph' 1846, 'Ceres' 1847, 'Crusader' 1849, 'United' 1851, 'Bystantium' 1855–56.

LARBALESTIER. Philip — 'Peggy' 1808.

LAUGIÉ, Edward — 'Cora' 1815.

LAURAINS. Charles — b. 1795, St H., son of Philip, 'Gulnare' 1836, 'Jersey Pkt' 1837, 'Zebra' 1841–46.

LAURENS, Jean — Master c. 1748.

LAURENS, Philip — 'London Expedition' 1774.

LAWRENCE, Abraham — a privateer captain, 'Lady Sarah' 1803, 'Hope' 1804.

LAWRENCE, P. — 'Wave Queen' 1900.

LEIGH, George — 'Elizabeth' 1780–96.

LEMPRIÉRE, Charles — b. 1798, St H., 'Jo' 1822, 'Hope' 1824, 'Good Intent' 1825, 'Union' 1825, 'Thetis' 1826.

LEMPRIÉRE, Clement — Captain of a frigate 1645, 'Jean' 1674.

LEMPRIÉRE, Clement — 'Prosper' 1774, 'Jersey' 1785.

LEMPRIÉRE, James — privateer captain 1692?, Master 1685, 'Dolphin' 1737.

LESBIREL, Clement — b. 1805, St J., son of Peter, 'Damon' 1835, 'Adventure' 1836, 'Bellona' 1840–43.

LESBIREL, James — 'Union' 1750–57.

LESBIREL, Thomas — 'Neptune' 1709, 'Numsley Castle' 1710.

LOVE, Robert — 'Kingfisher' 1822.

LOWE, Daniel — b. 1810 Isle of Wight, 'Medora' 1835–50.

LUCAS. Peter — Master's Cert. No. 22788, 'Brave' 1868.

LUCAS, Thomas — b. 1784, St Helier, 'Speedy Pkt' 1835, 'Henry' 1838, 'Rapid' 1839, retired from the sea 1839.

LUCE, Edward — 'Mary' 1715, 'Dolphin' 1737, 'Dauphin' 1743.

LUCE, Francis	b. 1859 Jersey, son of Jean and Ann Corbel, mar. Jane Elizabeth Bisson, Fruing captain, 'Mervenie', 'Century', 'Owny Belles', and 'Alliance' are some of the vessels he commanded.
LUCE, Francis John	'Ariel' 1850.
LUCE, George	lost with ship 1882, 'Sea Seal' *c.* 1882.
LUCE, James	'Enterprise' 1807, 'Anne & Mary' 1809, 'Charming Nancy' 1814.
LUCE, John	'Mary' 1729, 'Kingfisher' 1735, 'Postillion Pkt' 1745, 'Phoenix' 1756–65, 'Alexandre' 1774, 'William' 1778.
LUCE, John	'Ann & Mary' 1815, 'Escape' 1866, 'Herald' 1871, Master's Cert. No. 24692.
LUCE, Jean	b. 1805 St H., 'Ditto' 1836–39, lost with ship and crew 1839.
LUCE, Jean	Master 1677.
LUCE, Philip	'Success' 1738, 'Friend's Delight' 1744–47, 'Pretty' 1751.
LUCE, Thomas	b. 1797 St My., son of Edward. 'Damon' 1833–35, 'Guess' 1836, 'Farmer' 1842–43, retired 1847.
LUCE, ?	Master of ps 'Artic' when lost 27.9.1854, this vessel belonged to the Collings Line of America, Jersey Originaire?
LUEN, William	b. 1825 Colchester, lived St Malo *c.* 1863, 'Emily Cowlet' 1864, 'Eliza' 1868, 'Engineer' 1859. Captain Luen was presented with a silver teapot and a purse of gold by the Jersey Mutual Society for shipping for his meritorious conduct in bringing his vessel into Plymouth, under circumstances of great difficulty.
LUTMAN, William	'Queen Charlotte' 1822.
LYS, James	'Three Brothers' 1796, 'Harmony' 1803, 'Favourite' 1805, 'Young Peggy' 1807.
LYS, John	'Duke of Cumberland' 1744–54, 'Francis' 1747–48, 'Prince of Wales' 1748–51, 'London Pkt' 1754–65.
LYS, Philip	Master *c.* 1780.
MABILLE, Joshua	'Dolphin' 1805.
MACHON, Josué	b. 1808 St H., 'Loyal William' 1832, 'Amelia' 1836, 'Sylph' 1838, 'Napoleon' 1841, 'Bolina' 1844.
MAHY, Thomas	'Lively' 1860.
MAISTRE (LE), Abraham	'Mary' 1744, 1747, 'Friend's Delight' 1761.
MAISTRE (LE), Abraham	'Magdalene' 1804, 'Betsy' 1799.
MAISTRE (LE), Edward	Master's Cert. No. 43340, 'Circassian' 1860, 'Happy Return' 1871, 'Grace' 1872.
MAISTRE (LE), Francis	'Harmony' 1804, 'Calista' 1815, 'Fanny' 1816.
MAISTRE (LE), Jean	'Anne Mary' 1806, 'Two Friends' 1808, 'Flora' 1808, 'William Dumaresq' 1810–15, 'Dolphin' 1818.
MAISTRE (LE), Philip	lived Parade Road, St H., 'Siren' 1836, 'Island Queen' 1877.
MAISTRE (LE), Philip Th.	b. 1845 St H., mar. Matilda Cabeldu, d. 1900, lost with his ship, St Lawrence.
MAISTRE (LE), Pierre	'Courier' 1823–31, 'Guernsey Lily' 1829, died 1860s, lived St Lawrence.
MAISTRE (LE), William	lived Quebec 1787.
MALLET, George	'St Martin' 1843, 'Post Boy' 1848, 'Susan' 1849, 'Lady Douglas' 1862.
MALLET, Nicolas	a privateer captain, 'Mary' 1764, 'Defiance' 1778.
MALLET, Philip	'Kingfisher' 1785, 'Swift' 1803, 'Snowdrop' 1818, 'Herring' 1826.
MALLET, Thomas	'Mary' 1803.

MALZARD, Abraham	'Pigeon' 1737.
MALZARD, Abraham,	'Jane' 1812, mar. Anne Torré.
MALZARD, George	b. St Peter, d. 1890, bur. St P's cem., 'Damon' 1855, 'Prospero' 1859, lived Prospect House, St P. Captain Malzard took his vessel 'Prospero' up the River Amazon farther than any British ship had ever been before.
MALZARD, Henry	'Ellen Murray' 1846.
MALZARD, Isaac	'Peace' 1788–92, 'Lottery' 1803, 'Margaret' 1820, a privateer captain.
MALZARD, Jacob	'George' 1791.
MALZARD, John	'Nancy' 1803.
MALZARD, J.	lived Beaumont c. 1885, 'Chance' 1859.
MALZARD, Nicolas	'Mercury' 1790.
MALZARD, Philip	d. off Foo Chow, China ?, 'Betsy' 1814–20, 'Intended' 1831.
MANQUAIS (LE), Joshua	'Arichat' 1817, 'Betsy & Jane' 1819, 'Juno' 1820, 'Nestor' 1827, 'Lord Gambier' 1831.
MANUEL, Philip	'Pelican' 1822.
MARCHAND (LE), John	'Hebe' 1867–90.
MARCHAND (LE), William	'Two Friends' 1804–05, 'Queen Charlotte' 1806.
MARETT, Charles	'Bellona' 1813, 'Snowdrop' 1823.
MARETT, Edward	Master c. 1717, vessel confiscated Rouen.
MARETT, E.	'Surprise' 1900.
MARETT, F.	'Sydney' 1914.
MARETT, George	'Anne' 1790, 'Eliza' 1815, 'Father & Son' 1819, 'Hope' 1828.
MARETT, George	b. 1800 St Mtn., son of George, Master 1836–61.
MARETT, Jean	'Lyon' 1587.
MARETT, Jean	'Anne' 1790–95.
MARETT, John P.	'Union' 1862.
MARETT, Philip	'Phoenix' 1737.
MARETT, Walter Ernest	b. 1870, d. 20.2.1932. Yacht 'Charmion' 1904.
MARIE, Francis	a privateer captain, 'Hazard' 1813–14.
MARIE, George	'Jupiter' 1850.
MARINEL (LE), James	'Nancy' 1744.
MARINEL (LE), Matthew	Master 1797, d. 1858, bur. St J's cem.
MARINEL (LE), William	'Margarett' 1580.
MARMAUD, Hypolite	Master and shipowner in Cap Breton, from Jersey ?
MARQUAND (LE), Francis	Master of 'Gem' 1848.
MARQUAND (LE), George	'St Anne' 1842.
MARQUAND (LE), George Jas.	b. St H., mar. Mary Ann Coutanche, lost in storm from schooner 'Donna Maria', had settled Newfoundland.
MARQUAND (LE), George Jn.	Master of 'Milton' 1874.
MARQUAND (LE), Geo. Josh.	b. 1870 St H.
MARQUAND (LE), John	'Good Intent' 1806.
MARQUAND (LE), John	Master's Cert. No. 287, 'Recruit' 1870.
MARQUAND (LE), Josua	'Betsy' 1815.
MARQUAND (LE), Pierre	b. 1818 Jersey, d. 1901 Eskimo point.
MARQUAND (LE), Philip	b. 1790, d. 1872, bur. St P's cem.
MARQUAND (LE), P.	'Gladiateur' 1888–90, 'Red Gauntlet' 1900–06, 'Cicelia' 1908–10.
MARTEL, James	b. Guernsey, son of Philip, 'Canopus' 1836, 'Ceres' 1847, 'Mary Ann' 1852.
MARTEL, Peter	'Iris' 1874.
MASTERMAN, Robert	ss'Lord Beresford' 1824.

MASURIER (LE), Charles	b. 1794 St H., 'Dolphin' 1835, 'Harmony' 1840.
MASURIER (LE), Jean	a privateer captain, 'Papillion' 1806, 'Recovery' 1808, 'Peggy' 1810, 'Virginia' 1810, 'General Doyle' 1812, 'Betsy' 1812–15, 'Fanny' 1816.
MASURIER (LE), Jean	b. 1803 G., son of Jean, 'Mary' 1836, 'Nightingale' 1837, 'St Peter' 1840, drowned 1840.
MASURIER (LE), John	Master's Cert. No. 31904, 'Snowdrop' 1873.
MASURIER (LE), Josua	a privateer captain, 'Betsy' 1803–95, 'Duke of Argyle' 1805, 'General Doyle' 1809, 'Betsy' 1813.
MASURIER (LE), Peter	'Brothers' 1832.
MASURIER (LE), Philip	'Camelia' 1873, 'Casrelia' 1876.
MASURIER (LE), Philip	b. 1797 Ty., son of Philip, Master c. 1836–52.
MASURIER (LE), Thomas	brother of Philip ?, 'Camelia' 1884.
MAUGER, A.	'Reine Blanche' 1764.
MAUGER, Charles	'Centurion' 1838–60.
MAUGER, Charles	'Hazard' 1813.
MAUGER, C.	b. 1848, d. 24.6.1888, lived La Chaumiere, Millbrook.
MAUGER, David	'Elizabeth' 1790–92, 'Expedition' 1815.
MAUGER, Edward	'St James' 1758.
MAUGER, George	'London Pkt' 1754–65.
MAUGER, George	b. 1798 St L., 'Etton' 1833, 'Adelaide' 1836, 'Ninus' 1842–1843.
MAUGER, Helier	Captain or merchant before 1644.
MAUGER, James	b. 1861, d. 1931.
MAUGER, Jean	a privateer captain, licence granted 6.6.1692, 'Jersey Sloop' 1677–92.
MAUGER, Jean	'John' 1714–21, 'Duke of Cumberland' 1759, 'Good Intent' 1764.
MAUGER, Jean	'Bonne Esperance' 1715.
MAUGER, Jean	'Nancy' 1790, 'Neptune' 1803, 'Charlotte' 1809, 'Courier' 1818.
MAUGER, Jean	b. 1805 St O., d. 25.12.1844, bur. Green Street cem. 'Nameless' 1836, 'Swift' 1837.
MAUGER, Joshua	Master c. 1730, d. 1788.
MAUGER, Peter	a privateer captain, c. 1705.
MAUGER, Philip	a privateer captain, c. 1649.
MAUGER, P.	'City of Derry' 1778, 'Resolution' 1778.
MAUGER, R.	'Two Friends' 1796.
MAUGER, Thomas	b. 1806, d. 1862, bur. St C's cem.
MAUGER, Thomas	b. 1831 St C, d. 1909, bur. St C's cem.
MAUGER, Walter Chas.	no details.
MAYNARD, Francis	'Mary' 1744–61.
MAYNARD, Peter	'Willing Endeavour' 1737–57.
MEECH, Nathaniel	'Prince of Bouillon' 1836, 'Vigilant' 1838, 'Dapper' 1842–52.
MEHEU, ?	'Charles & Emma' 1859.
MENIE, Henry	'Rowcliffe' 1815.
MESSERVY, Charles	'Enterprise' 1808, 'Rowcliffe' 1817.
MESSERVY, Clement	a privateer captain, 'Ambition' 1752, 'Dragon' 1757, 'Active' 1778, 'St Charles' 1780. 'Jupiter' 1790, also 'Elizabeth' 1744–57. Captain Messervy, while master of the Guernsey privateer 'Dragon' was fined £200 for engaging crew from Jersey without permission.
MESSERVY, Daniel	'Molly' 1769–72.

MESSERVY, Elie   Captain or merchant before 1644.
MESSERVY, Elie   'Prince of Wales' 1788, 'Enterprise' 1794. Captain Messervy
                                was captured by the French 8.3.1794 and taken into Brest.
MESSERVY, Francis   'Jersey' 1776, 'Beaver' 1778.
MESSERVY, George   'Elizabeth' 1744, 'Delvarde' 1756.
MESSERVY, George   'Glance' 1869, also the 'Rescue' on the Australian wool run
                                1872, lived Georgetown c. 1832.
MESSERVY, H.   'Enterprise' 1780.
MESSERVY, Jean   lived St Aubin 1775, 'Elizabeth' 1744–57, 'Union' 1750–57.
MESSERVY, Jean   'Stest' 1803, 'General Don' 1810, 'Lord Charles Spencer'
                                1810, 'Dundas' 1813, 'Mars' 1815, 'Arichat' 1819–20, 'Betsy
                                & Jane' 1820–26.
MESSERVY, John   'Caroline' 1871
MESSERVY, Nicolas   lived Bulwarks, St Aubin, 1789, 'Phoenix' 1756–65.
MESSERVY, Noé   'Union' 1750–55, 'Phoenix' 1756–65, 'Mary' 1790.
MESSERVY, Philip   'Stagg' 1780–90, 'Friendship' 1790–92, 'Dundas' 1803,
                                'Hazard' 1820.
MESSERVY, Thomas   'Surprise' 1817.
MILLER, George   lived Rouge Boullion, St H., 'Pallas' 1831, 'Augia' 1836,
                                'Lightning' 1838, 'Rolla' 1841–52, retired 1852.
MISSON, Philip F.   lived Ty.?, 'Gladys' 1902, 'Resolute' 1905, 'Lady St John'
                                c. 1914.
MOIGNARD (LE), Amice   b. 1831 St J., d. overseas 1872, stone in St J's cem. Mar. Jane
                                Le Maistre, 'Asp' 1863, 'Century' 1866.
MOIGNARD (LE), Charles   b. 1814 St John, son of Amice and Suzanne Le Maistre, mar.
                                Anne Hocquard, d. St My. 1879.
MOIGNARD, James Chas.   b.1873 St C., d. 1905.
MOIGNARD, Philip   b. 1843 St C., d. 1923, bur. St C's cem.
MOIGNE (LE), Abraham   Master of 'La Bonne Societe' 1714.
MOLLET, Edward   'Welcome' 1878.
MOLLET, Francis John   'Galatea' 1864, 'Waverley' 1873.
MOLLET, Frederic   'Energy' 1874, 'Progress' 1877.
MOLLET, J. P.   'Wesley' 1876.
MOLLET, P.   'Polly' 1764.
MOLLET, Philip Josue   'Herbert' 1842.
MOLLET, Philip   'Pelican' 1825.
MOLLET, Philip   'Two Friends' 1876.
MONAMY, Clement   Captain or merchant before 1644.
MONAMY, Francis   'Fancy' 1826.
MONAMY, Thomas   b. 1788 St C., 'Traveller' 1825–31.
MOREL, Thomas   'Neptune' 1844.
MOSES, A.   lived Gorey, c. 1885, 'Gazelle' 1874.
MOURANT,Edward   'London Pkt' 1754 and 1765, 'Roy de Prusse' 1759, 'Adven-
                                ture' 1760–64, 'Neptune' 1764, 'Durel' 1778, 'Endeavour'
                                1785.
MOURANT, Jean   'Victory' 1806, 'Charming Nancy' 1815, 'Ceres' 1820, 'Hope'
                                1822–26.
MOURANT, Peter   a privateer captain, 'London Pkt' 1785, 'Guernsey Pkt' 1786.
MOURANT, Philip   'Three Friends' 1790, prisoner of war 1794 (escaped).
MOURANT, Stephen   'Hope' 1745.
MOURANT, Thomas Philip   b. 1850 St L., Master's Cert. No. 31452, 'Cygnus' 1874,
                                'Gladys' 1894–1900, d. St L. 1918.
NEEL, Elias   'Success' 1786.

NEEL, George	'Hope' 1785, 'Union' 1786.
NEEL, Guillaume	'Philip' 1737.
NEEL, James	'Two Brothers' 1778.
NEEL, Philip	'Molly' 1778, 'Southampton Pkt' 1785–90.
NEEL, William	'Philip' 1737.
NICOLLE, Clement	'Sukey' 1778, 'Hero' 1793, 1809 and 1813, 'Harmony' 1798.
NICOLLE, Elias	'Silk' 1826.
NICOLLE, F. G.	lived St Mtn., 'Almora' 1901.
NICOLLE, John	'Aurora' 1824.
NICOLLE, Joshua	'Nautilus' 1826.
NICOLLE, Matthew	'Kitty' 1809, 'Pink' 1811, 'Bellona' 1811.
NICOLLE, Peter	'Harriet' 1833.
NICOLLE, Philip	'Rose' 1804, 'Hero' 1807.
NOEL, Clement	b. 1807, d. 1859, bur. Green Street cem., 'Nautilus' 1816, 'Messenger' 1825.
NOEL, David	b. 1866 St Mtn., mar. Jane Eliza Buesnel of St S., schooner 'Maud' 1905?, ss 'Philotis' c. 1914, lost with ship in the Mediterranean.
NOEL, Edward	'Angelicque' 1780 and '96, 'Madelain' 1786, 'Mary' 1790–92, 'Le Heraux' 1815, 'Snipe' 1816.
NOEL, Edward Thomas	'Mary Ann' 1869.
NOEL, Francis	'Marie' 1786, 'Magdaleine' 1790.
NOEL, George	b. 1794, G., 'Nightingale' 1836, 'Ant' 1837, 'Commerce' 1848, 'Inch' 1849, 'Napier' 1850, 'Albert Edward' 1851, 'Hengiest' 1852, 'Christie & Jane' 1854, 'Engineer' 1855.
NOEL, George	b. 1829 son of Francis, 'Resolute' 1877, 'Rambler' ? also an American schooner ?.
NOEL, Jean	'Active' 1790–95.
NOEL, John	'James Harmer' 1877.
NOEL, Noel	b. 1800 St Mtn., son of Nicolas, Master c. 1836.
NOEL, Philip	b. 1801, St Mtn., son of Nicolas, Master c. 1836–51.
NOEL, Philip	Master's Cert. No. 23596, 'Flying Foam' 1866–79.
NOEL, Thomas James	b. 1812, son of Matthew, 'Speedy Pkt' 1836, 'Reward' 1848, 'Crichton' 1849–50, 'Eliza Jenkins' 1857.
NORMAN, George	'Dolphin' 1851–59, 'Eliza' 1867.
NORMAN, James	b. Jersey ?, to Newfoundland c. 1860.
OGIER, Abraham	'Jane' 1864.
OGIER, John	'William Pitt' 1846, 'Quickstay' 1859.
OGRAUD, John	a privateer captain c. 1710.
OLIVER, John	'Falcon' 1603.
OLSEN, George	'Commerce' 1786.
OLSEN, Lewis	'Fort Regent' c. 1885.
OLSEN, ?	lived Beaumont c. 1885, 'Ellida' 1859.
ORANGE, Edward	lived St B., d. 1845, bur. St B's cem., 'Oliver Blanchard' 1831–40.
ORANGE, George	b. 1811 St B., 'Surprise' 1836, 'Amelia' 1837, 'Amicus' 1841–45, retired 1845.
ORANGE, Jean	a privateer captain, c. 1705.
ORSATO, John Thomas	b. 1830, d. 1896.
ORSATO, ?	Master of 'Hero' 1840.
ORVIS, William	'Richard' 1846.
OSMONT, Philip	b. 1839, d. 19.8.1914, bur. Mont á L'Abbe cem., Master's Cert. No. 30165, 'Freeman' 1859, 'Media' 1871.

PALLOT, Charles	b. 1795 Ty., d. at sea 14.7.1874?, 'Calista' 1835, 'D'Auvergne' 1837, 'Ceres' 1838, 'Calista' 1839, 'D'Auvergne' 1843, 'Ceres' 1847.
PALLOT, Charles	b. 1835, St Mtn., youngest brother of Clement (shipowner), d. 1902, lived Elm Bank, Gorey pier, 'Autorise' for Gorey Harbour 1886–1901.
PALLOT, Clement	a privateer captain, 'Fox' 1778–79, 'Owners goodwill', Captain Pallot and 'Fox' appointed by the States Guard boat 1779.
PALLOT, Clement	l. St Mtn., Master c. 1880.
PALLOT, Deslandes	b. 1848 at sea, son of Josua and Ann Deslandes, Master of 'Bulla' 1873, d. at sea 1875, memorial Almorah cem., 1875.
PALLOT, Elias	younger brother of Clement, who married two sisters and lived together at Welton House, St Mtn.
PALLOT, James	'Sukey' 1763–64.
PALLOT, John	'Laurel' 1828, 'Traveller' 1835–40.
PALLOT, John	Master's Cert. No. 45492, 'Queen' 1859, 'Why Not?' 1862 (owner), 'Alexandre' 1864, also 'Morning Star' 1860.
PALLOT, Josua	b. 1794 Ty., d. 1861, memorial Almorah cem., mar. Ann Deslandes, Master of Jane 1848–53.
PALLOT, Nicolas	b. 1794 St Mtn., son of Philip, 'John' 1825, 'Charles' 1836, 'John & Mary' 1844, 'Queen' 1847.
PALLOT, Philippe	Master c. 1630, from Ty.
PALLOT, Philip	b. 1797, Ty., 'James & Ellen' 1836, 'Abeona' 1838, 'Rowena' 1840–50.
PALLOT, Philip	Master's Cert. No. 74680, 'Queen of the Isles' 1873.
PALLOT, William	son of Clement (shipowner), Master, went to live at Brightlingsea.
PARIS, Moses	'George' 1809, 'Rover' 1813–14, 'Active' 1814, lost with ship 1814.
PARK, Samuel Henry	b. 1849 Jersey, 'John Clark' 1878–79.
PASCAL, Duval	b. 1832 St C., d. 1856.
PASCOE, John	'Czarina' 1874.
PATEN, J.	'C. Columbus' 1851.
PATRIARCHE, Edward	'Bonaventure' 1587.
PAUMELLE (LA), Gyles	'Ann' 1693.
PAYN, James	'James' 1749–49, 'Providence' 1749–50, 'Squirrel' 1751–52.
PAYN, John	'Liberty' 1823.
PAYN, Josué	Master c. 1695.
PAYN, Philip	'Anne' 1737, 'Jersey Pkt' 1755–65.
PAYN, Philip	'Alliance' 1804, 'Success' 1804–10, 'Venus' 1813–14, 'Enterprise' 1824.
PAYN, Philip C.	b. 1784 St H., son of Philip, 'Marie Victoire' 1836, 'Samuel & Julie' 1837, 'Amity' 1838, 'Maria' 1839, 'Caroline' 1844, 'Pallas' 1850.
PAYN, Thomas	'Nancy' 1770, 'Charlotte' 1772–90 and 1804.
PAYN, Thomas	'Chestnut Farm' 1824, 'Ashburton' 1826.
PAYNE, H.	ss 'Brentford' 1887.
PAYNE, J.	'Grijalua' 1893 (not a Jersey ship).
PAYNE, Philip	'Othello' 1834, also 'Hilda'
PEARCE, Francis	'Chance' 1847.
PENINGS, John	'Esperance' 1814.
PEPIN, Clement	'D' 1848.
PERCHARD, Charles	'Young Peggy' 1811, 'Surprise' 1814, 'Young Peggy' 1814–27.
PERCHARD, Charles	'Indian' 1849, 'Sunda' 1851, 'Zarah' 1851.

PERCHARD, Elias   'Friendship' 1744–48.
PERCHARD, James   'Mariner' 1829.
PERCHARD, John Edward   Master's Cert. No. 72452, 'Heather Bell' 1867, 'Elfine' 1869.
PERCHARD, P. C.   'Enchantress' 1881, lost with ship 1881.
PERCHARD, Philip   'Hope' 1737, 'Seven Sisters' 1728, 'Friendship' 1744–48.
PERCHARD, Philip   'Elfine' 1900.
PERCHARD, Peter   'Mary' 1737–39.
PERCHARD, Peter   'Peggy' 1811–26, mar. Mary Sauvage, d. 1834.
PERRAND, Samuel   a privateer captain, 'Hope' 1703, 'L'Accident' 1721.
PERRÉE, Francis   'William Pit' 1840–45.
PERRÉE, Jean   from St My, 'Concordia' 1834.
PERRÉE, Philip   'Adventure' 1824, 'Dolphin' 1825–26, 'Doris' 1828.
PERRIER, Jean   'Fancy' 1806, 'Dapper' 1807.
PERRY, Henry   b. 1777, St H., 'Neptune' 1835, 'Damon' 1838, 'Amity' 1838,
                              'Sylph' 1839, 'Victoria' 1852.
PETIT (LE), J.   'Gazelle' no date.
PETIT, William   b. 1823 St J., d. 1856, bur. St J's cem., 'Origin' ?
PHON (Fondre ?), Michel   'Susan' 1587.
PICKSTOCK, Thomas   b. St H., a privateer captain, 'Queen' 1790–92, 'Herald' 1792
                              and 1798, 'Princess Royal' 1796, he died of yellow fever in
                              Surinam 1800. Captain Pickstock was famous for his fight
                              against the French in 1798, his sword is in Museum of
                              Société Jersiaise.
PICOT, Charles   b. 1807 St J., son of Philip, 'Phoenix' 1831–36.
PICOT, F. W.   d. 1914, memorial Mont á L'Abbe cem.
PICOT, George   b. 1844 St C., mar. Nina Mary Wimble, lived Wanstead, Essex,
                              Merchant Marine Superintendent, d. 1.6.1922, memorial
                              Mont á L'Abbe cem.
PICOT, J. F.   b. 1833, Lloyd's surveyor 1902, d. 1917.
PICOT (PYCOTT), John   captured by enemy 1579.
PICOT, Josua   b. 1804, d. Cape Colony castle 1846, Master of 'Judge
                              Thompson'.
PICOT, Philip   b. 1805, St H., son of Jean, mar. Marie Le Vesconte ? Master
                              1836, 'Harriet L' 1846.
PICOT, Philip John   b. 1836, lived Eden House, Maufant ? d. 1909.
PINEL, Charles   Master of 'Seaflower' 1735, d. of plague 1735.
PINEL, John   'Surprise' 1824.
PINEL, Philip   b. 1846, d. 1922, bur. Mont á L'Abbe cem., lived Janvrin
                              View, Stopford Road, St H., Master of 'Gladys' 1900.
PINEL, Thomas   b. 1800, St H., son of Jean, 'Mary' 1836–48.
PIPON, Charles   b. 1774, St B., d. 17.5.1841, bur. St B., a packet captain for
                              many years, 'General Doyle' 1809, 'Francis Freeling' 1811,
                              'Lord Sidmouth' 1815.
PIPON, James   'Seaflower' 1731, 'Pearl' 1733, 'Expedition' 1738, 'Tygress'
                              1744, 'Rowland' 1748, 'Pascal' 1749.
PIPON, Jean   'John' 1744–60, 1788, sailed from Shippegan as Master of the
                              St Aubin, 2 days after sailing Captain Pipon was washed over-
                              board and drowned with the mate and two other men.
PIPON, John   'Seaflower' 1717, 'Jersey' 1734–37.
PIPON, Josua   'Charming Nancy' 1746.
PIPON, Philip   'Golden Lion' 1668.
PIPON, Richard   a privateer captain, 'George' 1707, 'Capre Prince' 1708,
                              'Philip' 1737.

PIPON, Thomas	a privateer captain, *c.* 1705, Master of 'Thomas' 1730.
PIROUET, Abraham	Master's Cert. No. 12158, 'John Milton' 1865.
PIROUET, Francis	'London' 1794, 'Samaritan' 1796, 'John Bull' 1804, 'Swift' 1806.
PITMAN, G.	'Triumph' 1903, 'Silver Eagle' 1911.
PITMAN, R. R.	a G.W.R. Captain, ss 'St Patrick' and ss 'St Helier'.
PITMAN, W.	'Venus' no date.
PITON, Jean	b. 1796 St B., 'John & Mary' 1825, 'Neptune' 1826, 'Doris' 1831-33, 'Janvrin' 1836-39, 'Amelia' 1844, 'Canopus' 1849, 'Farrago' 1844, retired 1849.
PITON, Josue	b. 1795 St B., son of Josue, 'De Jersey' 1822-25, 'Doris' 1839, 'Charles' 1839, 'Three Sisters' 1839, 'Campbell' 1840, 'C. Columbus' 1851-53.
POIDEVIN (LE), Elias	'Minerva' 1873.
POIGNARD, Charles	'Venus' 1817, 'Clara' 1826.
POINGDESTRE, Charles	'Property' 1811.
POINGDESTRE, Francis	'Laurel' 1825.
POINGDESTRE, F. P.	Master, *c.* 1880 ?
POINGDESTRE, J. B.	'Gladys' 1900.
POINGDESTRE, Jean	'Jersey Flower' 1737, 'Two Brothers' 1747.
POINGDESTRE, Philip	'Habnab' 1811, 'Nancy' 1813, d. 1837, St B's cem.
POINGDESTRE, Philip	b. 1837 St L., d. Oporto, memorial St L's cem.
POINGDESTRE, Philip Fr.	b. 1816, 'Reward' 1841, 'Jane' 1850, 'Iris' 1853.
POINGDESTRE, Thomas	b. 1818, d. 28.4.1867, 'Flashy' 1858.
POISSON, Victor Peter	'Caroline' 1866.
PREVEU (LE), Daniel	'Willing Mind' 1748, 'Peter' 1749, 'Sarah' 1757.
PRIAULX, Edward	b. 1804, d. 1860, bur. St P's cem. 'Two Friends' 1844.
PRIAULX, John	ss 'Superb' 1850.
PRIAULX, John	b. 1837?, d. 15.8.1877, bur. St O's Methodist cem.
PRIAULX, Peter	b. 1790, d. 1883.
PRIAULX, Philip	b. 1808, son of Peter, 'St Aubin' 1836-46.
PROUINGS, John	'Ashburton' 1821
PROUINGS, John	b. 1834, d. 1866 Nasau, West Indies, memorial St My's cem., Master of 'Nameless' 1859.
PROUINGS, Thomas	'Industry' 1800, 'Good Intent' 1807, 'Anne' 1809.
PROUTEN, Edward	'Crown' 1876-1901, 'Wesley' 1905.
PURCHASE, Edward	'Integrity' 1826.
QUERÉE, Adolphos	'Louise Ernest' 1914.
QUERÉE, Philip	'The Trust' 1887.
QUERÉE, Wilfred John	ss 'Scapha', *c.* 1914.
QUERIPEL, Jean	b. 1798 St B., son of Elias, lost with ship and crew 1848, 'John' 1831, 'Castor' 1833.
QUERIPEL, Peter	'Seven Sisters' 1728-37.
QUESNE (LE), Clement	'Prudent' 1790-92, 'Suprise' 1794, 'Molly' 1803.
QUESNE (LE), Jean	'Nancy' 1790, 'Betsy' 1792.
QUESNE (LE), Joseph	'Papillion' 1807.
QUESNE (LE), Philip	'Tom & Mary' 1818.
QUESNE (LE), Richard	a privateer captain, 'Phoenix' 1757, 'Royal George' (Guernsey) 1760, 'Tartar' 1778.
QUILLER, Richard	'Flying Fish' 1793.
QUINTON, Thomas	b. 1781 Portsmouth, 'Dart' 1836, 'Telemachus' 1836, 'Providence' 1839, 'Green End' 1843.
RAMIER, C. W.	b. 1828 Jersey, 'Teaser' 1843, 'Centurion' 1848.

RAY, Thomas Boxer	'Neptune' 1818.
RAY (LE), ?	'Alderney Pkt' 1780–90, 'Postillion Pkt' 1790.
READ, J.	lived Val Plaisant 1899?, 'Flying Foam'?
REMON, Edward	'Industry' 1785.
REMON, James	'Triton' 1778.
REMON, Jean	'York' 1782.
REMON, Laurens	'Le Solide' 1790–92.
REMON, Thomas	'Dandy' 1826.
RENAUT, Philip	'Jane' 1835.
RENOUF, C.	'Canadian' 1778, 'Friends Endeavour' 1779.
RENOUF, Charles	b. 1836, Ty., d. 1901.
RENOUF, Charles	mar. Mary Ann Cosnard, Master of 'Belus' 1847.
RENOUF, Charles Hugh	'Industry' 1818–19.
RENOUF, C. P.	mar. Mary Ann Romeril, d. 16.4.1910.
RENOUF, Edward	b. 1826 St L., d. 1900, bur. St L's cem., 'Sultana' 1884–85.
RENOUF, Edward Amice	'Mars' 1826, 'Patruus' 1848, d. 1849 ?
RENOUF, Edwin Charles	b. 1881, d. Montreal, Canada 1977.
RENOUF, Francis	lived Coin Varin, St P., d. Australia?
RENOUF, Francis George	Master's Cert. No. 52500, lived Belmont Road, St H., 'London' 1855, 'Seabird' 1873.
RENOUF, Francis John	b. 1826, d. 12.3.1888.
RENOUF, Francis John	b. 1854?, d. 18.6.1929, lived Belmont Road, St H., ss 'Lydia' c. 1913, a L.S.W.R. vessel.
RENOUF, F. B.	Master of training ship 'Botha' (South Africa), 1921.
RENOUF, F. J.	Harbourmaster at St H., 1896–1926.
RENOUF, G.	Master, c. 1873.
RENOUF, Henry	'Britannia' 1819.
RENOUF, Isaac	'Friends' 1825.
RENOUF, J.	'Gaspé' 1815.
RENOUF, Jean	'Jersey Flower' 1756–63.
RENOUF, Peter	'Speedwell' 1745–46.
RENOUF, Philip	'Dundas' 1826, 'Ebenezer' 1831.
RENOUF, Philip	Pilot boat 'No. One' 1830.
RENOUF, Philip	b. 1842, d. 1919, Ty.
RENOUF, Philip George	Master's Cert. No. 30924, 'Vitula' 1871.
RENOUF, Thomas	b. 1781 St Mtn., son of Jean, 'Traveller' 1828–39.
RICARD, Edward	b. 1756 St O., son of Charles, lived La Robeline.
RICHARDSON, Jean	'Charming Betty' 1740–44, 'Friend's Delight' 1744, 'Fortune' 1786–90.
RICHARDSON, John	b. 1849, St My., d. 1896.
RICHARDSON, Leyghton T.	A G.W.R. captain for many years, retired to Weymouth.
RICHE (LE), Jean	'Hope' 1786, 'Mary Anne' 1790, 'Success' 1788.
RICHE (LE), Jean	'Concord' 1804.
RITSON, Edwin	ss 'Queen Mary' c. 1914.
RIVAILLE, Adolphos	Master, c. 1879.
RIVE, Jean	'Dashing Wave' 1860.
RIVE, Philip	b. 1796, St P., 'Friends' 1836, 'Geffrard' 1851.
ROBERT, Thomas	b. 1812, d. 1864, Master of 'Hope' 1840.
ROBERTSON, Peter	'Elizabeth' 1816.
ROBIN, Magdolain	1545–51, transported the artillery for the parishes of St P. and St L. 1551.
ROBIN, Philip	Master of 'George & Philip' 1737.
ROBIN, Thomas	b. 1711, d. 1781, Master of 'Philip' 1743.

ROISSIER, Jean	'Providence' 1790–1808, also 'Betsy'.
ROMERIL, Abraham	a privateer captain, 'Chance' 1813, 'Success' 1813.
ROMERIL, Edward	'Sultana' 1840.
ROMERIL, Edward	b. 1829, d. on voyage to the South China Sea, c. 1850s.
ROMERIL, George	lived St H.?, mar. Mary Ann Le Grand, 'Constant' 1810, 'Hero' 1821–24, 'Betsy' 1831–33, 'Dido' 1837.
ROMERIL, John	b. 1836, d. 4.3.1913, Master's Cert. No. 90580, 'Standard' 1874, also '85'.
ROMERIL, John	b. 1849, obtained Master's Cert. 1874, 'Century'.
ROMERIL, Philip	Master's Cert. No. 15190, d. 1891, bur. St C's cem. 'Kassa' 1868, also 'Kanagona'.
ROMERIL, Thomas	'Phoenix' 1756–65, 'Baron Hope' 1774.
RONDEL, Jean	b. 1820, Ty., 'Blue Eyed Maid' 1847, 'Rival' 1848–50.
ROSSIGNOL (LE), Augustin	'Resolution' 1817.
ROSSIGNOL (LE), Jean	Master of 'Bateau du Santé' (quarantine boat) 1742 and 1771.
ROSSIGNOL (LE), Jean	lived St O., 'William Dumaresq' 1800, 'Jersey' 1800, 'Resolution' 1806–10, 'Betsy' 1815, 'Swift' 1824–25, 'Duke of Wellington' 1826, 'Swift' 1835, retired 1835.
ROSSIGNOL (LE), Matthew	b. 1789 St H., lived Don Street, a privateer captain, 'Hazard' 1813, 'Property' 1815, 'Flora' 1815, 'Polperro' 1819–20, 'Jolly Tar' 1826–36, 'Aurora' 1844–46, retired 1846.
ROSSIGNOL (LE), Nicolas	Ceres' 1810, 'Laurel' 1823, 'Dispatch' 1829, 'Unity' 1840.
ROSSIGNOL (LE), Peter	'Crusader' 1848, 'Harriet L' 1855.
ROSSIGNOL (LE), Philip	a privateer captain, 'Swift' 1792–94, 'Success' 1803, 'Rocou' 1805, 'Masquerade' 1806–13, 'Charming Nancy' 1815, 'Experiment' 1825, 'Canopus' 1828.
ROSSIGNOL (LE), Philip	b. 1798 St H., lived St Savious Road, c. 1866. 'Rose' 1824, 'Clio' 1835, 'Commodore' 1845, retired 1845.
ROSSIGNOL (LE), Philip	'Harriet' 1855.
ROUGETEL (LE), Edward	'Rose' 1824.
ROUGETEL (LE), Jean	'Jersey' 1799, 'William Dumaresq' 1800, 'Jersey' 1807.
ROUGETEL (LE), Jean	b. 1808, G., d. 21.12.1844, 'Jersey Maid' 1836, 'Frederic' 1840.
ROUX, (LE), Jean	b. St B., a privateer captain, lived St Aubin 1775, 'Kingfisher' 1786, 'Felicity' 1780 and 1786, 'Vulture' 1803, 'Nelson' 1811.
ROUX (LE), Philip	'General Doyle' 1804, 'General Gordon' 1801, 'Providence' 1806, killed in action with a French vessel.
ROUX (LE), Pierre	'Dauphin' 1786–92, 'Dolphin' 1803.
ROUX (LE), Thomas	Captain or merchant before 1644.
ROY, D. J.	'Betsy' 1786.
ROY, George	Master c. 1901, died 1913.
RUEZ (LE), Abraham	Master of 'Robin' 1896.
RUEZ (LE), Edward	b. 1810, St O., 'Apollo' 1835, 'Tiphys' 1837, 'Rollo' 1837, 'Pelican' 1839–42, 'Swift' 1842.
RUEZ (LE), Jean	'Lively' 1818–21, 'Magdalen' 1822.
SALLAT, Andrew	'Lytella' 1587.
SAMSON, A. P.	'Accra', emigrated to New Zealand, no dates.
SAUVAGE, Francis Ph.	b. 1841 Jersey, d. 1893.
SAUVAGE, Philip	b. 1806, St H., lived Mont au Pretre, c. 1840, 'Jane' 1831, 'Seaflower' 1836–46, retired 1846.
SAUVAGE, Philip	b. 1816, 'Victoria' 1840, 'Jersey' 1851.
SAUVAGE, Philip Le Brocq	b. 1840, d. 1924.

SCARBOROUGH, William H.	b. 1797, 'Aurora' 1835, 'Lord Saumaresq' 1837.
SEALE, Peter	'Amité' 1603.
SEALE, Thomas	Captain or merchant before 1644.
SEBIRE, George	b. 1807, St P., d. 10.5.1852, Buenos Aires, 'Canopus' 1837, 'Clio' 1840, 'Ipswich' 1845, 'Leopard' 1848.
SEBIRE, Joshua	b. 1804 St P., son of Joshua, d. at sea 24.5.1843, 'Adventure' 1835, 'Damon' 1836, 'St George' 1837, 'Mastery' 1842.
SEELLEUR (LE), Frederic	b. St H., lived in the Parade, c. 1880, 'Annabella' 1828.
SEELLEUR (LE), George	b. 1797 St H., son of Jean, 'Watersprite' 1837, 'Princess Alexandrina' 1842–46, retired 1846.
SEELLEUR (LE), George	b. Jersey, d. 1889 Jersey, mar. Jenny Noel of St Mtn., made several voyages to Montreal.
SEELLEUR (LE), George	Master and owner of 'Conqueror' 1899.
SEELLEUR (LE), John A.	Master, c. 1851.
SEELLEUR (LE), Philip	'Graphic' 1874.
SEELLEUR (LE), Thomas	Master, c. 1851–1907.
SEELLEUR (LE), Thomas	b. 1840 St L., d. 1912, lived Devonshire Pl, St H., 'Nameless' 1877, a de Quetteville captain.
SEWARD, Philip	a privateer captain, 'Duke of Cumberland' 1757, 'Duke of Northumberland' 1757, 'Neptune' 1764, 'Charming Nancy' 1781.
SHEAN, Robert	b. 1808 Weymouth, 'Dove' 1836, 'Racer' 1846.
SHOOSMITH, Jean	Master of Bateau de Santé (quarantine boat) 1728.
SHOOSMITH, Philip	'Providence' 1780–96.
SHOOSMITH, Philip	a privateer captain, 'Jolly Sloope' 1704.
SIMON, Jean	'Young Peggy' 1800.
SIMON, Peter	b. 1793 G., 'Venus' 1822–31, 'Temperance' 1836, 'Lord Saumaresq' 1839, 'Don' 1840.
SIMON, Philip	'Expedition Pkt' 1804, 'Resolution' 1809.
SIMON, Thomas	'Queen Charlotte' 1806–07, 'Flora' 1809, 'Hope' 1815, 'George Mackintosh' 1822, 'Scartari' 1831.
SIMONET, Jacques	'Nancy' 1786.
SIMONET, Jean	'Betsy' 1775, 'Link' 1779.
SIMPSON, D.	'Unity' 1778, 'Liberty' 1785–90, 'Prudent' 1786' 'Goodwill' 1792, 'Providence' 1799, also 'Conway'.
SINCLAIR, Peter	'Constant Pkt' 1806, 'Royal Oak' 1815.
SLOUS, Elias	'Good Intent' 1803, 'Wag' 1816.
SLOUS, James	b. 1805 St B., 'Amity' 1836, 'Prince of Wales' 1858.
SLOUS, Jean	b. 1808 son of Elias, drowned at sea, lived St P., mar. Henrietta Slous (cousin ?) after Jean died she worked for Abraham de Gruchy's shop at St P., 'Habnab' 1836, 'Adonis' 1839.
SLOUS, Philip	'John & Mary' 1745.
SMALL, Richard	b. 1795 Devonshire, 'Vigilant' 1826, 'Flying Fish' 1844.
SMITH, James	b. 1803 St S., lived St H. c. 1840, drowned Honduras 1852, 'Crusader' 1836, 'Ceres' 1847, 'D'Auvergne' 1848, 'Ceres' 1848, 'Crusader' 1849–52.
SMITH, William Lane	b. 1786 Plymouth, 'Providence' 1836, 'Jersey Pkt' 1837, 'St Anne' 1838–50, 'Peace' 1850.
SMITH, William	'Samuel & Julia' 1820, 'Olive Branch' 1821, 'John & Mary' 1822–24.
SNOW, Thomas	a privateer captain, 'Marie' 1692, 'William' 1737–44.
SNOW, William	'William & Elizabeth' 1774, 'Charming Betty' 1776–78, 'Alert' 1779.

SNOW, William	a privateer captain, mar. Marie Mauger, built Lansdown House, Millbrook, d. 1750, 'Marie' 1704.
SOHIER, Jean	lived St H., 'Prince of Bouillon' 1826, 'Dapper' 1835, 'Prince' 1844–49.
SOHIER, Philip	'Jane & Louisa' 1838.
SOREL, Jean	b. 1815 St H., son of Thomas, d. at sea 1836, 'Brutus' 1836.
STARCK, C. E.	ss 'Athenic', c. 1914.
STARCK, Philip	Master, no details.
STEEL, Moise	'Liberty' 1786, 'Kingfisher' 1786–92.
STEEL, William	b. Sussex, lived Rose Cottage, Havre des Pas, 'Freedom' 1877.
STEVENSON, R.	lived Beaumaris, Anglesey and later in Jersey, but returned to Beaumaris, Master and part owner of 'Harmony' 1870.
SUEUR (LE), Abraham	'Friendship' 1786, 'Reward' 1792.
SUEUR (LE), Charles	b. 1839, mar. Leonore Noel, d. at sea while en voyage to Cardiff 3.10.1888, memorial St Mtn's cem.
SUEUR (LE), Clement	Master's Cert. No. 4893, 'Virgilia' 1866.
SUEUR (LE), C.	'Union' 1900–08, also 'Fanny Breslauer', d. on ship Halifax, Nova Scotia.
SUEUR (LE), Daniel	'Chazalie' 1877.
SUEUR (LE), Francis	'Anne' 1820, 'Guernsey Lily' 1841.
SUEUR (LE), Henry George	Master's Cert. No. 3768, 'Electra' 1875, 'Critic' 1877.
SUEUR (LE), James Thos.	b; 1829, d. of cholera Chittagong 14.2.1871.
SUEUR (LE), Jean	'Betsy' 1765, 'Jane' 1776–78.
SUEUR (LE), John	'Reward' 1783.
SUEUR (LE), John Fr.	'Cinderella' 1848.
SUEUR (LE), John Thos.	d. 1871, memorial Green Street cem.
SUEUR (LE), Joshua	'Conway' 1813, 'Angelique' 1816, 'Seaflower' 1820.
SUEUR (LE), Noé	a privateer captain, 'Mars' 1776, 'Young Mary' 1792, 'James & Nancy' 1794, 'Tartar' 1800 and 1815, 'Betsy' 1809, 'Friend-ship' 1809.
SULLIVAN, John	b. 1811 St H., son of George, 'Virginia' 1836, 'Janvrin' 1839, 'Souvenir' 1860.
SULLIVAN, Thomas John	'Flora' 1840.
SYVRET, Edward	'Ninus' 1852, 'Elizabeth Ann' 1862.
SYVRET, Edward J.	b. 1848, mar. Ann. Elizabeth Hamon, d. 28.10.1920, bur. Mont á L'Abbe cem.
SYVRET, George	d. 1846, in New Brunswick, c. 1830.
SYVRET, George Edward	Master's Cert. No. 26157, 'Jane' 1865.
SYVRET, Jean	b. St H., lived Peter Street. a privateer captain, mate on 'Hope' 1805, Master of 'Fox' 1803.
SYVRET, Jean	b. 1807, d. 1872, bur. St O. cem., Master of Arichat' 1842.
SYVRET, Peter	'Flower de Luce' 1600.
SYVRET, Philip	'Century' 1850, 'Jupiter' 1853.
SYVRET, Philip Edward	b. 1867, d. 22.3.1941, bur. Mont á L'Abbe cem.
SYVRET, Walter	'Hematope' 1896, drowned at sea.
TERRY, David	'Betsy' 1814, 'General Doyle' 1816.
TESSIER, Charles	'Pomona' 1831, 'Twenty-Ninth of May'.
THOMAS, Richard	'Queen Charlotte' 1810, 'Elizabeth' 1818.
TIBOT, Peter	'Dapper' 1805, 'Cap Breton' 1820.
TIREL, Servé	'Siren' 1840.
TOCQUE, F.	ss 'Duke of Normandy' c. 1928.
TOCQUE, Jean	'Corbet' 1778–79, 'Mars' 1780.

TOCQUE, Philip	b. 1804 St L., mar. Virginia Fruing, lived Elizabeth Pl., St H., 'Cap Breton' 1826–29, 'Commerce' 1831, 'Adonis' 1832–39, 'Patriot' 1839, 'Alice' 1847–50, 'Alliance' 1858, 'Chieftain' 1859, d. 1878.
TOCQUE, Thomas	Master of 'Ocean' 1827.
TONKIN, William	b. 1796 Cornwall, 'Susan' 1836, 'Lord Nelson' 1844, 'Zibiah' 1851, lost at sea.
TORRÉ, James	'Eagle' 1789–, 'Adventure' 1790–92.
TOUZEL, Charles	b. 1814 G., 'Commerce' 1840, 'Grouville' 1844–49, retired 1849.
TOUZEL, E.	'Two Brothers' 1778.
TOUZEL, George	ss 'Tirydail' c. 1914–18.
TOUZEL, John	b. 1801 St H., son of Philip, 'Exchange' 1826, 'Ann' 1835–44, retired 1844.
TOUZEL, Philip	'Mentor' 1817, 'Exchange' 1821, 'De Jersey' 1831, 'Ann' 1833.
TOUZEL, Philip	b. 1810 St C., son of Jean, Master 1836–49.
TOUZEL (LE), Philip Theodore	b. 1850, d. 1881, 'Royal Blue Jacket'.
TOUZEL, Thomas	'John & Caroline' 1824–26, 'Brandy' 1827.
TRACHY, Elias	'Elias & James' 1738, 'Neptune' 1749–55.
TRIGUEL, Clement	Master of boat at Gorey 1640.
VACHE (LA), Felix	Master of 'Harriet' 1828.
VALPY, E.	'Elisha Tupper' 1796.
VALPY, Francis	'Lord Nelson' 1805, 'Ceres' 1807, 'Roebuck' 1812.
VALPY, George John	'Bridesmaid' 1851.
VARDON, John	'Providence' 1819.
VAUDIN, Alfred	b. 1853, d. 1952.
VAUDIN, Charles	b. 1806 Trinity, son of Charles, Master 1836–47.
VAUTIER, Abraham	b. 1805, son of Jean, 'Hope' 1836, 'Argus' 1840, 'Aurora' 1852, 'Reward' 1855, retired 1855?
VAUTIER, Charles	'Don' 1836.
VAUTIER, Edward	Master's Cert. No. 48111, lived Agre House, St P.?, 'Bolina' 1877.
VAUTIER, Jean	'Seven Sisters' 1728–29.
VAUTIER, Jean	'Ant' 1804, 'Maria' 1831, 'Esther' 1833.
VAUTIER, Jean	b. 1801 St O., son of Jean, 'Hope' 1833, 'Argus' 1836–37, 'Eagle' 1838, brother of Abraham?
VAUTIER, Jean	Master of 'St Brelade' and 'Owny Belles' c. 1881, lived St B.?
VAUTIER, Nicolas	'Beazley' 1778.
VAUTIER, Philip	b. St O., Master's Cert. No. 23725, 'Storm' 1826.
VAUTIER, Thomas	'Success' 1810.
VENNEMENT, Daniel	'Spitfire' 1803.
VESCONTE (LE), Daniel	'Hind' 1824, 'Laurel' 1826.
VESCONTE (LE), Jean	b. 1790, 'D', 1829, 'Lion' 1839, 'Francis' 1835.
VESCONTE (LE), John	'Union' 1737.
VESCONTE (LE), John	'St Peter' 1794, 'Esther' 1803.
VESCONTE (LE), John Jas.	Master's Cert. No. 50916, 'Don' 1867.
VESCONTE (LE), Michael	son of Michel, 'Providence' 1737, 'Mary' 1747, 'Pretty' 1751.
VESCONTE (LE), Nicolas	'Three Brothers' 1737.
VESCONTE (LE), Nicolas Phil.	b. 1784 St J., 'Henry' 1835, 'Three Friends' 1839, 'Peggy' 1841, 'Green End' 1843, 'Peggy' 1844, 'Diana' 1848, 'Fox' 1848, 'Active' 1850.
VESCONTE (LE), Peter	'Homely' 1809, 'Pelican' 1815, 'Twig' 1821, 'Peter & Jane' 1823.

VESCONTE (LE), Philip	'Active' 1795, also 'Fiott'.
VESCONTE (LE), Philip Dolbel	d. 1831, bur. Green Street cem.
VESCONTE (LE), Philip	'Grampus' 1826, 'Hero' 1832, 'Turk' 1842.
VESCONTE (LE), Raulin	son of Michel, Master c. 1737.
VIBERT, Amice	Master c. 1840, mar. Marianne de La Perrelle.
VIBERT, Charles	Master of 'Francis John' 1869.
VIBERT, Edward	Master c. 1738.
VIBERT, Elias	b. St L.?, 'Nancy' 1763, 'York' 1786, 'Anne' 1816.
VIBERT, Helier	b. 1773 St My., 'Ann' 1817, 'C. Columbus' 1825, 'Larch' 1847–49, also 'Habnab'.
VIBERT, Jean	a privateer captain, 'Cornwall' 1786, 'Dumaresq' 1790, 'Marquis of Townsend' 1803–05, 'Grog' 1814–17, 'Brutus' 1826.
VIBERT, John Arthur	b. 1827, St B., mar. Sybil Shaw (Jean?) 1858. 'St Anne' 1852–57, 'James' 1845, lived Gaspé 1849–1880.
VIBERT, John	Master of 'Quick' 1865.
VIBERT, Nicolas	'Mary' 1747.
VIBERT, Nicolas	'Union' 1780, '96 and '99.
VIBERT, Philip	b. St P., d. 1784 in America, as pilot on HMS 'Quebec', merchant captain before joining Navy, 'Kingfisher' 1745–46, 'Postillion Pkt' 1762–63.
VIBERT, Philip	Captain Vibert was in command of the 'Gaspé' in 1830, when the vessel was lost, the captain's son and eight men were lost. 'Peirson' 1786, 'Elisha Tupper' 1790, 'Dumaresq' 1792, 'Anne' 1809, 'Maurice' 1821, 'Gaspé' 1824–30.
VIBERT, Philip	b. 1790 St J., 'Mars' 1823, 'Judith & Esther' 1831, 'Robert Watt' 1832, '36, 'Julia' 1844.
VIBERT, Thomas	'Constant Pkt' 1804, 'Betsy' 1805, 'Young Peggy' 1806, 'Neptune' 1807, 'Two Brothers' 1808.
VIBERT, Thomas	b. 1806, St My., d. 1887, 'Mayflower' 1836, 'Deslandes' 1837, 'Julia' 1844, retired 1847.
VICQ, Barnaby	'John' 1816, 'Beehive' 1817.
VICQ, Jean	'Ant' 1827.
VILLENEUVE, ?	'Charming Nancy' 1744.
VILLENEUVE, Gideon	'Unity' 1750.
VINCENT, Alfred	ss 'Greenland' c. 1914–18.
VINCENT, Amice	a privateer captain, 'Jersey Galley' 1744.
VINCENT, Francis	Master of 'Volant' 1868.
VINCENT, George	Master c. 1832.
VINCENT, John	b. St P., lived Lowlands, Master of 'Rachel' c. 1737.
VINCENT, John	ss 'Enterprise' 1872.
VINCENT, John A. F.	b. 1801 St P., 'Seaflower' 1836, 'C. Columbus' 1839, 'Homely' 1840.
VINCENT, Philip	Master's Cert. No. 10928, 'Isabella' 1838, 'C. Columbus' 1856.
VOIE, Jean	'Two Brothers' 1790, 'Favorite' 1792.
WALKER, James	from Lyme Regis, 'Bustler' 1813.
WALKER, Thomas	from Lyme Regis, 'Mary' 1803, 'Active' 1813.
WALLIS, ?	'J.F.' 1859, 'Brilliant' 1860.
WARREN, E. J.	Master and owner 'Fiona' 1904.
WEARY, Philip	lived St B., mar. Elizabeth Briard, Master of 'Grog' 1821.
WEARY, William	lived St B., at La Place, La Haule, Master c. 1851.
WESTLAKE, Thomas	'Active' 1821, 'Samuel & Julia' 1831.
WHEELER, George	'Olive Branch' 1859–60, 'Forest Lad' 1865.
WHEELER, James	Master of 'Star' 1856.

WHEELER, Philip Master's Cert. No. 73159, obtained 1878, 'Hernhut' 1877, 'Undine' 1878, lived Gorey.

WHITLEY, Charles E. 'Alabama' 1874–96.

WHITLEY, Elie Master *c.* 1830.

WHITLEY, John Charles b. 1862 G., d. 1924, bur. G.?

WILKINS, Henry a privateer captain, 'Flora' 1786, 'Johanna' 1790–92, 'Speedy Pkt' 1793–1809.

WINTER, Philip lived Bulwarks, St Aubin 1789, a privateer captain, 'Industry' 1745, 'Charming Nancy' 1749–79, 'Admiral Barrington' 1792.

WOOLDRIDGE, George 'Fortune' 1794, 'Cumberland' 1809, 'Unity' 1822–26.

WOOLDRIDGE, Thomas 'Friends' 1803, 'Sir Sydney Smith' 1812, 'Unity' 1817.

WRIGHT, John lived Gorey *c.* 1885, 'King' 1859.

WRIGHT, Philip Master of 'Harmony' 1792.

YOULTON, R. T. 'Lavinia' 1862.

YOUNG, George W. Master of 'Dart' 1874.

Figurehead of 'Rescue', 1187 tons. Owned by Philip Pellier of Jersey.

Appendix One

NUMBER AND TONNAGE OF JERSEY OWNED VESSELS

Year	Number	Tonnage	Seamen	Average Tonnage
1611	—	—	300	—
1685	40	—	—	—
1737	33	—	—	—
1768	34	1,300	—	39
1792	81	6,479	—	80
1807	76	6,655	556	85
1816	75	8,709	—	105
1817	79	8,167	787	102
1821	103	10,183	—	98
1826	172	15,651	—	90
1827	183	16,583	1,648	90
1830	205	18,611	—	90
1833	228	21,799	—	95
1835	243	23,221	—	100
1837	244	23,826	2,165	97
1840	269	26,593	—	99
1845	311	27,690	—	90
1850	347	32,330	—	93
1855	365	34,600	—	94
1860	418	41,048	—	99
1865	451	55,676	—	123
1870	343	35760	—	104
1875	275	22,712	—	83
1880	224	15,747	—	70
1885	172	11,655	—	67
1890	139	8,684	—	62

Appendix Two

AN AFFIDAVIT

ISSUED BY THE BAILIFF, HELIER DE CARTERET IN THE PRESENCE OF THE JURATS AND JUSTICES 29th OF JUNE 1537

Sworn by Guillaume and Nicolas de Soulemont, younger brothers of Thomas de Soulemont, sons of Pierre de Soulemont

Guillaume, a master, merchant and burgess of a certain ship called 'La Marie de Jersey', carrying a cargo of 50 barrels of salt or thereabouts, fetched from Ile de Re. These de Soulemont staying near Belle Isle, when mariners from Spain approached in two vessels and violently occupied, siezed and plundered the ship taking all the property of the de Soulemonts and furtively took the ship away contrary to the wishes of the de Soulemonts and their sailors.

The de Soulemonts humbly begged us to believe the Testimony of certain reliable men, which we agreed to do and they appeared before us.

Johannes Gomer — living in Jersey
Karolus Le Goupil — living in Jersey
Petrus Le Cornu — living in Jersey
Jacobus Valepy — living in Jersey
Guillemus La Nyerce — living in Jersey
Jacobus Le Cherf — living in Jersey
Hamon Carbecquet — living in Jersey
Matheus Pyel — living in Jersey
Willemus Lorbe — living in Fareham
Johannes Smyth — living in Yarmouth, Isle of Wight
Nicolas Lassy — living in Yarmouth, Isle of Wight.

The Spaniards stripped the sailors naked except for their shirts, and left them on Belle Isle.

This document is from the collection of papers from La Haule Manor.

Appendix Three

JERSEY CHAMBER OF COMMERCE

February 1768 saw the formation of the Jersey Chamber of Commerce, the first in the English-speaking world, by a group of mainly shipping merchants and owners to protect their interests: George Rowland, President, James Hemery, Secretary; Thomas Durell, Matthew Gossett, John Hue, William Patriarche, Thomas Pipon, Philip Robin. The early years were devoted to promote and protect shipping, which was natural in a society composed mostly of shipowners, and they agitated for improvements of harbours, both at St Helier and St Aubin. The Chamber took action in 1796, against the ruling by Britain that Jersey vessels proceeding to North American ports should first obtain clearance in Britain, in which they were successful, and to redress the wrongs of fellow Islanders in encounters with French interests. In 1788 the British parliament took action against the fraudulent exports of English wool. This act would have hurt the important Jersey knitting industry and its exports, so acting through the States, the Chamber was again successful in the restoration of the rights of the Islanders. Restrictions on the Tobacco trade in 1791 were lifted on the protestations of the local Chamber, which demonstrated to the merchants the usefulness of such an association.

Appendix Four

JERSEY BUILT VESSELS FOR OWNERS ON THE MAINLAND

Name	Date	Type of vessel	Builder	Tons	Owner
AGILE	1874	Schooner	Picot	88	
ALVINA	1874	Schooner	Aubin	57	
AMBERNYMPH	1859	Brig	Clarke	270	Scrutton & Co.
AMIRAL	1840	Schooner	Valpy	80	
ANGELA	1883	Yacht	Picot	7	
ANNE KAYE	1863	Barque	Deslandes	287	Th. Kaye, London
ANN HOLZBURG	1853	Ship	Clarke	705	Melhuish & Co., Liverpool
ANNIE	1860	Barque	Asplet	260	Ashton & Co., London
ARTHUR JONES	1835	Brigantine	Laing	212	an English company
BANGALORE	1843	Ship	Allen	900	
BRIDE	1877	Yawl	Picot	24	J. A. Lawe, Torquay
BRITISH MERCHANT	1847	Barque	Clarke	334	a Liverpool clmpany
BRITISH MERCHANT	1839	Barque	Deslandes	260	
CAMELIA	1876	Schooner	Bellot	65	
CAROLINE HUTCHINGS	1865	Barque	Clarke	440	
CHARLES GRAY	1863	Schooner	Le Sueur	65	
CHEETAH	1864	Ship	Le Vesconte	760	A. Robinson, London
CITY OF ADELAIDE	1838	Brig	Allen	250	
COMETE	1840	Brigantine	Valpy	?	
DAEDALUS	1839	Schooner	Le Masurier	78	
DELICIA	1848	Schooner	Le Sueur	79	
ELECTRA	1866	Yacht	Clarke	15	John Turner, Dartmouth
ELLEN	1872	Schooner	Le Sueur	78	
EVELYN	1864	Ship	Le Vesconte	762	Grierson, Cole & Co., London
EXCELLENT	1868	Ketch	Bellot	70	E. Seager, Shoreham
FAIRLIGHT	1858	Ship	Clarke	678	Redfern & Alexander, London
FAVONIUS	1874	Schooner	Le Sueur	74	
FAWN	1858	Schooner	Le Huquet	26	Williams & Co., Guernsey
F. C. CLARKE	1852	Ship	Clarke	648	Holzburg & Bowen, L'pool
F. E. ALTHAUSSE	1853	Barque	Clarke	430	a Liverpool company
FIFTEEN	1839	Brig	Deslandes	245	
FLASH	1866	Schooner	Gavey	59	
GENERAL DON	1828	Brig	Hamptonne	140	
HELEN HEILGERS	1854	Ship	Clarke	1,100	Melhuish & Co., Liverpool
HERO	1841	Brig	Esnouf	170	Tupper & Co., Guernsey

Continued on following page

Name	Date	Type of vessel	Builder	Tons	Owner
HERTHA	1857	Barque	Deslandes	257	
IRIS	1838	Brig	Deslandes	250	a Bristol company
JANE PRATT	1851	Ship	Clarke	729	Melhuish & Co., Liverpool
JEDDO	1859	Barque	Esnouf & Mauger	449	Reg. Hong Kong, 1866
JESSIE	1850	Schooner	Clarke	60	
JOHN MELHUISH	1850	Ship	Clarke	672	Melhuish & Co., Liverpool
JOSEPH HUME	1864	Screw brig	Clarke	450	Scrutton & Co., London
LABRADOR	1859	Schooner	?	94	
LARKINS	1826	Brig	Esnouf & Mauger	267	a London company
LINDA	1850	Barque	Clarke	450	a Liverpool company
LIZZIE	1857	Cutter	Aubin	50	
MARTHA	1836	Schooner	Esnouf	99	a Guernsey company
MARY	1858	Brigantine	?	203	
MARY & ELIZABETH	1836	Schooner	?	123	a Liverpool company
MATILDA WATTENBACH	1853	Ship	Clarke	1,077	Melhuish & Co., Liverpool
MATJE	1876	Schooner	Aubin	60	
MIGONETTE	1865	Barque	Clarke	284	Scrutton & Co., London
MIRZAPORE	1852	Ship	Allen	1,000	
MONTROSE	1861	Barque	Asplet	365	Scrutton & Co., London
NELLIE	1873	Ketch	Aubin	80	E. Seager, Shoreham
ORIENTAL	1842	?	Allix	?	for the Royal Navy?
PAGE	1856	Schooner	Valpy	109	
PERCY DOUGLAS	1861	Ship	Hayley	781	a Liverpool company
PRAIRIE FLOWER	1868	Cutter	Aubin	51	an English company
PROVIDENCIA	1872	Schooner	Deslandes	65	an English company
REBECCA JANE	1838	Barque	Esnouf	222	a Guernsey company
ROBERT BRADFORD	1849	Barque	Clarke	419	
ROSEAU	1857	Barque	Clarke	380	Scrutton & Co., London
ST VINCENT	1867	Barque	Clarke	462	Scrutton & Co., London
SALVADOR PACKET	1854	Barque	Clarke	362	a Liverpool company
SEVEN BROTHERS	1841	Cutter	Deslandes	30	
SEVILLA	1859	Barque	Clarke	598	G. Turnbull & Co., G'gow.
SYMORE	1836	?	Laing	300	
TIGHNAMARA	1835	?	Laing	?	
TRADEWIND	1841	Schooner	?	152	
VICTORIA	1837	Schooner	Hamon	125	a Guernsey company
VITULA	1871	Brigantine	Deslandes	147	
WAGOOLA	1856	Barque	Clarke	500	Redfern, Alexander & Co., London
WILLIAM COLE	1856	Ship	Clarke	952	Melhuish & Co., ?
WILLIAM MELHUISH	1859	Ship	Clarke	681	Melhuish & Co., Liverpool
W. W. SMITH	1857	Ship	Clarke	884	

NOTES AND REFERENCES

Chapter One

1. Mont Orgueil Castle, E. T. Nicolle, page 36.
2. Jersey's Parish Churches, Paul Harrison, page 38.
3. Ships of British Oak, A. J. Holland, page 118.
4. Bulletin of La Société Jersiaise 1969, page 65.
5. The Ships of the Port of Fowey, C. H. Ward-Jackson, page 39.
6. Actes des Etates 1795-98, page 29.
7. Almanac of La Chronique de Jersey, 1843.
8. Jersey Shipping Register.
9. Old Jersey Houses, vol. two, Joan Stevens, page 36.
10. Victorian Voices, Joan Stevens, page 187.
11. Jersey Shipping Register.

Chapter Two

1. Actes des Etat, 1660-75, page 82
2. Actes des Etat, 1689-700, page 104.
3. Actes des Etat, 1701-30, page 69.
4. Actes des Etat, 1746-54, page 39.
5. Actes des Etat, 1746-54, page 92.
6. Actes des Etat, 1788-90, page 72.
7. Actes des Etat, 1788-90, page 87.
8. Records of the Jersey Chamber of Commerce.
9. Jersey Shipping Register.
10. Chronology of Jersey, R. Mollet, page 56.
11. Town of St Helier, E. T. Nicolle, page 69.
12. The Bailiwick of Jersey, G. R. Balleine, page 34.
13. The Jersey Evening Post, reports of 1872, 1874, 1876 etc., also notes and maps loaned by Mr. Richard Mayne.
14. Act des Etats, 1524-96, page 50.
15. The Bailiwick of Jersey, pages 2 and 77.
16. The Bailiwick of Jersey, page 72.
17. The Bailiwick of Jersey, page 18.
18. Local Newspapers.
19. La Chronique de Jersey 1837-39.

Chapter Three

1. Jersey in the 17th Century, A. C. Saunders, pages 138-141.
2. *Ibid.*
3. A Biographical Dictionary of Jersey, page 9.
4. Information supplied by Mr. Michael Dun, also Transactions of La Société Guernesiaise.
5. A Biographical Dictionary of Jersey, page 535.

Chapter Three—*continued*

6. The Corsairs of Jersey, A. C. Saunders, Bulletin S.J. 1929 and Notes on Jersey Privateers, R. Mollet, Bulletin S.J. 1957.
7. *The Islander*, a local magazine 1939.
8. Quarterly of the Alderney Society.
9. Paper in the Library of La Société Jersiaise.

Chapter Four

1. The Church of St Brelade, Rev. John Balleine.
2. Jersey Settlements in Gaspé, Marguerite Syvret, B.A., Bulletin S.J. 1963.
3. Articles by W. A. Munn, in the Newfoundland Quarterly, 1934.
4. The Church of St Brelade.
5. Notes loaned by Mr. Michael Dun.
6. Old Jersey Houses, vol. two, Joan Stevens.
7. Local Newspapers.
8. Jersey Shipping Register.

Chapter Five

1. Bulletin S.J. 1928, page 51.
2. Bulletin S.J. 1928.
3. The Bailiwick of Jersey, G. R. Balleine, page xxiv.
4. Caesarea, a Discourse of the Island of Jersey, Jean Poingdestre.
5. A Biographical Dictionary of Jersey, page 486.
6. Old Jersey Houses, vol. two, Joan Stevens, page 39.
7. Local Almanacs.
8. La Chronique de Jersey, various reports.
9. Victorian Voices, Joan Stevens, page 244.

Chapter Six

1. Jersey Shipping Register.
2. Local Newspapers.
3. Jersey Evening Post.

Chapter Seven

1. Tombstones in local cemetery and local newspapers.
2. Lecture given to the Jersey Society in London, by Mr. Peter Robson, 1961.
3. Jersey and Guernsey Magazine.
4. Jersey and Guernsey Magazine.
5. *The Islander* Magazine.

OFFICIAL RECORDS

The Jersey Shipping Register, 1803 to the present, available at the Office of the Impot, St Helier.

The Jersey Merchant Seamen's Benefit Society, records held in the Library of La Société Jersiaise, St Helier.

Records of the Jersey Chamber of Commerce, Royal Square, St Helier.

Lloyds of London, Lists and other papers 1773, 1776, 1778, 1783, 1785, 1786, etc.

British Customs records, Bristol and Southampton.

Port books of Cardiff, Plymouth and Southampton.

BIBLIOGRAPHY

Balleine, G. R., *A Biographical Dictionary of Jersey* (Staples Press).

Balleine, G. R., *The Bailiwick of Jersey* (Hodder and Stoughton, 1951. Revised 1970).

Caesarea, or a Discourse of the Island of Jersey. Jean Poingdestre 1682. Société Jersiaise 1889.

de la Croix, J., *La Ville de St Helier* (Jersey 1845).

Saunders, A. C., *Jersey in the 17th Century* (1930–31).

Saunders, A. C., *Jean Chevalier and His Times* (Jersey 1936).

Stead, J., *Caesarea*.

Holland, A. J., *Ships of British Oak*. (David and Charles 1971).

Nicolle, E. T., *Mont Orgueil Castle* (Jersey 1921).

Nicolle, E. T., *The Town of St Helier* (Société Jersiaise 1931).

Harrison, Paul, *Jersey's Parish Churches*.

Stevens, Joan, *Old Jersey Houses*, vol. I (Jersey 1965. Reprint by Phillimore 1980).

Stevens, Joan, *Old Jersey Houses*, vol. II (Phillimore 1977).

Stevens, Joan, *Victorian Voices*.

Mollet, R., *A Chronology of Jersey* (Société Jersiaise 1954).

Turk, M. G., *The Quiet Adventurers in America* (Detroit 1975).

Turk, M. G., *The Quiet Adventurers in Canada* (Detroit 1979).

INDEX

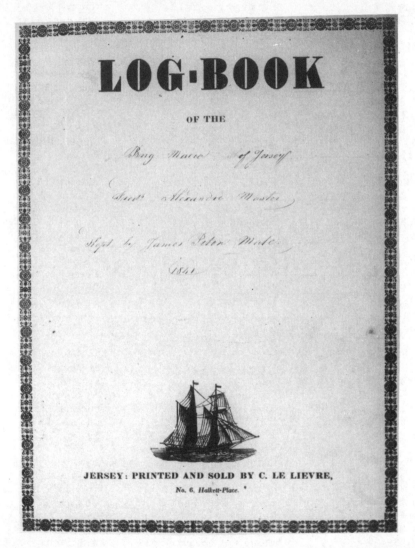

Log-book of the brig 'Maria', 1841.